Midwest
$27.94
P.O. 77921
12-13-01

W9-BBP-952

DISCARDED

Marriage

in a Culture

of Divorce

KARLA B. HACKSTAFF

TEMPLE UNIVERSITY PRESS
Philadelphia

Copyright © 1999 by Karla B. Hackstaff
All rights reserved
Published 1999
Printed in the United States of America

♾ The paper used in this publication meets the requirements of the American
National Standard for Information Sciences—Permanence of Paper for Printed
Library Materials, ANSI Z39.48-1984

Library of Congress Cataloging-in-Publication Data

Hackstaff, Karla B., 1954–
    Marriage in a culture of divorce / Karla B. Hackstaff.
    p.   cm. -- (Women in the political economy)
    Includes bibliographical references (p.) and index.
    ISBN 1-56639-724-3 (cloth : alk. paper). -- ISBN 1-56639-725-1
(paper : alk. paper)
    1. Marriage--United States Longitudinal studies. 2. Married people--United States
Interviews. 3. Divorce--United States. 4. Sex roles--United States. 5. Equality--United
States. I. Title. II. Series.
HQ536.H27 1999
306.81'0973--dc21   99-25159
                                                                         CIP

In memory of my mother

Contents

Acknowledgments

THIS BOOK pivoted upon the effort, time, and intellectual guidance of many people. Acknowledgments cannot fully indicate their contributions, or the extent of my gratitude and sense of good fortune for their helping hands, hearts, and minds.

Throughout the project, I have relied on inspiration and critique from many scholars. I am particularly grateful to those who have read the entire manuscript during various phases of production. Arlie Hochschild expressed an abiding faith in my project and in my ability to produce the book from its conception to its completion; I am forever grateful for and awed by her deft ability to balance criticism with compliment and emotional with intellectual support. Eli Sagan has been a beacon of brilliant insight throughout this project; his extraordinary teaching, unwavering support, and profound questions saw the project to completion. Also, my respect and gratitude are extended to Bob Bellah for his intellectual acuity and integrity, Nancy Chodorow for her analytic and interdisciplinary agility, Mac Runyan for his gracious critique, and Arlene Skolnick for her lively interest, feedback, and enduring support. The scrupulous readings and insightful criticisms of Anita Garey and Arlene Stein were irreplaceable early in the project; Terry Arendell's discerning and detailed comments and Ronnie Steinberg's astute recommendations were crucial in later phases. Since I could not incorporate all of their worthy advice, they are not responsible for the final version of the book.

I am indebted to institutions, which are always sustained through the efforts of key individuals. I am grateful to the Institute of Human Development (IHD) at the University of California, Berkeley and those employed there in the early 1990s—specifically, the director, Dr. Joseph Campos; Dr. Carol Huffine; Barbara Bureck; and, above all, my sponsor, Dr. Arlene Skolnick—for granting me access to the Intergenerational Studies data archive. To thank IHD is to thank the anonymous fifties spouses who appear in these pages for their remarkable commitment to social research. I am deeply grateful to Dr. Judith Wallerstein, Director of the Center for the Family in Transition, for hiring me and for allowing me to use interview material that I gathered for her research project on marriages. I received extensive financial support early in the project from the University of California, Berkeley, including the Department of Sociology

Mini-Research Grant, the UCB Regents Fellowship for two years, the Thomasin and Abigail Bellah Memorial Scholarship, and the Eli Sagan Scholarship. The Woodrow Wilson Women's Studies Research Grant provided crucial financial support. In recent years, Northern Arizona University supported me through Organized Research Grants that allowed me to write and craft this book, particularly during the summers. I am also obliged to the College of Social and Behavioral Sciences and Department of Sociology and Social Work at Northern Arizona University. I am particularly grateful to the dean of the college, Susanna Maxwell, and to the department chair, Richard Fernandez, who made a course reduction and other college and departmental support possible. I am thankful for two graduate assistants—Michelle Burgener, who provided formatting and proofreading assistance, and Jerret LeMay, who conducted literature searches and critical reading. And I thank the departmental staff for managing numerous copying and Federal Express requests.

I am indebted to many colleagues, friends, and reviewers for the labor, advice, ideas, or care they contributed at various phases of the project, including Bob Blauner, Dorothy Brown, Mary Damskey, Jeanne Ewing, Jeff Ferrell, Karen Ferrell-Lang, JoEllen Fisherkeller, John Foran, Bob Freeland, Cyndy Greenleaf, Phoebe Morgan, Karen Pugliesi, Brian Rich, Nick Townsend, and Angela Willetto. I also want to thank Michael Ames, editor at Temple University Press, for seeing potential in my manuscript, reducing its flaws, and assisting me throughout the book production process.

Above all, this book rests upon the generosity and time that the interviewed '70s spouses gave to me. While I have had to change their names and other identifiers to respect confidentiality, they remain vivid in my experience, and I hope the text resonates with the meanings that inhabit all of their marital worlds today.

Many other family members and close friends have sustained me in countless ways throughout the production of this book. I am forever grateful for the love, advice, and constancy of JoEllen, Cindy, and Philippe. So, too, my Dad and Mary have fully and lovingly supported my educational pursuits and aspirations throughout my life. My siblings continually express their love and encouragement. Finally, I am deeply grateful to my friend, mate, and husband, Bill Hathaway, who has supported me emotionally, financially, and practically. He has shared the trials and triumphs of writing this book that have necessarily brought troubles and joys into our marital life. Whether reviewing the manuscript, fixing dinner, or doing "marital work," he has been my sweetest companion throughout. This book is dedicated to him because it surely would not exist without him or his loving commitment to equality in marriage.

Marriage in a Culture of Divorce

Introduction

Watershed in the Meaning of Marriage

WHEN I was selecting earrings for my wedding, I was not thinking about my research. Nevertheless, it was inevitably an occasion for the expression of marital meaning. When I remarked that a particular pair was a bit too expensive, the salesperson tried to convince this reluctant spender by saying, "Yeah, but these are for once in a lifetime." Then, acknowledging the times, she added, "hopefully"—an adverb that even on the threshold of marriage nods in the direction of divorce. This was neither the first nor the last time that I heard such trailing adverbs. While the "once in a lifetime" signaled the enduring ideal of "marriage as forever," the qualification by the salesperson conveyed the doubt that attends marriage in a context of widespread divorce.

While rising divorce rates have been a concern in the United States in many periods (Riley 1991), a new tipping point[1] was reached by the 1970s, when divorce overtook death as the primary means of marital dissolution.[2] We no longer assume that a mother is a widow when she says in an ad, "He's crazy about my kid. And he drinks Johnnie Walker." When as many, if not more, marriages are expected to dissolve as endure in a generation's lifetime, the social context changes for everyone.

MARRIAGE CULTURE TO DIVORCE CULTURE

A numerical tipping point in divorce rates is only one sign of a larger, *qualitative* change in meaning that I refer to as the "marital watershed" of the 1970s. In part, this marital watershed refers to the decline of "marriage culture."[3] Marriage culture should be understood as a cluster of beliefs, symbols and practices, framed by material conditions, that reinforce marriage and deter divorce. It is constituted by three beliefs that reflect a stance toward marriage *and* divorce: marrying is a given, marriage is forever, and divorce is a last resort. These beliefs are expressed through people's talk. A husband reveals his belief in "marriage as forever" as he asserts, "Like I told people when I got married that this was going to be my one shot at it win, lose, or draw." These beliefs are also echoed in consumer culture. An advertisement for engagement rings

1

asks, "Is two months' salary too much to spend for something that lasts forever? A diamond is forever."[4] Although challenged, marriage culture remains a potent cultural force. We are in the midst of contesting ideologies today.

The "marital watershed" also refers to the emergence of "divorce culture." Divorce culture, framed by material conditions, should be understood as a set of symbols, beliefs, and practices that anticipate and reinforce divorce and, in the process, redefine marriage. Divorce culture encompasses three key beliefs: marrying is an option, marriage is contingent, and divorce is a gateway.[5] A television commercial for *Korbel* champagne reflects the terms of divorce culture when it pans a wedding reception and a toast to the bride and groom; as it focuses on two guests raising their glasses in the back of the room, one man whispers to another, "I give the whole thing two months." The champagne's quality, the ad suggests, will endure longer than the marriage.

Divorce culture is not just about more numbers representing divorce behaviors,[6] but about the emergence of alternative *meanings*. Cohabitation, domestic partnerships, gay and lesbian marriages, serial marriage, and parenthood outside of marriage, all contribute to the diversification of relationship ideals; however, divorce is the most widespread challenge brought to marriage in recent decades. One need not be divorced to talk the terms of divorce culture, nor do the married necessarily talk the terms of marriage culture. As Riessman (1990) demonstrated in her study of divorced women and men, many ex-spouses still believe in "marriage as forever." At the same time, as this study shows, many first-time married[7] spouses believe that "marriage is contingent." More than marital status, membership in a particular generation predicts whether a spouse talks in terms of marriage or divorce cultures. Those married in recent generations are increasingly talking and reproducing the terms of divorce culture. Moreover, gender ideologies consistently inform "marriage talk" and "divorce talk"[8] across generations.

THE CHALLENGE OF GENDER EQUALITY

Like divorce culture, gender equality challenges the status quo in marital meanings. In the last few decades, the ideology of gender equality has increasingly contested the reigning ideology of male dominance in marriage.[9] Along with divorce, the rise of equality changes the power dynamics in marriage. Although attempts to incorporate gender equality into marriage are hardly new, the challenge of gender equality has never been so widespread.

Because feminism, increasing numbers of women in the workplace, and divorce have "developed hand in hand" (Coontz 1992, p. 168), rising divorce rates have often been blamed on women. Increased participation in the labor force has provided women with economic alternatives to entering a marriage, staying in a marriage, or accepting the power dynamics in a marriage.[10] In addition, women have been found to be more approving of divorce than men (Veroff, Douvan, and Kulka 1981). Moreover, women are the primary initiators of divorce (Kitson with Holmes 1992). Although notions of "equality" have varied among feminists, critics of the recent women's movement have focused on the notion that equality emphasizes individual rights and have characterized feminists as individualistic.

Most basically, individualism is the belief that the individual comes first—before others or society. Consequently, divorced women have been more easily perceived as self-interested individualists abandoning "marriage as forever." I have been puzzled for some time by implicit and explicit claims that *women's* individualism is causing divorce. Women, who are frequently the primary parent and provider for children after divorce, have never struck me as particularly individualistic; by shouldering relational responsibilities their actions seem more self-sacrificing than self-interested. Individualism seems a more pertinent characteristic of the numerous uninvolved fathers.[11]

Although we need to attend to men's individualism, we still need to ask whether women are becoming more individualistic. Some are. I will argue, however, that because we proceed from a history of male-dominant marriages, individualism does not *mean* the same thing to women and men. For men, putting the self first remains a way to sustain male dominance in marriage. For women, putting the self first is a way to counter male dominance in marriage.

Defining equality inside or outside marriage is enormously problematic. Equal to whom? According to what standard? Still, for more than a century gender equality has been expressed through two main and competing strains of thought.[12] There is, first, equality that minimizes differences between the sexes and emphasizes individual rights. This version of equality aims to secure for all women the independence that has always been more available to white men, including political rights and economic opportunities. This is "rights equality." Second, there is "relational equality." This is equality understood as equity, which challenges rather than embraces the white masculine standard. This version of equality recognizes gender and racial difference and would have us revalue ideals and practices associated more often with white women and people of color (Collins 1990). These ideals include responsibility, interdependence, and relationality. While relationality will vary by class and race or culture, it is most generally "a stance which emphasizes expressivity and takes others into account not as 'other' but as important in themselves" (M. Johnson 1988, 68).

Both strains of gender equality contest male dominance and are apparent among the members of recent generations, in particular the generation that came of age in the 1970s. I am not the first to argue that the high divorce rate reflects the introduction of gender equality into a marriage (M. Johnson 1988, 261; Goldscheider and Waite 1991). For example, Goldscheider and Waite (1991, 14) argue that some part of the high divorce rate "reflects the working out of the sex-role revolution." They document increasing egalitarian attitudes among young adults of the 1970s and they show how a family background of divorce predicts egalitarian practices, particularly among men. However, aggregate statistics of individuals' responses leave some questions unanswered. What does women's independence *mean* to wives and husbands? How does gender equality influence the power dynamics in a marriage? My research reveals these meanings and illustrates the microdynamics of gender equality and divorce culture within marriages. The rise of gender equality has contributed to divorce, not because women are too individualistic, as some scholars emphasize, nor because gender equality is inherently destabilizing in marriage. Rather, it is the *transition* to gender equality that unsettles institutional arrangements, including marital commitments. Gender equality (whatever the context or definition) has rarely been achieved with ease, or finality. And today we see more wives asserting their visions of marital relationships.

THE IMPULSE FOR THE RESEARCH

While I have never been divorced myself—a fact that people find curious when they learn that my research is on divorce culture—I am a child of divorce. I vicariously experienced the decline of stigma in my white, middle-class surroundings from my kindergarten to high school years. The divorce of my parents by 1960—before stigma and other disincentives lost their power to deter divorce—meant that I was alert to both enduring and dissolving marriages. During my elementary school years, peers who had divorced parents were few and far between; explanations concerning where my father lived or my mother's different last name were required. By my high school years in the early 1970s, many more peers had divorced parents and such explanations were unnecessary. The stigma I sensed in my early years had all but vanished by adulthood. Further, by the late 1970s, I had witnessed and embraced feminist critiques of marriage and had practiced "living together." My derivative experience of "divorce" and marital alternatives suggested to me that the meaning of marriage and divorce had changed significantly in my life span—extending beyond those who divorced. The impulse for this research, then, was my initial sense that there were important differences in the meaning of marriage and divorce for those who came of age in the 1950s and their "baby boom" children, such as myself.

THE RESEARCH PROJECT

My study of married couples grew out of the literature on divorce, rather than that on marriage. Most of the literature on divorce observes that everyone's life is touched by divorce in one way or another. Despite the frequent appearance of this truism in the divorce literature, the majority of research projects have in fact focused on the implications of divorce for the divorced population or the children of divorce. I was curious about the meaning of this "prevalence" for those other than the divorced. I assumed that widespread divorce affected people whether they were single, married, divorced, cohabiting, remarried, a child of divorced or married parents, a grandparent with reduced contact, a teacher who does not know which home address is relevant, or an employer who must garnish wages for child support.

Unlike many scholars of marriage and divorce, I was not primarily interested in predicting divorce. To my knowledge, no one had explored the *meaning* of divorce for the married. I wanted to discover how people talked about, constructed, and interpreted divorce in the context of marriage.

My central questions were: How are wives and husbands shaping and being shaped by a new marital context marked, above all, by a high divorce rate and demands for gender equality? Would gender make a difference? Has prevalent divorce similarly affected the meaning of marriage for women and men? Would generation matter? Would couples married before and after the 1970 watershed construct different meanings?

To shed light on the shifting meanings of marriage and divorce, I investigated two generations of married couples.[13] I analyzed in-depth, longitudinal interviews conducted in 1958, 1970, and 1982 with wives and husbands born around 1928 and married around 1950. I collected the archival data at the Institute of Human Development at the University of California, Berkeley, during the fall of 1991. I compared these interviews to my own in-depth interviews with matched wives and husbands born around 1953 and married after 1970.

I refer to these two groups as the '50s couples (or Older generation) and the '70s couples (or Younger generation), respectively. Both generations were primarily middle-class people—although class backgrounds varied. Because of racial/ethnic limitations in the original archival data, the '50s spouses were 85 percent European-American and 15 percent African-American.[14] Among the '70s spouses, 62 percent were European-American, 15 percent were African-American, 15 percent were Asian-American, and 8 percent classified themselves as bi-racial. I analyzed interviews with 26 individuals in the Older generation (12 couples and 2 former spouses for comparative purposes) and I conducted interviews with 34 individuals in the Younger generation (17 couples). (See Appendix: Methodological Notes for more information on the samples.)

I interviewed the '70s wives and husbands separately at a place of their convenience. I asked what was good, surprising, bad, disappointing, challenging, and hopeful in their marriage. I asked for the story of their relationship. I asked about sex, work, leisure, gender, parenting, and fairness in the marriage. Because I wanted to discover and not presume whether, when, and how divorce might be relevant to them, I waited for the respondents to bring up divorce and then pursued their lead. After the in-depth individual interviews, I conducted a joint interview with each couple in their home, asking more about their family backgrounds and the ups and downs of their marital lives. (See Methodological Notes for more information on the interviews.)

Although I also interviewed various "experts" on marriage and divorce and analyzed symbols that had emerged in popular culture by the 1990s, the culture of divorce is apparent, above all, in the talk of married couples from the Younger generation.

THE POWER DYNAMICS OF (RE)CONSTRUCTING MARRIAGE

To analyze beliefs about marriage and gender, I looked for patterns among two generations of married couples. How did '50s couples talk about divorce and gender equality as the decades proceeded? Were they primarily reproducing or contesting "marriage as forever"? How did they construct male dominance, if at all? Were '70s spouses constructing "marriage as forever," too? How did '70s spouses' marital ideologies interact with their gender ideologies? Did these ideologies matter in the power dynamics of the relationship?

First, I found some spouses who can be described as traditionalists—that is, they believe in "marriage as forever," that men should have the final say in marriage, and that the breadwinner-homemaker division of labor in marriage is most desirable. These spouses eschew the trends toward easier divorce and gender equality. Avoiding these trends becomes more difficult for the '50s spouses over time, and is most difficult for the '70s spouses. The power dynamics of traditional couples are partially set by the belief in male dominance, yet a traditional marital ideology means that wives' power is located in the institutional basis of marriage, which theoretically guarantees that husbands will honor their commitments.

Second, some spouses are trying to introduce notions of gender equality based upon relational responsibilities and interdependence, even as they aim to maintain "marriage as forever" and "divorce as a last resort." They are trying to reconstruct it by divesting marriage of its historical association with male dominance. However, because of the legacy of gendered work in families and society—enduring occupational segregation, pay differentials, and the division of labor in housework and child care—this pattern is not easy to sustain. Such couples resemble the "near peer couples" described by Schwartz (1994); spouses can aspire to gender equality, but lack the social resources to achieve it. This can tip the balance of power in favor of men.

Third, a few spouses express support for male dominance, but also believe marriage is contingent and conditional. Marriage becomes contingent, then, on the conditions set by the husband. Such a pattern of beliefs represents a male-centered model of marriage because it advances men's power and options in a marriage. It represents a "cautionary tale" for women. A wife caught in such a marriage must abide by her husband's terms or risk being left by him. While some wives still support male dominance in marriage, such wives are most likely to also view marriage as forever, not as contingent.

Finally, there are some wives—and husbands—who support marriage as contingent and believe in gender equality. These spouses represent new dynamics that have emerged in marriage with the rise of divorce culture and gender equality. They talk in terms of optional and contingent marriage, and they portray divorce as a gateway. They are more likely to talk about "rights equality"—that version of gender equality based on individual independence rather than about explicit notions of equity or interdependence. This dynamic can represent a "cautionary tale" for husbands; if wives cannot secure independence through marriage, they can pursue it through the divorce option. Yet, if marriage is explicitly contingent upon independence and equality, there are implicit relational contingencies as well.

Spouses in both generations only approximated these patterns. Indeed, there is great variation within each generation. However, this analysis of the '50s and the '70s couples revealed that belief in marriage culture and male dominance are on the decline, while beliefs in gender equality and divorce culture are on the rise.

OVERVIEW OF THE BOOK

The first chapter previews the changing cultural meanings of divorce and marriage for the two generations by looking at the points of greatest contrast between the '50s couples and the '70s couples. Three key changes are apparent: 1) divorce culture and egalitarianism are on the rise among the '70s spouses; 2) while among the '50s couples it was the wives who took care of or monitored the marriage's well-being, among the '70s couples a full-blown "marital work ethic" is espoused by both wives and husbands; 3) finally, it is the '70s spouses who actively *reproduce* divorce culture.

In Chapter Two, I depart from marital stories to describe the social, demographic, legal, and economic conditions that have been necessary for the rise of divorce culture. I address the cultural influences conventionally associated with marriage culture: religion and male dominance. I also discuss the newer cultural influences associated with divorce culture: therapeutic culture and gender equality. I argue that since the women's movement, therapy has become more women-centered. I show how gender equality and therapeutic ideals are shaping the redefinition of marriage and divorce, within a culture of divorce.

In Chapters Three through Six, I return to the longitudinal data on the '50s couples, married over 30 years by their last interview. In Chapter Three, I analyze how spouses' "talk" about marriage, divorce, and gender changes over time. The prevailing patterns reflect the traditional terms. The '50s wives and husbands are both more likely than the '70s spouses to support male dominance and marriage culture, and more likely to perceive gender equality as an issue relevant to the "public" sphere, rather than to marriage. The '50s spouses certainly register the rise of divorce culture over time, but they do not *reproduce* divorce culture to the same degree as the '70s spouses. Moreover, '50s wives, more than husbands, are *thinking* divorce, suggesting discomfort with the marital bargain of their times.

Beginning in Chapter Four, I explore case studies of '50s couples who depart from the prevailing pattern of traditionalism. The Dominicks of Chapter Four reveal the power dynamics that emerge when male dominance is sustained and divorce culture enters into the husband's marriage talk; the wife "thinks" divorce, but marriage culture beliefs leave her powerless to produce change. This pattern is virtually without reward for wives. The Hamptons of Chapter Five initially believe in marriage culture and male dominance, but over time become increasingly egalitarian in their ideology and practice. Marie Hampton's enduring belief in marriage culture keeps the marriage going until Henry Hampton's talk of gender equality increases. Finally, the McIntyres of Chapter Six represent the turn toward egalitarianism and divorce culture among the '50s couples. The McIntyres' marriage, like that of the Hamptons, reveals the difficulties of changing ideologies midstream; however, their changes are more sweeping and more gratifying than the Hamptons'. Martha McIntyre's belief in divorce culture empowers her to assert her marital ideals; Michael McIntyre chooses to respond to her change. In short, wives are changing more quickly than husbands, but, in general, neither wives nor husbands of the Older generation are changing as fast as the Younger generation.

Chapter Seven explores perceptions of the '50s era. The '50s spouses' retrospective accounts of marriage are informed by contemporary practices. The younger group's constructions of marriage in the 1950s reflect well-known stereotypes of the era, which is, by and large, their parents' generation. From the viewpoint of the '70s spouses, divorce in the 1950s was not simply a *last* resort, but *no* resort. The '70s spouses tend to "locate" marriage culture in the past and divorce culture in the present, and in so doing they reproduce the terms of divorce culture.

In Chapters Eight through Eleven, I analyze data from in-depth interviews with the '70s spouses, who were born in the early 1950s and married in the late 1970s and early 1980s. Chapter Eight describes the '70s spouses' increasing divorce stories and divorce anxiety, as well as strategies used to contend with divorce culture. Central among these strategies is the "marital work ethic"—a belief in the need to work on marriage in a culture of divorce. The proportions of those who support gender equality and reproduce divorce culture are greater in the Younger generation. Gender equality has become an issue within the "privacy" of the home as much as in the public world of work. Chapter Nine illustrates how the Clement-Leonettis and the Walkers rely upon external social commitments to bolster gender relations within their marriages. The Clement-Leonettis employ therapy toward the end of a gratifying and equal marriage. The Walkers show how religious commitment can advance marital work and egalitarianism. Chapter Ten looks at the Greens and shows how a '70s couple sustains traditional beliefs of male dominance and marriage culture in a social context challenged by new ideologies. The Greens face a different marital context than the '50s traditionalists; they are surrounded by and must contend with the countercurrent of divorce culture. Finally, I address how the blend of male dominance and divorce culture is generally imputed to other's beliefs and lives rather than one's own.

In Chapter Eleven, I address how matched wives and husbands are more likely to hold different beliefs among the Younger generation. I begin by discussing the Nakato marriage, where the husband is changing faster than the wife. I argue that this is less problematic for marriages than the reverse; paradoxically, he can use his power to advance gender equality. In most cases, however, wives seem to be changing faster than husbands (Hochschild with Machung 1989). As the Kason-Morris marriage illustrates, tensions plague such asymmetry. While the power of a husband who believes in male dominance and divorce culture is amplified, so, too, is the power of a wife who believes in equality and divorce culture. Because wives like Roxanne Kason-Morris are on the increase, '70s wives are more likely to say, perhaps to *do*, what '50s wives only *thought*. Until the social context affirms wives' marital visions, the power of divorce culture will be crucial for wives who seek to redefine marriage. In the final chapter, I discuss the promise and problems of divorce culture for women, men, children, and society.

1   Marriage and the Construction of Ideology

From Marriage Culture to Divorce Culture

IN their classic article, "Marriage and the Construction of Reality: An Exercise in the Microsociology of Knowledge," Berger and Kellner (1964) provided a detailed and insightful portrait of how marital "realities" are constructed over time. Marriage is described as a "dramatic act in which two strangers come together and redefine themselves." Socially constituted selves inevitably change as the spouses' once separate social circles gradually merge. Marriage entails constructing and objectifying a shared subworld embedded in the private sphere and serves to siphon off surplus, potentially disruptive energy. In Berger and Kellner's account, the narrowing and stabilization of personality brought about by marriage is described as "functional" in a society that rigidly controls conduct and often requires geographical and social mobility.

Three decades later, feminist researchers immediately perceive two problems: the invisibility of gender power relations and an artificial split between private and public spheres. Feminist research on marriage has revealed how power relations influence the constructions of selves in the service of marriage; historically, becoming a wife and becoming a husband have not meant the same thing. Bernard's (1972, 1982) classic analysis of "his" and "her" marriages was one of the first works to portray the disjuncture in spousal experiences and highlight the legacy of male dominance in marriage. Patricia Zavella's (1987), Miriam Johnson's (1988), and Hochschild's (1989, 1997) books are more recent analyses revealing gender power relations. In these and other works, feminist researchers have also challenged the idea that the construction of marriage occurs within a bubble called the "private sphere," apart from the influences of the wider society, by uncovering the multiple ways in which social structures—from the economy to the legal system—enter into marital and family dynamics (Ferree 1990; Lopata 1993; Thorne and Yalom 1982). In recent years, however, feminists have affirmed Berger and Kellner's theoretical orientation by increasingly taking a social constructionist approach in the study of gender and families (Thompson and Walker

1995; West and Zimmerman 1987). Rather than just focusing on macrosociological structures that subordinate and victimize women, feminists are analyzing the ways in which women actively create, contest, and resist microsociological structures of dominance in a variety of contexts (Gerson and Pleiss 1985). This book reflects Berger and Kellner's social constructionist approach toward marriage, but also brings feminist insights to bear upon marital dynamics. Spouses concurrently construct heterosexual marriage and gender as the following accounts of the Stone and the Turner marriages suggest.[1]

THE '50S STONES: CONSTRUCTING TRADITIONALISM

Katy and Evan Stone are a white, upper middle-class couple enjoying an intensely gratifying marriage by their 30th anniversary in 1982.[2] Indeed, Katy Stone apologizes for making her marriage sound like a "Doris Day movie plot" at this time. When Katy is asked how she would explain the high divorce rate, she asserted:

> This isn't going to be a popular answer. I think it's because the roles are pretty badly messed up. And, for a gal to get the same salary for her to be able—when she is on her own, be able to have equal job opportunities and things, I have no problem with that. But in a marriage—my mother said something that was just neat [...]* 'Somebody has to be the boss, and it really is better if it's the man.' And I think that says it in a nutshell. I think marriages that really try to be equal in a way that there is a total partnership that one is not really stronger and in authority over the other, I don't personally feel that works that well, and I think that most women are longing for a strong man. I think most women when they get out of line would love to be told in a loving but firm way to sit down and shut up. That's the way I feel . . . .

In this passage, Katy *interprets* the rise of "gender equality" as a cause of divorce. She has also made sense of the trajectory of her own self-development and her marriage. Because Katy and Evan Stone were interviewed in 1959, 1971 and 1982, we can trace the evolution of their marriage. It has not always been "a Doris Day movie plot."

Like many couples married in the 1950s, Katy Stone refers to parents when asked what encouraged or discouraged her initial marriage to Evan. Katy explains that when she was 24 years old in 1952, her parents invited her to their beachfront vacation home, along with family friends and their marriageable son. "This was," she says, "a plan worked out by my

*Ellipses within brackets indicate omitted text; ellipses within quoted copy indicate a pause in speaking.

father, who unquestionably thought I was getting along in years and should be married." Katy and Evan announced their marriage three months later.

Evan credited the "era" with propelling him into marriage.[3] When asked about the influence of his parents' marriage, Evan says: "I don't think I really thought about it too much. [...] I grew up in an age where we did things 'cause they was to be done. I mean, I went to school because it was supposed to be done, I got married because it was supposed to be done." Evan's talk about entering marriage reflects the talk of his generational peers. This is "marrying as a given."

In 1959, after seven years of marriage, Katy Stone discussed her initial, difficult years as an Air Force pilot's wife. During Evan's leaves from the service, she'd discovered, with each visit and each pregnancy, that sex and affection were separate for him and awkward for her.[4] She confided, "I was fond of him, but I was hurt. But the philosophy of the Air Force housewife is 'You make your man happy.'" She had relied heavily on the support of the other Air Force wives in his absence. When he returned for good, she missed the support of the wives and was "frightened" to have him home all the time.

Upon Evan's discharge from the service, Katy "did a snow job on him" so he would pursue a promising sales job. She wanted him to be independent from his family and the family business, to build confidence. She wanted to redefine family ties for the sake of the marriage. She describes their relationship coolly, in terms of "fondness," and then asserts her resolve regarding the marriage: "We were fond of each other in spite of strains which had never been discussed, and I made up my mind I was going to do everything to make this marriage work."

Katy's Marital Monitoring

In addition to redefining family ties, to make the marriage work, Katy lowered her expectations and worked to secure her husband's affection. She noted in 1959: "Intellectually he has all the good ideas in the world, but it's old pedestrian me who has to plan the picnics, the beach parties, tracking in the sand, etc. Gradually he has become much more comfortable with the [children]. He and I are on a very frank basis now. We're both very fond of each other. He has learned to be more affectionate. I have learned to expect less from him than I did at first." Regarding his affection, Katy admitted that "it wasn't easy for me to beg for attention, but I've learned to do it in ways that aren't humiliating to either of us." Katy would hint of her upcoming birthday—by remarking that she felt old or by prompting the kids to convey the fact— to avert his forgetfulness, his guilt, and her sense of being neglected.

In these passages, Katy describes the work of monitoring a marriage, which is basic to the production of her eventual "Doris Day movie plot." While this marital monitoring is neither as explicit nor as salient as it will become among the '70 couples, its elements are apparent and it is, above all, wives' work. Monitoring partly entails "kin work," or the conceiving, creating and maintenance of kin ties (di Leonardo 1987, 442–43).[5]

Monitoring a marriage also means doing "emotion work." This entails inducing or suppressing "feeling in order to sustain the outward countenance that produces the proper state of mind in others" (Hochschild 1983, 7). Katy was clearly suppressing her expectations of Evan. She also tried to induce a "proper state of mind" in him by actively attempting to redo or remake her gender for her husband: "And I said [to Evan], 'Let's make me the kind of woman you'd like to be married to, what would she be like?' And he was laughing, and said, 'she'd be attractive, physical-wise.' When we were first married, physical appearance was very important to him; now it has taken much of a back seat. [And he continued] 'She'd be able to keep her mouth shut, but also know how to ask the right questions and bring people out. . . . ' " Katy reports a history of being a leader: "I just had long habits of competence and with anybody but a person of Evan's temperament I could have gone on and been a bossy lady to my lack of satisfaction."

In a supplemental interview three years later (1962), Katy is still working to keep her "mouth shut." She has been emotionally depressed. She feels excluded and "empty." Complying with Evan's ideal reveals an internal struggle:

> Basically, Evan and I have changed roles. He's the one with the confidence now and I am without it. I've always known he's had to win his confidence by his own achievements and not what I could do for him. But in spite of knowing this I felt terribly excluded because he's not one to talk things over easily. But then he never has been. He took me on no trips except one. A man and his wife and Evan and I went to a meeting. The man and I [sat together] and got into a discussion about some [current events] and I was feeling good being included again and was having a fine time till all of a sudden Evan turned around and said "you talk too much." I was chagrined at his criticism of me. [. . .] Evan has told me he feels I monopolize conversations when we're out to a social gathering and don't give the other people a chance to talk and *I've gotten so self-conscious and so uncertain that I don't feel like me anymore. I feel empty—I don't know who I am anymore* [emphasis added].

After ten years of marriage, Katy has managed to reverse the roles, yet her very identity is at stake in her attempt to approximate the image of the good wife.

The image of the wife, particularly in white, middle-class culture, has historically and legally implied "inequality, taking a back seat, economic dependence, being a provider of personal service, and loss of self" (M. Johnson 1988, 41). Katy's talk reveals that there is nothing "natural" about a wife's subordination; rather, it emerges through a process of social construction. As Bernard (1982, 39) observed, "It involves a redefinition of the self and active reshaping of the personality to conform to the wishes or needs or demands of husbands." This is Katy's struggle as she works to suppress her assertive voice. At this time, Katy and Evan share the ideology of a male-dominated marriage, but their practices, particularly Katy's practices, fall short.

Katy's Divorce Thoughts

Despite these difficulties, Katy was not thinking or talking divorce in 1962. Only nine years later, in 1971, does she toy with the thought of divorce and the appeal of independence. All five children are teenagers, and her husband is facing maximum career demands. After 19 years of marriage, Katy reviews her imaginative experiment with independence from marriage.

> I think this last year when I sort of pulled away and I sensed that he was kind of struggling and he was sort of pulling away, I became . . . you know, quite disenamoured with the whole thing and I just went through a little period of all my little feeling sorry for myself times, that I just felt, "Well, I'm really independent, I could just pull away from this without a look back." Well it was a great thought while it lasted. [. . .] but these were not serious—these were not really thoughts that I really believed inside, but they were—they were *there* which they hadn't been for many, many, many years.

Although Katy was miserable in 1962, she only begins to think about divorce in the 1970s, as the divorce rates approach a "tipping point" in society at large.

Katy never does pursue divorce. She contains her distress by minimizing its prevalence over time: "You know you're always going to have the percentage of times when what you need they're not able to give." If her needs cannot be met now, they will be at some future point. This is Katy's compensation, and a vital underpinning to the belief that "marriage is forever." It is a belief in reciprocity beyond the "give and take" in any one moment of a marriage; it suggests that the sacrifices will be worth it. It is also a belief that erodes as the Younger generation scrutinizes the gendered nature of "give and take" within marriage.

The privileged context of an upper-middle-class marriage may suggest that Katy must rationalize her disappointments and stay in the marriage for financial reasons. Yet, more than most wives, Katy could be financially independent because she has an inheritance. She asserted that she "never was interested in anything else other than marriage." Minimal employment experiences before marriage and raising five children were likely deterrents to divorce. She explains, "I'm strictly a one-man woman and I—having a happy husband and happy kids, you know—that's real important to me." She is not only deterred by her marital ideals, but also by her gender ideals: "Evan is [the] one that is that strength between us, where he is definitely—he is male and I'm a female." She repeatedly remarks on Evan's "total masculinity." Katy yearns to be comfortable in a heterosexual, male-headed marriage; she doesn't link the lack of emotional sustenance to the structure of power in the marriage.

Evan's Divorce Thoughts

Evan Stone did not have thoughts of divorce in 1970, but by 1982 he admitted to considering divorce around 1973–74. His family was "crumbling," partly because of his intense involvement in his work.[6] When asked what prompted thoughts of divorce, he declares: "That I wasn't the boss." Like many '50s spouses, by the 1970s Evan verbally supports women's equality at work in the public sphere; however, in marriage there has to be a boss.

When Evan is asked what he likes least about his wife, he jests that "she's female." After relatively cautious responses to his female interviewer, he "quit beating around the bush" and asserted: "Oh gosh, she walks a very delicate line. [Interviewer: Between?] Between being a wife and at the same time not being dependent. She has to be her own person, but I probably can't express that. I want her to be independent and yet be a wife. I don't want her whining or whimpering. I want her strong, but at the same time I want her as a wife." Evan's difficulty articulating support for Katy as a strong person, and dissatisfaction with this strength in a *wife*, epitomizes the catch-22 situation that exists for many women, especially strong women. He wants her to be "independent" without losing the characteristics attributed to "traditional" wives: dependence, submissiveness, and subordination.

Turning to Religion

The Stones draw upon religion to solidify their gender and marital ideologies. While Katy had always believed in God and had been Protestant, by 1982 she reports "finding Jesus" as her "personal savior" back in 1974. Katy was initially influenced by two of her children, who began going to church with neighbors; then Evan went. They were drawn to a neighborhood church and soon after, they "found Jesus," drawn by fundamentalist tenets more than by organized religion.

Katy explains how the scriptures taught her to be open to what Evan needed. The Word helped her to understand "how God laid down the male and the female" and, therefore, she "stopped being good" in areas such as household financial responsibilities and making sure things got done, so that Evan could be good in them instead. She reports that "the Lord was really talking to me through the Bible, saying 'drop back, let him make decisions, he needs your respect'"—a lesson for her marriage that she learned "in the nick of time." Katy's religious commitment augments her monitoring of the marriage and legitimates her emotion work— that is, suppressing her competence and bolstering Evan's authority.

Katy's efforts, as well as finding the Lord, helped Evan realize his authority as husband. Evan acknowledges that it was Katy who monitored and steadied their marriage when it was at its most vulnerable. The "needs" to which he refers below include his needs to be the head of the household and his need to realize his masculinity in work without her interference: "And I just thank the Lord that she was able to recognize in our marriage needs that I had, and was able to meet those needs. In other words, when things were getting a little shaky, why, she'd take the steps to keep our marriage together."

He knows Katy is happy because "we are able to communicate now, and share." Evan adds that "gradually, as time has gone along, I've become more of a proper husband and father, and taken responsibilities that I should." Later in the interview, referring to the Bible he reiterates: "I found the healing from my family in there, the healing for my concern about the world in there, I found the ... my function as a father image and a helper to people in the scripture."

By 1982, the Stones' practices align with their ideals of a male-dominated relationship, marked by the terms of marriage culture. Constructing the marriage of their dreams has been a process of persuasion, conversion, and above all, Katy's monitoring. Paradoxically, this religiously anchored, male-dominant marriage is not without feminist and therapeutic elements. Bolstered by religious tenets, Katy has drawn on a traditional institution that validates relational concerns; it is a strategy that not only reflects a nineteenth-century inclination to credit women with "moral superiority," but also a twentieth-century strategy of trading control of the household for relational and emotional concessions from men.[7] Katy has worked to be "the kind of wife" Evan would like her to be—a wife who affirms his dominance.

Ironically, by the time Katy and Evan forge the 1950s ideal of a male-headed family, the ideal has lost its hegemonic grasp in the greater society.

As for other '50s couples, for the Stones "marrying was a given," marriage was presumed to be "forever," and divorce only a "last resort." This last resort depended upon Katy monitoring the marriage and reconstructing herself for Evan. Male dominance and marriage culture are nearly hard-wired for them. Their divorce talk is telling in this regard. Echoing Katy's explanation for widespread divorce in 1982, Evan asserts: "it's hard for me to see a marriage surviving when woman becomes the dominant force."

By 1982, the Stones construct ideologies asserted by half of the '50s couples: marriage culture and male dominance. The Turners, in contrast, are among the third of '70 couples who challenge the old terms and forge new marital meanings through innovative strategies in a new marital era.

THE '70S TURNERS: RECONSTRUCTING MARRIAGE IN DIVORCE CULTURE

Nick and Mia Turner defy all the "sequences" associated with "marriage culture": they were lovers, then friends, then roommates, then lovers, and finally they married—not because anyone proposed, but because their friends were asking them if and when they were going to get married. For the Turners, marrying was experienced as an option. Married for ten years by 1992, they were raising three children, including a daughter from Mia's first marriage. This was Mia's second and Nick's first marriage. Mia is Japanese-American and Nick is African American.[8] Both spouses are college educated, middle class, and work full time.

Describing their marriage, Nick Turner succinctly states, "it's *not* a symbiotic relationship." He describes a period before their marriage when Mia withdrew from the relationship. His attitude was, "Fine. Bye. She's not interested. I got to take care of myself." Nick emphasizes "independence" and "options," talking the language of divorce culture as he addresses marital tensions between Mia and himself: "But I guess my basic view or philosophy is, there's *a way to work this out*. If it doesn't work out, then it doesn't work out. *There are some other options.* The last thing I want somebody to tell me is that 'no, this door is closed on you, you can't use this door.'" Nick's "basic view" means he is willing to "work" and flexible enough to look for options within the marriage. Still, he wants doors, including the divorce gateway, to remain open. The option to marry, to stay, to leave, also punctuate Mia's talk about marriage.

When I asked Mia Turner what is good about her marriage, she initially says, "everything." She elaborates that it is good "sexually," provides "emotional support as far as career-wise, [. . .] there's no really set role of who does what, you know, everyone does everything." The latter represents the egalitarian model of her marriage; the Turners share work and home responsibilities. Next, Mia asserts that "independence" is good, but when she immediately adds "even though I'm married," she begins to convey the idea that her independence is possible not because of, but in spite of, being married. Part of being independent is the freedom to make decisions, she explains: "When I have to make a decision . . . I think of as a couple, but I also think of myself, I would say first—what is good for *me*—and I know if I make that decision that it'll fit right in. Not that I run over him or anything, but it's nice to know that you can do that." When Mia explains that she does not "run over him," but "it's nice to know that you can do that," she implies that her aim is not to dominate, but to avoid being dominated.

When I ask Mia about the biggest surprise of her marriage, she offers a typical repartee of divorce culture, and then conveys her amazement that Nick puts up with her independence: "One of the surprises is that it's lasted this long. [Laughs.] No really, it's like I feel like 'who is gonna put up with me?' You know? Because at this point in my life, it's like, you take me like I am or else forget it, because I'm not going to be in the same situation as I was *in my first*, where I did everything to please a person and lost myself, you know. So I'm just going to be the bitch I am and you take me, or else you're gone." Mia's individualism is clearly a reaction to her experience with sacrifice and subordination in her first marriage. She refuses to "lose" herself again.

In Mia's view, the problem in her first marriage was her husband's "traditionalism." She complained that "it was mainly, you know, the place of the woman's at home." Being a housewife was "not me," according to Mia. Her first husband "went into a rage" about the lack of cleanliness in the house when she was bedridden. When he raised a cooking pan at her, she says, "it was the excuse that I needed." As Mia tells it, "it really wasn't violent, it was a fit of temper, but it was enough." Mia pursued divorce and now her marital commitment is contingent upon happiness defined as an equality rooted in independence.

Individualism and/or Relationality?

Mia Turner repeatedly equates independence with "happiness" and views this equation as a criterion for marriage and divorce. When I ask about any divorces that should have been, Mia suggested her parents should have divorced, rhetorically asking: "Why stay together if you're not happy?" Mia explains that marriage "put a stop" to her father's adventurousness in his younger days. For Mia, individual happiness, rather than obligations or children, justifies marital endurance.

As Mia recounts the divorces she has witnessed, we learn that she gives advice consistent with her belief in "divorce as a gateway." When her sister-in-law was trying to decide whether to divorce, Mia not only provided support, but successfully advocated divorce: "I was always encouraging her, you know, 'Hey, this is your lease on a new life. Do whatever you feel is right! [. . .] It's like these things happen, you know. Are you happy?'"

Mia's speculation about her parents' marriage, her advice to her sister-in-law, and her own divorce account suggests that Mia is a clear-cut individualist—she believes that one's self and happiness should come first. Individualism clearly informs her marital and gender ideologies; in fact, it serves to bridge these ideologies. Marriage, divorce, and de-gendered roles are all rooted in and contingent upon individual choice or rights equality and personal happiness.

Yet, several contradictions suggest that happiness means more than independence and personal happiness to Mia—that Mia harbors *relational* concerns. While individualism is a stance that puts the self first, relationality emphasizes expressivity and attunement to the needs of others. Relationality, rather than individualism, informs many a '70s wife's ideal of marriage. Rights and relational equality are easier to sever in abstract theory than in actual practice. Three aspects of Mia's interview suggest this ideal: her story of an unexpected divorce, the Turners' own brush with divorce, and Mia's marital disappointments.

An Unexpected Divorce

Despite a remarriage based on independence and de-gendered roles, Mia retains an "image" of successful marriage that leaves her open to what I call the "unexpected divorce." Such divorce stories reveal a new "structure of surprise": the unexpected divorce represents the dashed hope that marital endurance is predictable. Mia states:

> And then this couple, I saw socially [. . .] they were like the only high school couple to still be together. [. . .] I kind of thought that was a good, you know, marriage, they have two kids, you know, a beautiful home, he's in computers, you know, she didn't have to work [slight laugh]. [. . .] But um . . . *shocked all of us when they got divorced.* [. . .] For me it was something because, you know, all these years, and you're talking about maybe 20 years, [. . .] and they had two kids and um . . . I thought it was sad only because the kids were beautiful and we just thought like "wow, they have everything going for them."

With the exception of the marriage's longevity, the reasons for Mia's shock were puzzling. After her first marriage, Mia repudiated the breadwinner/homemaker model she described in the foregoing account. For Mia, being a "housewife" in a "suburb" was, as she said: "absolutely horrible." She loves her work. She does not espouse staying together for the kids. Yet she mentions the "kids" three times and was saddened because the "kids were beautiful."

Mia's disbelief at this divorce reveals her personal ambivalence and how the "ideals" of marriage culture and male breadwinning endure, even in the midst of divorce culture and gender equality. Ultimately, however, this divorce story works to affirm Mia's belief that traditional roles undermine marriages today. Furthermore, Mia's story of an unexpected divorce—especially her repeated reference to the kids—reveals Mia's relational concerns about divorce. These concerns also surface as she discusses a "near divorce" from Nick.

Divorce Options: Turning to Therapy

Two years ago, one of the Turner's children was hit by a car when each spouse thought the other spouse was watching the child. While their daughter has generally recovered, the incident represented a family communication problem to both spouses.

One evening, during this traumatic period, a new crisis emerged when, as they both attested, Nick "erupted," getting drunk and violent. When I ask about the biggest surprise of his marriage, Nick begins to relate his version of this event. He replies, "I guess the . . . *we're still together after I erupted one evening,* you know, I had too much to drink and one thing set me off and I went on a screaming rampage." This "near divorce" was averted because, with some resistance, he conformed to her conditions. As Mia reported, her conditions were: "I go, 'okay, you know, you go see the therapist *or I'm out of here.'* You know, I wasn't gonna wait around for him to put his mitts on me. That was . . . that's all it took for me, you know. And uh . . . but you know, it was just so out of character for him. But you know, like I said, I think it was all that internalizing." Mia goes on to frame the "violence" not only as pivotal, but exceptional: "it was just so out of character." It was "Dr. Jekyll and Mr. Hyde."

When Mia demanded that Nick go into therapy, she put into practice the belief in a "marital work ethic." The "marital work ethic" is the belief that one must *work* on a marriage if it is to survive. This belief was almost universal among these '70s spouses. In contrast to the ethic, "marital work" is the practice; it involves the ongoing reflexive and relational work necessary to create, sustain, and reproduce a gratifying marriage. If relationality is the aim, the marital work is the means—a means typically infused with therapeutic culture. Mia not only forged a direct link between Nick's non-communication and his explosive behavior that night, she also expected Nick to share the emotion and expressive work of marriage. While *she* feels the freedom to communicate, she conveys frustration that "he doesn't share a lot of his uh, deeper feelings." She wanted Nick to learn the expressive and relational skills for the survival of the marriage. Or else.

What I want to emphasize here is that Mia used the power of independence to produce relational ends. Divorce culture became a means to marital endurance. Mia defined the terms of marital contingency and used the divorce option to redistribute the emotional division of labor in the marriage. Apart from her adamant demand for independence, Mia desires a relational marriage.

My data on '70s wives suggest that women's increasing independence and their attempts to redistribute the "marital work" are a mark of *women changing faster than men* (Hochschild with Machung 1989). For '50s couples, marital monitoring was done by and expected of wives. In the context of marriage culture, such monitoring led to wives' accommodation *within* the marriage. Among '70s couples, both spouses talk about and believe in a marital work ethic; in the context of divorce culture, reflexivity about marriage is unavoidable. Despite shared talk, and because of wives' conventional responsibility for monitoring marriage, '70s wives must enlist husbands into the practice of the marital work ethic. To bring about relational ideals in their marriages, more wives must engage the power of independence. Wives' individualism should be understood in the context of these relational ends. Independence may be crucial for redefining marriage in an egalitarian direction; even so, wives need husbands like Nick, who are willing to reciprocate.

Nick was reluctant to go to therapy, but he recognized that "I got some stuff out of it." Nick admits: "Sometimes I should say stuff and I don't, other times I say half things and don't cover it all." He isolated "communication," as the biggest "challenge" of the marriage. Nick was still struggling, but he continued to "work on" communication.

Relational Disappointments

When I ask her what is most disappointing about this marriage, Mia begins by returning to her disappointment about communication. Her faith in the "marital work ethic" tempers this disappointment. She asserts: "The communications thing, that is a little bit disappointing, but I don't think it's something that we can't um ... work on and I just hope, you know, that we don't get to the point where we don't try ... you know? And his mother, recently shared that with me, recently because I always thought outwardly they had a great relationship, but she said something to me about 'we really don't talk much.' And it's like, *oh god, I don't want to get to that point."* When Mia moaned, "oh god, I don't want to get to that point," she conveyed her absolute dread of a noncommunicative marriage. "Communication" and "talk" are marks of her relational criteria for marital happiness; she does not simply want independence, she wants to feel connected.

Mia goes on to express disappointment in the relationship between her husband, Nick, and her daughter, Jeri. As was the case with other parents and stepparents I interviewed, making a whole family out of part-relations for the Turners entailed a great deal of effort, frustration, and variable rewards. For the biological parent, in this case Mia, there can be disappointment that their deep and unconditional love for their child is not shared. Despite the declining emphasis on "staying together for the sake of the children," and the increased emphasis on the spousal relationship, children remain a part of the equation in marital happiness. For Mia this is a relational, rather than an individualistic, disappointment.

Mia's third marital disappointment also testified to her relational concerns in the marriage. More than that, it symbolized her sensitivity to Nick's concerns, because it was identical to Nick's expressed marital disappointment in his interview. She is disappointed, like Nick, that he is not happier with his work. While Nick has a high-paying, stable job, he has always wanted to be an interior designer. They each express the hope that Nick's dream will become financially feasible in the future.

In sum, despite Mia's individualistic "talk" and a marriage contingent on independence, her disappointments and desires are implicitly relational.

Mia's Hidden Agenda

Nick's participation in the "marital work" augurs well for the Turner marriage. Nevertheless, Nick's expressed disappointments are fewer and less relational than Mia's. In line with Bernard's (1982) report that "his" marriage is better than "hers," Nick appears more satisfied with the marriage as it is. Because Nick is content, he is less inclined to monitor the marriage. However, an inclination to underestimate the fact that for Mia, happiness does not just mean "independence," but also means communicating "deeper feelings," could result in Nick's being one of those former husbands who "didn't know what happened." In Kitson with Holmes' (1992) suburban divorce sample, a notable difference was discovered in the frequency of the marital complaint "Not sure what happened"; for ex-husbands it ranked third, for ex-wives it ranked 28th.[9] In short, Nick might miss the import of Mia's "hidden agenda."

Given Mia's expressed tributes to independence, Nick might believe that recognizing her independence is sufficient. Mia privileges independence to counter the pull of wifely subordination—because she has known the power of socially structured roles, in spite of herself. Because we proceed from a history of male-dominated marriages, individualism does not always *mean* the same thing for women as for men. Individualistic wives are often trying to counter male dominance in marriage. As Miriam Johnson (1988, 261) succinctly observed: "What most women seek is not power but the absence of domination." Wives fear being subordinated in a way that husbands do not. Thus, for Mia, an equality based upon independence is crucial for the survival of the marriage. Although it is necessary, it is not sufficient. While Mia is deeply aware that the combination of independence with marriage is a boon not to be taken lightly by women, relationality informs her vision of a fulfilling marriage.

Forging an egalitarian marriage based on independence and measured by relational fulfillment has depended upon at least three factors: Mia's use of empowered independence, Nick's willingness to recognize Mia as fully his equal and to monitor his marriage, and finally, a well-stocked tool kit of strategies to contend with the option of divorce.

A Tool Kit of Strategies

Both of the Turners, as we have seen, engaged the "marital work ethic." This strategy was most prevalent among '70s spouses. Such relational and reflexive work toward sustaining a marriage is compelled by contingent marriage. Regardless of gender, spouses today feel vulnerable to divorce. However, because wives have conventionally been responsible for monitoring marriage, it is their task to enlist husbands' participation. Although not all '70s wives did so, Mia secured Nick's participation. The Turners went to therapy. They "worked on" their communication. Beyond this *activist* strategy to contend with contingency, the Turners also employed *interpretive* strategies used by '70s couples to contend with marital contingency.

First, '70s spouses use *gender ideology* as a shield against divorce. The Turners' marital commitment is contingent upon an equality rooted in independence, but gender ideology also represents a guarantee of marital happiness. "Gender ideology"—a belief in traditional or egalitarian roles—is a frequent interpretive strategy used by spouses to ensure marital happiness, or conversely, to predict marital demise. While Katy Stone was convinced that gender equality undermined marriage, Mia believed traditionalism did so. The Stones believed male dominance would sustain their marriage, yet as a strategy this was relatively rare among the '50s spouses because marital endurance was more assumed. For the '70s spouses, strategies to secure marital stability are evident. A few '70s spouses still see traditional roles as a guarantee of marital stability, but the proportions have declined. Most '70s spouses talk about equality as crucial to marital happiness. If marriage culture and male dominance were nearly hard-wired for the Stones, divorce culture and gender equality are nearly so for the Turners.

Many '70s spouses, regardless of marital stability, talked about trials when their marriage was on the line, but they *passed the test*. At one point Mia conveys the tentative nature of today's commitments when she says, "That's what I feel marriage is all about. [. . .] [You] enter the relationship as strangers and then you don't really know until you get into it and you're put to the test." Nick and Mia were hardly strangers upon marrying. Yet, the experimental nature of their relationship over time is undeniable: they were lovers, then friends, then platonic roommates, then lovers sharing parenting, and then they married. They shared neither racial/ethnic nor class backgrounds in their childhoods. There is no predicting the relationship. Marriage is a "chance" affair; it begins as a contract and continues as a test. Their "commitment by choice" reflects the tentative quality of their "contract": it could change at any time. So far, they have "passed the test." As Nick remarks: "We've survived some stuff."

The *hypothetical divorce* is an interpretive strategy which comes up briefly in Nick's interview as he discusses a previous relationship where he got "burned." A hypothetical divorce is an imagined divorce that would have taken place had the person married an earlier partner. It is psychologically important, because, by the 1990s, all spouses feel more vulnerable to divorce and its increasing unpredictability. It allows spouses to resolve their ambivalence about divorce. The hypothetical divorce essentially "contains" their potential for divorce; this allows their current relationship to "contain" their chance at marital endurance. For those who have divorced, like Mia, a corollary is found in the *illusory marriage*. Mia explains, "the first marriage, I went into for the wrong reasons, you know, it *really wasn't a marriage*." Akin to the Catholic Church's concept of "annulment," which proclaims that a marriage never took place (Phillips 1991, 2), the illusory marriage suggests the previous marriage was wrong—to the wrong person or for the wrong reasons. Mia was not the only remarried spouse to deny "the reality" of a first marriage. By reconstructing an earlier relationship, '70s spouses can confer authenticity and resilience upon their current relationship.

These strategies are indicators of a generalized "divorce anxiety" among 1970s spouses. Paradoxically, to engage these strategies is to contend with and construct divorce culture at the same time. This distinguishes the '50s spouses from the '70s spouses; while we see the '50s spouses "register" the rise of divorce culture by the 1970s and 1980s, the

'70s couples not only register, but reproduce the tenets of divorce culture and its language of individual choice.

Divorce culture is marked by a language of individualism. However, individualism does not mean the same thing for husbands and wives. Husbands have had more room for independence within male-dominated marriages; by definition, they have had more power to assert their marital ideals. Now, more wives are asserting their marital visions. In contrast to Katy Stone, who "lost" her self for a male-defined marital ideal, Mia put her self first in her remarriage. Still, the individualistic talk of some '70s wives can obscure a vision of relationality that often conditions the option, the contingency, the gateway.

While marital monitoring was apparent among '50s wives, a full-blown "marital work ethic" has become a pervasive strategy among '70s wives and, increasingly, husbands. The '70s couples use more strategies to reconcile the desire for an enduring and gratifying marriage with a belief in contingency—a belief fostered by a changed social context. A new social context means that few spouses can escape divorce thoughts and all must be reflexive. In the next chapter, we look at the changing social conditions—demographic, economic, legal, and political—that have informed and interacted with these generational changes in marital meaning.

2 The Shifting Grounds for Divorce
Structural and Cultural Conditions for Change

New Structural Conditions for Divorce Culture

DIVORCE is only one thread in the fabric of family and social change we have witnessed in recent decades. Demographers Ahlburg and De Vita (1992, 1) remarked that "The family has changed so much in just a few decades that it is difficult for individuals and social institutions to keep up." In addition to divorce, salient developments have included cohabitation, domestic partnerships, gay and lesbian marriage ceremonies, blended families, single parenthood, and dual-job couples. All have contributed to the diversification of relationship ideals and the decline of the reigning ideal. While they are all distinct developments, together they question fundamental assumptions about the nature of marriage. Cohabitation and single parenthood suggest one need not marry at all; lesbian and gay marriages suggest marriage need not be heterosexual and, along with dual-job couples, that labors need not be divided by gender; blended families suggest that marriage is not necessarily forever and relationships can be redefined. Divorce, however, remains a crucial thread that both unravels and secures the nature of marriage on a widespread scale. A number of demographic, economic, legal, and social conditions help explain the dramatic changes in marital practices in the United States between the 1950s and the 1990s that enabled and reflected the rise of divorce culture.

The Demographic "Tipping Point"

Today, nearly everyone's life has been touched by divorce. Witnessing divorce has become a common experience. By the 1960s, divorce could no longer be said to be "a functional substitute" for death (Stone 1989), and by the 1970s it had became more common for an adult to lose a spouse (or a child to lose a parent) through divorce than through death (Glick 1979; Sweet and Bumpass 1987). In 1970, the U.S. Census Bureau acknowledged the antiquated assumption that the end of a marriage was caused by death when, for the first time, it introduced the question of *how* a person's marriage ended (Sweet and Bumpass 1987).

Writing of a 1970 marriage cohort, Cherlin (1992, 24) reported that "by 1977, only seven years after they had married, one-quarter of these couples had already divorced. In contrast, it was 25 years before one-quarter of those who married in 1950 had divorced." It has been predicted that 51 percent of marriages begun in 1970 will eventually end in divorce. Predictions of divorce for marriages contracted in more recent years run from slightly less than one-half to two-thirds (Cherlin 1992, 24).

While divorce rates during the twentieth century have been increasing overall, the divorce rates of the 1950s were unpredictably low. Cherlin (1992, 22) pointed out that to compare the rates of the 1950s with those in the 1970s and 1980s is to compare a period of relatively low rates with a period of relatively high rates. In this sense, the 1950s were, in the long term, the unusual decade; the 1960s and 1970s represent the resumption of long-term trends.

Divorce scholars speculate that the very high numbers of divorces may be more than indicators; they may have some kind of intangible power of their own to affect the social context of marriage and divorce. Because divorce is so prevalent, Goode (1993, 3) remarked, "the *average* divorce in the West is less explosive now than in the past, but the summed impact on the society may be even greater because the number of divorces is so much greater." Cherlin (1992, 48) observed that divorce behaviors preceded attitude changes in the 1960s, but these divorces probably influenced the clear change in attitudes: "Once attitudes toward divorce began to change markedly—probably at the start of the 1970s, give or take a few years—then the shift in people's beliefs may have provided a new stimulus for further rises in divorce." Finally, Phillips (1988, 617) suggested that divorce could have a "hypothetical feedback" effect. Relying on a double negative to emphasize the tentative nature of his claims, he argued: "It is unreasonable to suppose that divorce laws and the divorce rate, and the increasingly high profile of the divorced population, have had no impact on the perceptions and behavior of the married population" (633).

The Legal Upheaval

The legal regulation of marriage and divorce has changed radically since 1970, when California introduced "no fault" divorce—now incorporated into the legal systems of all 50 states. This innovation liberalized divorce by abolishing grounds and deeming fault irrelevant.[1] Because spouses are no longer required to establish fault, a moral framework has given way to an administrative one; punishing a party who assumes guilt for breaching the marriage contract is no longer relevant. Unlike under traditional law, it is not necessary to disclose or devise grounds for divorce—it is enough to declare "irreconcilable differences," or "irretrievable breakdown." This has reduced the adversarial climate that attended divorce in the past. Perhaps most indicative of the permissive nature of the new law, where it applies, is the "no-consent" rule, which permits one spouse to decide unilaterally when spousal differences have become "irreconcilable." The power of divorce lies with the spouse who wants it for whatever reason; the resistant spouse can no longer rely upon "fault-based grounds" as leverage to deter or to be compensated for the divorce.

Weitzman (1985, 368) elaborated on how these changes fundamentally redefined marriage: "The new rules shifted the legal criteria for divorce—and thus for viable marriage—from fidelity to the traditional marriage contract to individual standards of personal satisfaction. They thereby redefined marriage as a time-limited, contingent arrangement rather than a lifelong commitment." The legal messages of "contingency" and "individual standards of personal satisfaction" cannot be seen strictly as "causal." To a great extent, no-fault divorce was interpretive; that is, it adapted to behavior already going on and encoded this behavior into the law (Glendon 1987, 142). Divorce behaviors began to climb in the early 1960s, more liberal attitudes toward divorce followed, and then, after no-fault divorce was introduced in the 1970s, there was no apparent effect on divorce rates (Cherlin 1992, 48, 56). Yet, as Weitzman (1985) argued, this redefinition of marriage promoted individualism by providing incentives for acquiring self-sufficiency and investing in oneself rather than in a relationship. Such effects are not necessarily measured by an immediate leap in rates. Moreover, evidence suggests that other adult roles, primarily occupational, seem to be gradually displacing the salience of marriage and family relationships (Hochschild 1997; Sweet and Bumpass 1987; Spanier 1989). Finally, beliefs in "contingency" were reflected in a 1977 survey finding that a majority of people do not believe that most *other* people expect to remain married today (Yankelovich 1981, 96). These new rules, like law in general, should probably be understood as constitutive as well; laws influence how we perceive reality, how we legitimate and feel about our behaviors (Glendon 1987, 9, 142).

In recent years, we have witnessed an effort to use legal reforms to influence how we perceive divorce (Sugarman 1998; Kay 1990). A small but notable move to introduce "covenant marriages" into family law has been occurring at the state level. Louisiana was the first state to institute covenant marriage in 1997, and Arizona followed in 1998. The laws aim to reconstitute the cultural norm of marital commitment in three ways. First, couples who choose such marriages must seek premarital counseling—religious or secular. Second, in the event of divorce, the couples must meet grounds for divorce set by the state (such as adultery). Third, couples who wed under covenant marriage must abide by a pre-set waiting period before the divorce is finalized (*San Francisco Examiner,* November 23, 1997). So far, covenant marriage does not replace, but exists alongside, no-fault divorce law. Covenant conditions could reinforce "marriage as forever," though they could also evoke the fault-finding and hypocrisy that characterized many divorces before the 1970s.

While the main motivation of the initial Family Law Act was to eliminate hypocrisy and to reduce litigation over fault-finding, and *not* to effect equality between men and women per se, the provisions relating to "equality" or "gender neutrality" have been at least as consequential as the intended effects, if not more so (Kay 1987, 300–301). The traditional criterion of gender was replaced by the principle of equality to determine the distribution of property awards, spousal and child support awards, and child custody (Kay 1987; Weitzman 1985). The substitution of gender-neutrality for a gender-specific approach to these issues eliminated the long-standing legal support for gender-differentiated responsibilities. It was no longer assumed that only the mother was eligible for custody. Nor was it assumed that the father should be solely responsible for the children's economic welfare. Finally, it was no longer assumed that a man should support his former wife; both spouses were responsible for self-support.[2] In short, the legal base for the "doctrine of separate spheres," that is, the belief in a breadwinning, dominant husband and a caretaking, child-raising, and submissive wife, was essentially dismantled at this time.

The downward mobility of divorced women and children has been well documented (Arendell 1986, 1987; Colletta 1983; Duncan et al. 1984; Kurz 1995; Mason 1988; Newman 1988; Peterson 1996; Weiss 1984; Weitzman 1985).[3] Sometimes these effects have been blamed on no-fault divorce. However, these consequences may stem more from attempts to create legal gender symmetry in an asymmetrical social context (Fineman 1991). Weitzman (1985, 35) explained that the attempt: "to treat men and women equally—or *as if they were equal*—at the point of divorce [...] ignores the *structural inequality* between men and women in the larger society. Divorced women and divorced men do not have the same opportunities: the women are more likely to face job and salary discrimination and more likely to be restricted by custodial responsibilities [emphasis in original]." Assumptions concerning gender-neutrality and self-sufficiency have had ironic effects. The new laws and the sheer prevalence of divorce have played a major role in rendering visible women's continuing economic dependence on men. Under these conditions, women's locations in the sex-stratified labor force, their lower wages vis-à-vis men, and unjust governmental policies became highly salient.

These legal changes have had different generational effects. The generation married in the 1950s is more likely to feel that "they've changed the rules in the middle of the game" with the introduction of no-fault divorce in 1970 (Weitzman 1985, 30).[4] Since the middle-class wives of the 1950s were more likely to be career homemakers, they have been exceedingly vulnerable to the new laws that counsel "self-sufficiency." Eleanor Smeal observed about these women: "They discover the false security of marriage: they can be fired from their job at a moment's notice, with no unemployment compensation, nor retirement benefits, no profit-sharing" (cited in Weitzman 1985, 210). For '50s husbands as well, the deference and caretaking conventionally accorded the breadwinner is lost with wives' potential capacity to earn a living and to "divorce on demand" (Glendon 1987). The bargain has changed for both spouses.

While the rules of the game have not changed midstream for '70s wives, who married under the new legal conditions and are much more likely to be employed, they remain primary parents in a context that has yet to change the male-defined occupational structures. Child care has not been sufficiently institutionalized and, for women, "using child care is almost an entirely unavoidable condition of employment" (Anderson and Vail 1999; Uttal 1996, 294). Furthermore, many jobs are still arranged around the prototype of the man with the support services of a wife in the home (Hochschild 1975, 1997). In short, social structural conditions remain unequal for the '70s couples as well.

It is ironic that attempts to introduce gender neutrality into the legal process of divorce have had the effect of re-gendering the experience—exacerbating as well as exposing long-standing inequities. In tandem with the law, and as a result of legal changes, economic conditions are de-gendering marital rights and responsibilities.

The Economic Shift: Manufacturing to Services

The shift from a manufacturing economy to a service economy, global competition, and a slower rate of economic growth have all contributed to the changing financial circumstances of family members over the last fifty years. Family members have become accustomed to, if not entirely accepting of, the increase in two-earner families, temporary work, and the gap between the rich and the poor. If the 1950s became known for postwar prosperity and affluence, the 1970s became known for the oil crisis and economic "stagflation."

The decline of manufacturing and rise of the service sector has been a long-term shift occurring over many decades, but the shift accelerated in the 1970s (Coontz 1992; Ehrenreich and Piven 1984). The decline of manufacturing jobs meant that high wages—"family wages" secured by decades of union struggle—were becoming scarce by the 1970s. As many social historians have documented, men actively constructed the "family wage" through the struggles and eventual cooperation of labor unions and capitalists in the late nineteenth century and the early decades of the twentieth century (cf. Ferree 1990, 872; May 1988; Hartmann 1976). Not all men had access to this "family wage." However, this wage created economic security for women married to men who did and laid a foundation for the "male provider role." It also reproduced a system that presumed women's dependence on a male wage. This presumption worked to legitimize wage discrimination and occupational sex segregation; this has plagued working women, particularly single women and working-class married women, ever since. It has effectively reinforced the ideal of marriage as a career for women—an ideal from which working-class men and women and single women can only fall short.

In the 1950s, the expanding economy created conditions for upward mobility, at least for some segments of the population. The economic prosperity of the 1950s has been overplayed, glossing over the fact that the benefits varied by race/ethnicity and class (Coontz 1992; May 1988). However, the era was marked by an improving standard of living. While in the mid-1940s one-third of U.S. homes did not have running water and half did not have electric refrigerators, the postwar economic boom brought relative affluence. The median family income rose 42 percent in the 1950s and another 38 percent in the 1960s (Cherlin 1992, 35). Many of the new suburbanites had working-class roots, but the family ideal was middle class (Skolnick 1991) and the suburbs were primarily white. The middle-class nuclear family ideal was intertwined with owning a home—a tangible asset that, in turn, depended upon economic conditions and government policies.

Stephanie Coontz (1992) observed that the upward mobility experienced by large sectors of the 1950s cohort was marked not only by an expanding economy, but by government assistance. Government assistance in the form of the G.I. bill and new regulation and financing through the Federal Housing Authority and the Veterans Administration combined to create home ownership and educational opportunities. The rapidly expanding economy and governmental assistance together provided the context for upward mobility, the enduring myth of "self-reliance" notwithstanding.[5]

Among the factors used to explain the unexpected trends of the 1950s—high marriage and birth rates as well as low divorce rates—"affluence" has been a favorite. However, affluence and a low divorce rate have not been consistently associated. Cherlin (1992, 43) observed that the economy continued to improve into the 1960s, yet age at marriage and divorce rates were going up, not down. Conversely, affluence has been used to explain high divorce rates. Elaine Tyler May (1988, 9) has observed that the variables commonly used to explain behavioral changes in the 1960s and 1970s—affluence and the expanding employment and education of women—existed "at the peak of the domestic revival" in the 1950s. In sum, affluence cannot fully explain cohort or period changes.

Cherlin (1992, 31–43) noted that most explanations can be categorized as either *cohort* or *period* explanations. Cohort explanations focus on those experiences distinctive to a particular birth cohort, such as the experience of the Great Depression or the absolute size of a birth cohort, such as the baby boom. Period explanations emphasize social changes that seem to affect everyone at once. Two cohort explanations for the trends of the 1950s incorporate affluence into their accounts—those of Elder (1974) and Easterlin (1980). However, Cherlin argued that neither Elder's emphasis on the social and psychological effects of the economic climate nor Easterlin's emphasis upon cohort size explain the characteristics of all groups that fall under their purview. Cherlin concluded that "it is clear from the vantage point of the 1990s that period effects have dominated trends in marriage, divorce, and childbearing in this century" (32). When marriage and divorce rates have been high, they have been high for all; when low, they have been low for all, regardless of age. Cherlin provides a careful critique of "cohort" analyses, showing that behaviors such as women's participation in the labor force rose for all ages. Still, there is a difference in the degree, the class status, and the meaning for women of the baby boom generation.[6]

The number of women in the labor force was increasing in the 1950s, in part because jobs in the expanding service sector were perceived as "women's work" (Oppenheimer cited by Cherlin 1992, 149). May (1988) accurately observed that women's education and employment were rising in the 1950s. However, the rise affected middle-class women of the '50s and '70s generations at different points in their life cycle, changing the meaning of wage work.

One of the most notable changes that occurred between the 1950s and 1970s was the "revolutionary" rise in the number of married mothers in the labor force. With the continued expansion of the service economy and its reliance upon nonunionized, cheap labor, more mothers were drawn into the labor force. McLaughlin and colleagues (1988, 94) reported:

> In 1950 the labor force participation rate of women with preschool-age children was 11.9 percent, and the rate for women with children aged 6–17 was 28.3 percent (Michael 1985; Hayghe 1984). By 1980, however, these

rates had increased to 45 percent for those with preschool-age children and to 62 percent for those with older children. These changes represent increases in labor force participation of nearly 300 percent for women with young children and over 100 percent for women with older children during the thirty-year period.[7]

Today, two-job couples comprise the majority of married couples.[8] By 1995, 91 percent of the fathers and 67 percent of mothers in married couple families with children under age 18 were employed (U.S. Bureau of the Census 1996, 7).

The rise in women's participation in the labor force has been particularly steep for white, middle-class married mothers. They have followed the lead of working-class mothers of all races/ethnicities who have, more often than not, had to secure wage work. Stacey (1990, 11) pointed out the gender and class ironies that occurred with the decline of manufacturing jobs and the male "family wage":

> Escalating consumption standards, the expansion of mass collegiate education, and the persistence of high divorce rates then gave more and more women ample cause to invest a portion of their identities in the 'instrumental' sphere of paid labor. Thus, middle-class women began to abandon their confinement in the modern family [in the 1960s] just as working-class women were approaching its access ramps. The former did so, however, only after the wives of working-class men had pioneered the twentieth-century revolution in women's paid work.

Because so many factors changed simultaneously, mothers' participation in the labor force should not be seen as the cause of higher divorce rates. Still, most scholars agree that women's participation in the labor force deserves emphasis as a crucial determinant in changing marital practices (Cherlin 1992, 63).[9]

The change to a postindustrial economy which redefined women's and men's economic opportunities had a significant impact on family patterns by the "watershed" era of the 1970s. At one and the same time, this shift changed the conditions for entering, conducting, and leaving a marriage. The economic context of the 1970s marital cohort's experiences can be sharply distinguished from that of their parents. After an affluent childhood in the aggregate, the 1970s generation faced a sluggish economy. From an economy of manufacturing jobs based on production that provided a "family wage," we moved toward a service economy based on consumption that provided minimum wages. Some of the economic changes, such as the development of an advanced industrial society and women's participation in the labor force, have been cumulative. Other changes, such as the oil price shock of 1973 and stagnant wages, have been specific. As crucial as economic shifts have been, however, Cherlin (1992) suggests that changes in marital patterns cannot be reduced to economics—the social and political climates must also be considered.

Contrasting Social and Political Climates

From a period famous for McCarthyism and incipient civil rights struggles to a period famous for the Vietnam War and an array of social protest movements, there is no doubt that pervasive, but distinctive influences were at work in families' lives in both eras. Most scholars' explanations for the high marriage, high fertility, and low divorce rates of the 1950s and the low marriage and fertility and high divorce rates of the 1970s include reference to the unique social and political contexts of the times.

After World War II, millions of people seemed to have a "pent up" need to marry and have children after postponing this during the war. Many analysts have reasoned that the trials of the proceeding decades left Americans "exhausted" and influenced their turn inward toward family lives (Phillips 1988, 618, citing Seeley et al. 1956). In *Homeward Bound,* a study of 1950s marriages, Elaine Tyler May (1988, 208) reasoned that the cold war of the 1950s itself influenced people to turn toward home life. According to May, foreign and domestic political policies were a key factor in conservative domestic behaviors: "In private life as well as in foreign policy, containment seemed to offer the key to security. With security as the common thread, the cold war ideology and the domestic revival reinforced each other." As May concluded, containment, security, conformity, and domesticity marked the decade.

Even as their participation in the labor force reached all-time highs, the domestic ideal intensified for women (Cherlin 1992; Coontz 1992; May 1988; Skolnick 1991). In her "critique of 1950s social science," Wini Breines (1986, 86) revealed how researchers of the times *perceived* gender equality, despite countervailing evidence. Because gender contradictions were obscured, only in retrospect has it become evident that "the 1950s contained the tinder of gender conflict and change of the next thirty years."

The tinder of gender contradictions in marriage predated the recent women's movement, according to Ehrenreich (1984). She argues that this tinder began to spark for men even during the 1950s, tracing what she called a "male revolt" against the family breadwinner role back to early "gray flannel" dissidents, the inception of *Playboy* magazine, and the Beats. These outlets for men were marked by a defensive masculinity that guarded against the ever-present threat of being labeled homosexual or deviant. While "conformity" was a key issue for white men, the "problem with no name" was a more central issue for white women (30).

With the publication of *The Feminine Mystique* in 1963, Betty Friedan articulated white, middle-class women's vague discontent as wives and mothers and called it the "problem with no name." Friedan found fault in society, including the mass media, the educators, and the psychologists, who had promoted the "feminine mystique" and stifled women's development by preventing their participation in the public world (Skolnick 1991, 115–16). Friedan's book marks the beginning of white women's break with the "suburban family ideal."[10] This break was fueled by the rising political ferment of the times.

The Civil Rights movement of the 1950s had inaugurated an agenda that challenged inequality, injustice, and the violation of individual rights. The challenge to the status quo and the assertion of individual rights were translated into a challenge to the concept of "woman's place" and an assertion of women's rights. The Civil Rights and New Left movements were followed and accompanied by the women's movement, the sexual liberation movement, and a budding gay and lesbian movement—the three movements to have the most direct impact upon redefinitions of marital meanings.[11] These movements exposed the contradictions between ideals and practices, tutored women in the skills of political organizing, and finally, compelled recognition that the "personal is political."

The women's movement as a whole initiated a rethinking of women's lives and identities as workers and family members. While the movement was largely homogenous by class and race/ethnicity (white and middle class) it was constituted by a broad political spectrum of liberal, radical, lesbian, socialist, and Marxist feminists. All these branches of feminism pursued some notion of "equality"—though they differed in how to define and achieve it. Issues that had been largely suppressed for women and men in the 1950s became increasingly visible and problematic—from wage discrimination to marital norms.

The recent women's movement crested in the mid-1970s (Skolnick 1991). This was in part due to its success, which, in turn, generated the rise of opposition movements. It was also due to its own internal flaws: young, white, middle-class women's failure to take the needs of all women into account, particularly working-class women and women of color (Davis 1981; hooks 1981; Hull, Scott, and Smith 1982; Moraga and Anzaldua 1981), as well as the needs of wives and mothers (Rosenfelt and Stacey 1987; Snitow 1990). Yet, even as the high tide of the movement subsided and women became reluctant to label themselves feminist, the support for feminist ideals conveyed by the recent women's movement has become unmistakable and probably irreversible.[12] In a 1989 poll, 85 percent of African-American women, 76 percent of Hispanic women, and 64 percent of white women said that the United States needed a strong women's movement. Young women between the ages of 18 to 29 were among those most likely to make that assertion (Renzetti and Curran 1995, 502, 505).

When compared to attitudes in the 1950s, beliefs about gender, sexuality and family life have changed remarkably. A trend toward egalitarianism is evident in survey data collected since the 1960s and 1970s (Mason and Lu 1988; Simon and Landis 1989; Thornton, Alwin, and Camburn 1983). By 1976, 70 percent of women and 65 percent of men condoned "married women earning money" (Moen 1992, 16). Attitudes embracing the male-headed household were also on the decline. Only 32 percent of wives disagreed with the belief that "most of the important decisions in the life of the family should be made by the man of the house" in 1962, while 78 percent of the same wives disagreed in 1985 (Thornton 1989, 876).

Attitudes toward diverse sexualities also began to change in the 1970s. Sexual identity politics have evolved notably since the "gay liberation" movement was sparked in 1969 by the Stonewall riots and since the lesbian feminism of the 1970s (Stein 1997). Yet, unlike the women's movement, social movements for sexual minorities do not seem to have crested. Lesbian and gay couples have been fighting for the right to marry or the right to marriage benefits, the right to custody, and the right to new family forms through the courts and legislative bodies (Weston 1991; Stacey 1998). In so doing, they contest a still tenacious legal assumption about marriage: heterosexuality.[13] If marriage were to include same-sex couples, this could help challenge gendered patterns of inequality associated with the institution (Stacey 1998).

The "sexual revolution" significantly liberalized views toward premarital sex and sex unrelated to marriage.[14] The numbers and acceptance of cohabiting couples increased (Cherlin 1992; Gwartney-Gibbs 1986; Thornton 1989). By the mid-1980s, half of the married population aged 30–34 had cohabited at some time, in contrast to only six percent of those over 60 years of age (Goode 1993, 159).[15] Cohabitation across classes appears to account for declining marriage and remarriage rates, even as it is conducive to divorce (Bumpass, Sweet, and Cherlin 1991). Bumpass (1990, 488) observed: "both marital instability and cohabitation are part of, and contribute to, the reduction in the perceived necessity of marriage."

Critical attitudes toward remaining single (perceived as "sick or immoral, too selfish, or too neurotic") declined markedly between 1957 and 1976—from 53 to 34 percent of respondents (Veroff, Douvan, and Kulka 1981, 147). More recently, only one-third of adults under 25 agreed that "it is better to be married than to go through life single" (Bumpass

1990, 488). While young people still expect to get married at some point (Thornton 1989, 880), from 1976 to 1992 there was an increase in the percentage of high school seniors who agreed that "one sees so few good marriages that one questions it as a way of life" (Glenn 1996, 26). Increased acceptance of sex before marriage and the option of cohabitation are conducive to later marriage, no first marriage, and no remarriage—even where children are involved (Bumpass, Sweet, and Cherlin 1991). More than one child in four is now born outside of marriage (Thornton 1996, 74), and single parents are as likely to have never married as to have been divorced (Bureau of the Census 1995b, xvii). Attitudes and practices reflect how the lock-step sequences in dating, marrying, and bearing children, adhered to in the 1950s era, have clearly been on the decline since the 1970s. Marrying became an "option" as attitudinal changes provided leeway to have sex, live together, and live a singles life without the sting of stigma prominent in the 1950s.

Finally, "marrying as a given" is likely to mean something different when escape from a marriage is decreasingly deterred by social or legal constraints. Changing attitudes toward divorce itself have been striking. In her small-scale study of divorcing adult children and their parents (i.e., grandparents), *Ex-Familia,* Colleen Leahy Johnson (1988, 47) found that "almost three times as many divorced parents as grandparents agreed that divorce was a 'growth experience.'" [16] Johnson also found that about twice as many of the divorced parents in her sample said a woman's "first responsibility was to herself rather than to her family" compared to the still-married grandparents (47). This is related to the decline in the belief that spouses should stay together for the "sake of the children."

Thornton's (1989) longitudinal study revealed that in 1962, 51 percent of women disagreed with the statement that "when there are children in the family, parents should stay together even if they don't get along"; by 1977, 80 percent disagreed. Thornton concluded from his data: "There has been a dramatic and pervasive weakening of the normative imperative to marry, to remain married, to have children, to restrict intimate relations to marriage, and to maintain separate roles for males and females" (873). What had been deviant in the 1950s—children born out of wedlock, cohabitation, divorce, working mothers, and childlessness—was more acceptable by the 1970s. The stigma we attach to divorce, among other behaviors, has declined (Gerstel 1987), while our emotional expectations of what marriage should deliver have been on the rise.

Expectations of marriage have been on the rise since the turn of the century (May 1980). These expectations have continued unabated, yet they had also become increasingly fluid by the 1970s. Spouses were less likely to construct uniform definitions of "the" marital situation. Boundaries between social norms and social deviance were harder to discern. Vocabularies of norm and deviance—"courtship," "shotgun weddings," "shacking up," "illegitimacy," "old maids,"—began to lose their meanings as family forms diversified. The message conveyed by no-fault divorce—that marriage is a "time-limited, contingent arrangement"—was increasingly reflected in rates and attitude surveys. Because the experience of divorce liberalizes attitudes, as the divorced population has multiplied, the "tipping point" in numbers gradually contributes to the watershed in marital meaning. Although it has become harder to believe that "marriages are forever," just what marriages should be contingent upon has been contested.

The debate over what marriage should be contingent upon has been evident in ongoing cultural debates involving religious and secular beliefs about the meaning of marriage, as well as gender ideology. While "marriage culture" has held its own in these debates, "divorce culture" has been fortified by cultural developments since 1970.

OLD AND NEW CULTURAL GROUNDS FOR MARRIAGE AND DIVORCE

Historically, one can discern two sets of belief systems that have, through various institutions, contributed greatly to debates about marital meaning in the United States. Both marital ideologies—marriage culture and divorce culture—dynamically interact with and are informed by two other systems of meaning that are not necessary to them, but have become associated with them through the particulars of Western history. Marriage culture has historically been supported by the Judeo-Christian tradition, as well as by an ideology of male dominance. In contrast, divorce culture has been fortified by two other belief systems: therapeutic culture and gender equality. These beliefs systems clearly influence lives and institutions beyond marriage; they are also capable of interacting with marital ideologies in complex and sometimes contradictory ways.

All these belief systems have informed and interacted with one another. Yet, the strength of that interaction has varied. Thus, marriage culture, the Judeo-Christian tradition, and male dominance have tended to "go together." It is crucial to note that I am not claiming, for example, that all Judeo-Christian traditions repudiate gender equality or divorce. Also, I am not claiming that divorce culture is a cause or effect of gender equality (or, marriage culture of male dominance); rather, I am claiming that *beliefs* about gender equality and divorce culture have complemented one another because they share similar presuppositions. Also, I am not claiming that therapeutic culture and gender equality bear *no* relationship to the beliefs of "marriage culture;" as we will see in later chapters, beliefs in marriage culture, religious culture, and gender equality can converge. However, I am claiming that, historically, these relationships have been weaker.

Marriage Culture and the Judeo-Christian Tradition

Marriage culture can be understood to be associated with Western religious culture in at least four interrelated ways: (1) historically, religious institutions have regulated marital practices, sanctioning marriage and censuring divorce; (2) the marital practices of the religiously committed suggest that divorce is experienced as a last resort more often; (3) theoretically, religion has given meaning and purpose to family practices, especially marriage; and (4) religious institutions have generally reinforced the link between male dominance and marriage culture.

The beliefs of "marriage culture" have their historical moorings in religious culture and, in the West, these moorings have been the Judeo-Christian or biblical tradition (Bellah et al. 1985). While there are notable variations within the biblical tradition with respect to marriage and family, there are also shared themes.[17] The Judeo-Christian tradition has primarily supported, if not exalted, marriage: marriage has been framed as necessary, as fundamentally for the procreation of children, as heterosexual, as monogamous, and as lifelong.[18]

Most teachings in the Judeo-Christian tradition have promoted "marriage as forever" and have denounced or discouraged divorce or remarriage. An earlier phase of "marriage culture," when divorce was virtually "no resort," echoes in Christ's mandate: "what God hath joined let no man put asunder" (Matt. 19:6). The belief in divorce as "no resort" endures in some faiths;[19] however, the latest phase of "marriage culture" in the twentieth century has ushered in the more prevalent belief in "divorce as a last resort" in most U.S. congregations. Even the traditionally divorce-resistant Catholic Church became more liberal between the 1950s and the 1970s: All "religious groups became more tolerant of divorce, but Catholics demonstrated the greatest amount of change, with the result that Catholic attitudes are much closer to those of non-Catholics in 1971 than they were in 1958" (McCarthy 1979, 181). In the light of traditional strictures, the growing number of annulments and divorces among Catholics suggests that "last resort" beliefs are far reaching.

Aldous (1983) pointed out that the number of divorces is too large for divorce to be reserved for the nonreligious. Nevertheless, religious membership still differentiates divorce rates. Ammerman and Roof (1995) document the tendency of some churches to cater to traditional families. Still, the association between marriage culture and religious culture is represented by lower rates of divorce among the religiously committed, though the correlation is weakening.[20] Albrecht, Bahr, and Goodman (1983, 83) found that religious couples are more likely to remain married, particularly if they are married in a religious setting, if they are religiously active, and if the spouses share the same faith. Alternatively, those wed in civil ceremonies, the nominally religious, and those in interfaith marriages reflect higher divorce rates.

Bellah and colleagues (1985) elaborated on the collectivist incentives and moral premises that augur for maintaining marital commitments among the religiously committed. Speaking about marriage for those within the Christian tradition, they observe: "It is, first a commitment, a form of obedience to God's word," it "rests less on feeling than on decision and action," and its permanence is possible "only by having an obligation to something higher than one's own preferences or one's own fulfillment" (97). They point out a distinction in marital meaning for those who embrace Christian values: "Of course, these Christians seek some of the same qualities of sharing, communication, and intimacy in marriage that define love for most Americans. But they are determined that these are goods to be sought within a framework of binding commitments, not the reasons for adhering to a commitment" (97). Here, they isolate a traditional, theoretical link between "marriage culture" and "religious culture." Among other commitments, marriage is a commitment that is sustained for purposes beyond the couple. Thus, "the reasons for adhering to a commitment" expand. Marital breakdown is more likely to be recognized if the marriage interferes with the "larger purposes of life" or obedience to God, rather than under conditions of noncommunication or estrangement. Because religious culture assumes a community and a reality prior to the individual, it advances shared substantive ends and individual choices that are delimited by a morality of practices seen as intrinsically good (Bellah et al. 1985, 333–35).

In addition to divorce, recent changes in gender norms and ideologies have been one of the greater challenges for religious institutions and their members. Christianity did not invent male dominance and, in some ways, challenged it by according women a role in the church. Yet, as D'Antonio and Cavanaugh (1983, 142) pointed out, "the societies within which Christianity grew"—Hebrew, Greek, and Roman—"provided the major patriarchal ethos that so strongly shaped the nature of the family down to modern times." The ideology of "male dominance" has not been supported by all denominations,[21] yet it has been a salient and tenacious gender ideology within the Judeo-Christian tradition.

Women's equality and independence has been problematic for religious institutions in the same way it has been problematic for families (Ammerman and Roof 1995). Values associated with religions and families have been in tension with the values of freedom and equality advanced by political democracy and the values of competitive individualism reinforced by a capitalist economy emphasizing individual achievement, self-reliance, and self-interest. Despite the individualistic strain inherent in the Protestant Reformation, religious institutions, like families, have conventionally advocated the values of collectivism, commitment, caring, cooperation, obligation, and self-sacrifice (Aldous and D'Antonio 1983; Bellah et al. 1985; Hargrove 1983). Yet, it has been women, above all, who have been expected to sustain commitment, do the caring, and sacrifice for family members. As Bellah and colleagues (1985, 111) point out with respect to marriage, "women today have begun to question whether altruism should be their exclusive domain." Thus, if the values advanced by religious cultures have been "good," they have not been equally good for all family members.

In sum, religious traditions in the United States tend to uphold a model of marital commitment that reinforces conservative gender beliefs and practices as well as "divorce as a last resort." In contrast, "therapeutic culture"—relatively new in Western history—offers an alternative framework for reevaluating gender issues, redefining marriage, and reframing "divorce as a gateway." With crucial exceptions,[22] therapeutic culture has been increasingly conducive to a more fluid model of gender and sexual relations and has often validated women-centered concerns, aspirations, and values.

Therapeutic Culture and the Language of Individualism

"Therapeutic culture" designates a culture of shared meanings that privilege a psychological and individual perspective for interpreting and making sense of our existence and experiences.[23] It is characterized by a rise in psychotherapy (therapists, clients, organizations), therapeutic forms (such as support groups and advice books), and a therapeutic language (such as "growth" and "self-fulfillment"). Therapeutic culture is associated with divorce culture in at least three suggestive ways: (1) the growing numbers of conflicted or divorcing spouses using therapy and therapeutic forms; (2) the individualistic presuppositions these domains share; and (3) a countervailing tendency for therapeutic culture to advance affective or relational ideals in marriage.

Therapeutic culture, in the form of therapy, advice books, and support groups, is increasingly used by individuals to make sense of their marriages and their divorces. A substantial increase in various kinds of counselors between 1975 and 1985 is one indicator of the increasing appeal and use of therapy. Philipson (1993, 58, citing Robiner 1991, 428) reports: "During that period, psychiatrists increased their numbers by 46%; psychologists by 80%; social workers by 140%, and marriage and family counselors by a shocking 367%. In just one decade, the number of practitioners dispensing mental health services increased over 100%." Along with practitioners, users of therapy have increased in the last two decades. Bellah and colleagues (1985, 121) estimated that probably three times as many Americans saw mental health professionals in the 1980s as in the 1960s. Arendell (1986, 4) suggested that the "rapid growth of the counseling profession is doubtless due in part to the increase in the divorce rate." Kitson with Holmes (1992, 344) found that within the suburban divorced sample, 45 percent had sought assistance from therapists at some point in their marriages; in contrast, within their married sample only 12.4 percent had sought assistance.[24]

But the relevance of therapeutic culture to the meaning of marriage and divorce extends far beyond the married and divorced going to therapy. The therapeutic ethos is increasingly reflected in our magazines, advice books, newspapers, and television programming. In her analysis of self-help books, Simonds (1992, 51) documented the proliferation of advice books on managing relationships: "More than ever before, our language is saturated with the dramatic, self-oriented vocabulary first popularized by the human potential movement; we discuss having our needs fulfilled, working at our relationships, growing emotionally through various involvements." Simonds reported that self-help has found a large audience in female readers and "it is in self-help books addressed to women that heterosexual relationships in their totality are deconstructed most fully" (171). Whether the books counsel "how to save your marriage," or "how to know when your marriage is over," they roundly preach that growth is a goal and solutions lie with the individual's determination.[25]

Finally, magazines and newspapers regularly run articles on "therapeutic" approaches to marriage and divorce. After *Cosmopolitan* compiled the results from its survey of divorced women, the February 1992 issue announced, "20,000 Readers Reveal the Main Reasons for Divorce." The "number one marriage killer," we learn, is "the lack of a basic emotional connection between husband and wife." A later issue of *Cosmopolitan* conveys a therapeutic ethos in its cover story, "Finding a Good Therapist to Save Your Marriage—and When Not to Bother" (August 1993). While such advice articles in magazines are not new, the messages are changing. In her analysis of magazine articles on marriage from 1900 to 1979, Cancian (1987, 43–45) documented an increase of themes advancing self-fulfillment, flexible roles, and intimacy—particularly between 1960 and 1979.[26] Self-expression, intimacy, and flexible roles—hallmarks of relationship ideals today—are therapeutic themes found in almost every vehicle of popular culture.[27]

One cultural vehicle by which people publicly wonder about the proper basis for marriages is nationally syndicated advice columns, such as "Dear Abby" and "Ann Landers." Both columns reflect the therapeutic ethos and regularly recommend therapy, particularly in divorces of "last resort" characterized by "abuse" and/or "alcoholism." For example, Ann Landers responds to a wife's complaints about her alcoholic husband and her interfering mother: "Get into counseling at once and find out why you insist on hanging onto an alcoholic, abusive, unemployed liar. When your counselor gets to the word 'rebellion,' listen with a third ear. Tell yourself, 'I've got to grow up and stop using this lousy relationship to punish my mother.' Then do it" (*Los Angeles Times,* September 10, 1991). Another wife writes: "After many brutal beatings that put me in the hospital, my minister reminded me that the Bible said, 'Turn the other cheek.' Of course my husband continued to beat me, thinking it was his right as the head of the household. Thank God, I finally came to my senses and divorced the bully." Abby responds: "There is hardly a passage in the Old or New Testament that hasn't been interpreted in more ways than one. I would never advise turning the other cheek if the first one was black and blue. Nor would most clergy in the 1990s" (*San Francisco Chronicle,* October 6, 1991, Sunday Punch). Another wife writes that her husband finds sex "too much trouble," is a slob, and is not listening in therapy. Abby responds: "If, as you say, he is already in therapy but 'isn't listening' and you put up with him, you need the therapy more than Al" (*San Francisco Chronicle,* April 6, 1992). In these cases, the necessity of taking care of one's self and a willingness to relate or listen to others anchors the advice.

Therapeutic culture offers a secular alternative for assessing conditions for marriage and divorce. All the premises of divorce culture—"marrying is an option," "marriage is contingent," and "divorce is a gateway"—address whether and how to marry and divorce. Individualism links and underlies these premises. As Bellah and colleagues (1985, 334) revealed, therapeutic culture is informed, above all, by the tradition of "expressive individualism." Expressive individualism "holds that each person has a unique core of feeling and intuition that should unfold or be expressed if individuality is to be realized." Expressive individualism conveys the messages and values of self-reliance, individual choices and needs, and personal integrity.

Bellah and colleagues (1985) argued that the danger of individualism arises when individualism is not restrained by substantive ends. Similar to Durkheim (1951), who submitted that "egoism" and "anomie" become dangerous when they overwhelm the currents of altruism, Bellah and colleagues suggested that we face an imbalance: that declines in both the biblical and republican traditions within American culture have led to an individualism unchecked by traditions with substantive ends that bind social life. When individualism prevails, moral criteria for actions change: "Utility replaces duty; self-expression unseats authority. 'Being good' becomes 'feeling good'" (77). An overemphasis on individual feelings, they argued, obscures our dependence on the sociocultural context both as a source of our limitations and of our potential. Moreover, when individual feelings conflict, sustaining commitments is problematic: "Now if selves are defined by their preferences, but those preferences are arbitrary, then each self constitutes its own moral universe, and there is finally no way to reconcile conflicting claims about what is good in itself" (76). The problem with stressing individual needs in the context of marriage is transparent; when the nearly inevitable conflicts in marriage arise and there are no shared ends to resolve the claims—whether God, the common good, or even the sake of the children—then either a stalemate is reached or resolution devolves onto the individual with the greater implicit or explicit power to effect his or her needs.

Yet the idea of shared ends is also problematic: who decides what is "good in itself"? As we have seen, marriage culture has been tightly linked to the patriarchal ethos of religious culture; conflicts in marriage have too often been decided by the preferences of husbands.[28] Given the gendered oppression that has transpired in the name of substantive ends, it is not surprising that therapeutic culture is increasingly resonant for many women. Instead of the conventional advice telling them to set their needs aside, women are counseled to attend to their own needs, their own feelings, and to take responsibility for their lives. The therapeutic ethos promises moral autonomy, self-reflection, honed communications skills, and feelings of self-worth. While both women and men are subject to the dangers of an individualism understood as self-interest, for women therapeutic culture advances a promise of self-determination that historically has been denied them.

Cancian (1987) argued that analysts across the political spectrum, including Bellah and colleagues, have too severely criticized therapeutic culture for individualistic tendencies and underemphasized the degree to which therapy advances love as well as self-development. She noted that therapy itself can be a means to, and a model of, affection, commitment, and interdependence. Because the therapeutic ethos encourages interdependence and mutual support, Cancian argued, it is not necessarily opposed to marriage and family bonds. Today's relationships manifest the trend toward "self-development" and are a vast improvement over the waning "companionship" blueprint of the 1950s, which emphasized traditional gendered duties and the subordination of women. Cancian described two new models of relationship since the 1950s: the "independent" and the "interdependent" models—both advance more flexible roles and a more androgynous model of love. In Cancian's view, Bellah and colleagues (1985) focus on the "independent" types. These types, she agrees, are more individualistic and see self-development as a precondition to love. However, the other new model, the "interdependent couples" who see love as a precondition to self-development, are more prevalent today.

This suggests that therapeutic culture advances a double message: in addition to the language of individualism, therapeutic culture advances relationality. Relationality has been defined as "a stance which emphasizes expressivity and takes others into account not as 'other' but as important in themselves" (M. Johnson 1988, 68). This definition of relationality revalues feelings and validates them as a form of knowledge, akin to the nongendered "ethic of caring" among African-Americans (Collins 1990); however, in Euro-American culture relationality is frequently constructed as feminine (Gilligan 1982). Of course, historically there have been some individualistic women and relational men across racial/ethnic groups; still, individualism has been masculinized and relationality feminized in dominant white, middle-class culture.

While theorists vary in their evaluations of "therapeutic culture," most theorists agree that the ideals advanced by therapeutic culture are informing today's relationships. Furthermore, they concur that "self-development" has been differentiated by gender and partially determined by economic and social structures. Historically, men's individualism under capitalism depended upon women's self-sacrifice and caretaking (Bellah et al. 1985, 40). As white, middle-class men and women deconstruct these ideals under the purview of therapeutic culture, gender and marital "terms" become contested, unstable, and uncertain. By advancing degendered ideals of caretaking and achievement, therapeutic culture simultaneously contributes to and resolves these instabilities. Still, instability and conflict are to be expected as we undo gender associations in the quest for equality.

THE QUEST FOR GENDER EQUALITY

In the last few decades, the cultural ideology of gender equality has increasingly contested the ideology of male dominance. This conflict continues unabated, yielding redefinitions of family roles and marital responsibilities and revisions of gendered power relations (Ferree 1990). This is not to say that the ideal of gender equality in marriage is new. Equality and role-differentiation have been core, if contradictory, ingredients of the companionate marriage throughout the twentieth century (Cancian 1987; Riessman 1990, 73). There have always been pockets of people who have tried to incorporate gender equality into marriage culture, despite the contradictory press of role-differentiation and the constraints of social structures.[29] As important as such precedents are, they have been culturally marginal efforts until recently. The quest for equality continues.

Gender equality and divorce culture do not share historical roots as male dominance and marriage culture do. Scholars have, however, tried to relate the two phenomena. Research has shown that the experience of divorce tends to foster egalitarianism (Furstenberg and Spanier 1987, 77; Kitson with Holmes 1992, 74). Attempts to identify a reverse influence of gender equality upon divorce have yielded mixed and inconclusive findings. Gender ideology or sex-role attitudes do not seem to predict later divorces (Thornton, Alwin, and Camburn 1983, 224). Nevertheless, there is a widespread "hunch" that the push for gender equality is "associated with" divorce. Goldscheider and Waite (1991, 14) observed: "It is likely that some part of the high divorce rate reflects the working out of the sex-role revolution, in which couples have become increasingly dissatisfied with their original bargain, but cannot find a way to change the terms without dissolving their marriage." Inconsistent findings regarding the effect of gender equality on divorce may be due to three complexities: "original bargains" change over time, men and women are ambivalent about changing gender relations and ideologies, and spouses do not necessarily share ideologies about gender or marriage. Such dynamics are difficult for surveys or public opinion polls to capture.

The complex relationship between gender equality and divorce culture is examined throughout this book. Here, I want to focus upon one central way in which these ideologies are associated: both divorce culture and gender equality *challenge* the status quo in marital meanings and, as such, change the power dynamics in marriage. As challengers to the status quo, both divorce culture and gender equality tend to threaten the enduring, though substantially weakened, ideal of the male-headed household. A number of conditions have had to converge for the challenge of gender equality to become widespread, but most important among these is that wives have had to secure financial independence to weaken the link between marriage culture and male dominance. The potential or actual self-sufficiency of wives can ease departure from the marriage for both spouses. As the economic linchpin of marriage eroded, so too, did the forced interdependence—the economic and emotional bargains—that characterized the "ideology of separate spheres." The "affective individualism" marking white, middle-class marriages in the last century became more problematic by the twentieth century. The gendered split between husbands' "individualistic" rights and wives' "affective" responsibilities became more visible.

Given women's historical identification with family, it should be no surprise that blame for the demise of "marriage culture" has often been directed at women, rather than at social structural changes and the difficulties of wresting equality from men who are reluctant to cede prerogatives of a bygone era (Goode 1982). Beyond women's growing participation in the labor force and its implied increase in independence, women have been associated with rising divorce for other, related reasons. Ever since Jessie Bernard (1982) uncovered the "his" and "her" perspectives of marriage, research has continued to find that women do not benefit from their marriages as much as men, nor are they as satisfied with them (Faludi 1991; Glenn and Weaver 1988; Lee, Seccombe, and Shehan 1991). Moreover, on the whole women are more approving of divorce than men (Veroff, Douvan, and Kulka 1981). Finally, women are the primary initiators of divorce and are thus more likely to be seen as abandoning "marriage as forever."[30] For all these reasons, women have been more easily perceived as "the problem," than have men or institutions that have failed to change.

Yet, as I argued in the Introduction, the tendency to highlight women's individualism is peculiar, given divorced women's enduring family involvement as primary parents and breadwinners; this suggests that they are not simply exchanging relational responsibilities for individual rights. Focusing simply on women's initiation of divorce may obscure a deeper problem: the degree to which women may initiate divorce because of the negligent or provocative actions of husbands (Kurz 1995). Men's widespread abandonment and/or nonsupport of children after divorce suggests that individualism may be a more serious problem for some men.[31] Furthermore, holding women responsible for divorce rates ignores the oppression of women in marriage in the past and overlooks impediments created by the current social structure. Structural inequities suggest that women's "individualism" does not resemble men's "individualism." As Coontz concluded, the problematic changes in families are "caused not by the equality women have won but by the inequalities they have failed to uproot" (Coontz 1992, 168, citing Faludi 1991).[32]

Increasingly, men believe that women's rights have been won and men's rights have been lost (Faludi 1991). While data suggest that gender inequality has not been overcome, Goode (1982) explained that men resist equality partly because, as superordinates, men are more likely to view small losses of deference, advantages, or opportunities as large threats. A 1989 *New York Times* poll revealed that although a majority of women "believed American society had not changed enough to grant women equality, only a minority of men agreed. A majority of men *did* agree, however, that the women's movement had 'made things harder for men at home'" (Faludi 1991, 61). Recent signs that men want to sustain the authority historically associated with the male provider role in marriage culture include calls from some quarters for husbands to lead and wives to submit in marriage—expressed by the Promise Keepers and the Southern Baptist Church. These calls reflect the finding that many men and women still invest a great deal of symbolic value in the male provider role, in spite of its decline (Faludi 1991, 457). Such movements also indicate that our cultural conceptions of "masculinity" are in flux and contested (Arendell 1995; Bernard 1982; Messner 1997). As women make claims on the provider role—including the prerogatives associated with it, such as individualism—what constitutes "manhood" or "masculinity" is less clear. Contending with the force of a spouse's individualism may be a familiar experience for many women, but it is new for most men and involves issues of relative power, status, and identity (Arendell 1995, 35).

The enduring individualism of men and the emergent individualism of women needs to be understood in a historical, economic, and politically gendered context. Often, "equality" is understood in terms of equal individual rights, but equality is in fact a much more complex concept. Like therapeutic culture, gender equality manifests a tension between the ideals of individualism and relationality. While divorce culture advances individualism on a manifest level, among some spouses it may be a means toward the goal of relationality on a latent level. Divorce culture signifies a conflict between gendered ideals, not only between male dominance and gender equality, but also between interpretations of gender equality itself.

Equality Versus Difference

As women and men increasingly claim and try to incorporate gender equality into marriages, scholars have debated just what "equality" should look like. Known as the "equality versus difference" debate, it has been relevant in a variety of contexts, including marriage. Those who support a strict and "objective" notion of equality tend to emphasize gender similarity (or alternatively "gender-neutrality"), which "minimizes" gender differences. For these scholars creating equality is a matter of extending to women rights that more men have always enjoyed as "individuals" in the liberal tradition. Such a position tends to rely upon what has been, until recently, a standard of rights available to and defined by white men. From this perspective, an egalitarian marriage is a contract to ensure fulfilled needs between two free, autonomous and identical individuals, while divorce is the result when the interests of one party are no longer served. If women assert their individual rights and needs, both within and by leaving marriages, the question arises of whether they are modeling themselves after a problematic, if hegemonic, model of masculinity. On a manifest level, "rights equality" shares an affinity with divorce culture through the legal language of individual rights and the cultural language of individualism.

In contrast to equality understood as similarity, difference theorists question male-defined standards, or any standards that have ignored marginalized discourses, whether by gender, race/ethnicity, class, or sexuality. As bell hooks (1984, 18) rhetorically asks: "Since men are not equals ... which men do women want to be equal to?" Such theorists "maximize" the issue of difference on the dimensions of race/ethnicity, class, sexuality, and gender.[33] Positions on this debate vary enormously, depending upon whether the focus is on "difference" between women and men or among women. What difference theorists share, however, is that they want to reinstate values such as relationality that have heretofore been marginalized and excluded from the notions of the "liberal individual" that have informed the ideal of equality. This view accords room for alternative notions of equality—including an egalitarian marriage based upon an equality of responsibilities, caretaking, and self-sacrifice—that presume relational connection and interdependence. In short, devalued meanings constructed and practiced by marginalized groups are revalued and inform this ideal of equality.

In my view, the similarity/difference dilemma is not necessarily an "either/or" issue; rather, women and men are both alike and different. In another context, Patricia Hill Collins (1990) called this a "both/and" position.[34] And Scott (1988) sees equality versus difference as a false dichotomy, arguing that equality means indifference to differences. We would not even be concerned with equality if people were not in some way different. "Placing equality and difference in an antithetical relationship has, then, a double effect. It denies the way in which difference has long figured in political notions of equality and it suggests that sameness is the only ground on which equality can be claimed (766). We need, as Scott argues, to reject this dichotomy even as we analyze how it operates in people's lives.

From the minimizers, we can learn how women and men are more alike than different, and that the differences are socially constructed and require power to sustain. With the increased salience of gender equality, more women are demonstrating both their capacity and their desire for autonomy, independence, and individual rights. This suggests that eventually both love and work can be de-gendered.

The maximizers teach us that qualities associated with women—as nurturing, expressive, and responsible caretakers—must be revalued and, as historical and cross-cultural analyses reveal, are not specific to women (Collins 1990; Mead 1935; Moraga and Anzaldua 1981; Nobles 1976; Spelman 1988). Indeed, this is how we know that gender differences can be reconstructed. However, if it is clear that we need to construct new, flexible, and inclusive standards, it remains unclear how this will be achieved. Revaluation of qualities and practices associated with white women and/or people of color will depend, in part, upon privileged men engaging their capacity for relationality and sharing emotional responsibilities—toward their own families and through social institutions that enable rather than impede care.[35] Despite the assertion of some "maximizing" theorists that gender differences are essential, gender differences need not be construed as "natural." Still, these socially constructed differences are experienced as "real" and inform the expectations and interpretations of heterosexual marriage.

New Relational Grounds for Marriage and Divorce

The literature on marriage and divorce suggests that relational responsibilities may be as crucial to understanding marital stability today as individual rights. What is distinctive about marriage today is that its affective quality has become increasingly central to its viability. There is evidence from survey research that new cultural grounds for divorce, related to emotional standards, are emerging. In *Portrait of Divorce*, Kitson with Holmes (1992, 3) suggested that as marriage is increasingly assessed by "the ability of the partner or relationship to foster the individual's or couple's growth," a "new type" of divorce has emerged. They found:

> The importance of affection and companionship in relationships today is highlighted in the data from both the suburban divorced and the married samples. Both groups yearned for more communication with and support and concern from their partners. [...] There appears to be a growing recognition that such *relational complaints are acceptable grounds* for ending a marriage. This was also illustrated by the reports of the suburban divorced respondents that they and their spouses had grown apart [emphasis added, 341].

As Kitson and Holmes observed, to highlight the new factor of "relational complaints" is not to deny that traditional factors still account for many divorces; but it is to recognize a new ingredient affecting divorce rates.

This increasing emphasis on the affective qualities of marriage reflects a decline in the institution's economic and other functions. It may also reflect women's increased assertion of their marital ideals. Research on marriage and divorce consistently finds that heterosexual men and women seem to want and expect different things from their relationships. Women tend to want more intimacy, more talk, more sharing (Cancian 1987; Duncombe and Marsden 1993; Rubin 1983; Thompson and Walker 1989). In their review of the marriage literature, Thompson and Walker (1989, 846) found: "Women tend to complain that their husbands do not care about their emotional lives and do not express their own feelings and thoughts." Riessman (1990, 69) found similar variations upon analyzing women's and men's divorce accounts. She reported that in men's view "the marital relationship was not self-contained or was not primary enough to the wife." And she found that men blame themselves for not living up to "women's standards" of emotional intimacy. Divorced women's main complaint reflects this standard: "[f]or women, marriage flounders because husbands fail to be emotionally intimate in the way wives expect them to be" (69).[36]

Riessman's discussion of women's standards of intimacy echoes Cancian's argument that love has been feminized and that we need to redefine love. Cancian (1987) contended that it is not therapeutic culture, but "feminized" love that troubles love relationships today. She argued that since the nineteenth century, our notions of love have excluded qualities associated with masculinity.[37] With the exception of sex, "masculine" qualities, such as the practical giving of help are ignored in our cultural constructions of love. Instead, love is associated with "feminine" qualities such as nurturance, sensitivity and the expression of feelings. Cancian argued that we need to redefine love because this constructed split reinforces power differences between women and men; it conceals men's relational capacities and emotional needs, while it denies women's work and "naturalizes" their relationship to love. When it is believed that women are "love experts" by their very nature, then the material basis of women's dependency is obscured. Cancian asserted that we need to redefine love to de-gender both love and self-development.

While this call for redefinition of "love" is laudable, it may underestimate the tenacity of gender constructions as well as the economic and political inequalities that impede redefinition. It suggests that women and men alike need to apply themselves to these redefinitions and that they have the same recourse to resources to do so. While this will certainly vary among women by class, race/ethnicity, and religion, on the whole women seem to be embracing "self development" and masculinist responsibilities more rapidly than men are embracing the responsibilities of "feminized love." Research suggests that women do appreciate the practical giving of help—particularly on the "second shift" (Hochschild with Machung 1989). Moreover, most research finds that women are still responsible for monitoring marriage (Kitson with Holmes 1992; Thompson and Walker 1989). As wives increasingly shoulder conventionally masculine responsibilities, such as productive labor, they increasingly and understandably want to share reproductive and emotional labor as well. In short, perhaps men should attend to these "feminized" standards.

For men to attend to feminized standards does not mean making men feminine; rather, it means reconstructing ideals of femininity and masculinity altogether. With the decline of the male provider role, a key anchor for masculine identity and status has been lost. While this "crisis in masculinity" (Kimmel 1996) may threaten some men, it is also an opportunity to incorporate heretofore alternative and marginal masculinities—broadening the horizons for men as well as women (Connell 1987). Given how central the affective qualities of a marriage are to its viability, sharing this relational work may be crucial to redefining marriage in an age of divorce.

Miriam Johnson (1988, 259) argued that "as women gain power as people" (e.g., through their participation in the labor force, through divorces enforcing and enabling autonomy, and through extended autonomy determined by their long lives), they are more likely to "gain power within marriage itself." Like Johnson, I believe that marital instability is a cost—perhaps temporary—of the quest for gender equality in marriage (261). Johnson also argued that due to the problematic legacy of male dominance in heterosexual relationships, egalitarian marriage should be patterned upon women's relationships with women. Or, we might consider employing patterns of relationship where power has been equalized and de-gendered, such as some sibling and same-sex relationships. The challenge of gender equality—particularly if it is reconstructed in terms of a female standard—is how to contest domination without dominating. Johnson succinctly noted that "what most women seek is not power but the absence of domination" (261). While many wives may want to share an equality of sacrifices and relational responsibilities, they may find it easier to secure an equality of nonsacrifice and individualism.

FROM '50S MARRIAGE CULTURE TO '90S COMPETING CULTURES

In sum, social, economic, legal, and demographic conditions have contributed to, and are evidence for, the emergence of divorce culture since the 1970s. While these developments cannot fully reveal how this changed context has affected the *meaning* that women and men confer upon marriage and divorce, they do reveal the outlines of a new social context. The shift to a service- and consumer-based economy from a manufacturing-industrial economy has had enormous consequences for gender and marital relations as women's participation in the labor force has grown and the male wage has declined. By the 1970s, legal structures supporting the breadwinner/homemaker division of labor and the position of the male as head of the household had been dismantled by no-fault divorce. Social movements questioned the status quo and confronted social issues such as women's reproductive rights, unequal pay, the sexual double standard, and the contradictions of equality and role-differentiation that had constituted the "companionate marriage" since the nineteenth century.

Some scholars argue that marital breakdown has been historically constant, and that only what people do about it has changed. In this view, divorce rates are an accurate reflection of the amount of breakdown that has always been present in the West, but has been obstructed by legal and economic constraints. Like Roderick Phillips (1988), however, I would argue that marital breakdown has increased as well as divorce. In line with Phillips (639), I see the changing social and economic structures as redefining marital expectations and, therefore, changing the very meaning of "breakdown." Kitson and Holmes (1992) provided evidence for a "new type" of divorce based on "relational complaints"; this suggests that divorce rates do not simply reflect increased accessibility to divorce, but new meanings for marital "breakdown." In the past, men have had more power to define marital viability. Today, more women are empowered to assert their marital visions. Putting these visions into practice, however, has been a slow process, taking more than one generation.

The changing structural and cultural conditions across the generations should not simply be seen as a backdrop to marital lives. Whether or not spouses actively participated in or were victims of political events, whether or not their own practices reflected the prevailing demographic patterns of their time, and whether or not they embrace religion or therapy, shifting historical conditions actively reverberate through people's lives. Whether we are only aware of our personal choices, or also able to engage a sociological imagination to "grasp history and biography and the relations between the two within society" (Mills 1959), we engage our personal agency within the constraints of our times. Our choices are made from a particular menu or structure of choices,[38] and that menu changes as the result of the great and small initiatives in our everyday lives. If a woman "chooses" to stay married or to divorce her husband, she has tacitly assessed the meaning of her marriage for her children, her job and income potential, her religious commitment, her health, her sanity, her family relations, her friendships, and her dreams. Likewise, if a man "chooses" to stay married or to divorce his wife he, too, must assess an array of ramifications. These assessments depend upon whether there is a world war, whether there are job opportunities, what kinds of transportation options are available, government policies, and whether one will be embraced or shunned by social networks. In general, '70s wives and husbands experienced a different menu than their '50s counterparts—a more complex and contradictory menu that, by the 1990s, has come to include marriage and divorce cultures. For '50s spouses, marriage culture prevailed because of the structural and cultural menus of their times.

3 The Push of Marriage Culture Among '50s Spouses

FROM the early years of their marital commitment, the '50s couples have watched the clouds of divorce gather on the distant horizon. Over the decades, the clouds have grown in number, changed their shape, and moved closer to home. From the time of the first adult interviews in 1958, when the U.S. divorce rate stood at a low (relative to a surge after World War II) of 2.1 per thousand population, to the early 1980s when it had more than doubled to around five per thousand, the volume of divorce increased tremendously (Cherlin 1992; Glick and Sung-Lin 1986).[1] Whether these clouds seemed menacing or promised a rainbow, it is a change in the marital climate which most of the Older generation have "ridden out." The relative lack of divorce among the '50s couples has contributed to stereotypes about the 1950s.

In recent years, many family scholars have rightfully pointed out that our stereotypes of '50s families are just that: stereotypes (Breines 1986; Coontz 1992; May 1988; Skolnick 1991). The ideal of the married, heterosexual couple dividing breadwinning and child rearing along gender lines and living in a suburban tract home was only fortified when translated into images during the early days of television. In *The Way We Never Were,* social historian Stephanie Coontz (1992, 29) insightfully noted: "Contrary to popular opinion, 'Leave It to Beaver' was not a documentary." She proceeded to document the diversity of marriage and family experiences by social class and race/ethnicity, as well as the gendered conflicts that seethed below the surface within white, suburban families. Moreover, the 1950s was a peculiar slice of history because couples married younger, had children younger, had more children, and divorced less often than would have been predicted given previous trends (Cherlin 1992). And they did all this even as the rate of women's participation in the labor force continued to grow—though the rate of growth was still low relative to the 1980s.[2] In short, the realities were much more diverse and complicated than the image would suggest. Nevertheless, the stereotypes are based on observed general tendencies among '50s adults and on shared ideals that endure even now.

These images of the 1950s tell us a great deal about American cultural ideals, whether we deride or extol them. At the least, they convey the ideals and meanings of marriage within middle-class families. Referring to the middle-class family, Skolnick (1991, 22) asserted, "Its domestic ideals and practices have been culturally dominant in America, defining what is normal, natural, and moral." Majority beliefs about marriage, divorce, and gender supported the nuclear family ideal and were largely critical of variations (Thornton 1989; Veroff, Douvan, and Kulka 1981). Today, in many ways, the middle class is following the marriage and divorce patterns once more prevalent among the working classes and some communities of color; however, because the white middle class defines what is "normal, natural, and moral," the middle class changes the meaning of these patterns. As Peters and McAdoo (1983) have observed, when the white middle-class population exhibits these patterns—such as divorce or working mothers—what was once seen as "deviant" is now more likely to be framed as "alternative."

The middle-class and predominantly white '50s couples in my sample wed when a belief in "marriage as forever" prevailed. The belief that "marriage is forever" may seem to be the flip side of the belief that divorce is a "last resort." However, the former premise captures adherence to the vow "till death do us part." Divorce as a last resort, on the other hand, captures the deterrents that prevent divorce from being a first or second resort. These deterrents change in number and substance over the decades and determine how readily divorce becomes a thinkable option. For those within marriage culture, deterrents to divorce include financial interdependence, social and familial networks, stigma, religious convictions, and above all, the "children's sake." By the time these couples are celebrating anniversaries of twenty to thirty years, shared histories and caretaking are added disincentives to divorce.

Divorce culture is on the rise around the twentieth anniversaries of the members of this marital cohort. A new cluster of convictions are surfacing to suggest that marrying is rooted in freely chosen bonds, marriage is contingent, and divorce is less destructive than marital conflict and may even be an affirmative act—serving as a gateway to a more fulfilling life. Divorce culture is characterized by choice—whether to marry or to divorce and how to work and raise children. The belief in the primacy of individuals is not new, but within the family, the most conservative and traditionally hierarchical of institutions, its democratization is noteworthy.[3]

By the time the '50s couples have reached their thirtieth anniversaries, marriage culture has lost its hegemonic hold. Divorce culture, made possible by individualism, is a sign of new marital and familial ideals in the making. The Older generation has been challenged by, and to some extent has contributed to, the "watershed" in marital meanings.

In this chapter, I focus on the patterns shared by the Older generation. I review the '50s couples' marital lives by tracing the rising discourse on divorce within this sample. How has the growth of divorce affected this generation? How do couples cope with the prospect of divorce—in their own or other marriages? In the late 1950s, the talk of divorce is minimal and focuses on their parents. By the early 1980s, divorce discourse has multiplied with reference to parents, friends, family, society, and self.[4] As the divorce rates rise and divorce talk increases, individuals joke, distance themselves from, and moralize about divorce. They increasingly see long-term marriage as an achievement. Even so, some spouses, especially wives, are "thinking divorce." I analyze wives' accounts and both spouses' responses to the challenge of gender equality brought by the women's movement. Before illustrating these findings, it is important to note both the characteristics and the limits of my sample of '50s couples.

THE SAMPLE OF '50s SPOUSES

I selected 12 couples (and 2 former spouses) from a longitudinal data set archived at the Institute of Human Development at the University of California, Berkeley. My sample is a subset of a larger sample of 248 individuals born between January 1928 and June 1929 in the San Francisco Bay Area who were regularly studied throughout their lives. In 1958, when they were 30 years of age, they were interviewed about their educational, occupational, marital, and parental careers. At this time, subjects' *spouses* were included irregularly. Between 1969 and 1971, when the original subjects were about 40 years of age, they and their spouses were each interviewed in depth for a second follow-up on their adult lives. Finally, between 1981 and 1983, both subjects and spouses were recalled for a third follow-up, composed of both a structured interview and a clinical interview with each spouse.

I selected ten couples in their first marriage on the basis of marital satisfaction scores compiled in 1982 because I wanted to see if "divorce talk" occurred for happy and unhappy spouses alike. Three couples scored in the top third on marital satisfaction, five were in the middle third, and four were in the bottom third. In all, I reviewed the marital histories of 26 individuals; 24 were part of matched couples and two were former spouses.

The socioeconomic class of the selected couples varied slightly but was primarily middle class by adulthood.[5] Eichorn (1981, 41) pointed out that by the adult interviews 90 percent of the longitudinal samples were middle class due to such things as funding restrictions, deaths, and selective attrition. Above all, this generation experienced significant upward mobility in their lifetimes. Thus, my desire to select ten first-married couples that would be demographically diverse—including by class and race/ethnicity—was partially limited by the nature of the longitudinal sample and by my selection of respondents by marital satisfaction scores.

The variation by race/ethnicity was minimal in the larger sample. Because the initial respondents were selected from a survey sample consisting of every third birth to Berkeley residents in the late 1920s, the race/ethnicity of respondents was a function of the surrounding area. This sampling also preceded the westward migration of many African-Americans around World War II. Although the study is "representative" of the region at that time, the area was predominantly Euro-American. Speaking of the Intergenerational Studies, Clausen (1993, 44) notes: "Afro-Americans, Hispanics, and migrants of Asian origin are not represented except for a very few blacks. These minority groups were present in the populations of north Oakland and of Berkeley to only a limited extent at the time the study started." Of the 26 individuals whose cases I sampled, 22 were Euro-American and four were African-American. There was no intermarriage by race. Three individuals who were Euro-American identified themselves as ethnically Jewish, but only two had had some religious training and none adhered to Judaism as adults. Most of the 26 individuals were affiliated with Christianity at some point in their lives. Three were Mormon, eight were Catholic, and the remaining thirteen were Protestant.

The earliest marriage occurred in 1946 (for one individual who subsequently divorced) and the latest was 1954. The mean year of marriage was 1950. The mean age at first marriage was 21.7. The mean number of children was three per couple and no couple was childless. One couple had six children, and a few had two. By 1970, their children were generally teenagers, though some were fully grown. By 1982, their "nests were empty" and they were speculating about retirement.

TALKING DIVORCE

Talk about divorce—one's own or among family and friends—was minimal during the first series of interviews in the late 1950s. Most of the couples in my sample had been married for six to ten years at this time and were raising children. The salient absence of divorce discussion is partially explained by the format of the interview. A mostly structured interview, focusing on personality traits of oneself, one's spouse, and one's parents, meant that divorce was not addressed specifically and would arise only if the respondent brought up the subject voluntarily. Today, an interview schedule addressing marriage and family relations without questions about divorce would seem flawed. But in the 1950s this was not an oversight.

After a relatively dormant and atypical phase through the 1950s, the divorce rate was barely beginning to accelerate in 1958 and 1959. Stigma was still strong, and the probability of one's own divorce, as well as divorce among one's social circles was significantly less than we witness today—particularly among middle-class whites. Only 3 of 24 individuals in this sample had separated or divorced parents by the time they were 30 years of age.

In these early interviews, only one-fifth of the interviewees brought up divorce explicitly. One wife, Susan Anderson, referred to her in-laws' separation; she reported that her husband's father virtually abandoned his mother, but did not go into details (her husband was not interviewed at this time). Another wife, Doreen Dominick, lamented her parents' divorce, and yet another, Linda Finley, brought up separation and divorce as options averted by her parents, despite martial tensions:

> The importance of the family was always stressed in my home also. There was no separation, at any rate, although maybe there would have been if there had been more money [laughs]. And there was a little discontent but in neither home it was not *great* enough to split the family. The pattern was one of strong family ties. There was no separation or divorce, although there was some strain. And there is not any with us, either at least not yet. There are times when we don't agree, but they're never serious enough to involve the children or long term.

Her talk suggests that the ideology of "strong family ties" overcame mild discontent. By 1982, however, another version had emerged regarding the severity of strains in her parents' marriage—that her parents "hated each other" and that her mother "was miserable" and "suicidal" in the course of the marriage. Although she laughs, given her lower-middle-class background, perhaps "money" was a crucial obstacle for her parents.

Finally, one couple, Gary and Pat Holstein, brought up his parents and siblings' divorces and remarriages. Gary, whose childhood was distinguished by divorces and remarriages—as well as a transnational upbringing—reported that the divorce was hard on his sister. Pat relates in 1958 that all the divorces in his family influenced her parents' reception of Gary: "My parents' attitude was that you get married, you make your bed and you lie in it. You don't change. It just isn't their religion; religion only emphasizes it. My mother has learned about [Gary's father] . . . and was horrified, privately. She has this business about 'like father like son.'

I really think she had some visions of Casanova about Gary. [...] We really fall in with my parents' way of doing things." In 1959, Pat firmly believes that she and Gary "fall in with her parents' way of doing things." In ten years, however, they will separate and divorce. Their divorce will be "more in line with Gary's parents' way of doing things," yet the divorce will be more clearly initiated by Pat, in spite of her Catholic upbringing.

Undoubtedly, more discussion about divorce could have been elicited from these respondents in 1959 had direct questions been put to them. Yet, because the probability of divorce in one's immediate circles has shot up in recent decades, it seems likely that in an interview today about marriage, family, and life's highs and lows—with the same interview format and at the same life stage—the topic of divorce would arise more frequently. While the interview schedule I administered to the younger couples explicitly addressed divorce late in the interview, most of the individuals raised the topic voluntarily early in the interview.[6]

Divorce Discourse: Increasing Volume

In 1970, when these spouses are about 40 years of age, more is mentioned about divorce as the growing divorce rate increasingly touches the perimeters of their own lives. The rise in "others'" divorces, is not only noted, but is becoming an occasion for humor, sorrow, distancing, and pride. When Ted Mitchell is asked in 1970 who his closest friends are, he mentions a couple of friends and then modifies his response: "Well, the woman—they got a divorce. She's remarried and so I don't know him too well." In 1970, Roger Finley observes: "We see a lot of our friends' marriages breaking up, so we're grateful to each other, isn't this nice it didn't happen to us. Aren't we lucky. We're still compatible and see no reason to break up, so we admire each other over that. We admire our relationship." Widespread divorce makes "admiration" and "achievement" possible. The "admiration" expressed by Roger is premised on the voluntary maintenance of a marriage. In the past, when a marriage did not endure, it was more frequently due to the death of a spouse. Marital endurance in the context of widespread mortality does not carry the same meaning as a long-term marriage in the context of widespread divorce. "Luck" may be felt in both contexts, but admiration, pride, a sense of achievement are not. Marital endurance becomes an achievement only as divorce becomes more thinkable, widespread, and accessible. Individual will is assumed to underlie the marital "success." These are conditions for pride.

Daryl Anderson's first child is about to depart for college in 1970 when he is asked about his expectations once all three children have left home.

He remarks that he and his wife will go on short trips, perhaps bowl, but he still will really enjoy spending time with the kids and with friends. He mentions some very close friends: "We have a good friend—he was my best man—and we've been buddies all our lives. And they have a little financial setback and they can't do much—so we usually go camping and water skiing with them and things like that, but they pretty much can't do anything now. And uh . . . I like to be with people who are my long time friends—is what I like to be with more than acquaintances." In 1983, these same good friends come up once again and Daryl laments their divorce. He explains that this man had been his buddy since high school and they'd been each other's "best men" at their respective weddings: "We were—we are extremely close. We raised our kids together, and uh, uh . . . planned to do many things together after retirement and unfortunately after thirty-four years of marriage they divorced. Kind of was hard to take because we had a lot of love for both of them, you know." Daryl's wife, Susan, also mentioned these friends in 1970 and is distressed about their friends' divorce in 1983: "I just felt like she had died [laughs] you know, because we just kind of lost contact completely with her but we're still in contact with her husband. But it just hasn't been the same since she's been gone." That there is some anxiety as well as grief attached to this divorce is suggested by the "jokes" they attempt. Susan laughs as she notes it was as if the wife had died. And as Daryl discusses involvement in a canoe club, he jests: "I just bought it. It is a real nice canoe, and uh . . . I went with a group of guys and their wives, about three divorces since we've joined the group [laugh]."

By the 1970 and 1982 interviews, the spouses in this older generation are more regularly giving both solicited and unsolicited responses that refer to their own potential and others' actual divorces. Recall that it was 1970 when the Census Bureau realized it could no longer assume that the end of a marriage implied the death of a spouse and thus introduced a question concerning *how* a respondent's marriage ended (Sweet and Bumpass 1987, 176). Likewise, the very fact that researchers chose to ask respondents whether they had ever considered ending their marriage and what had kept their marriage together is itself a sign of changing times.

Oscar and Daisy Wilson represent the trajectory of increasing awareness of divorce among the '50s spouses. When asked in their individual interviews in 1982 if they had ever considered divorce, both responded in the negative. Oscar was also asked if there was anything he would change about his life if he could. He replied:

I do regret sometimes that I didn't do something else where I coulda made a lot of money, and comfortably do some of the things that . . . you see your contemporaries doing . . . think nothing of a month in Europe . . . two week cruise and a couple other vacations a year. [I:⁷ Mm hm] We've never—we've always been comfortable. We've always had a little recreations and, a boat or a trailer or something. I don't know, I don't know whether those people end up getting divorced [laughter].

Oscar's joke, like Daryl and Susan Anderson's jokes, is a means to distance himself from the threat and to compensate for his regrets. If he is less well-to-do, perhaps he is at least happier and shielded from divorce. The interviewer picked up on the topic and then explicitly asked Oscar about the high divorce rate. He initially asserted that his daughters' and his own marriage were fine and then added:

None of our close friends are divorced either. We seem to gravitate toward those kinds of people. [I: People like yourselves.] All of our best friends that we ran around, we don't see more often now, but the ones that we did buddy around with while we were single and when we first got married they scatter out, every one of 'ems still married. [I: Your sister was divorced?] Yeah, my sister was. But the . . . I don't know what . . . I don't know what's causing the divorces now. [. . .] Oh, there's no stigma about divorce anymore. [I: Uh huh.] Well, I was telling you that some of these fellahs that work there, they're paying child support to one or two ex-wives and their present wife is receiving child support from one or two previous marriages, I don't know how they do all the bookkeeping. Maybe everybody ends up breaking even [laughs].

Oscar would prefer to identify himself with the still-married friends whom he no longer sees very often than with his sister or his coworkers at the fire station, whom he sees daily. Despite his gratifying marriage with Daisy, he is uncomfortable with the widespread divorce around him; he would like to distance himself from it, but it also gives him opportunity, like Roger Finley, to be proud of his marital endurance. By the early 1980s, couples in the Older generation are not only mentioning, joking about, distancing themselves from divorce and expressing pride in their achievement of a long-term marriage. They are also moralizing about divorce more.

When Oscar is asked how his parents' marriage influenced his own marriage, he describes the physical and financial adversities faced by his parents and asserts:

[My] parents had stable marriage, both only married once. Their marriage endured despite their ups and downs and physical problems. I think I acquired the values. I don't have a casual attitude toward marriage. I think lots of people today do. For me, if you take the marriage vows you should

stay with it if you can, unless it is a *totally unacceptable situation*. I think
I acquired values in that regard [emphasis added].

As Oscar refers to the "totally unacceptable situation" that would justify
a divorce, he is speaking the language of marriage culture. Divorce is a
"last resort" for intolerable circumstances; otherwise, marriage is forever. Under the terms of divorce culture, one might say that the qualifier
"totally" could be dropped.

Just what constitutes an acceptable or "unacceptable situation" for
divorce is in flux by this 1982 interview. As the legal grounds of divorce
have shifted from the likes of "adultery" to "irreconcilable differences,"
so too have the cultural grounds for divorce. What justifies divorce? How
are help and harm distributed? The injury done to others versus the self
has always been part of the equation of whether a divorce is acceptable
or not; however the figures on each side of the equation are changing.

In 1982, Henry Hampton is asked what has kept his wife, Marie, and
himself together after 30 years of marriage. Henry responds, "I'd say two
things, really," and continues by generalizing the glue for his own marriage to others' marriages: "The children are the main thing that keep people together and then as they get older they substitute economic reality,
a decent place to live, secure income, someone to take care if something
happens. These are strong forces. If none of these forces existed it is a
matter of conjecture what would happen." In these few lines, Henry outlines three features—children, finances, and caretaking—that strongly
deterred divorce for many in this generation. Familial and financial deterrents are strong forces indeed; social interdependence marks these deterrents to divorce, as do marital goods. Add stigma to these deterrents and
the disincentives grow. Together they inhibit divorce by privileging social
and personal relationships over the individual. Yet, not all family members forfeited their individual desires to the same degree. In short, this
formula tends to obscure how social interdependence manifested itself for
the 1950s marital cohort.

The recent expansion of "unacceptable marital situations" can be
traced to at least two factors: (1) people redefining what is damaging
to the self and others[8] and (2) greater weight given to the individual's
well-being—for all family members. First, redefining "damage" has followed from the growth of therapeutic culture. The reach of a therapeutic
viewpoint, inside and outside religious institutions, emphasizes the secular and psychological self whose health depends upon met needs and
"functional," rather than "dysfunctional," relationships. As the compass of "dysfunctional" relationships expands, so too do unacceptable
marital situations.[9]

Second, we are redefining what is damaging to children. Studies increasingly conclude, and many parents concur, that marital conflict may be worse than divorce for children (Amato and Booth 1997; Block, Block, and Gjerde 1986; Kelly 1988; Kitson with Holmes 1992; Stewart et al. 1997). Our concerns are migrating from "the children's sake" within marriage to the "best interests of the child" after divorce.

Finally, redefining "damage" has arisen because women's voices are entering the discourse. Concerns over family violence—primarily wife battering and the sexual and physical abuse of children—are most salient among family behaviors decreasingly tolerated because of feminist analyses and advocacy. While violence, adultery, and alcohol and drug abuse were not approved by the Older generation and could enter into "totally unacceptable" accounts, they were not readily perceived to be grounds for divorce either. With the rise of divorce culture, the destructiveness not only of divorce, but of marriage, becomes part of the equation. Women, whose independence has been denied by and whose survival has been ensured by marriage, are sensitive to the destructive potential of marriage.

Despite this sample's general adherence to the premises of marriage culture and the endurance of their marriages, their discourse on divorce proliferates in tandem with the rates around them. In this context of proliferating divorce and divorce talk, I traced whether any of these spouses were "thinking divorce" in relation to their own marriages.

Who Is "Thinking Divorce?"

In the 1970 and 1982 interviews, of the 20 individuals reviewed (i.e., 10 couples who remained in their first marriage), 11 explicitly claim that they had never considered divorce. Among the 11 who had not contemplated divorce, 2 had high, 6 had middle-range, and 3 had low marital satisfaction scores. Of the 9 remaining individuals, who confided that they *had* considered divorce, 5 scored in the lower third, 2 scored in the middle, and 2 scored in the highest third on marital satisfaction.

In sum, marital satisfaction scores (based on 1982 data) differed only slightly between those who had or had not considered divorce at some point in their marriage. The group who had "divorce thoughts" was constituted by a few more of the least satisfied, as might be expected.

Much more than marital satisfaction, spouses having had divorce thoughts were differentiated from those who had not had divorce thoughts by their gender. Of the eleven noncontemplators, only three were women. Of the nine contemplators of divorce, only three were men.[10] Moreover, of the two couples selected who had divorced and remarried, the divorce was initiated by the wives—and caught the husbands by surprise. What could it mean that women are considering divorce more in this sample? And how was divorce averted?

WIVES MONITOR MARRIAGE

These '50s wives are either contemplating divorce more or reporting on their contemplations of divorce more than are the men. This gender difference may seem curious, particularly since marriage and family have been a veritable career for women in generations past. Moreover, are not women supposed to be more relational and attentive to relationships than men (Chodorow 1978; Gilligan 1982; di Leonardo 1987)? Paradoxically, considering divorce seems to reflect a concern for the relationship and for the spouse, as well as for the self. To consider divorce is to monitor the marriage. Ironically, women may consider ending marriage because of its importance to them. I argue that because women are more likely to define themselves in relation to others, they are more likely to sense and respond to a deteriorating relationship. As they register the decay, they reevaluate the relative destruction of marriage versus divorce.

These wives' accounts of why they considered divorce suggest that it is not so much "independence," but "interdependence" that is missing in their marriages. As Martha McIntyre explains, "I felt very much alone." Janet Johnson cites her husband's "inability to interact with the kids and do family activities" as a reason for her thoughts of divorce. A few of the wives explain their divorce thoughts by the fact that their *husbands* were unhappy at the time. Marie Hampton explains: "He was very unhappy with me and I felt it was my problem that I wasn't suitable for him. The kids were young and I was trapped, as it were." And despite her own unmistakable misery, Doreen Dominick points to "his unhappiness." For this generational sample, these reasons suggest relational concerns, rather than the self-centered concerns that many critics have argued lead to divorce.

Yet, the '50s wives may also be considering divorce more because they experience the strains of marriage, and may sense that they have less to lose with respect to physical and psychological health.[11] Gendered variation of divorce thoughts within marriage is in keeping with the related findings that "his" and "her" versions of marriage diverge and that "his" is generally more gratifying (Bernard 1982). It is also in line with the repeated finding that marriage serves to protect men more than women from ill-health and mortality (Durkheim 1951; Hu and Goldman 1990). Precisely because wives, and not husbands, are traditionally responsible for the well-being of family members, wives are more likely to recognize the strain of the emotion work, kin work, and caretaking they perform, while men invisibly benefit from it. In short, this aggregate "social fact," if it is sensed at all, is more likely to be felt by women than by men.

Finally, women "thinking divorce" is in keeping with the assertion that women may be "changing faster" than men in the twentieth century (Hochschild with Machung 1989). As most research confirms, women appear to suggest and to initiate divorce proceedings more often than men (Kitson with Holmes 1992, 93; Wallerstein and Blakeslee 1989, 39).[12] Perhaps "thinking" by older women foreshadows "doing" by younger women.

Younger generations are entering their marriages as divorce is more thinkable, acceptable, and doable across gender. Younger wives can more easily turn their thoughts to actions as they are surrounded by more economic responsibilities and options and influenced by lower thresholds for divorce. In contrast, the 1950s husbands and wives experienced nearly two decades of a predominant marriage culture before the rising challenge of divorce culture in the 1970s. The older wives, with fewer economic options and beliefs grounded in marriage culture, may think divorce, but stay the course, trying to transform marriage from within.

The centrality of gender to divorce discourse in this sample is twofold. First, while all the respondents increasingly "talk divorce," by the early 1980s, the nature of their talk about divorce varies by gender. While more men talk about others' divorces, more women are considering their own potential divorces. Second, gender arrangements are part and parcel of the new marital terms; both men and women are actively confronting and reevaluating gender arrangements in their marriage. The '50s couples have lived through tremendous shifts concerning gender ideology and marriage. How do they contend with the challenge of gender equality?

MARRIAGE AND THE "MALE-HEADED HOUSEHOLD"

In the last decade, the notion of a "male-headed household" has become increasingly ambiguous. Today, we are just as likely to assume that the term refers to single men or households headed by divorced fathers as we are to assume that it signifies the husband in a married-couple family. Since 1980, the Census Bureau has designated the householder as "the person in whose name the housing unit is owned or rented and can be either spouse in a married-couple household." Before that census, the household head referred to "the husband in a married-couple household" or the person "recognized as such by the other members of the household" (Santi 1988, 511). When used to refer to married-couple households, the phrase "male-headed household" both reflected and reproduced the cultural ideals of earlier generations; it also served as another manifestation of the legal and governmental scaffolding supporting male-dominated marriages. While there are instances of resistance to the structure in generations past, in recent decades the structure has been more fully and more pervasively dismantled.

The demise of the use of the term "male-headed household" to signify legal power in a marriage, and the rise of its use as a term to complement "female-headed household," signifying a family structure, demonstrates how one buttress of male dominance has collapsed under the weight of social change. This is not to argue that male dominance prevailed within every marriage in the past, nor that it has been eclipsed today. My focus here is on the ideal, rather than adherence to the ideal. Regardless of actual behaviors, in the past couples laid claim to the "male-headed household." The husband/father was said to make the "final" and the "big" decisions; it was he who had, at the very least, veto power. Whether the husband dominated decision making or not, couples seemed to search for evidence to support his dominant position. The nature, the size, the result of the decisions were central to distinguishing between his decision making and hers.

In contrast, today, again regardless of behaviors, more people want to claim equality in marriage. Egalitarianism competes with male dominance in the married-couple household. The hegemony of the male-headed household has lapsed. It is no longer a legal given, a statistical majority, or *the* cultural ideal.[13] However, for the generation marrying around 1950, the ideal continued to inform their marriages into the 1980s. Although legal or social ideals never entirely describe people's behaviors, people are put in the position of having to respond to ideals and norms. Ideals necessarily shape accounts and inform strategic action.

Of the 12 couples in this sample, 9 clearly assert that the husband dominates and is the head of the household in the first interviews, conducted between 1958 and 1960. For example, in 1959, the interviewer of Susan Anderson remarked in the record that out of the entire interview, the only statement she made with any feeling, was that her "husband is head of household." Over the course of the decades, five of the wives make the additional point that women in general often respect a husband who can "control" them.

In 1960, Marie Hampton has been married to Henry for six years and has had three children. Asked whether Henry or herself is more dominating or submissive, she replied: "I blow off steam, but he's the one who makes the decisions. If I get my way, it is because he decides it. We discussed it early in our marriage, and I said I'd just as soon he did. I had several fellows whom I could step all over, and I didn't like it. We don't do anything that he doesn't want us to do. I get mad about it, but I'm really glad he does."

Martha and Michael McIntyre have been married for nine years and have had four of their six children by the 1958 interview. Asked about her husband's faults as a parent, Martha replies: "Maybe he's too strict at times, beyond the limits of reason. Actually I think he's a terrific father. He is the real authority in our home, and I think that's the way it should be. That was something I had to work out, but I know now that if it were the other way around I wouldn't be happy. Being strong-willed myself, I need someone to tell me when I've gone off the deep end."

Pat and Gary Holstein have been married for eight years in 1958. During this interview, when asked who is more dominant and who more submissive, Gary asserted: "I think I like to be in a more dominant position if I can help it [he laughs] [. . .]. She likes to be boss about some things around the house. For example, anything concerned with domestic aspects of the family—*minor* items—oh, like daily menus—*small* household items. *Major* items she doesn't like to make decisions on—*big* appliances or anything like that" (emphasis added). When Pat is asked who makes the decisions, she indicates that the final decision is always Gary's and says, "I felt for a time that I dominated Gary, like my mother . . . but my mother bought everything, and Gary and I . . . our home is us . . . both our personalities." She notes that Gary recently bought a new refrigerator and exclaims, "It was just fabulous. Gary has assumed a very *masculine* role . . . he has bought all the *big* items for the house . . ." (emphasis added).

LOCATING EQUALITY OUTSIDE THE HOME

The degree to which this ideal of the male as head of the household infuses the marriages of the '50s couples, as well as their response to the burgeoning women's movement from 1970 to 1982, reveals the unique challenges confronting this marital cohort with respect to the distribution of power by gender. The women's movement arises at a time when these couples' children are nearly grown. Life-stage adjustments become intertwined with reconstructions of gender as more wives return to work. Spouses increasingly contend with the society-wide attempts to redefine gender. In 1970, men's "freedoms" are more salient than "women's liberation," though the widespread movement begins to insinuate itself into their gender accounts. By 1982, the diffusion of feminism is more evident. Many couples strive to incorporate the principle of "equality," even as they retain a "male-headed household."

During the in-depth interviews conducted in 1970, both spouses are asked: "What are the good things about being a man (woman) versus a woman (man)?" This elicits spouses' perceptions of gender arrangements at this point in time. That families are constituted by gender-differentiated roles remains both an assumption and an ideal. This question about gender immediately becomes a response about family. The breadwinner/homemaker differentiation is salient in their accounts—despite 7 working wives out of 12 by 1970. Women most frequently mention having children and being taken care of as a good thing about being a woman. Men's responses indicate an awareness of their prerogatives, most explicitly, their "freedoms." Above all, there is an unguarded quality to the men's responses—a sense that gender roles and arrangements are "as they should be."

When Roger Finley is asked this question, he echoes the late 1950s talk about "heading the household" and delineates the privileges of being a man:

> It's still a man's world any way you look at it. I think I enjoy it. Trying to compare a man's world with a woman's world, I can see that a woman usually tends to be dependent on a man, in many things. And I'm glad I'm not in that position. I just feel that men are better than women. (Well, shit) I mean they're luckier anyway. They've really got more going for them. Being a little facetious [laughter] [...] I mean, I like making decisions, important decisions, things like business. I like being the head of the house; even though I think all our household decisions are made mutually. It's not that I'm telling my wife what to do or anything like that. But I like to be looked up to as head of the house. I like earning the money that supports the whole household, rather than me sitting home and cooking and washing dishes and my wife out working. That would be too terrible to contemplate.

So far, Roger preserves the title of household head, yet his peripheral awareness that change is afoot is captured in the word "still." If "it's still a man's world," it is subject to possible change. While being head of household undoubtedly yields certain privileges for Roger, it may be that the "title" or "rank" of being "head of the household," may be as important as any power actually exercised. Roger is glad he's not in the position of being dependent, yet his wife Linda says in 1960, "He's never lived by himself and he is dependent on somebody to take care of his household routine a great deal. He kind of goes all to pieces when he's left [laughs] for any length of time." Essentially, Linda reciprocates a patronizing attitude when she laughs at his ineptitude.[14] She also describes the context that allows for Roger's freedom of choice. Roger enjoys prerogatives as a man in "a man's world," precisely because of what Linda enables and provides at home (Ferree 1990; Thorne with Yalom 1982).

Gendered inequality at work becomes increasingly difficult to justify; gendered inequality on the home front, however, still resonates for many of these couples. The challenge of gender equality ensuing from the women's movement and women in the work force is more easily accepted, at least ideologically, for these couples than is any deconstruction of gender differentiation at home. As these couples increasingly presume, the public sphere is where the quality of "equality" is seemingly located.[15]

Many respondents speak favorably of women's opportunities at work, but do not extend these changes to family relations—even in 1982. The distinction between private and public becomes a convenient vehicle for their ambivalence, even though it is a boundary that is more illusory than real, as feminist scholars have shown (Ferree 1990; Thorne with Yalom 1982). This pattern emerges in these examples as spouses are asked in 1982 how they feel about the movement to change women's roles in society:

I have some pluses and minuses. I have had some experience as an employer seeing what problems women can have with the way they're treated, and I have a real sympathy with that. And I think legislation, and we've changed to a lot of women to be individuals. But at the same time within the marriage structure, its hard for me to see a marriage surviving when women becomes the dominant force [Evan Stone].

I'm not a women's libber, but yet I feel women should be given fair treatment in the working world [Irene Mitchell].

I got mixed emotions. I think women should be paid equal, but I don't think that their role, they should still be treated as a lady, because, in other words, if the man should open the door for her and things like that, but there are going to be certain times when she's going to be number two, and she can't have her cake and eat it too [Ted Mitchell].

Money-wise—women getting equal pay for equal work is good. But I also have been raised that the husband should be the head of the household. It's kind of hard to change the thinking on that. Also in our religion, the husband is the head of household. [I: How about your feeling on education and career opportunity?] I think it's great the way women are doing so well. I think, they've come a long way. I'm all for it [Susan Anderson].

Larry Frank, in his second marriage, feels that the movement to change women's roles is "terrific." His wife, Nancy, has worked full-time her entire life and is proud of her occupational achievements, given that she never finished high school and married for the first time at age 16. When Larry is asked if the movement has influenced their marriage, he echoes the Virginia Slims advertising campaign of the 1970s that proclaimed, "women have come a long way":

Well we agree upon everything that a woman should do in as far as women's lib. There are some minor things that we don't see eye to eye, but they're very minor. [I: Has that influenced your marriage?] It has helped us a lot. My wife believes in women doing a lot that a man can do. And I agree with her. I feel there is a place on earth for women, and they can do some of the men's jobs. Naturally they can't do them all, and we agreed on a lot of these [. . .] [I: And that's been a good influence on your marriage?] Well it's helped us a lot because I feel that it is a big question or big point in life at this time in people's lives. Women have come a long way in the last 10 years.

Even as Larry voices support for the women's movement, he relies on a male standard for evaluating women. When he asserts that women can do "a lot that a man can do," and that "there is a place on earth for women," men are the yardstick. He perceives that the movement is a "big point in life at this time," yet assumptions regarding male prerogatives linger in the discourse. When "equality" is understood as women being equal *to* men, it is manifest only when women do as men do; thus, participation in the labor force outside the home resembles and stands for equality. Like the Mitchells, the Andersons, and the Stones, whom we met in Chapter One, most couples deal with their ambivalence about gender changes by projecting the issue of gender equality onto the public sphere and the next generation.[16]

LOCATING GENDER EQUALITY IN THE NEXT GENERATION

Another strategy for recognizing the issue but keeping it at a distance is for spouses to project the issue of gender equality onto the next generation. When Linda Finley is asked what she thinks about the changes in women's roles, she states:

Well, I think it's inevitable. Because women have, by necessity, to move out of the place where they were. Financially speaking, it's a matter of survival, not just for them, but for their families, at this point. [I: Do you personally relate to it?] Not as strongly as I might have. If I'd been born in this generation, then I would feel the need. The need was not there as directly, somehow, in my young married years. And we were able to make enough money so that it hasn't ever been a critical thing finally to do it, and I've never been career-oriented to a point where I was terribly involved in my own stride and things.

When Linda Finley observes that financial need and cultural permission for women to have their "own stride" underlie the shifts among the younger generation, she points to the changing social environment. Like most wives, Linda returns to work part-time after the '70s movement and after her children are grown. Pursuing her "own stride" any earlier or any more vigorously would have created tension with Roger who, it might be recalled, "like[d] to be looked up to as head of the house" and perceived homemaking as "too terrible to contemplate." Linda may intuit the cost of challenging Roger's authority and control, for those qualities "are buttressed by institutional sources outside the family"—from religion, law, and custom to economic institutions (Chafetz 1980, 410). The private/public distinction is more illusory than real precisely because these institutional supports do not stop at spouses' doorsteps. Nevertheless, through their projections onto the public sphere and the next generation, they are able to reconcile ambivalence and potential conflict and distance themselves from the challenge of gender equality.

Linda Finley is among the majority of '50s spouses (15 out of 24) who contend that their marriages have *not* been influenced by the movement. However, the meaning of noninfluence varies. For two couples, "noninfluence" means an egalitarian marriage to begin with. For example, the African-American Stevenses did not assert the male-headed ideal to the same extent as did other, primarily Euro-American couples in the 1950s. When Julia Stevens is asked about decision making in 1959, after seven years of marriage, she says, "Well, we talk it over. I guess the *major* ones are his, but we always discuss them" (emphasis added). While she echoes the common assumption that the "major" decisions are the man's, she also discusses her independence. And after claiming that she is more independent, she is asked about her husband's independence: "I think he's fairly . . . I don't know, though. When he's left alone he won't cook. That's like most men. Anyway, he's most always independent." And when asked "Who is boss?" in the 1970s, Sam Stevens objects that he does not believe that is the "correct terminology." Julia Stevens, like many scholars, directly relates the fact that she was not influenced by the women's movement to the fact that she is African-American.[17] When asked about the influence of her race/ethnicity, she observes: "The black woman has always been somewhat different [. . .] because we've never been put in that role of a nice little feminine woman who stayed home and took care of her kids." The Stevenses talk leans toward egalitarianism well before the development of the women's movement among primarily white women.

For others, "noninfluence" implies an active repudiation of the trend. The white, upper-middle-class Stones, whom we met in Chapter One, are the prevailing model. Their talk suggested a defensive response, as their positions on the male household head hardened in response to the trend toward gender equality. The white, lower-middle-class Wilsons, married for over 30 years, also denied being influenced by the women's movement. When asked if her marriage was influenced by the movement,

Daisy Wilson asserts, "I don't think it has. It has affected some marriages, but not in mine." Her husband Oscar agrees: "Not much at all." Although spouses do not construct the ideal of male dominance to the same degree in 1982 as they did in 1958, by and large they do not embrace the ideal of gender equality advanced by the women's movement either.

Finally, a few spouses downplay the women's movement, but realize that change is in the air. Pat Ross[18] reluctantly admits to being influenced by the women's movement:

> I would like to say no. I would prefer that things happen outside of me are not things that govern my life. But in reality, it has. I think we're all changing, including men. [My son] made the comment to me that when he gets married, his wife will have a career. It is just presumed that his wife will have a career—it doesn't occur to him that his wife is going to be a housewife. He talks about participating in raising the children. He's already looking at life like that. So this has influenced me.

Pat echoes Linda Finley's view that gender equality has greater relevance for the next generation. And while the focus remains on women moving into the labor force, there is also recognition that her son may participate in the labor at home. For this generation, then, spouses primarily contend with the challenge of gender equality by projecting it onto the public sphere and the next generation.

4   The '50s Dominicks

Dominating with Divorce Culture

WHILE I was conducting my research, I had a chance encounter at an airport with a man who was about sixty years old. Upon hearing that my research was about divorce, he said, "I've told my wife she better do as I say, or I'll divorce her and she'll find herself in the poor house." In the same breath, he both showed his knowledge of many women's downward mobility after divorce and demonstrated how the combination of male dominance and divorce culture can work. For those whose beliefs are rooted in divorce culture, the door to divorce is always open. A husband who believes in male dominance in marriage and uses the divorce option as a threat has enhanced his power to define the terms of the marriage. This power is augmented if such a husband's wife believes in marriage culture and views divorce as a last resort. A spouse who believes that marriage is forever and divorce is a last resort is more likely to accommodate the wishes of the spouse who uses divorce as an ever-present option.

MALE-DOMINATED DIVORCE CULTURE: A CONTRADICTION FOR WIVES

Spouses who believe in male dominance and divorce culture simultaneously are logically more likely to be men than women. Divorce culture is based upon individual needs, growth, and gratification; all three premises of divorce culture assume some degree of individual autonomy and choice. A male-dominated marriage, in contrast, confers autonomy primarily on husbands, not wives. In short, male dominance has different implications in the context of divorce culture than it has in marriage culture. To join male dominance with divorce culture is a contradiction for wives; they cannot assume the autonomy presumed by divorce culture and the subordination presumed by male dominance simultaneously. Conceivably, a wife could believe that if she divorced her husband she could secure greater male dominance in a remarriage. Yet, such an action would simultaneously reveal her independence and ability to depart from roles. Wives who feel free to use the divorce option as a lever and set the terms of marital contingency in relation to their needs and ideals of a gratifying marriage are more likely to believe in egalitarianism, which also affords them a measure of autonomy. Alternatively, the wife who leaves her husband because of his inability to perform his duties as a household head—due to affairs, alcohol, or unemployment, for example—is more likely to support the terms of marriage culture and see divorce as a last resort.

Traditionalist wives who abide by the terms of marriage culture and male dominance are most vulnerable to the power of divorce culture if they are married to husbands who feel they have the prerogative to threaten divorce. Such wives, I argue, have little leverage to secure their marital ideals. Submissive wives will be reluctant to leave the marriage and more likely to feel, if not be, more financially and psychologically dependent upon their husbands. Therefore, they will be more subject to husbands' power and conditions. Moreover, believing in male superiority implies that husbands are, in some sense, "better"—better decision makers, better wage earners, better in a variety of ways that legitimate the dominance. If the wife believes her husband is "better," then she not only sees herself as "less than" him, but she is also unlikely to perceive his flaws or his dependence.

Thus, male dominance attached to divorce culture represents a "cautionary tale" for wives; if they do not abide by their husbands' terms, they risk being left for another woman. Of course the belief in male dominance is not new, but the new context changes its meaning. Traditionally this belief has been marked by the redeeming virtue of commitment—a responsibility to others set ideological limits on the power of the husband.

To view divorce as a gateway can foster the stereotyped, mostly male prerogative of leaving one's wife for "a younger model." The husband who pursues a younger woman not only reinforces male standards of sexual attractiveness as crucial to a desirable wife, but also augments the power attached to being a man with the power attached to being older. But whether a husband relies upon his sex, age, or economic resources, such husbands can use the divorce option as a lever to set the terms of marital contingency.

In my sample, this male-centered strategy is still more likely to be attributed to "others," rather than recognized in oneself—perhaps because this sample is primarily constituted by enduring marriages, and perhaps because the concept of serial marriage for the purposes of one's own gratification remains unsettling and even objectionable. To the degree that people's acts follow their beliefs, those who believe in male dominance and divorce culture are probably more prevalent among the divorced. Still, a husband can express these beliefs without acting on them; he can simply threaten to leave his wife in the "poor house."

While the pattern or "ideal type" represented by the Dominicks—that is, a pattern reflecting male dominance and divorce culture—provides a tool for comparison, these are dynamic patterns and cannot be thought of as hard and fast—above all because people are not types, and beliefs change over time. Still, isolating such patterns enables us to see that, on the whole, among '50s couples husbands and wives were more likely to hold the same beliefs about marriage and gender. While among the '70s couples, 6 out of 17 (about one-third) contained spouses who expressed different beliefs about gender or marriage, only 2 out of 12 couples (one-sixth) in the older generation contained spouses who expressed distinctly different beliefs about marriage, divorce, or gender. The Dominicks are one of these two couples.

THE DOMINICKS: '50S TRADITIONALISTS GROW APART

The Dominicks are a white, middle-class couple, who have four grown children by the 1980s. Vincent Dominick had a working-class background; however, he became a successful insurance salesperson and lifted his family into the middle class. Doreen Dominick was a homemaker until her children were in junior high school, when she went to work. The Dominicks' complaints across the decades, and their low marital satisfaction scores in 1983, reveal a largely unsatisfying marriage.

Sketchy evidence in the 1950s interviews suggests that both spouses began with traditionalist beliefs, including marriage culture and male dominance. Doreen Dominick maintains a belief in marriage culture. However, over time she is decreasingly content with male dominance and gravitates toward egalitarian ideals. In contrast, Vincent Dominick gravitates toward divorce culture; he maintains a belief in male dominance, but over the decades increasingly sees divorce as a gateway to his happiness.

Vincent will ultimately stay in his marriage, yet he seriously considers divorce for reasons more in line with divorce culture: his own happiness. At the same time, he actively resists Doreen's desire and push for equality. Doreen's efforts represent the difficulty of introducing equality into a relationship founded upon male dominance. This difficulty is acute not only because of his resistance, but also because of her loyalty to marriage culture. Her convictions about lasting marriage are, in part, a reaction to her childhood experience.

Married for nine years in 1959, Doreen Dominick designated her parents' divorce as the "low" in her life. Because her parents divorced, Doreen was one of the few people to bring up divorce in the early interviews. Interestingly, she interpreted the cause of the parental divorce to be problematic gender relations. She suggested that in her parents' case, her mother was too passive, her father's dominance was too severe: "My mother wouldn't speak up to my father. She would just go along [. . .] I think it would have been better if she had stood up to him. He was very domineering. [. . .] *I still think that the father should be the dominant one in the family.* I think a woman respects a man who does that. I think it's about 75–25 percent between me and Vincent—that's too much." Like most of the '50s wives, Doreen "still thinks that the father should be the dominant one in the family." However, Doreen foreshadowed her gravitation toward egalitarian ideals when she said that 75 percent dominance by her husband was "too much." When asked at this time what she expected of marriage before she married, Doreen remarks: "Well, I wanted a very happy marriage. The last thing I wanted was a divorce." Doreen never does frame divorce as a gateway, but rather sees it as a constantly hovering threat.

The Challenge of Equality in Mid-Marriage

Most of the '50s wives in this sample contributed to the rise in married women's participation in the labor force in the 1970s. And they did so as the women's movement emerged. These developments represent the option of greater financial and political power for wives. How do the Dominicks cope with this new marital context?

Like many '50s husbands, in 1971, when asked about the good things about being a man, Vincent Dominick highlights "the freedoms that a man has":

> Oh, I think the freedoms that a man has, probably the greatest advantage in a simple-minded way of looking at it. Regardless of the equality and all that they talk about, a man certainly has much more freedom than a woman. Unless the woman has little or no morals, and this has been an argument at home, because as I say, I do like to take off. I have about seven or eight fishing cronies and we like to get out about four or five times a year and go for three or four or five days, and Doreen can't do this. She can't pick up with a girlfriend and take off four or five times a year. As I said, this is sort of a simple-minded way, but I think that as far as advantages, if you're speaking of the career female, they have really as many advantages as a man at this particular point. They certainly have brought that out as far as the [company] is concerned. All the gals that I had anything to do with promoting have all been outstanding girls that I don't think you could find in many cases, males that would be anywhere near as capable.

Vincent's response reveals a lot about the workings of power and sexuality in male-dominated marriages. Vincent readily admits that "a man certainly has much more freedom than a woman." He assumes this freedom is "natural." To naturalize any behavior is to legitimate it. It is inconceivable to Vincent that Doreen might "take off four or five times a year." Being inconceivable means that neither society nor Vincent is visibly obstructing her potential desire to take off; rather it is simply assumed that she will not do so. Vincent's male dominance can be described as "hegemonic" precisely because it is a commonsense belief that seems given, appropriate, natural, and without contradiction (Gramsci 1971; Komter 1989).

What makes Doreen's seeming inability to "take off" natural? Vincent's response suggests that this "naturalness" is rooted in sexuality. When Vincent says that only women who have "little or no morals" take off, the moral concern is not about going fishing. Perhaps a woman "taking off" is neglecting her domestic responsibilities. More important, she is a woman on the loose. Fear of her sexual freedom lies just below the surface. This fear stems from the Western roots of patriarchal[1] marriage, which guaranteed paternity. For Vincent, this fear may also stem from his own projections. When he takes off for weekends in future years, Vincent will not just go fishing. Yet, sexual difference is not ultimately rooted in "natural sexuality," rather it is rooted in the ability or *power to define* sexuality as naturally different.

Still, Vincent's power is being culturally challenged and he knows it. The power signified by working wives and the women's movement suggests that '50s husbands cannot entirely ignore the claims for equality. Vincent grants that there are "outstanding girls" in business. He also wants to believe that "the career female ... really [has] as many advantages as a man at this particular point." Like other husbands and wives of this generation, Vincent is willing to allow "equality" in the workplace. Yet the workplace functions like a dam—preventing the flood of egalitarian demands from invading his home. In order to reconcile a marital bargain founded on the assumption of male dominance with the new marital terms of women's equality, these spouses repeatedly rely on the artificial split between the public and the private (Lopata 1993). Yet, precisely because the distinction is artificial, the waters of egalitarianism necessarily spill over into homes.

We learn from Doreen in these 1970 interviews that Vincent has finally permitted her to return to work. Doreen reports that after much resistance, Vincent changed his mind because "he's heard enough of it," and as long as the kids "are taken care of and he doesn't suffer" she can work: "he made me understand that he wasn't about to help out at home, because it wasn't necessary that I work, and uh, if I could do it all, fine. Go ahead and go. Otherwise, don't do it." His *permission* suggests his power, yet her persistence suggests her increasing sense of entitlement. Doreen's response reflects wives' resistance to the confines of home and their pursuit of freedom in the world of paid work. However, it is a pursuit premised on sustaining responsibilities at home. In this context, prevalent among white middle-class wives in the '50s cohort, Doreen's "second shift" is her priority. Vincent's account not only echoes husbands' assertions about male freedoms on the domestic front, but in combination with Doreen's account, it suggests that Vincent is setting the terms.

By the 1980s, when Doreen is asked whether the women's movement influenced her marriage, she explains that "it made it rocky," because of "not being there all of the time and doing my own thing, my own interests outside the home . . . having my own money." Doreen would not have gone to work as readily, she asserted, if it had not been for the women's movement. She pursued a job for the "independence," rather than for the money. While money enabled independence, neither spouse saw Doreen's work as necessary for survival. Vincent confirmed that the women's movement and Doreen's return to work led to "deterioration at one point [in the marriage] because it came on all of a sudden and she went from one extreme to the other."

The challenge of gender equality has left its mark on the Dominick marriage. It is important not only because equality was a point of contention—there are a number of other threats to their marriage—but because its failure represents how a wife's unwavering commitment to marriage blunts the ability to create equality, just as a husband's belief in divorce culture hones the power of male dominance.

The Brink of Divorce: Conditions of Last Resort

Doreen and Vincent Dominick may have the most troubled marriage of the sample—seemingly more troubled than those of the two couples who divorced. In part, their marital endurance points to the tenacity of marriage culture. In part, it points to their ability to reconstruct their marital accounts over time. Doreen's account changes in interesting ways between the 1970s and the 1980s—"divorce thoughts" are always present, but they migrate over the course of time.

When Doreen is asked in 1971 whether she has ever been seriously worried about her marriage, her response, like Katy Stone's, reflected the disruptive effects of military service for marriages in their infancy—a common problem for this generation:

Uh . . . maybe *right at the beginning*, within the last, well, when he came back from [overseas]—he'd been gone for 21 months or something like that [I: Oh, wow] So then, you know, things go on there so that they're kind of in a fog so that when he came back—he'd been gone so long—I guess nervous pressures or something and I wondered then . . . at that time . . . and when he took on the house responsibility and I became pregnant—things were a little jagged—you know, and I might have thought about it, but I really didn't think seriously. [Emphasis added.]

Doreen admits and discounts these "divorce thoughts" early in her marriage. However, it is clear that she was attuned to the "jagged" edges of her marriage.

By 1983, when Doreen is asked when her marriage was at its *best*, she says when they were newlyweds. Given the 1971 account that suggested difficulties "right at the beginning," this is surprising. Perhaps these early thoughts have been overshadowed by her more recent thoughts of divorce. When asked about divorce considerations in 1983, she states: "I thought of it, but never did it," claiming that she thought of it *two* years ago. When asked to explain the conditions for these thoughts, Doreen simply states that it was because of "*his* unhappiness" (emphasis added). Doreen may have been denying her own unhappiness and projecting it onto Vincent. Yet, Vincent *was* unhappy. She was clearly attuned to his needs—monitoring the emotional quality of the relationship just as other '50s wives did.

Vincent reports in 1983 that he had thought of divorce because of "being miserable." Vincent is the other husband among the '50s couples, besides Evan Stone, who admits to having thought about divorce. What threatened the Dominicks' marriage in Vincent's account? Vincent reports that they have seen "marriage counselors, psychologists," because of "sexual problems," but this "hasn't made a hell of a lot of difference." Vincent further disclosed that they had separated for a couple of weeks once. Asked what caused the separation, he replied, "Inability to communicate. She was fearful that I was going to be violent physically and abuse her. [I: She left?] Mmm hmm." We never do learn if Vincent's report of Doreen's fear was based in reality; that she does not mention physical abuse is no reason to assume it did not happen. Unless questioned directly, many battered wives do not readily admit abuse, given what it implies about their spouses, their marriages, and themselves. It is possible that Doreen's fears were ungrounded when she left. Regardless, communication and sexual problems clearly existed by both accounts.

The Dominick's marital tensions do not start and stop with botched communication, fear of physical abuse, or sexual problems. Their marriage has been plagued by Vincent's extramarital affairs and has also been stressed by a handicapped child. One wonders what has kept the Dominicks together.

Accounting for Marriage

By 1983, spouses were regularly asked what kept them together. This question is itself a sign of divorce culture—suggesting that staying together should be accounted for. Riessman (1990, 14) points out that "it is only in untoward situations that behavior needs to be 'accounted for'" and that "getting divorced is such an instance, because of the ideology of marriage as forever." Yet, with the rise in numbers and acceptance of divorce, "staying married" must also be "accounted for"—particularly when staying in a hostile or destructive marriage is increasingly framed as problematic or "dysfunctional." This will be more apparent among the younger couples. Still, mirroring those who divorce, the Dominicks want to legitimate staying married.

When trying to justify a decision to stay married or to get divorced, the tendency is to imagine "the path not taken." Most people giving retrospective accounts strive to affirm the paths taken, and the Dominicks are no exception, despite some regrets. Doreen primarily draws upon her belief in marriage culture; Vincent selectively draws upon the terms of marriage and divorce culture to legitimate his choices.

When Doreen is asked what has kept her marriage together she replies, "love." Despite the conflicts and the strains, she wants to claim a "good" marriage. However, these claims are suspect when she keeps returning to the topic of divorce: "We've had a good marriage. We've had our problems, but we've had a good marriage. And we've had ups and downs, a lot of ups and downs lately, in the last few years. But hopefully now we can—I thought we might have to get a divorce." Reference to the "ups and downs" echo Katy Stone's observation that there will be a "percentage of times" when all will not be satisfying in a marriage. Yet, Doreen's reiteration that they have had their "ups and downs," suggests the repeatedly precarious nature of their marriage. As the interviewer probes to find out whether divorce has been ruled out altogether at this point, Doreen replied that "There's always that *possibility,*" primarily if "someone comes into *his* life, which I don't think has ever happened."

However, it has happened. Doreen's suspicions and fears are not ungrounded in this case. Vincent admits that he's had occasional affairs. He confides: "I'm not promiscuous by any stretch of the imagination. Probably . . . my first time around was four years ago . . . yeah; about that [. . .] I guess you know my upbringing and I have an awful lot of respect for Doreen [. . .] I was uh oh about a year ago quite serious with a . . . gal that was considerably younger. She was a divorcée and if she didn't have a youngster, I think I'd have probably run off with her." Doreen's report that there have been "a lot of ups and downs lately, in the last few years" coincides with his report that his first affair was "around four years ago." Doreen could be refusing to confide in the interviewer or wanting to deny her own suspicions.

The affairs may be both a cause and a consequence of failure in sexual therapy and communication. It is curious, but not unusual, that Vincent remarks on his respect for Doreen while discussing his affairs. Rubin (1983), among others, has discussed the madonna/whore complex in some men. Rubin found that sometimes for men "sex is easier, less riddled with conflict, when it comes without emotional attachment" (117). Vincent's last affair was a seeming exception to this pattern; in this case, the "youngster" mitigated "divorce as a gateway" for Vincent. Vincent gravitates toward the individualistic themes of divorce culture when he admits that this lover's responsibility for a child—a responsibility he did not want to share—was a primary deterrent to divorce.

Yet, there were other obstacles at the gateway of divorce as well—obstacles that reflect marriage culture. When Vincent is asked what has kept them together, three issues figure prominently: family, Doreen's "kin work," and the sake of the children. "Kids. My father. Her mother. [I: How?] She is probably closer to my father than my sisters and brothers. It would destroy him if something happened. With [our] youngest son, he is more or less on his own, but I felt an obligation that we be together. He's had enough problems in life with his handicap and his accident. And he didn't need that." Their son was not only born blind, but was brutally beaten and robbed at knifepoint in his adolescence. Vincent states that if it were not for their son "needing, you know, some cohesion at home and my father, uh, I think I'd have left you know. I'm not happy and I think I would have just packed my bags and moved out, but too many hassles about a lot of things; it's improved since the kids moved out and we don't have all these pressures and all the rest of that bit but uh we don't have an awful lot in common. . . ." Vincent suggests that divorce might have been a gateway to happiness—that is, he relies upon divorce culture—when he implies that he could have been a whole lot happier outside of their marriage. Yet, he also points to the "sake of the children," a key deterrent to divorce under the terms of marriage culture.

As Vincent continues to justify his marriage, he seems to emphasize the endurance itself as a reason to stay together:

> But I guess you know after, what? Thirty-two years. You look back at a lot of happy things and you have a lot to be thankful for; you know the kids have been good kids and uh they're concerned you know. They recognize that our relationship is strained and uh, you know, they're concerned about that. But we'll all live through it . . . I was a real achiever when I was younger, from a career standpoint, and that—she resented that you know; she was left out and I didn't want her to work. Yet I put all my energies

into my job to get ahead and I got all the recognition and she got nothing and you know all that routine, things turned around . . .

Despite Doreen's "resentment" and the conflicts recognized by the children as well as himself, Vincent points to "a lot to be thankful for," and notes that "the kids have been good kids." These are the perceived rewards of enduring marriage. Yet his account not only represents the resilience of old terms, but also the increasing press of the divorce option. Under the terms of divorce culture, the marriage must deliver some happiness, some gratification; Vincent attempted to evoke this when he claimed that there have been "a lot of happy things." Yet Doreen's "resentment" and the conflicts, recognized by the children and himself, suggest otherwise. When Vincent said, "I got all the recognition" and "she got nothing," he recognized that Doreen had sacrificed a great deal—a sacrifice that is more apparent with the rise of new terms and a new generation. However, his concluding comment regarding "all that routine, things turned around" suggests this is a begrudging recognition.

With thirty-two years and their children in common, Vincent pulls back from the brink of divorce. When Doreen discusses her reasons for staying in the marriage, she remarks that the kids are "all supportive of the two of us being—they don't want their parents divorced." According to Doreen, the kids have made this clear. Doreen, like Vincent, has "stayed together for the sake of the kids."

THE LEGACY OF MALE DOMINANCE

In the end, Vincent Dominick chooses to remain in his marriage and provides reasons considered legitimate under the terms of marriage culture. Vincent claims he stayed together for "the sake of the children" and other family relations. Given the adversity experienced by one of their four children, this emphasis upon parental responsibility is admirable, despite and even because of the conflicts that plague their marriage. Yet these claims ring a bit hollow, given Vincent's admission that he would have divorced if his lover had been childless. Moreover, his divorce thoughts were always attached to his unhappiness, not Doreen's. It was Doreen's loyalty to enduring marriage that kept this marriage alive.

"Marriage as forever" has been an explicit goal of Doreen's since she was a child. Doreen has an aversion to divorce rooted in her Catholic background and her parents' divorce. Recall that the worst low in Doreen's life by 1959 was her parents' divorce. It may be that this childhood injury has fortified her resistance to divorce; she has felt the damage of divorce and refuses to inflict this on her children. This suggests that children of divorce do not necessarily repeat their parents' behaviors, but also react against them. Yet, Doreen's unwavering adherence to marriage as forever may impede her efforts to effect change; she cannot threaten to leave, has little leverage with which to redefine the neglect, abuse, emotional impoverishment, or inequity she feels. Paradoxically, she needs equality to inject equality into the marriage. Without much leverage, she represents the difficulty of introducing equality into a marriage founded upon male dominance.

Both the Dominicks interpret changing gender relations as a cause of marital upheaval. Gender becomes salient for them through the women's movement and Doreen's return to work. By resisting Vincent's established authority when she went to work, Doreen challenged the terms of male dominance. Nevertheless, the minimal change in her marriage reveals the limits of Doreen's power and the extent of Vincent's "hidden power."

In her study of married couples in the Netherlands, Komter (1989) uncovered several dimensions of power: manifest, latent, and invisible power. Manifest power, which refers to the ability to enforce one's will even where there is resistance, can be tracked in terms of visible outcomes. When Doreen wanted to go to work, she persisted despite Vincent's resistance, and ultimately fulfilled her desire; while she finally received Vincent's permission, her work was on his terms. Vincent's terms were also a form of manifest power: he was not going to help her desire and did not want to see any disruption in "second shift" responsibilities.

Vincent never exercises his manifest power quite to the extent of the traditionalist Evan Stone. When Evan threatened to divorce Katy if he did not remain "the boss," he explicitly used divorce as a lever to set his terms. Manifest power clearly indicates who makes the decisions and what will or will not occur. However, the threat of divorce can also be used under conditions of latent power.

Latent power refers to the ability to thwart a potential problem or to avert threatening issues. Whether he was abusive or not, Doreen's fear that Vincent might physically abuse her speaks to her anticipation of his power. And whether Doreen knows of his affairs or not, her suspicions underlie her fear of divorce. She can hardly threaten divorce to obtain her desires if she suspects he will take her up on the offer. Moreover, her concern with "his unhappiness" means she cannot rock the boat. Komter (1989, 212) found that both manifest and latent power worked to the advantage of the husbands because usually wives wanted change and husbands did not, resulting in conflict, or because wives avoided pressing for a desired change, anticipating negative consequences. In short, these powers reinforced the status quo of traditional gender beliefs and practices.

Invisible power may be more insidious because it is rooted in prevailing cultural beliefs that go unquestioned. Neither the powerful nor the disempowered are aware that it is operating. Komter (1989, 213) observed: "The ideological underpinnings of inequality in marital power that are confirmed by means of invisible power do not reflect accidental beliefs and opinions, but express cultural and societal hegemonic values about women, men, and what is appropriate and natural." Vincent's observation that women do not have the freedom to go away four or five times a year to fish is stated as if it could not be otherwise; the power this accords him and withholds from her goes unrecognized. That society provides men, but not women, with leisure time is just part of everyday reality; it is not perceived as what it is: a greater valuation of men and their autonomy. Vincent's valuation of his own happiness is represented in his pursuit of affairs; this allows him to maintain his dominance and his freedom in a way that Doreen cannot. Both Vincent and Doreen speak as though Vincent is entitled to more happiness than Doreen. Vincent may be entitled to more happiness than he has, but it does not seem to occur to either of them that Doreen is, too. Such cultural ideals invisibly enhance Vincent's power and undermine Doreen's. Doreen's belief in "marriage culture" also invisibly enhances Vincent's power. When promoting divorce as a very last resort is combined with the traditional gender expectations of male dominance, Doreen must make the sacrifices, must put her needs aside.

Social change, however, has a way of making the invisible visible. By the 1980s, even Vincent grudgingly realizes that he "got all the recognition." The women's movement and wives' participation in the labor force potentially influence all three levels of power. The movement promotes alternative ideological resources for wives; paid work provides financial resources for wives. Yet, to access these resources on a manifest level, wives must be willing to assert their needs and desires. To access these resources on a latent level, wives must be able to recognize when they are anticipating their husband's needs at the expense of their own. When the very definition of being a "wife" has been to subordinate one's own needs to the needs of one's husband, learning to address their own needs can be difficult for wives. Finally, to make these resources visible requires that a husband anticipate and become attuned to a wife's needs. Indeed, because monitoring the well-being of the marriage has been wives' conventional responsibility, to recognize and value women's needs, desires, and interests is to redefine marriage.

The high threshold for divorce set by the terms of marriage culture has not served Doreen. The Dominicks separate, possibly experience violence, pursue therapy, and weather extramarital affairs; although these adversities are not automatic mechanisms for divorce, they can be conditions of "last resort." If Doreen were not so loyal to "marriage as forever," she might question her sacrifices, refuse to countenance the threat of violence, imagine that not only divorce, but marital conflict can be bad for the children, and finally imagine a truly egalitarian marriage, in which she, too, is entitled to happiness. Of course, however entitled he may feel, Vincent has not secured happiness—perhaps reflecting a cost of male dominance for men (Messner 1997).

5 The '50s Hamptons and Other Couples

Redefining Marriage Culture in Terms of Gender Equality

UNLIKE the Dominicks or the traditionalist Stones, some '50s spouses take advantage of changes in women's roles to redefine their marriages in terms of gender equality while retaining their belief in "marriage as forever." Divorce culture and gender equality become salient at a time when the '50s couples are well into their marriages. By and large, the children have been raised and occupational demands have subsided. In short, incentives and deterrents to divorce have shifted in relation to the life course. Because the gendered division of labor regarding child rearing and wage earning can become less central in later years, one might hypothesize that gender equality would be easier to attain. However, this change appears difficult to effect—indeed 6 of the 12 couples never even try. For those who do try to redo gender relations while maintaining marriage culture, there are inevitable references to the "ups and downs in marriage."

The effort to weave a new pattern—integrating the new warp of egalitarianism with the old woof of marriage culture—is evident in the dynamics of three couples (a quarter of the '50s sample): the first marriages of the Hamptons and the Stevenses and the remarriage of the Franks. In all three couples, the wives have worked since the 1960s. I begin with the first-married Hamptons because the *process* of change is more apparent in their discourse. Although I focus on the Hamptons, I discuss these other cases to reveal the variability that can be found even when all couples embrace gender equality and "marriage as forever."

These couples' level of marital satisfaction by 1982 suggests some difficulty in weaving marriage culture and egalitarianism into a whole. The Hamptons and the Stevenses reflect a middle level of satisfaction, while the Franks reflect a lower level of satisfaction.[1] In contrast to traditionalists, none of the couples in this category are highly satisfied. This does not mean that couples who believe in gender equality and marriage culture are never happy; however, these cases suggest that the *transition* to equality can strain a relationship and threaten to unravel a marriage.

THE HAMPTONS: RIDING OUT THE YEARS WITHIN MARRIAGE CULTURE

The Hamptons are middle class, Euro-Americans, who have rejected Protestantism by adulthood. In 1960, they have been married for eight years and have had three children. Henry has a college education and is working as a medical technician—a job that has compelled the family to move several times. At this time, Marie asserts that "if I get my way, it is because he decides it." She also admits that "being a housewife is not enough." She continues: "Henry doesn't like it if I'm home; I get moody. He feels I should get out. He's really the big pusher on it." This suggests Henry's egalitarian inclinations early in the marriage, though as we will see, "getting out" does not necessarily mean going out to a paid job.

When Henry is asked about the good things about being a man in 1971, he echoes Vincent Dominick: "A man has more freedom in society, I guess." The interviewer asks, "In what ways?" and Henry replies: "Well . . . in the sense that . . . just from the time you're in school where a boy asks a girl on a date or something, a man is the one who takes the initiative, you know. A woman reacts to things. Although I guess that's changing. But . . . in the fact that a man would perhaps make decisions where a woman—you know, has a stronger influence in running things. That isn't true in my case actually, but I guess for a lot of men it is." Henry is recounting the ideal by which husbands are supposed to be the "decision makers," and wives are supposed to carry these decisions out. Asked who makes the decisions, Henry responds: "she thinks I would make most of the decisions, but I would say generally speaking it would be half and half or something." Henry's awkward and conditional phrasing reflects the lack of fit between the reality and Marie's ideal. Marie confirms the marital confusion in 1971 over who is making and who is carrying out decisions: ". . . actually he wears the pants in the family. He used to decide everything we bought. But as we get older, I'm getting a little more pushy I guess. He's maybe bending a little more. [I: But you said you make the decisions.] I make the minor decisions about everything. And I sort of try to influence him on the major ones. [...] And I help him make up his mind to what I think he wants." Marie works to retain Henry's position as household head—his wearing of "the pants." Even as she "influences" Henry on the "major" decisions and helps him make up his mind about what she thinks he wants, she is reluctant to acknowledge her active control in family affairs. The male-headed household remains a powerful ideal, even as their marital lives produce evidence to the contrary.

By 1971, Marie has been working for about five years—since her youngest child went into kindergarten. Married for 17 years with three children, Marie is asked if she ever thought her marriage would not work out. She says, "Well, often. Off and on over the years." As the interviewer probes, asking "But you never got to the point—?", Marie responds with the deterrents associated with marriage culture: "No, the kids come first, with both of us. No matter how mad you might be." She admits considering marital counseling, but when she brought it up to Henry, "he got furious," and "I got over it."

While she does not pull the two observations together, her contemplation and rejection of divorce occurred after her sister got a divorce. In 1982 we learn that her sister divorced in the late sixties and Marie has been alienated from her sister ever since. Marie and Henry were close to their brother-in-law, and Marie disapproved of the divorce. Marie claims, "If she would get over her self-centeredness, I'd like to be a closer friend to her, but as long as she's so wrapped up in number one, it's difficult." Implied in this statement, as well as her assertion that "the kids come first," is that her sister's divorce can be explained by her selfishness—a critique that had, and still has, more power as a divorce deterrent for women than for men.

Married for 28 years in 1982, Marie again acknowledges marital problems, but asserts: "We have our disagreements and they pass; you don't have to go and get a divorce over them." Asked if she ever thought of divorce, she says "yes" and refers back to earlier years: "He was very unhappy with me and I felt it was *my problem* that I wasn't suitable for him. The kids were young and I was trapped, as it were. [I: Who thought about it?] I did." Like Doreen Dominick, who was concerned about "his unhappiness" when she thought of divorcing Vincent, Marie locates the problem in herself as she contemplates divorce. Her concerns are relational rather than individualistic. Marie also asserts in 1982 that "I had some preconceived idea of 'his work' and 'her work'—they had to be ironed out. They caused problems when we were first married." Ironically, Marie initially objected to Henry's assistance with housekeeping: "I took it personally when he got a hold of a broom, and now I take it as a compliment." She essentially felt that Henry was invading her territory—but Henry grew up in a motherless family and expected to help out. He also had higher standards for cleanliness than Marie.

"The children," and the presumption of women's responsibility for them, deters a divorce that might have been. It is a deterrent that leaves time for adjustment. This becomes fortunate for Marie because, in the meantime, feminism emerges to support her predilections to be more than a housewife and eventually define a more satisfying marriage. She notes that she and Henry argued regularly when she went to work—he resented the authority that her work gave her at a time when he was "lacking in authority." But they fought it out, and the "phase" passed. Asked about her thoughts on the women's movement and whether it influenced her marriage, she observes:

> I guess I'm an aberration. I've done it already. I think in some cases women are trying too hard to be both and they're going to lose their parenthood in the shuffle if they're not careful. I think men are having a real problem with their identity, the young ones I see. I didn't marry a macho type, and he's changed all to the good in the years we've been married, as I have changed toward the equal thing, but he was pretty equal anyway, so it's not been a problem.

When Marie asserts that she has "done it already," she is referring to her years in the labor force. Her statement that women might "lose their parenthood," again reflects her relational concerns, even as she is concerned about equality. Marie appropriates the language of the women's movement in her references to the "macho type" and the "equal thing"—an appropriation that has made it possible for her to dispense with the idea that marital instability was her problem, that she was not suitable for her husband.

Henry's response when asked whether the women's movement has influenced their marriage reflects his flexibility: "I think it has in small ways. I don't do a lot around the house but I certainly agree that men should do some of the work and I do more than I used to."

When asked what has kept them together, Marie reiterates an assertion from 1971: "We come from a long line of married couples. We have the mental set for staying with one person." This is the belief in "marriage as forever." Also in 1982, Marie elaborates on her divorce thoughts, and the influence of family relations emerges:

> Oh, I thought for a while, you know, we were so ill-suited; I obviously was never, ever going to be the kind of wife he wanted, and, bug out and get out while I could, but he got the kids. I went that far [chuckles] and never went through with it. I couldn't go home, because my mother thought he was so neat, it would be terrible. If I ever went home, that would be the last place I'd go. 'Cause she'd take his part, so. [chuckles] But, you know there are ups and downs in marriage; it's not smooth.

After 28 years of marriage, Marie has overcome their martial difficulties and asserts that her relationship with her husband has "returned a lot since the kids are gone." She also explains that after her husband had a heart attack, she was sitting in the hospital with him and realized: "I would really like to ride out my years with him; it would really be terrible if I didn't." Doreen Dominick's unwavering support for "marriage as forever" seemed to impede her efforts to incorporate equality; in contrast, Marie's support for this belief allows her to "ride out" the conflicts that eventually result in a more egalitarian marriage.

The beliefs in "marriage as forever" and the "good of the children" kept Marie and Henry going when the going got tough—particularly when the children were young and as Marie started working. By the time their children are grown, they have mostly left the ideology of a male-headed household behind. By 1982, both spouses insist there is no boss. They have also reinvigorated a marriage that was vulnerable in the early child-rearing years. As other studies have suggested is common, their marital satisfaction rebounded after the active child-rearing years had passed (Cowan and Cowan 1998; Rollins and Feldman 1970). As Henry notes, if "forces" did not exist to deter divorce, "it's a matter of conjecture what would happen." Those forces, sustained by marriage culture, are seriously challenged in the 1980s. If the Hamptons were twenty years younger and had the same conflicts around authority, children, and work, a divorce might have been more likely. On the other hand, the push of marriage culture may well have sustained this couple.

The Stevenses: Parallel Equality

I might have presented the Stevenses for in-depth analysis instead of the Hamptons, but their change as a couple is less salient. Like the Hamptons, the Stevenses are middle class and in their first marriage. In each couple, the wives "think divorce" while the husbands do not, and the wives have changed more over time. Both marriages reflect a middle range of satisfaction and blend marriage culture with egalitarian ideals. However, the Stevenses contend less with the *change* toward gender equality because they never asserted the male-headed ideal to the same extent as other couples.

Julia and Sam Stevens claim that their household is mutually headed over the decades; this may be related to their religious beliefs and African-American ethnicity.[2] Egalitarianism may be more valued and practiced within some African-Americans' marriages than it is among other races/ethnicities, though this is still debated in the literature. Recall that when asked "Who is boss?" in 1970, Sam Stevens said that he did not believe that was the "correct terminology." Recall, too, that when Julia was asked in 1983 whether the women's movement influenced their marriage, she explained that its influence was minimal "because the black woman has always been somewhat different." She observed, as have many African-American scholars (Collins 1990; Davis 1981; Hull, Scott, and Smith 1982; Lewis 1977; Staples 1982), that black women cannot relate to the women's movement "because we've never been put in that role of a nice little feminine woman who stayed home and took care of her kids. . . ." Further, Julia asserts: "We really did a shared parenting." Sam does not indicate whether they shared parenting, but he does note his support for the movement to change women's roles and says that it has not influenced his own marriage. Their definitions of "love in marriage," provided independently in 1970, suggest that an equality of sacrifice is intrinsic to love:

> Giving and taking and sharing on a fairly equal basis—but there has to be a lot of giving and you have to care enough for the other person to really give [Julia].

> I—one thing is to be able to understand and be able to give, of yourself, not expecting a return always [Sam].

In spite of these shared ideals and their shared love, for Julia the marriage falls short of the ideal in later years.

By 1983, the Stevenses are emotionally distant but do not impede one another as they each pursue their independent interests. When Sam is asked what has kept their marriage together, he responds: "I can only speak for my own self. I think—my parents were married for a long time, didn't believe in divorce. They were patient; I'm very patient. I accept things a lot easier . . . I don't, we don't pry at each other. We share a lot of things together. I think that has a great deal to do with it. . . . We have arguments, but we never really, we never fight, we never have any physical, verbal [fighting]." While Sam perceives the separateness of their lives as an asset ("we don't pry at each other"), Julia perceives it as cause for concern. By this time, Julia has "thought divorce" because "we're into such different areas right now." There are indications that Julia is changing faster than Sam: "I seem to go off in different areas and I seem to change in the things I do, influenced by the things that happen to me, but that doesn't seem to influence him that much; he seems to go the same particular level." The factors that have kept them together are "love" from Julia's viewpoint; from Sam's perspective, it has been the ability to "accept things" and "the ability to make a commitment and stay with it." In sum, Sam emphasizes that "marriage is forever" more than Julia. Julia deters herself from divorce when she adds, "you can't expect everybody [to] move at a pace you may" and asserts, "hopefully we'll be able to work it out." Clearly, whether they can find more areas of overlap in their lives, the strains are not at the level of last-resort grounds, such as affairs or physical abuse. There are faint echoes of divorce culture in Julia's talk. One senses that Julia wants an equality that is *more* than parallel independence—an equality that reflects shared growth and change.

Julia seems to enjoy an independence associated with rights equality, but has not been able to secure the expressive interdependence associated with relational equality.

Marriage Culture and Equality Among the Divorced: The Remarried Franks

Larry Frank and Nancy Frank had been married for 17 years by 1983. The Franks are white, have a high school education, and have working-class roots, though they are home owners and financially secure by the 1980s. The Franks are in a remarriage; both have been divorced. Their case study is interesting because, despite divorces, Nancy Frank does not talk in terms of divorce culture.[3] Some social science research indicates that divorce tends to "liberalize" individuals' beliefs, but Nancy shows that this is not always the case. Also, the Franks, like the Dominicks, represent a couple whose beliefs are at odds; eventually, Larry talks divorce culture and Nancy does not.

Larry was intensely family-oriented, would not have pursued his earlier divorce, and reconciles himself to his divorce only years after his remarriage. He would have stayed in his first marriage "forever." His second wife, Nancy was childless and left her first husband due to severe and repeated intimidation and wife-beating—clearly a legitimate reason for divorce on the basis of last-resort terms implied by marriage culture. She seeks family relations in this second marriage on the terms of marriage culture and more egalitarian relations. Larry also tentatively accepts egalitarian terms. While they both know by experience that marriage is not forever, they still frame divorce as a last resort in the 1970s.

In 1971, Nancy has been married to Larry for almost seven years, when she is asked what is behind all the divorce: ". . . I'm sure that everybody says this, that before your marriage got along so beautifully and you'd listen to one another and you're very obedient to one another, and it's a shame that things like this happen—as you grow together that you can't talk to one another and I think this is a great part of falling out in marriage." Nancy suggests that verbal intimacy becomes difficult to sustain after marriage.[4] Nancy wants to share interpersonal talk with Larry, too.

Nancy is not anticipating another divorce, but she admits that she is worried about the future because of their inability to talk to each other. Yet, in 1971 she rapidly adds, "I would *never, never* think of doing anything like divorcing him or anything like that. I don't think I could be the same person without him" (emphasis added). This assertion reproduces her enduring belief in "marriage as forever" and reveals how marriage defines her identity. Yet it also reflects an aversion to divorce rooted in her own divorce experience. Her divorce made her "bitter" and "afraid"; she resolved that "if there was going to be a next marriage that I was going to have one that wasn't going to be domineering, or try to run my life or slap me around, and it is exactly what I found [laughs]. I was fortunate enough." In short, she repudiated the dominance implicit in the abuse.

Nancy's experience reminds us, as Kurz (1995) has documented, that domestic violence frequently feeds into divorce—that divorced wives have often been battered wives. Kurz found that 19 percent of the divorced women in her representative sample explained that they divorced their husband because of his violence. Kurz also documented that even when this reason was not the one provided, 54 percent of women experienced violence by their husbands two to three times or more and that this violence seemed to be in response to wives efforts to be independent (52, 67). Even now, in an era when wife-battering is more widely recognized and criticized, it is difficult for battered wives to leave their husbands—due to threats of violence, greater rates of violence upon separation, and downward mobility. The costs of divorce remain great, but were perhaps even higher in Nancy's time, when wife-battering was less recognized and other reasons for divorce less legitimate.[5]

Nancy describes her divorce as "the worst period of my life." When the interviewer affirms that it sounds "pretty tough," Nancy states: "Because saying that I was divorced bothered me. Because I had somewhat of a religious background and I know that we marry once and that's supposed to be it, so it bothered me a lot, and um . . . being married, and then all of a sudden being able to do exactly what you wanted to do was a tough road. And the way people took advantage of you, you know, it's kind of hard." Nancy is describing the pain of stigma, the strain of acting against her religiously anchored belief in "marriage as forever," and the feeling of rootlessness that accompanies letting go of the structure of marriage. In short, for Nancy, divorce is not framed as a "gateway," but rather an escape of "last resort." She was not seeking independence through her divorce—indeed, "being able to do exactly what you wanted to do was a tough road." Her divorce was characterized by a "freedom *from*" (dominance and violence) at least as much as a "freedom *to*" (run her own life).

In 1971, Nancy feels "fortunate enough" in her remarriage. Asked what is satisfying about Larry, she says: "Oh, gosh. A lot of things please me about him, but I can't . . . he's a good provider, he's uh . . . a good family man. He thinks about his children, his wife. He doesn't go out and drink on Friday nights with the boys or stop at the bar and have a drink. He's home every night at the same time." Her statements reflect the expectations of the traditional working-class wives Rubin (1976) described—expectations grounded in marital roles. But Nancy also has flagging hopes for more intimacy: "I'd like a lot more understanding, but someone else is going to have to, I'm afraid, show him, because he just doesn't listen to me as far as things like that."

In 1971, like Henry Hampton and Vincent Dominick, Larry Frank remarks on the liberties of men when questioned about the benefits and advantages of his gender. There is some confusion in his response:

> I don't know if there is any [both laugh]. I never gave it much thought to be honest, I . . . sometimes I . . . well let me put it one way, I feel sorry for a woman that has children at home and has to take care of them and I look at it as if . . . a lot of men don't look at it like I do . . . I know fellas that work down at work, fellas that work with me, they feel that they work 8 to 9 hours a day, they're working real hard, that hard, that they should be entitled to go someplace near over the weekend, hunting, fishing, to Reno, do these things, but I think, there again, that they [are] forgetting the other part of their life and that's the woman. She's home all day long with the children, taking care of the house for them and taking care of his children, they should be entitled to the same thing they are. If *one's going to go, one could go and* . . . I, like I say, I've never given it any thought about being, the difference between a man and a woman, I . . . feel that there's no difference because—the opposite sex, naturally, I've never given it any thought [emphasis added].

It is possible that Larry falters after his aborted description of what a fair weekend getaway might look like for men *and* women ("one's going to go, one could go and . . . I've never given it any thought") because he is registering the ramifications for his own (re)marriage. It is a response indicating that men's roles and accompanying freedoms are still a given in 1970, and yet there is a tentative attempt to admit equality into the marriage.

By 1983, Larry perceives the women's movement positively and believes "women have come a long way in the last 10 years." It may be that Larry's experience with divorce and remarriage has deepened his appreciation for the tasks of women. He was single for about a year and was an active divorced father. He is also amazed that his new wife, who has worked all of her life, married him at all because of his responsibilities of alimony and child support.

Asked in 1971 if he was surprised when his marriage broke up, Larry frames his own divorce as an "unexpected divorce" among his circle of friends:

I was ... let me put it in ... *shock* at the time because ... I felt that, like I said before that people felt that we were just the ideal couple [...] people are just amazed and ... I was utterly *shocked* because I never felt that anything like this could ever happen to me and uh ... I was really, it really bothered me, I was really hurt by it and uh ... I'm not sure that I got over it but, I guess that was one of the biggest *shocks* in my life because I felt that, at the time, the children were right at the present time, were right at the age where they needed a father and I felt that I could do more at that time than at any time in their life, even though I was working. When you get to that age, you've got to have somebody with them and this really bothered me and really hurt me ...

The divorce took Larry by surprise; he repeats his shock three times in the above passage and reemphasizes the amazement of others in his life.

Larry's account, here and in other interviews, suggests that he was "monitoring" the children—and his job—rather than the marriage. His reference to the children's need for their father implies that he would have sustained the marriage for the sake of the children. In many ways, children *were* the marriage for Larry. Larry stated in 1958 that he "always wanted to get married young and raise a family." Yet, Larry is slow to apply what he has learned—that a spouse must also monitor the marriage. When asked if divorce changed his point of view about marriage, Larry responds:

Well, I learned a few things, let's put it that way. I learned to take an interest in ... my wife more [...] But right now, I feel that I still sometimes lack these qualifications whereas I come home and I'm tired and ... eat, read the paper and I fall asleep, my wife feels at the present time that she's there by herself, living by herself [...] This isn't right on my part, and I know it and, I try to correct myself when I do these things and I do, and uh, my wife right now isn't hard to push, she's very easy to please, she doesn't ask for the world.

He knows that he needs to reciprocate the attention Nancy gives to the marital relationship. He upholds the ideal even as he admits he falls short of it. Larry *talks,* though sparingly *practices* relational equality in the marriage.

The fact that Larry's change is only partial is, perhaps, because Nancy is "very easy to please." Moreover, she swears she would "never, never" divorce him. Larry can relax his efforts if there are no conditions attached to the marriage. A few years after this 1971 interview, he takes the traditionally male privilege and engages in extramarital affairs (Lawson 1988).[6] Larry will explain these affairs in terms of "communication"—that the low point in their marriage derived from "physical attractedness to other people that I could communicate with, which at that particular time in my life I didn't have it at home."

Larry's use of "communication" has become central to his "vocabulary of motives" at this point. He uses it to explain his divorce, his remarriage, and his affairs. When Larry is asked what has kept them together in 1983, he asserts: "Well we've had brief moments where we have a little problem, but we do communicate an awful lot, and we have a lot in common. I feel basic communications is a way of life."[7] Justifying marriage in terms of "communications" (rather than "commitment," for example) has the ring of divorce culture, and while neither Larry nor Nancy has ever pursued therapy, it also reflects the rise of "therapeutic culture."

Another sign of therapeutic culture emerges as Larry reframes the meaning of his earlier divorce. Rather than conveying the shock and the losses (particularly vis-à-vis his children) as he did in 1971, Larry emphasizes the benefits in 1983: "And, as it turned out for me, it never really hurt me. It, in fact, *made me a better person*, really, and like I say, earlier, I was very fortunate when I met Nancy, which is my present wife, in that we . . . we struggled through the first couple of years, you know, naturally, but after that, why, the puzzle became . . . together" (emphasis added)."

Divorce culture—divorce as a gateway—infiltrates Larry's account as he retrospectively values the experience of divorce for his character development. Interestingly, Larry's behavior is not all that different from that of Vincent Dominick—though there is no sign of physical violence in this case. However, his therapeutic language suggests different ideals and a shifting worldview. Also, he is not really considering divorce in this marriage.

In 1983, Nancy reports having considered divorcing Larry in the early 1970s when she found out that Larry had been seeing another woman. Nancy reveals her husband's affair to explain their brief separation eight years ago. Asked why she decided not to get divorced, Nancy replies: "Had a lot at stake, and he straightened up his act, and the love was never gone. But I would have anyway. I would have divorced him anyway. [I: If he had continued . . .] Yes." This resolve indicates an increasingly "contingent" view of marriage for Nancy. Her stance has changed since her assertion that she would "never, never consider doing anything like divorcing." Nevertheless, extramarital affairs are "last-resort grounds." Given Nancy's experience in her first divorce, her age, her attachment to her stepson, and her enduring belief in "marriage as forever," the difficulties of pursuing even a last-resort divorce are substantial.

The remarriage reflects male dominance to a degree—primarily in Larry's behavior. Yet, it is also clear that the gender relations in this mar-

riage are more egalitarian than in either Frank's or Nancy's first marriage—a situation that is in line with other research findings on remarriages (Furstenberg and Spanier 1987; Smith et al. 1991). It is also hard
to compare an early and later marriage because of their different locations in the life course. Larry himself addresses this difference in 1983
when asked about the major turning points in his life:

> Well, I believe it was the time of my second marriage, when I remarried the
> second time. [I: So it was the second marriage itself that was the turning
> point?] Turning point, yes ma'am. [I: Can you tell me something about
> that?] Well, my first marriage I was married and had the four children,
> which is a *different way of life* than my second. First marriage was primarily
> raising the children, to do things right in this world, and to show them the
> right way of doing it. The second marriage, I never had the children, and
> became more independent and more secure to do the things that I wanted
> to do ... [emphasis added].

Larry asserts this independence despite the remaining child in his home,
whom he and Nancy have raised together. Still, child rearing responsibilities have declined, enabling Larry and Nancy to aspire to an egalitarian ideal at this stage of the life course. These midlife conditions allow
for shifting ideals. Nancy manages to retain a belief in marriage culture
despite her earlier divorce. Over the years, Larry increasingly talks in
terms of divorce culture. This might help explain why they make only partial change toward equality. Both Nancy and Larry increasingly voice
egalitarian ideals, yet Larry's behavior is at odds with his stated ideals.
His "manifest power" has been met by Nancy's threat of divorce; yet there
are indications that latent and invisible power endure. Beyond his extramarital affairs, Larry defaults to a traditional division of reproductive and
emotional labor.

THE POWER OF MARRIAGE CULTURE

The power of marriage culture might be described as the power of
patience. For both wives and husbands, the beliefs of marriage culture sustain the relationship during phases that threaten to unravel it at the seams.
Marie Hampton "rides out" the years with Henry. Julia Stevens says "you
can't expect everybody to move at a pace you may." Sam describes himself as "patient." Both Julia and Sam recognize the "give and take" of
marriage. In these ways, the power of marriage is shared by both wives
and husbands and as such can foster an equality of sacrifice, rather than
nonsacrifice.

As the examples in this chapter suggest, patience is not necessarily passive, though some of the relevant activity is invisible. Patience entails

"emotion work" to absorb the "ups and downs of marriage." Marie may have "gotten over" her desire for marital counseling when Henry "got furious," but she had to sacrifice, or press down, her desires for relationality. And this signifies how the patience of women and men can be different. Sam Stevens is clearly patient but, unlike his wife, he is not patient in spite of divorce thoughts, or at least he does not report them. Indeed, the waiting of wives is more notable because they all had "divorce thoughts." Patience enabled Marie, Julia, and Nancy to table their "divorce thoughts," and wait for Henry, Sam, and Larry to change.

The contexts of and motivations for the patience of these wives are not identical. Marie waits for Henry's move toward the "equal thing" and aims to avoid, and perhaps even fears, the label that she has applied to her sister: "self-centered." In contrast, Julia has not had to wait for rights equality because she and Sam had a more egalitarian vision of marriage to begin with. Still, Julia appears to be waiting for a more relational equality, for Sam to be "influenced by the things that happen" to him. Finally, Nancy's context and motivations are also different. She wants to avoid another divorce; the first divorce was, after all, the "worst period" in her life. She demands that Larry "straighten up his act" with respect to his affair, yet may still be waiting for his behavior to reflect his egalitarian talk.

Marriage culture empowers women and men to varying degrees, due to the legacy of male dominance in marriage. While any number of factors can threaten heterosexual relationships—from financial strain to sex—conflicts over gender ideology and practice are fundamental. Until no-fault divorce was instituted—20 years into the marriages of most of these '50s couples—many "gender rules" were written into the law. Gender has shaped marital interactions like a rulebook and, therefore, has been intrinsic to marital interactions, including the meanings of financial strain, sex, or child rearing.

To become a traditional wife or husband has entailed "doing gender" in particular ways to adhere to conventional rules (West and Zimmerman 1987).[8] Similarly, to become a nontraditional wife or husband entails "undoing" or, perhaps more accurately, "redoing" gender. Because power has been unequally distributed between wives and husbands, the move from male dominance to gender equality must be approached differently by women and men. A wife or a husband is empowered if their spouse believes in "marriage as forever" because they can count on the spouse to ride out turbulent transitions. Yet in the transition to gender equality, it is particularly important for wives to have husbands who believe in "marriage as forever," because it is largely wives who desire and initiate the change to gender equality. Marie resisted Henry's power, fighting for her own authority by going to work over his objections. A *shared* belief in marriage culture empowered Marie. Because Henry believed in marriage culture and the "forces" that deter divorce—from children to care taking—Marie could press for equality without fearing Henry's departure.

Of course, marriage culture does not inevitably empower. It is important to recall the dynamics of the Dominicks. Clearly, Doreen's patience undermined her power. This was, in part, because Vincent's commitment to male dominance was stronger and his commitment to marriage culture was in question. In short, when husbands are drawn to divorce culture, marriage culture is disempowering for wives. We witness this dynamic between the Franks, when Larry chooses to have an affair during a period when Nancy would "never, never think of divorcing" him. This transition to gender equality ultimately depends upon the dynamics between wives and husbands. Indeed, the power of marriage culture is not simply located in spouses' willpower or individual agency; it is also located in the dynamics between wife and husband.

By the 1980s, one senses that '50s spouses who have aimed to redefine marriage in terms of gender equality are in marriages that are "good enough." The marital endurance of '50s couples who try to incorporate egalitarianism into their marriage is a tribute to the wives' patience as well as husbands' receptivity toward equal relationships. Their marital endurance is an achievement in two senses. They have been able to harness the power of marriage culture in spite of the transition to gender equality and in spite of increasing divorce. Yet, there is a notable luster in the marriages where we see wives engage the power of divorce culture. We turn to this dynamic in the next chapter.

6   '50s Spouses Secure Equal Footing in Divorce Culture

BY THE EARLY 1980s, the generation marrying around 1950 has traversed the conformist 1950s, turbulent 1960s, and experimental 1970s and entered a decade nostalgic for, but hardly a duplicate of, the 1950s. These couples married when marriage culture prevailed. Yet the longer their marriages have endured, the more divorce proliferates around them, the more stigma recedes, the more legal and economic hurdles are lowered, and the more gender equality marks cultural expectations. Marriage culture and male dominance are losing their hegemonic hold. Still, only a few '50s spouses challenge all the old terms. These spouses talk in terms of optional and contingent marriage and portray divorce as a gateway. Gender equality is primarily understood in terms of individual independence, rather than explicit notions of equity or interdependence. In general, the discourse of these spouses emphasizes self-development as essential to the marital relationship (Cancian 1987).

Pat Holstein, later Pat Ross, illustrates this new talk. During her 1958 interview, she expresses the feeling that she and Gary "fell in line" with her "parents' way of doing things"—"that you get married, you make your bed and you lie in it." This is "marriage as forever." Instead, after nearly 20 years of marriage, Pat divorces Gary, in part because she yearns for more passion in her life. By the 1972 interview, after she has been married to Neil Ross, her second husband, for two years, Pat is asked what was wrong with her first marriage. She replies:

> I don't know … I don't know … I don't know … I think that what was, probably was lack of passion, in a nutshell. [I: Physically, you mean?] Yeah, probably. Not only physically, I think. I think that Gary and I would have been fantastic as a brother and sister, I think the world of him, I really do, you know, I would go to any length for him, you know, today, he's a unique person. Gary is unique. And he'll always be unique and he'll never change for me. […] I think that what was wrong with our marriage was passion, I had no jealousy for Gary, nor did he have for me. […] We had a wonderful working relationship where we truly like each other, truly, but it didn't have the passion it should have had, it never had, and that's what dissolved our marriage, we were doomed to be good friends from the beginning, I believe this.

Pat implicitly knows that this is not a divorce of "last resort." As she constructs an account of her divorce she moves from uncertainty ("I don't know") to self-assurance ("I believe this"). Her initial claims of ignorance suggest her sense that her account may not be legitimate to her listener. Will the interviewer interpret her divorce as justified? Pat proceeds to build a case. She relates that they had "a wonderful working relationship," but their relationship lacked the sexual passion that she has found in her remarriage. By the end of the passage, she emphasizes the inevitability of divorce—they were "*doomed* to be good friends."

As the interviewer probes in 1972 to find out what else contributed to the divorce, Pat explores the problems in her first marriage compared to her second:

> I think that what happens to people, they get to a certain point, and something has to happen, you see, there's a physical momentum of nature, you know, we have to have changes of season [. . .] This is what a good fight helps occasionally, you *need something to stir* and change and I think that was not happening in my marriage with Gary, I don't think it would happen for Gary, Gary was very *ritualistic,* he saw—now this is what I see, not a fact, this is my fact,—he saw me as *mother-wife,* that was the label on that one. [As a] child, child sort of thing. I think that Gary had us all put into these situations, I don't [think] Gary saw me a lot as a woman, I think, you know, the role I played was the—more than the woman. [In contrast,] Neil doesn't see you in a *role,* he sees you as a woman and relates to you that way all the time, that's first, he doesn't see you in roles at all which this bothered me about Gary and I probably treated Gary like he was in one of these boxes right away. I think Gary is happier now, I believe this, although I think it was very hard for him to get out of the family unit and I think that's been very difficult for him, but I think that Gary needed freedom, he never had it, I really believe that [emphases added].

Pat accounts for her divorce in terms of a basic need in human nature: they both needed change. Nothing would "stir" in her marriage. Gary resisted change by his "ritualistic" orientation. In line with Miriam Johnson's (1988) depiction of the "wife" role, Pat articulates the inequality intrinsic to these "roles" when she describes Gary's treatment of her as a "child." Nevertheless, she admits that she probably put Gary "in one of these boxes" as well—an admission verified by her 1958 interview in which she asserted with pride that Gary "has assumed a very masculine role" in their household. Unlike Gary, her second husband, Neil, does not see her in terms of the roles of wife and mother. She feels *recognized* and able to assert her individuality in her remarriage. She justifies Gary's post-divorce difficulties by asserting that freedom was something that *he* needed too—a position he grows to embrace as well.

Pat has found one way to meet the challenge of gender equality in marriage. Through divorce and remarriage, Pat overthrows the roles that were seemingly resistant to transformation in her first marriage. She draws upon divorce culture to achieve her ideal of a passionate, de-gendered, and vital marriage. Indeed, by the early 1980s the Ross' remarriage scores in the highest third in marital satisfaction. However, another way to transform gender relations in marriage is to draw upon the beliefs of divorce culture to transform relations within the same marriage. This is the way of the McIntyres.

THE '50S MCINTYRES: CHANGING ALL THE TERMS MIDSTREAM

The McIntyres are the only other couple of the Older generation who can be described as integrating divorce culture and gender equality into their marriage by the early 1980s. Again, one does not have to be divorced to advocate divorce culture. The focus is on the beliefs and not the behaviors—though the two are interrelated. Martha and Michael McIntyre radically redesign their marriage in terms of divorce culture and gender equality.

Martha and Michael McIntyre are Euro-American and upwardly mobile. In 1982, they score in the middle range of marital satisfaction after 32 years of marriage and five children. Martha acknowledges the "social pressure to get married" when they did—marrying was given. And Michael recognizes the "independence" and "opportunity" available to their children's generation that was unavailable to them. Both describe great change in their marriage. Michael McIntyre continues to frame divorce as a last resort in his *own* marriage, though not his children's marriages; it is Martha who places the couple at the forefront of change by importing new terms into the marital relationship.

The outward shape of Martha's marriage is conventional, from her age at marriage to her role as housewife and rearer of five children. Yet, by 1970 it is clear that Martha is an unconventional woman, ahead of her times in many ways. She pursues therapy and enlists her husband, returns to school, begins a career, has an affair that she is convinced has fostered growth in herself and the marriage, and readily asserts that she is the "boss" in their family. Feminism, as both Martha and Michael agree, strongly influenced their marriage. Their marriage endures not because they cling to the shores of marriage culture and the male-headed household; rather they brave the rapids of social change and, in time, chart a new course altogether.

A "Marriage on the Rocks"

Asked in 1982 when the marriage had been at its worst, Michael says after the end of the first 10 years (around 1959), as he was starting his business. Martha expands the period. She claims that their marriage was no good from 1953 to 1970—"a long time to have a terrible marriage." As with the middle-class Stones and the Hamptons, the difficulties were centered firmly in her child-rearing years and his most challenging business years. The constructions of gender embedded in larger social structures contribute to the trajectory of their marriage and some of their difficulties.

In 1958, Martha and Michael have been married for eight years and have had four of their five children. Martha indicates at this time that Michael is the "real authority in our home, and I think that's the way it should be." She describes him as "one hundred percent man." She reports that the early years of marriage have been a "big adjustment." The marital adjustment in these years is partly due to disparate backgrounds and different emotional styles in their families of origin. While both are Euro-American, their differences are notable. Her upper-middle-class, ethnic Jewish yet atheist background initially conflicts with his working-class, Irish Catholic upbringing. His opportunities are made possible by the G.I. bill—an avenue of opportunity that lifted many families economically in the 1950s (Coontz 1992). These social and economic disparities are exacerbated by events that destabilize many marriages: financial straits, illness, and death.

The McIntyres begin having children immediately. At one point, Michael has difficulty securing steady employment. They temporarily move in with his parents. Eventually Michael begins his own business, entailing long hours. Their infant daughter becomes deathly ill and is hospitalized for months—affecting Martha's feelings of attachment to her. Then Martha's mother dies. During this time, Martha states, "I really felt my marriage was on the rocks." While she seeks psychological counseling at this time, Martha speaks as though the worst has passed by 1958.

By 1971, we learn that Martha has been working for her husband's business since 1959. She assumes responsibility for over-the-phone sales and bookkeeping. When the hired receptionist divorces and then departs the area, she puts more hours into Michael's business. Not long after, Martha also considers divorce. When Martha is asked in 1971 how she thinks she would deal with widowhood, she voluntarily brings up divorce, replying:

> Course there was a time I was thinking about life without him anyway because I was so mad at him. [I: Uh huh. That was —?] And I felt that really

we just didn't have anything to keep us going together so—this was right in this particular *bad* period of his devotion to the business, for one thing and all the time away, and I had—really was faced with the problems of [. . .] the children and I felt very much alone, and I just felt "Well, gee—I could do just as well on my own." [I: Uh huh.] "I'd be happier." [I: This was three or four years ago?] Three or four. It was the worst part of this period, but I was feeling less dependent. Earlier than that I was feeling too dependent because the children were so small and there were so many of them, but as they were growing up I thought maybe if I had to, I would go it alone. [pause] But that was—that was before therapy [emphasis in original].

Therapy may have saved this marriage. We learn that extensive family and marital therapy as well as involvement in support groups follow upon one child's growing drug problems, which created havoc in the family. Martha describes "role-playing" in therapy: "mostly getting in touch with your feelings and constantly the question is 'how do you *feel* right now?' No feeling is in retrospect. No digging up ancient history. We don't go back to how did your mother treat you or how do you feel you were treated as a child. We talk about the here and now" (emphasis in original). Asked what she thinks would have happened if they had not sought psychotherapy, Martha responds: "I think it would be just the same old drag that it was. The same old hang-ups and the same disturbing things present and the same inability to work through problems. Our main problem was lack of communication, or being able to communicate. The feelings that were strongest. And I think nothing would have changed. . . ." For Martha, like Larry Frank, communication is a key word. Communication's absence or presence is increasingly being cited as the source of and solution to their problems. Martha credits "excellent therapy" for the family's ability to enjoy and communicate with each other.

However, Martha is less comfortable with Michael as the "authority" of the household than she was earlier in her marriage: "And . . . he's got sort of this father image about him though, you know, sort of an *authoritarian thing* which the kids pick up and I pick up and sometimes he can get this—he can act parental to me, and I *just* flip my lid over it . . . because I can't stand having him treat me like a—like he's my parent . . ." (second emphasis in original). Martha is also displeased with some of his assumptions regarding "her second shift"—such as expecting a hot dinner at 10:00 P.M. She states: "And I have this little thing in me saying, 'Why should I cook a meal for the family and clean it all up and then at the end of the day fix yours too? [laughs] I mean you come home on time and you can eat with the rest of us.'"

Yet, Martha senses that change is afoot. According to her, Michael is "beginning to re-evaluate" his own "value systems" because of the kids. And with respect to goals for their marriage, she says:

> ... we're *growing* together and I just want to see this continue, and I would like to see a really—really beautiful, *open* relationship which we haven't really arrived at yet. You can see it—you can begin to see it taking shape, but it isn't there yet, and we still have a lot of areas where we can improve probably.... Michael has a harder time expressing his negative feelings to me than I have and he keeps—when he's angry it's much harder for him to overcome the anger than it is for me and ... but this is changing too. So I just like to see more [I: Relationship?] the *relationship grow,* and I'd also like to get really involved in some kind of a project—something that we're doing together [emphasis added].

Martha's displeasure with Michael's "authoritarian thing" and her marital ideal of a growing and open relationship indicate a shift toward new terms. She appropriates the language of therapeutic culture to nurture her vision of intimacy in their marriage and the emotional flexibility she increasingly expects from her husband. In contrast to the early years, Martha feels that "he's much more understanding and accepting of things now."

In 1971, Michael confirms that there were many years of marital conflict and a more recent sense of resolution. He notes that he had "little difficulty with people" until his marriage. Then, "I got involved in these intense feelings with my wife" and "could get along with everybody except her." He continues: "Now, I, it's sort of a growing up or a maturing process in the marriage where it ends up that some of those things that seemed to be pretty painful at the time have been converted into a lot of deep love and affection." Here, Michael describes his marital relationship as a context for his own growth. In the transition to an egalitarian marriage, Michael's talk reflects an equality based on "interdependence" as often as "independence." Michael confirms that they started out trying to get therapy for their daughter, Emily, and "ended up getting help for ourselves." He continues: "It's ... had an unusually constructive ... it's not only helped Emily, but it's certainly helped us ... getting to understand one another, and Martha's feelings for herself ... in other words, she can say now that she accepts herself as a person, and would always say before that she couldn't do that." He describes Martha as a woman who has had a lot of "negative feelings about herself, which she seems to be surmounting." *Her* personal development is important to *his* marriage. Asked about his goals in marriage, he wants to "be able to understand each other" and to have a life that "isn't entirely surrounding the children."

When Michael is asked about the advantages of being a man in 1971, he does not refer to the "authoritarian thing" mentioned by Martha, but does note men's "freedom." His reply, marked by numerous pauses, reveals some uncertainty regarding the nature of the freedom: "[Pause] Oh . . . I might just say the freedom to get around . . . just the things that . . . physically . . . might be over women. Other than that—[laughing]. I feel there is a greater, a little less . . . inhibition or less pressure . . . I feel, as a man I can . . . have a certain amount of self-reliance, that maybe a lot of women don't have and don't want. But I can set a course, and a direction and do it, and not feel—and just feel that I can physically do it." It is ambiguous whether the freedom which men enjoy over women, is biological ("physically" able), psychological ("less inhibition"), or sociological (able "to get around"). Ambiguity may reflect ambivalence here. Michael implicitly knows there are contextual differences for the genders, but he is reluctant to discriminate. He is reevaluating. There is a nascent sense of the social psychological and social structural barriers that many women face—a sense that is undeveloped at this time, but more salient by the 1980s.

Securing "Equal Footing"

By 1982, Michael asserts that Martha's career pursuits—*after* working for him—have had a "positive" effect upon their relationship; it has procured empathy and mutual understanding and "has had a monumental influence on her growth as a person." He says:

> I've always wanted her a success, and wanted her *growth* and I think maybe it was a little difficult for her to—she seems to have an awful lot of friends whose husbands resented their *independence*. And I felt it a little bit risky, on the other hand, I felt that it was worth a gamble to me—it would be much better for me to risk her having—her independence, than to object to it, and have a—not a happy relationship. I was—I was completely willing to gamble that if she were happy, we'd both be happy. At any rate, I think maybe my total support of what she's doing, maybe it was a factor in our becoming closer [emphasis added].

Michael recognizes that Martha's independence can strengthen rather than threaten the relationship; his "risk" is rewarded by a "happy relationship." In addition to validating the importance of Martha's autonomy made manifest by her work, Michael also credits the women's movement. When asked if it has affected their marriage, he asserts that it "probably influenced my wife to want to have more independence, both financial and personal, and motivated her to go back to school and seek a career. I suspect she might have done it anyway but the women's movement erased any indecision on her part."

While Michael increasingly values Martha's independence, he also values his own. In 1982, he describes their early power struggle and its resolution:

> Martha is a very *strong-willed* person, too, but I'm not easily dominated. And there's a strong tendency to be dominating, but I couldn't accept that. I've always felt that—I wanted my family, but I also have to live *for myself*, so, I'm willing to make compromises, but I am not willing to be completely overridden by Martha, and so I didn't give ground, I didn't easily give ground. I think I gave—I think we both gave ground, we both stuck to what we believed in and we both had to work it out. And that, I think that was very *healthy* and I—I would have been disappointed in my marriage relationship if I didn't have a strong-willed person who did believe in certain things and want to stick by them. But I had the same kind of personality, so that brought [laughs slightly] about some confrontations in how we did things, and in the end it seemed to work out very well, but it was difficult to learn to live with each other having these strong ideas.

Michael's accounts reveal men's dilemma in the "companionate marriage" with the challenge of gender equality. Michael McIntyre and Evan Stone share the same struggles; their resolution, however, is quite different. Evan wanted his wife to be strong, but he also wanted a "wife"— that is, a role-differentiated marriage in which the wife's will is ultimately subordinated to her husband's. Michael, in contrast, emphasizes a balance of power between *persons*, rather than a division of power between gendered *roles*. Equality, rather than role differentiation, is implicit throughout his account. He tries to forge mutuality in marriage, yet he does not forfeit the chance to "live for myself"—that is, his own individual autonomy. He sees their struggle as "healthy."

In essence, Michael presents what Jessica Benjamin (1988) describes as an "intersubjective" view of a relationship, wherein the "tension" between "assertion and recognition" is sustained, rather than allowed to degenerate into dominance and subordination. Together, Michael and Martha "gave ground" as they each pursued their individuality. Benjamin argues that while it is avoidable, for the most part, the "breakdown of the tension between assertion and recognition becomes associated with the polarization of gender identity," and "implicated in control and submission" (84–85). The McIntyres attest to the possibility of an intersubjective relationship avoiding the gendered pitfalls of dominance and submission. But the balance is precarious.

In retrospect, the premise advanced by marriage culture—that "divorce is a last resort"—serves the McIntyres early in their marriage as they face adversity and negotiate their power struggle. Even by the 1980s, Michael still talks in terms of divorce as a last resort; he states that, unlike other couples, he would not just "give it up" when "there's a hard, difficult conflict" and "I wouldn't just run down to my lawyer for a divorce." And Michael reports that in spite of the strains, "none of the things shook me as far as having the right decision about who I married. Nothing in our conflict ever made me question that decision." Michael heartily agrees with the interviewer that the conflicts helped him understand himself as a person, and adds that "all of this was part of a growth process."

Asked what factors he thinks helped him to work through their marital conflicts, Michael says, "Geez. I think our own desire to work through it and our refusal to let our problem down, and I think the fact that we loved each other and the children, as well." In this statement, Michael communicates shared conflict and resolution when he refers to "our" desire and "our" problem; in his odd phrasing of "our refusal to let our problem down," he suggests that they had a responsibility to the problem—a challenge that had to be met. When he is asked when his marriage was at its best, he responds: "It's been at it's best for the past 7 to 10 years. [I: Why?] Because my work interests and professional interests no longer overshadow my wife's. We've been on *equal footing*. And particularly *her growth* and confidence as a person has a tremendous lot to do with it" (emphasis added).

In sum, Michael's claims have changed with the times: "equal footing," mutual "independence," and "growth" have become key words for characterizing their marriage. The only premise unchallenged from "marriage culture" concerns "divorce as a last resort." Yet, Michael does not claim high thresholds for divorce. In reference to his children's marriages (current separations and potential marriages), he avows that if they make marital mistakes, "that's part of life and that's growing up." Speaking generally about the younger generation, he says, "I'm very accepting." Michael observes, "There's a lot more freedom to express oneself, and a lot more independence, and that sort of thing, but given the opportunity, we would have behaved the same way [laughs]." He recognizes that he did not enjoy the same options available to his children. Yet, he has flexibly adapted to the changing marital environment—marked by the rise of options afforded by divorce culture. Yet, as Michael confirms, Martha has changed more and actively redesigned their marriage in terms of this new marital environment.

With the exception of one key issue (her extramarital affair), by 1982, Martha's and Michael's accounts of their marriage, family, and each other are remarkably congruent. In her 1982 interview, Martha asserts that "right now," is the best time in their marriage because they "have grown together and have a lot of powerful history together." Both assert that the early years were the most troubled. Like her husband, she speculates that their early quarreling may explain the extreme closeness they can see between all of their children. Like Michael, Martha claims at this time that she has never had thoughts of divorce (we know, however, from earlier interviews that this is a reconstruction). Financial and emotional dependence may have held Martha to the marriage, yet once she was "independent," the nature of their relationship changed. Martha affirms that "initially it was need" that kept them together, but now it is "genuine qualities that we see in each other. Caring and companionship and respect and an active sex life."

Martha talks extensively of her own "growth" as a person. Not unlike Katy Stone's attributing responsibility for her religious conversion to her children, Martha reports that "my daughter started me in my own inner growth process," around 1968. Through family and individual therapy, Martha "began to find my own self." She was drawn by the compassion and caring intrinsic to a "humanistic" psychology and knew she wanted more of it in her life. She felt that she was "on the brink of a great kind of self-discovery." Spiritual growth followed psychological growth as she became involved in various workshops and retreats. In these pursuits, she found an "inner peace."

Between 1968 and 1976, Martha returned to school and began to work in the area of public policy. Since then, her "career has just exploded." Asked whether the women's movement has affected their marriage, Martha replies: "I have been a part of the whole movement by moving out and becoming a part of the work force. I am very conscious of any kind of sexism or discrimination against women, particularly when it affects me. I will often call my husband on it when he makes a sexist remark, whether it has to do with me or not." She also sincerely recognizes that her husband provided a great deal of support as she pursued her career.

It was at work, however, where she met Ken. Martha would not tell Michael about Ken, because of her "own selfish motives." She concedes that Michael would be bothered by the betrayal more than the sexual infidelity and would probably leave her. And she explains: "I don't want to break up the marriage. [...] And my relationship with Ken has enriched me, I think in the sense that I'm enriched by it, it had enriched Michael's and my relationship." Martha sees her self-development as a precondition to a good marriage: "And we enjoy being together. I mean this has not been true for all the years of our marriage at all. I mean this is something that has—since *I* became a person and a human being, since *I* began to take care of myself, and to become a self-managing individual, that is when our relationship has grown" (emphasis in original). Martha and Michael both refer to their joy in "being together." And both attribute this enriched relationship to Martha's independence. Mutual recognition and assertion characterize their relationship after 33 years; however, it is a recognition that is sustained through one very important lie in a society that supports monogamy.

The McIntyre marriage reflects the benefits, deficits, and contradictions of a relationship that traverses marriage and divorce culture. Martha and Michael weathered incredibly conflicted years; their endurance is a function of "marriage culture" (particularly divorce as a last resort), as well as the economic realities of rearing five children on a lower-middle-class income in the early years. Now, they remain committed to one another and their powerful "history" together, even as they begin to speak the language of "expressive individualism" (Bellah et al. 1985). As feminism, new-age psychologies, and career prospects expand, the McIntyres can take advantage of new tools with which to make sense of their marital struggles. Once they have become a dual-career couple, firmly among the middle-class, and in their middle years, their marriage begins to change with the times. And this transformation has depended upon and developed out of Martha's assertion of independence, as well as Michael's support within a social context of inequality.

Martha has availed herself of that greater "freedom to express oneself" and "independence" that Michael observes in the younger generation. Both comment upon her growth. Their communication and sex life are better by both of their accounts. Yet, this is a portrait of a marriage that bases its equality on a masculine standard. In a sense, Martha has appropriated prerogatives that were once the preserve of men; like Vincent Dominick, she takes the "liberty" to have an affair within the confines of marriage. In this, she puts herself before the marriage. She legitimates this choice, however, in terms of "relationality." Whereas Vincent Dominick and Larry Frank justify affairs in terms of what was *missing* from their respective marriages, Martha legitimates her actions in terms of what it *provides* to her and, therefore, to her marriage. Martha affirms her individuality through her sexuality, her therapy, and her work. Her account of how her affair has "enriched" her marital relationship is persuasive—particularly in combination with Michael's testimony of improved relations. But it rests upon a shaky foundation, precisely because she has not told Michael of her infidelity for fear of marital dissolution.

Martha believes that if Michael were to learn of her infidelity, he would be shocked, hurt, and angry. I would further speculate that his response would be framed in moral as well as therapeutic terms. He would not only be disillusioned by her dishonesty, but might also conclude that Martha had not, in fact, "grown" as much as he had presumed. The elasticity of therapeutic language—embedded in much of divorce culture—becomes apparent when "growth" serves as a residual category to account for the strong and weak marriage alike. As Bellah and colleagues (1985) have observed, the paradox of expressive individualism—the backbone of therapeutic culture—is that commitments are sustained only as long as they "feel good." Early in their marriage, the McIntyres' commitment to one another was based on more than "feeling good." Commitment to their five children was a shared tie, and commitment to divorce as a last resort was a salient value for both. But their children are grown and the terms of their marriage have changed with the times. If we accept Martha's assessment of Michael's response, their marriage would no longer "feel good" if he were to discover her affair.[1] Would shared history or professed love sustain their marriage? It is impossible to say. Clearly, there can be a precarious quality to securing equal footing on the terms of divorce culture.

POWER DYNAMICS BETWEEN '50S SPOUSES

The preceding chapters have shown how '50s couples respond in patterned ways to the rise of a new marital context marked by "divorce culture" and "gender equality." There are couples, such as the Stones, who retain a belief in "marriage as forever" and male dominance. In contrast to the Stones, the McIntyres are more likely to see marriage and divorce as optional, to speak the language of therapeutic culture, and to be influenced by a different cluster of divorce deterrents. Unlike either the Stones or the Dominicks, the McIntyres embrace equality within marriage. However, the McIntyres' mutual insistence on equality contrasts with the Hamptons' more muted version of equality. The McIntyres and the Rosses reflect the ideals of divorce culture and gender equality among the '50s couples by the 1980s—though we will see more of such dynamics among the '70s spouses. Of course, even traditionalists who resist divorce culture must respond to it, as the choice "to stay married" increasingly calls for legitimization once expected only of the divorced.

In general, changes in marital and gender ideologies have been incremental and are visible only among half of the '50s couples. While I reviewed only one strictly traditional couple, the Stones, it should be recalled that 6 out of the 12 couples embraced male dominance and marriage culture in this conservative sample. This suggests that sustaining older, established terms is easier. Still, even these older terms must be actively reproduced, as we saw with the Stones.

Also, the beliefs of spouses within each marriage differed more in degree than in kind. Within each couple, beliefs converge more than we will find in the Younger generation; spouses' ideologies were most at odds within the Dominicks' and the Franks' marriages. The general tendency toward shared beliefs may be a function of years together—after all, they have had nearly three decades of a "marital conversation" to construct the meaning of their marriage (Berger and Kellner 1964). This convergence may also be related to the historical location of their formative years: The 1950s were marked by intense pressures to conform (Lindner 1956; Breines 1986). When there were exceptions to the monogamous, heterosexual, nuclear family (and there were), those who departed from the marriage culture and the male-headed household risked stigma. While variations became more acceptable over the decades, the 1950s may have left an imprint on many among the Older generation. My sample suggests that it has.

Nevertheless, some couples did change substantially and, for the most part, the changes were initiated because of the monitoring and ideals of wives. It is interesting to note the timing of these changes: Marie Hampton thinks of divorce around 1970, after her sister's divorce; Martha McIntyre has divorce thoughts after the receptionist divorces; and all these contemplations of divorce occur primarily as the divorce rate reaches a tipping point and as the ideology of women's independence is prominent in public discourse. It is also essential to note, however, that for this generation these historical events converge with a point in the life course when the pressures of parenting and providing are at their greatest. Still, for the most part, thoughts are not turned to action.

Trying to reconstruct a marriage on an egalitarian model is both a material and psychological effort. Most of these wives are working by the 1970s, and they voice concerns with handling both the first and second shifts. Yet, there is also a psychological effort to redefine power. The wife role has been a subordinate role. While wives may seek not power, but rather the absence of domination (Miriam Johnson 1988), it is nevertheless difficult to depolarize and de-gender the dominance and submission attached to gendered roles (Benjamin 1988). Whether under the terms of marriage culture (for example, the Hamptons or the Stevenses) or divorce culture (for example, the McIntyres or the Rosses), efforts to grapple with gender equality are an attempt to build a new kind of marriage altogether. While equality becomes emphasized over and above role differentiation by some couples, this shift seems more successful in those marriages that talk the terms of divorce culture.

Among those who bring an increasingly egalitarian lens to marriage, the McIntyres (and Rosses) appear to be more egalitarian and more satisfied than the Hamptons (or Stevenses and Franks). The McIntyres have accepted, if not embraced, divorce, pursued therapy, and changed gender patterns; among these spouses, marital monitoring is eventually shared. Those who pursue gender equality while retaining marriage culture have changed, but less notably. Changing gender relations while still abiding by marriage culture seems to be the greater challenge. While the Hamptons talk equality, they do not seem to practice it to the same degree, their marriage is more lackluster, and their marital satisfaction score is slightly lower.

How might we explain this result? There seem to be two related explanations. Much has been made of divorce as an outcome of women's individualism, as symbolized by the women's movement and women's increasing participation in the labor force; however, as I have argued, this analysis overlooks men's (un)willingness to change with women, as well as women's attempts to redefine the meaning of marriage from within. If we compare Michael McIntyre to Vincent Dominick or Evan Stone, it is clear that husbands must also be willing to change. Yet their willingness to do so may be influenced by wives' resources and willingness to press for change.

While wives have always had sources of power within a marriage, the willingness to leave a marriage is undoubtedly empowering if one wants to redefine the terms. It can force interactive engagement. This is the power of wives like Martha McIntyre, but less salient in the accounts of the wives like Marie Hampton. The partial change within the marriages of the Hamptons and the Stevenses may reflect the difficulty of pressing for a relational equality without the lever of the divorce option, which requires putting the self first. As I argued in Chapter One, it is more difficult to secure relationality than to model individualism; the former requires interactive participation and the latter does not. Ironically, individualism becomes an important means to relationality.

Divorce culture functions to "make sense" of diverse marital histories by relying upon the language of individualism. Although divorce culture is new and radical, individualism is, in some ways, traditional rather than radical. Divorce culture, grounded as it is in individual choice, inherits the promises as well as the problems of individualism (Riley 1991). One promise is the innovation that individual choice can foster. Another promise is the ability of women to take control of their own lives; this promise, I am suggesting, may make it easier for wives to redefine the terms of their marriage—whether the ends are individualistic or relational.

Nevertheless, problems are apparent. Individual needs are bound to come into conflict. And children, who are not party to the marital contract, do not necessarily experience divorce as a gateway. Historically, women have been expected to reconcile individual family members' needs (Degler 1980). While women still do most of the marital monitoring (Thompson and Walker 1989), even as they share in the providing, some of these wives, such as Martha McIntyre, suggest that women are less and less willing to shoulder the entire responsibility for the kin work and emotion work involved in monitoring marriage. Can such crucial responsibilities be redistributed without threatening the relationships upon which they are based?

A second problem with divorce culture is also the promise of marriage culture. When commitment is defined as contingent, long-term goals are problematic. As I have suggested, for some of these spouses who have contemplated divorce (for example, the McIntyres and the Hamptons), the belief in "marriage as forever" in their early years—along with economic constraints and child rearing that were present for all of the marriages—seemed to sustain them through rough periods for later relational rewards. Paradoxically, while marriage culture allowed Marie to "ride out" the conflicts that eventually resulted in a more egalitarian marriage, it also seemed to impede Doreen Dominick's efforts to incorporate equality. She could not resist male dominance when she was willing to stay in the marriage at any cost. Yet, there were other factors keeping Doreen in her miserable marriage—from religious convictions to her victimized son. Also, Doreen's experience as a child of divorce seemed to fortify her very strict terms of last resort. Yet, it is not just within wives' purview to redefine marriage. Husbands' responses and willingness to share responsibilities for marital monitoring are crucial to introducing equality. Vincent Dominick did not respond. Michael McIntyre did.

While the '50s spouses respond to social change in various ways, their adjustments contrast with the '70s couples. In the next five chapters, we turn to the marital and gendered constructions of '70s spouses, who come to adulthood in a very different era.

7   The '50s Era in a Rearview Mirror

THE FIRST divorce 39-year-old Patrick Reeves can recall is that of an older cousin who divorced in the early 1960s. Patrick, who was about 10 years old at the time, replays his reaction: "Whoooa, it shook me to the core that that could happen. *And* they had children—*small* children—even to me at that time." From the vantage of the early 1990s, Patrick describes a ripple effect through his extended family after this cousin's divorce: "That like broke the logjam or something and then the next five years, there must have been probably three or four [divorces]. And eventually it reached the point where those, those divorces and stuff went up through the higher [i.e., older] levels of my father's family."

Patrick goes on to speculate about the meaning of divorce for the older generation: "There was a time there where divorce was real *powerful* and *liberating* for this generation of people who just, once you got married, that was it. Strict, Christian brokering you know, *they had no alternative.* But eventually—maybe that was in the '60s or '70s, probably the '70s, that wasn't true anymore—and that it was okay now to get divorced. So some of 'em did. And one of them was one of my aunts" (emphasis added).

In this passage, Patrick explicitly links the "private trouble" of his aunt to the "public issue" of divorce developing in the 1970s (Mills 1959). As he does so, he reproduces the terms of divorce culture to account for the shift. The expanding authority of divorce culture is captured in the recognition that by the 1970s, "it was okay to get divorced." To perceive divorce as both "powerful and liberating" is to construct it as a gateway. When Patrick speaks of "no alternatives," he implicitly relies on the terms of marriage culture. He links the absence of alternatives to the associated domain of religion when he refers to "Christian brokering." Past images are redefined by Patrick from the vantage of the present. The seemingly tautological account, in fact, depicts a historical process; it is the changing social context that makes "marriage culture" visible.

The ripple effect in Patrick's white, middle-class family is reflected in the rise of divorce rates across race and class, though lower-income families remain the most vulnerable (Cherlin 1992; Kurz 1995).[1] Moreover, Patrick depicts the ripple moving from a younger generation into an older generation. While there have been notable increases in divorce among older, long-term couples in the last three decades—as suggested by the talk of the '50s couples—the '70s spouses, such as Patrick, witnessed an expanding divorce context before they were ever married. In this chapter, I focus on the '70s couples' direct experiences with the "ripple effect." First, I examine how, by the 1980s, rising cohabitation and divorce affect the '50s spouses' accounts of getting married in the first place, and then I compare these accounts to those of the '70s spouses. Next, I look at the '70s spouses' evaluations of marriage among their parents' generation. How does the generation born in the 1950s and married in the 1970s compare the marital context of the 1950s to its own? And how has the rising tide of divorce informed the '70s spouses' own marital practices?

RETROSPECTIVE VERSIONS OF MARRYING: THE '50S SPOUSES

Social constructions of what makes or breaks a marriage are easily overshadowed, and even disguised, by individualized, personal accounts. For the '50s spouses, a social understanding of their marital choices emerges only in retrospect. There is a "truth" about the 1950s, and their own decisions to marry, which becomes a shared cultural conception in this marital group by the 1980s. The influence of love, sex, and romance, the push of parents, and the pull of jobs do not disappear in their accounts, but a *new* reason does appear. They realize that their peers and their times shaped their choices. It is a social account coauthored by their generation only in hindsight.

During the 1982–83 interviews, when the '50s spouses were in their mid-'50s, they were asked how their parents' marriages affected their own. They were also asked what factors influenced them *to* marry and what factors influenced them *not to* marry when they were younger. By far the most common inducement to marriage, virtually unmentioned in any of the earlier interviews, was that "marriage was the thing to do," or that it was "the times." Some of their responses to these questions include:

> It seemed to be what everybody else was doing. There was a lot of social pressure to get married, and I wanted to get married, and I was scared about having to support myself [Martha McIntyre, married 32 years].

> I was heading in that direction, I'm sure. And of course I was ... during an era where that was the thing to do. You got married, you had kids. You moved to the suburbs. That's exactly what happened [Linda Finley, married 34 years].

> All our friends were getting or were married [Irene Mitchell, married 30 years].

Most of my friends were getting married; it seemed more socially acceptable to be married [. . .] I was finishing school and getting a job and everything [Ted Mitchell, married 30 years].

I suppose friends getting married probably did. And I suppose there was a
certain amount of anxiety on the part of my parents, too, I think, for marriage [Janet Johnson, 33 years married].

As in Janet Johnson's reference to her parents, family relationships
were a related theme in this generation's accounts of what encouraged and
discouraged them to get married. Recall that Katy Stone reported that
"this was a plan worked out by my father who unquestionably thought
I was getting along in years and should be married." And Evan Stone similarly reported, "I got married because it was supposed to be done."

Those who had divorced and remarried also referred to their first marriage in the 1950s as a decision influenced by the times:

I didn't want to [marry], but I did anyway. It was the thing to do [Nancy
Frank, divorced and remarried, reflecting on her first marriage].

I married marriage. I had been in the service and finally felt that everyone
was supposed to get married and settle down and I felt that was my function. I had been in the service and I had no roots and in 1946 I felt that was
the thing to do [Neil Ross, twice divorced, reflecting on his first marriage].

Whether happily or unhappily married, whether married once or more,
in 9 out of the 12 couples at least one of the spouses acknowledged "the
times" in their marital accounts.

The power of social eras to shape our choices often remains hidden in
the present, while we actively, blithely, or painfully make and explain our
individual lives. For the '50s couples, a new account of their marital decisions only becomes visible with hindsight. Retrospective accounts are frequently disparaged because of the memory's ability to alter the facts.
However, this critique begs the question of how "facts" and "accounts"
are constituted in the first place.

At least two factors shed light on the "emergent motive" of "the
times." First, motives may be actively suppressed or denied because of a
disinclination to credit or blame society, a kind of "social denial." To recognize the power of social and cultural influences seems to diminish the
scope of our autonomy, mock our individuality. In a highly individualistic society, the inclination is to highlight internal and personal motives to
account for one's experiences and choices, from marriage to occupation.
Hindsight provides a safe distance to allow the power of social influence
to emerge. However, in this case, we cannot simply claim that "social
influence" was always there and was finally admitted to consciousness

later. While social forces were always "there"—indeed, for this cohort social influence was more embraced than repudiated—the social interpretation implicit in evoking "the times" could not emerge until later.

A second factor accounting for an initial inability to perceive the impact of social forces concerns the constraints of our sociohistorical location. Until we have traversed "the times" and witnessed the next generation's ascent to adulthood, our location is obscured. The '50s couples, like "immigrants through time," have watched this shift from the predominance of marriage culture to contested cultural beliefs.[2] From the vantage of the 1980s, those who married in the 1950s cannot fail to notice the spectrum of options that were largely unavailable to them—except by default or at great risk.

The comparatively low rates of singleness and of divorce in the 1950s retrospectively shape the Older generation's justifications for marriage. "Not marrying" was no more an option for many in this generation than "divorcing." Their marital accounts by the 1980s reflect the 1950s social science portraits of social character—emphasizing conformity to and popularity among peers in an increasingly consumer-oriented society (Breines 1986; Riesman, Glazer, and Denney 1950; Seeley, Sim, and Loosley 1956; Whyte 1956). The '50s couples' marital accounts begin to sound like the "other-directed" type described in Riesman and colleagues' *The Lonely Crowd*. The social press for conformity, however, was more taken for granted in the 1950s; only in the 1980s did the social press become salient to the '50s couples. Over time, members of the Older generation adjust to the rates of cohabitation and divorce by revising their marital motivations.

Today's alternatives create a "vocabulary of motive" that is generationally specific (Mills 1940). Mills explains that a vocabulary of motive requires a sociological understanding: "over against the inferential conception of motives as subjective 'springs' of action, motives may be considered as typical vocabularies having ascertainable functions in delimited societal situations" (904). The emergent motive of "the times" or "the thing to do" accounts for the marriages of the Older generation in terms understandable not only to themselves, but also to their progeny in the 1980s. Both generations recognize that the younger set have entered marriage aware of competing options—from cohabitation, single parenthood, and domestic partnerships to remarriages and more employment opportunities for women. This spectrum of alternatives provides the contrast by which members of the Older generation can and do impute new motives for their marriage. At the same time, the spectrum precludes appropriation of this justification by the Younger generation; to explain one's marriage as motivated by social expectations is less legitimate for '70s spouses. Too many other options abound.

MARRYING: FROM A GIVEN TO AN OPTION

When these primarily middle class '70s spouses compare their marital experiences with those of their parents' generation, their descriptions became an occasion for highlighting the tenets of marriage and divorce culture. These respondents' parents, with some exceptions, were born in the late 1920s and married in the late 1940s to early 1950s—like the '50s couples I have been analyzing. How do the Younger generation's retrospective accounts regarding marrying in the first place compare to those of the Older generation?

The marital entrance, no less than the marital exit of divorce, is marked by increased choices for the Younger generation. As the '50s spouses retrospectively attribute marriage to the "times," they substantiate the widespread belief in "marrying as a given" in the '50s era. Among the '70s spouses, in contrast, about half of the 34 individuals claim they did *not* anticipate getting married when they were young adults. For many more '70s spouses, marriage was neither a given trajectory, nor the expressed ideal.

For example, Naomi Rosenberg reports that she did think of marriage as a teen, but her main aspiration was "leaving home" and going to college. Her parents' lifestyle and enduring marriage seemed "too insulated" and did not appeal to her. She asserts: "I saw marriage as constricting and suffocating, which is maybe why I didn't respect the institution of marriage." Naomi explains that her mother regrets not pursuing a career and was constrained by her times—a constraint Naomi wanted to avoid.

Once at college, where she was influenced by the feminist movement, Naomi began to think about marriage more seriously. After a number of years and a series of relationships in which the men she met were not "monogamous or committed," she met Ira. Ira, she states, "was really the first person who was even realistically here to have a commitment relationship." Nevertheless, she remained "cautious" about the relationship. They dated for two years and lived together for two years. She reports that "I was pretty critical of the institution of marriage, per se, so maybe six months into the relationship I fantasized about living together." She was not sure of how "egalitarian" the "arrangement" would be with children, and she was not keen on taking on someone's chores. As a lawyer by this time, she had seen "disastrous fallouts." Eventually, she married in order to have children, gain legitimacy as a parent, and accommodate Ira's desires. Naomi explains that Ira "has more respect for the institution of marriage than I do. He likes marriage in its own right." Naomi's desire for children and a "monogamous and committed" relationship led to her eventual decision to marry in spite of her critique.

In this account, it is clear that Naomi wanted a committed relationship. But she did not want marriage to constrain her as, in her view, it had constrained her mother. And the "disastrous fallouts" she had seen made her cautious. For many like Naomi among the '70s spouses, living together represented both a critique of the institution of marriage and a cautious stance based on witnessing marital fragility. In this '70s sample, 11 out of 17 couples—22 spouses in all—lived together briefly (six months) or extensively (twelve years) before marriage. Among the 22 spouses, 14 lived together before their first marriage; the remaining 8 spouses cohabited together before their second marriage. This generation's growing reliance on cohabitation before or apart from marriage is overrepresented in this sample, yet reflects generational trends (Thornton 1988; Goode 1993). Goode (1993, 161) reported: "In the mid-1980s, only 4 percent of U.S. couples were in cohabiting unions, but 16 percent (of all ages) had cohabited before their first marriage, and 25 percent had ever done so (this includes remarried couples). However, half of the married population aged 30–34 had done so at some time, in contrast to only 6 percent of those over 60 years of age."

Of course, because of my sample parameters, all these cohabiting couples eventually married. How was marriage raised as an option? Seven husbands proposed marriage in the traditional fashion, although some noted that "there was no bending knee." Seven couples said there was no proposal and described the process in terms of "should we get married?" Three couples said that there was no proposal, but did not elaborate. Five wives said they would have ended the relationship if their partners had not planned to marry. While some of these assertions elicited male proposals and others became joint decisions, women's suggestions of marriage were framed as ultimatums by both spouses, rather than as proposals. Upon launching a marriage we see lingering gendered constructions of proposals; if women suggest marriage it is seen as a threat and if men suggest marriage it is seen as a proposal. Why might this be the case? Do middle-class women feel a greater "need" for the institution of marriage than men?

Wives' accounts of launching marriage did suggest that they felt a greater need for marriage—particularly for being mothers or anticipating motherhood. Wives' marital proposals/ultimatums revealed a desire for commitment, not only for themselves, but especially for children. In contrast to a stated unwillingness to *stay together* for the sake of the children, children are still a central reason to *enter* marriage. Enduring issues of legitimacy and, even more important, the labor and resources required to rear children, deter many of these middle-class women from choosing single parenthood. One woman living with her partner, and with one child from a previous relationship, gave her partner a "deadline" for marriage. They were contemplating a second child and she reports saying to her husband-to-be: "I was not going to be a single parent to two children. That was not my idea of happiness. I could do this with one child and that's because I had the support of my ex-in-laws. But I was not going to do it with two children, because I knew my emotional limits." Her "deadline," in fact, yielded a proposal; while she is critical of marriage elsewhere, it is a criticism related to the role of a wife, more than of a mother (M. Johnson 1988).

Lynn Shepard and Stanley Flynn are a white, middle-class, dual-job couple who have been married for ten years and have two children. Stan is an active Quaker; Lynn describes herself as a nonbeliever. This is Stan's first marriage and Lynn's second. The couple had cohabited for a year before their marriage. After much hesitation, they finally decided to get married out of concern about how their future children might deal with "illegitimacy," as well as out of a desire to please their aging parents and involve their respective communities in a joint celebration, and, finally, because they could orchestrate the ceremony.

In their individual interviews, both Stan and Lynn express a commitment to one another unrelated, and almost in opposition, to marriage as an institution. Stan notes that he did not and does not "have any use for marriage." He prefaces this remark with the observation that his "folks had a terribly unhappy marriage." Neither he nor his wife have been into "marriage for marriage's sake—and still aren't." He repeats his cousin's maxim that "marriage is a terrific institution, if you happen to enjoy living in an institution."[3]

On the one hand, Stan argues that "marriage would [not] make any difference in terms of keeping us together because of some piece of paper." On the other hand, Stan relates that they both felt that if marriage was going to change anything, then "forget it." He clearly feared that the "institution" might overwhelm the relationship as they sought to define it. Stan accurately remarks that Lynn had similar feelings because of her first horrible marriage and had resolved, in fact, never to marry again. In her individual interview, Lynn confirms that she had been sure that she would never marry again after her first divorce; however, after a while she knew that her relationship with Stan would be "forever." Lynn and Stan still value the "forever" commitment—but are wary of its packaging in marriage and are critical of "forever at any cost." In their practice and their verbal critique of inevitable and eternal marriage, the Flynn-Shepards reflect the view of some of their contemporaries—that commitment is possible in spite of, not because of, marriage.

The Fenton-Harrington marriage is a first marriage that has endured for seven years. They are a Euro-American, middle-class, nonreligious, dual-career couple raising one child. For Beth Fenton, cohabitation represents an implicit critique of and reaction to the conventions of "marriage culture." Her peers supported her critique of marriage in young adulthood. In the course of telling me about a friend who had divorced, Beth mentions that he was unusual among their community of countercultural peers because he was one of the first to get married. She states: "He got married and he didn't want to tell anybody he got married because he was embarrassed, because it was against our culture to get married [. . .] he got married secretly and only one person knew." Here, Beth portrays the "stigma" of marriage in some social circles of the early 1970s—a stigma based on a critique that Beth shared for some time, in part because of her parents' marriage.

Beth states that "egalitarianism" is the linchpin of her relationship with Adam and that it was missing in her parents' marriage, despite their claims to the contrary. She fervently asserts several times in her interview that it was not marriage she sought, but a "marriage-like relationship." Beth implies, like Lynn and Stan, that commitment might be undermined rather than reinforced by conventional marriage. The critique that Beth expresses is reflected in the nine-year tenure of Beth and Adam's relationship before marrying. Caution is more apparent in Adam's account. Beth's husband, Adam Harrington, both credits and blames his parents' divorce for his personal development. He credits his parents' divorce for his shift toward more progressive political views. He also theorizes that he was "reluctant toward a permanent relationship" because of his parents' divorce—that what he "took from them was a great skepticism about relationships."

In the Younger generation, the shift from "marrying as a given" toward "marrying as an option" was marked by increased skepticism, critique, and caution. The fallout of divorce seemed to foster a wary attitude about entering marriage. More '70s spouses than '50s spouses expressed caution about marrying and more '70s wives were critical of male dominance in marriage before they ever married. Entering marriage was increasingly portrayed as a threat to, rather than a guarantee of, commitment. More '70s than '50s spouses were skeptical about the patterns of marriage practiced by the generation preceding them.

'70S SPOUSES' PERCEPTIONS OF THE 1950S: NO OPTIONS

The 1950s are known for an intensification of and increasing behavioral conformity to a normative nuclear family ideal. (Breines 1986; May

1988). Many sociologists have established that much about the 1950s has been mythologized and idealized because of a preoccupation with the experience of the white, middle class, notorious television symbols such as "Ozzie and Harriet," and a myopic view of the historical and socioeconomic context (Coontz 1992; May 1988; Skolnick 1991; Taylor, Chatters, and Tucker 1990). To what degree do these 17 middle-class couples reiterate and thereby reproduce this mythic vision?

Many respondents, like Patrick Reeves, described their parents' generation as having "no alternative" to enduring marriage. One wife, Iris Sutton, reports that despite her parents' conflicted marriage, there was some stability because there was "little divorce" in her Catholic, working-class neighborhood. Her husband, Ben Yoshida, states that a marriage "had to be very broken up" to end in divorce in his parents' generation. Lynn Shepard asserts, "My parents married for life." And her husband, Stan Flynn, concurs that for his parents, "you just don't get divorced"— despite their marital turmoil. Echoing Stan, Dennis Garcia asserts that in his parents' era "you don't get divorced."

Spouses frequently mentioned how long their parents had been married to convey the meaning of marital endurance for their parents' generation. For example, when Debbie Nakato is asked if she and her husband share the same idea of what it means to be married today as members of her parents' generation, she replies: "His parents have been married, I think it's 45–44 years, and my parents, they're going on 39, you know—that strong family belief in marriage and, you know. 'Cause we were having dinner one day at his parents' place and they go 'I think the worst word in the dictionary is divorce.'" Speaking of their parents, Debbie's husband, Paul, confirms in the joint interview that "in their generation it was unthinkable to get divorced." Like Debbie Nakato, Rosemary Gilmore depicts marital endurance like a family tradition: "My grandparents were married for 54 years before my grandmother died. My father and mother were married for 38 years before my father died. Marriage has been a very important thing in our lives. My father was married very briefly before, but he and my mother were together for many years, so I saw that as being a way to stay together, because they worked together."

The '70s spouses' depictions of the marital climate of the 1950s reproduced familiar portraits of that era, when "marriage was forever." These portraits were drawn in spite of the fact that not all of the respondents' parents remained married. The '70s spouses separate their parents' ideals from their parents' behaviors as they describe the era. Furthermore, the '70s spouses' stereotypical descriptions conceal their evaluations; they are not necessarily nostalgic for the 1950s. In contrast to their *descriptions,* their *evaluations* of the era were more varied and were often shaped by their reactions to their parents' marital experiences. Most '70s spouses are ambivalent, some criticize, and a few idealize the second tenet of marriage culture: "marriage as forever."

An Ambivalent Evaluation of the 1950s

Dennis Garcia is in a long-term first marriage to Margaret Garcia. Margaret is a homemaker, training for a job, while Dennis is an engineer and often works a side job to maintain an upper-middle-class lifestyle. Dennis is Latino/Euro-American and Margaret is Euro-American. While neither are religiously committed, Dennis was raised Catholic. Dennis and Margaret are among the 22 respondents whose parents remained married throughout their childhood.[4]

The marriage of Dennis's parents endured despite his father's extramarital affairs, his mother's emotional estrangement, and marital conflict in general. However, Dennis's parents eventually divorced in 1988—when he was 35 and well after he had formed his own family. Dennis has been married to Margaret for 17 years and has two children. When I ask Dennis if he thinks the times were really so different for his parents' generation compared to his own, he replies:

> Well, they just don't treat it—I mean people don't treat marriage like *I treated* marriage—and perhaps my dad even and my mom *treated* marriage. You're married and that's it. *You don't get divorced.* And you *ride it out.* I think it's certainly a helluva a lot *more healthy now.* To say good-bye. But unfortunately, in the same regard, you end up getting married and know that if it doesn't work out, you can just say good-bye. I don't know I—I certainly wouldn't stick with it as long as my parents did just for the sake of the kids. [KH: Uh huh, you wouldn't ...] *You screw up the kids anyway.* [KH: So um ... so you feel like your parents stayed together mostly for their kids ...] Uh huh—and maybe *how it looked.* There wasn't a lot of divorce in their group of friends. Today, Jesus, *if you're not divorced, it's pretty unusual* [emphasis added].

Ambivalence marks Dennis's evaluations. When he says that "unfortunately ... you can just say good-bye," he is implicitly critical of the ease of divorce. Framing his own and his parents' belief in "marriage as forever" in the past tense locates marriage culture in the past. And by relying upon the past tense, he inadvertently allies himself with the those who do not "ride it out."

Dennis's tendency to locate the ideals of marriage culture in the past reemerges later in the interview as he describes his male friends' behaviors at bachelor parties and their weekend trips to "Mustang Ranch." He is "amazed" by the husbands who engage in extramarital sex and "betray" their wives. He remarks that he does not "understand the norms *anymore.*" The "anymore" suggests that this behavior is new. Of course, his father's extramarital affairs should suggest to Dennis that this is not so new; but this interpretation is possible for Dennis, in part, because he sees his father as an exception in the 1950s and himself as the exception in the 1990s.

Despite his parents' eventual divorce, Dennis perceives his parents' effort as based on "marriage as forever"—a marriage sustained almost 40 years in part for the kids and for "how it looked," that is, to avoid the stigma of divorce in the 1950s. By the 1980s, both stigma and the kids are moot—the kids are grown and the social climate is changing. The portal of last resort, firmly latched for over 35 years, becomes a final escape, if never a gateway, for his parents. While his parents abided by the terms of marriage culture, the tolerance associated with divorce culture may have eased the passage.

Dennis's representation of the "typicality" of being married or divorced is radically transposed in these two eras: divorce was atypical in his parents' generation; remaining married is atypical for Dennis's peers. Dennis is saying that the stigma surrounding divorce in the 1950s is not relevant today, but he is also implying that staying married has become nearly deviant when he remarks that in the 1990s "if you're not divorced, it's pretty unusual." This dichotomized perception of marital eras and the felt, if not actual, marginality of staying married is implied by others in his cohort. Another '70s spouse defensively quips: "What's wrong with having a good married relationship?" The lapsed hegemony of marriage culture is salient for many among the Younger generation, and ambivalence is the most common response to this context of contested marital ideals.

A Critical Evaluation of the 1950s

In contrast to the Garcias, Lynn Shepard and Stan Flynn are critical of the belief in "marriage as forever." Both Lynn's and Stan's parents remained married until death. Lynn relates that her mother knew her father for a total of three months before she married him at age 20, and they stayed married for about 55 years. Lynn's marriage to Stan is her second, and her critique of "marriage as forever" seems to issue from her own divorce after a childless first marriage lasting two years.

Lynn reports that "the idea of my being divorced" was "shocking to my parents." When she divorced in 1972, it was "still kind of unacceptable." As the topic of divorce came up over the years, her mother would repeatedly assert: "I just don't think people try hard enough to work it out" and Lynn would respond, "Well mom, would you rather I'd be with

Tom [first husband]?" Invariably, her mother would say no. Lynn astutely comments that it was as if her mother was talking about "some concept of the ideal," rather than about Lynn, when she talked about divorce. Her mother was, in fact, talking the ideals of marriage culture. I would infer that Lynn's mother wondered whether Lynn was sufficiently unhappy to justify divorce on the last-resort terms of marriage culture.

Stan's parents also remained married until death, but Stan's critique of "marriage as forever" and "divorce as a last resort" issues from witnessing years of parental conflict. Stan regrets that his mother was "always struggling" because "she knew that she had made the wrong choice for herself." After Stan reached adulthood, his mother tried separation from his father for over a year, but she was plagued by guilt. The experience of witnessing this turmoil in his parents' marriage leads Stan to declare, "I believe in divorce." He rapidly adds, "I also believe in working on relationships." He grants that divorce gets more "complicated" with children, but he also does not "believe in prolonging poisonous relationships because of the children or something like that." For the happily married Flynn-Shepards, protecting their children from marital conflict has not been an issue.

While Stan asserts the importance of working on relationships, he actually depicts his marital relationship as relatively free of work. What Stan expresses in his interview—that "it's been an incredibly conflict-free kind of marriage"—is affirmed and demonstrated in the joint interview. If the condition for staying together under the terms of divorce culture is happiness, they meet it. Despite their deep satisfaction with their relationship, they believe that divorce should be an easy option; and, paradoxically, because of their deep satisfaction with their relationship, they continue to wonder whether the weight of the "marital institution" might crush their relational commitment.

Idealizing the '50s Era

The upper-middle-class, Euro-American Weisses have been married for 17 years and have two children. Their gender arrangements, their religious practice, and their belief in "marriage as forever," are all drawn upon to substantiate their claim of being "traditional." Aron is an investor; Susan focuses on raising their two children and is involved in community associations and clubs. They are Jewish and keep a kosher household. The Weisses feel marginal in today's social context of competing cultures. In her individual interview and again in their joint interview, Susan Weiss maintains: "He and I think we both really fit back in the 1950s."

Their sense that they belong in the 1950s—and their strong adherence to the ideals of marriage culture—may seem curious given that Aron's parents divorced and Susan questions whether her parents should have stayed together. During their joint interview, Aron and Susan Weiss talk about her parents' rocky marriage, and they offer the times and children as reasons her parents evaded divorce:

> SW: My parents had a horrible marriage and they just stuck together . . .
> AW: *'cause of their generation.* [SW: because . . . Yeah.] Her parents had a—loveless marriage? [SW: Yeah.] For fifty years?
> SW: But yet there's an adaption of, not love, but companionship. [AW: Need.] That warm body.
> AW: Yeah, my parents alternated between extreme love and extreme hate. I think her parents were sort of in the middle ground of—"well we're stuck with each other so we gotta make it work."
> SW: *And for the kids.*
> AW: And for the kids . . .

While Susan and Aron explain her parents' marital endurance in terms of the era and children, they do not acknowledge that this explanation falls short when it comes to his parents' willingness to divorce. A belief that marital commitment should be contingent on happiness would help to resolve this contradiction. Aron's parents' marriage was marked by separation, divorce, and living together in the 1970s after divorce. In contrast to many respondents' parents, Aron's parents became increasingly nontraditional in their relationship over time. Aron does not "really understand what motivated them to live together," but he recognizes that "they were happier unmarried. They were happier living together. They just seemed to get along better that way." Here, Aron suggests that the underlying reason for his parents' marital rearrangements was happiness. Yet Aron repeatedly expresses the belief that (un)happiness is not sufficient justification for divorce.

When I ask Aron how parenthood changed his own marriage, he asserts that having children "takes away any doubts you have about whether or not you're going to stay married." As he says that there is no "backing out" once children are born, he immediately acknowledges the limits of such certain and absolute statements today:

> Clearly if something fundamental happens, you know, marriages can break up with the children, they do all the time. But within the normal confines of what people want to do [. . .] changes in ways that are irritating, but trivial, that's not a good enough reason, I think. And I sort of think, I guess the model I have in my own mind is, you see and read about

> so many marriages breaking up because "I'm sort of displeased," you know. And that's not, you know, that's not good enough. You gotta be one heck of a lot more displeased, before you destroy three people's lives.

For Aron, divorce remains a "last resort," rather than a "gateway," and he sees divorce as destructive of relationships. While spousal happiness is not sufficient justification for divorce here, it clearly underlies his account of his parents' divorce.

When I ask Aron how his parents' divorce affected him, he replies: "It probably, it probably drove me to be more—[have] more personal security craving than I might otherwise have had." At another point, he searches to capture his feelings: "I wasn't happy about it—probably not happy—not embarrassed particularly—but sort of sad. Maybe angry, I don't know." Aron resists criticizing his parents' behaviors directly; however, he conveys an implicit criticism as he discusses how divorce would negatively affect his two children—he presumes an emotional impact that he cannot capture in his own experience. And in the course of discussing the context for his children, he reproduces an image of being surrounded by divorce:

> I mean whenever Susan and I have an argument or something, our son bursts into tears, "you're going to get a divorce." And that kind of—it's so—because they see them at school. He's now at the age where every year there's a parent, one or two, the families are breaking up. And, you know, the husband has found someone younger, a secretary, this or that, you know, and "I'm gonna to do what I want to do," and so divide. You know, so you sell the house and move to—I think they all move to the Valley. [...] That's where half goes; that's where the women go with the children.

Aron's repeated talk about marriages with children breaking up "all the time," and "so many marriages breaking up," and his sensitivity to the fact that at his son's school every year, there are "one or two—the families are breaking up," suggests that Aron is alert to and feels the advance of divorce culture, in spite of his own adherence to marriage culture.

In sum, the Weisses support the ideals of marriage culture, and they tend to locate the source of their ideals in the 1950s. Their parents' experiences inform their beliefs to an extent. The formation of Aron's marital ideals seems to be a reaction against the marital patterns of his parents. Despite the nontraditional behaviors of his parents and the problematic tensions between Susan's parents, they locate marriage culture in the 1950s because they imagine a supportive context for themselves there. They sense that cultural support for "marriage as forever" is waning. The 1950s ideal—more than their parents' examples—underlies Susan and Aron Weiss's support for marriage culture. Their sense of marginality is captured when they ask, "have you interviewed anyone else like us?" I assure them that I have.

The Resilience of Marrying as a Given

As Susan and Aron Weiss's interviews suggest, marriage culture is still alive and well for some '70s spouses. Aron Weiss says that when he was a teenager, he planned to marry and have children. Aron and Susan did not live together. Aron proposed marriage. Half of the '70s spouses assert that they knew they wanted to marry and have children when they were teens or young adults. Six couples did not live together before marriage. And relational "commitment" is ensured, not threatened, by marriage for these couples.

Bill and Rosemary Gilmore have been married for 13 years and have two children. They are a dual-job couple, both work full-time, and they have been upwardly mobile. He works as a maintenance supervisor, and Rosemary's job is in services at the telephone company. They are both African-American. While Rosemary is active in a Christian congregation, Bill is not as active.

When I ask Bill whether he imagined himself married when he was a teen, he replies: "Yeah. I have always relished the idea of being a bread-winner, care provider. The guy that you look forward to coming through the door." Asked whether he's worried about divorce, he responds: "No, it's like, I've got that commitment, vows and stuff." Later, as he speaks about his wife, Rosemary, he asserts: "I think both of us have the same mindset with regards to marriage. This is it. Like I told people when I got married that this was going to be my one shot at it win, lose, or draw, and I think I meant that. I really believe it's not something to enter into lightly." Bill also reports that they "never lived together" and that there was never any debate about children: "I wanted children. Rosemary wanted children. So we basically decided that we'd have one child right away." Their first child arrived in time for their first anniversary. But Bill's adherence to the ideals and sequences of marriage culture are also a function of his parents' experiences. Bill implies, and Rosemary affirms, that the death of both parents by the time he was a young teen fueled Bill's longing for a family. Bill repeatedly describes his marriage as a "commitment to family." As his wife Rosemary puts it:

> I think both Bill and I have a strong sense of family, not only with our kids, but even with our outside relatives—he has a niece that came into the mar-riage with us. [...] I remember when we were dating and entertaining the thought of getting married and stuff. I automatically saw her as being part of that package. I know—I remember Bill telling me about this family. He

didn't have the normal traditional-type family life like I had, the upbringing, I guess, since he lost his parents at an early age. It seemed like that was something that he always wanted. It's funny because when we were thinking of getting married and stuff, I said, "That's one thing that I want to make sure that he has, that sense of normalcy with a mother, father, kids, that kind of thing."

While Rosemary's talk on one level proffers the "nuclear family" as normalcy, on another level and in practice their marital commitment threads its way through the fabric of their extended family. Only three couples in the '70s sample had participated in raising a sibling's child—a niece or nephew—and two of these couples were African-American, including the Gilmores. In this case, Bill was already taking care of his niece before his marriage. The Gilmores represent both the support for family members in need and the added responsibilities for African-American married couples with resources to assist in child rearing. This reflects research findings concerning the enduring ties of obligation among African-Americans for family beyond the nuclear family, into the extended family (McAdoo 1988; Taylor et al. 1990). Rosemary comments here that the niece was "part of that package." And Bill remarks elsewhere that extended family responsibility "just goes with the territory."

Although less prominent than among the '50s couples, the premises of marriage culture have *not* been discarded by this cohort. Yet even among those who primarily talk the vocabulary of marriage culture, there is keen awareness that the marital context has changed considerably since their parents' early years. Cultural pressures to marry and stay married have ebbed in response to the rising tide of divorces surrounding them.

CONCLUSION: MARRIAGE "WAS" FOREVER

The '70s spouses have been in the thick of redefining marital meanings. While '70s spouses' descriptions of their parents' era are often stereotypical, their evaluations differ; they are variously ambivalent, critical, or admiring of the perceived reign of marriage culture in the 1950s. As respondents draw comparisons between their own and their parents' generation, many of them tend to perceive members of their parents' generation as constrained by or victims of "marrying as a given" and "marriage as forever." Their portrait of divorce in the 1950s, moreover, is less one of "last resort" and more one of "no resort." One of the hallmarks of marriage culture—staying together for the children—has lapsed as a hegemonic reason for marital endurance for some couples in this sample, certainly not all couples, as represented by the Weiss and Gilmore marriages. Many respondents still grapple with the questions over the nature of commitment, the degree of "displeasure" that justifies divorce, and the extent to which children should "complicate" divorce.

Respondents view the 1950s through their parents' experiences and use those experiences to define and make sense of the marital environment today. Most spouses tend to locate marriage culture in the past—as if "marriage *was* forever," but is no longer. There is a converse tendency to locate divorce culture in the present. Neither tendency is quite accurate. The seeds of divorce culture can be seen as a marginalized cluster of beliefs that was present in, but has evolved since the 1950s. In fact, as we have seen, both clusters of beliefs can be found in the 1950s and the 1970s cohorts, but many of these respondents rightly intuit the change in relative strength of marriage and divorce cultures.

The change in relative strength underlies the perception that getting divorced is no longer stigmatized and staying married can be experienced as deviant. Tensions between the cultures of marriage and divorce are evident. Most spouses still see children as a central reason to marry. Yet, critique of the marital institution is more salient among some '70s spouses—whether in their repudiation of staying together just for the children's sake or concern about male dominance in marriage. Above all, the "broken logjam" of divorces described by Patrick Reeves at the beginning of this chapter fosters caution among all '70s spouses.

8   The Pull of Divorce Culture

Divorce Anxiety Among '70s Spouses

As Bill Gilmore discusses the models for his marriage, he notes that his "perception of marriage" is drawn from his "parents and other people." The "other people," he explains, were "who I associated with that were married when I wasn't married . . . who for the most part aren't married anymore." Bill remarks that an era followed when they were the "odd couple out" because all their "friends were single or divorced and we were married." He reports that among his friends "the majority of people that we associate with *now* are married" and that "there are no visible signs of strain." As if to leave room for "invisible" strains, Bill adds: "But then one of the [model] couples that I associated with when I was single, they were married *nine* years before they decided to get divorced." He attempted his hand at "marriage counseling" with this couple, but it "went down the tubes." Bill admits: it was "a very traumatic experience for me because I really cared a lot for these people [. . .] it was a real sad point in my life when they parted company." He observes, "I mean, you hear about other people getting divorces and that, but in my lifetime, that was the most up close and personal view I've had of divorce. It was pretty dirty."

Bill's account signals the concerns of this chapter—the prevalence of divorce, the impact of witnessing unexpected divorces, and some of the difficulties of defining a model marriage today. Despite his attempt to counsel the friends who informed his perception of marriage, they eventually divorce. An issue faced by many of these married couples is how to sustain an enduring marriage when everyone appears vulnerable to divorce. Maintaining a marriage is more difficult for the Younger generation because of a climate of contingency. Contending with contingency is a conundrum because the younger cohort frequently support, or even advocate, divorce and yet desire stable marriages. Even as people are cynical about the potential permanence of others' marriages, they hope their own marriage will endure (Blumstein and Schwartz 1983, 28). How do '70s spouses cope with marital contingency?

To a degree, the '70s spouses reflect the responses we saw among the '50s spouses: divorces become an occasion for humor, sorrow, pride in one's own marriage, and distancing. Yet '70s spouses also feel vulnerable to divorce. Their stories of others' "unexpected divorces" and their own "survival" suggest there is a new "structure of surprise"[1] surrounding marital endurance and dissolution. Even as these stories represent unpredictability, '70s spouses implicitly theorize about what prevents or circumvents divorce as they strategize to sustain their marriages. Spouses employed at least four strategies to contend with the specter of divorce, including: (1) "hypothetical divorces," or divorces they might have experienced, but have evaded in their own lives; (2) "passing the test," or stories of adversity that signify their marital resilience; (3) seeing "gender ideology as a shield" against divorce; and (4) belief in a "marital work ethic" for sustaining marriage. Taken together, the surprises, stories, and strategies suggest that it is not only the divorced, but the married who are constructing divorce culture.

SURROUNDED BY DIVORCE, MARRIAGE IS THE SURPRISE

The average year of marriage for the Younger generation is 1979. A poll conducted in 1978 found that 60 percent of respondents did *not* think "most couples getting married today expect to remain married for the rest of their lives" (cited in Yankelovich 1981, 96). This captures the contingency in the air for the newly wed '70s couples. By their interviews in the 1990s, the members of the Younger generation have had to contend directly with the "contingency" of marriage.

The '70s spouses feel surrounded by divorce in a way that was less evident in the '50s spouses' talk. This is particularly apparent if the generations are compared by age; when the Older generation was near 40 years old in 1970, their divorce talk was sparse compared to that of the Younger generation when they neared 40, in 1991. An environment of divorce is really not apparent for the '50s spouses until their 1982 interviews. Among the '70s spouses, the number whose parents had divorced is more than double that among '50s spouses. And for the '70s spouses, the list of peers—divorced siblings, friends, cousins, and coworkers—is more extensive. In short, the felt prevalence of divorce is unmistakably greater and is reflected in their multiple stories of divorce. The "ripple effect" of divorce touches both generations, but at different points in the life course.

Some respondents began to feel the "ripple effect" of divorce in the early 1970s. Margaret Garcia is in her first marriage with Dennis. She recalls that when she was in high school, around 1970, "I had friends whose parents were getting divorced right and left. I remember saying to my friend—her parents were solid too—that I just felt like she and I were the only people in the world that had a solid family." And when Adam

Harrington's parents initially divorced in high school, he did not tell anyone for a year; as he saw more and more divorces, he realized his experience was hardly unique.

Other respondents began to feel the ripple effect in the late 1970s. We heard Bill Gilmore report that: "Somewhere along the line, things started happening. People got divorced, and I got married, and then we were the odd couple out because all our friends were single or divorced, and we were married." Lynn Shepard recalls a time when her brother, two cousins, and herself were all separated from their spouses, sharing the Christmas holidays, and commiserating about life being "rocky." Nick Turner discusses the divorces of his twice-divorced cousin and thrice-divorced brother. At the conclusion of her interview, Mia Turner, the first in her family to divorce, remarks, "the way it is now, you can't ever find a family that's not blended."

Andrea Skinner and Leon Kramer were both previously married, but consider their current marriage stable. They note that their parents—and their parents' generation in general—had stable marriages. Andrea states: "I'd have to say none of our generation had stable marriages; we had [sic] the most stable marriage in our family." As if to illustrate, Andrea and Leon go on to discuss the divorces of three cousins and the two divorces of Andrea's sister. While Leon initially asserts that his relatives are all in stable marriages, he moves on to the exceptions of his cousin and aunt. They agree that most of their old friends see their marriage as solid, and Leon quips, "because nobody stayed together." Andrea objects, "One couple did." The broken "logjam" that Patrick Reeves described at the opening of the previous chapter floods the talk of '70s couples.

The prevalence of divorce was not only reflected in their numerous stories of divorce, but also in their own awareness of their eligibility for divorce, which is often laced with humor. When I opened the interview with the question "what's good about your marriage?" one wife quipped, "that we're still married." When, at the close of the joint interview, I said that I might be in touch for a follow-up interview in the future, several spouses asked, "to see if we're divorced?" When I raised the question "what's the biggest surprise of your marriage?" the most common rejoinders were: "that we're still married," "that it's lasted this long," "that we've made it this far," and "that it's lasted." Sometimes respondents were joking and sometimes they were serious and referred to a period of conflict that brought them to the threshold of divorce. Another common rejoinder was surprise that "the longer we're married, the happier it is," or that "it's gotten better over time," or "that it's gone so smoothly." The expectation of marital discord or divorce—expressed in the 1978 poll—clearly lurks in the background of these statements.

As spouses discussed divorces surrounding their lives, they expressed divorce anxiety—a tangible *uncertainty* regarding their own and other marriages. This sense of uncertainty seems to be fostered by *witnessing* family or friends *going through* a divorce; simply meeting somebody who had previously divorced did not carry the same impact as watching married parents, friends, or peers divorce. Those whose parents had divorced often contended with this "uncertainty" earlier; however, it was not limited to those with divorced parents, to previously divorced spouses, or to unhappily married spouses. Widespread divorce means more spouses witness divorces, and this seems to elicit divorce anxiety. Witnessing the "unexpected divorce" had the most impact of all.

The Unexpected Divorce: "It Could Happen to Us"

If the surprise of marital endurance represents the expectation of divorce, the "unexpected divorce" represents the dashed expectation that divorce is predictable. The "unexpected divorce" conveys the message that divorce could happen to the seemingly happiest of couples, which implies, in turn, that "it could happen to us." That spouses feel eligible for divorce comes across not only in their jokes about the surprise or deviance of remaining married, but in their explicit expressions of anxiety or fear. The belief that "it could happen to us," led couples to make sense of why some marriages endured and others dissolved.

Fourteen spouses told stories of an "unexpected divorce." The "unexpected divorce" generally revealed an inadequate set of assumptions about what makes for an enduring marriage. Among the factors that characterized divorces that were deemed "unexpected" were marital longevity, the presence of children, and home ownership. A long-term marriage, in particular, seemed to suggest that a couple was on its way to "marriage as forever." Stories of "unexpected divorces" not only illuminate spouses' ideals about marital endurance, but also their coping mechanisms in the midst of unpredictable divorces.

Paul Nakato is in a happy first marriage of five years to Debbie. They have two young children.[2] When I ask Paul if he has known anyone divorced, he discusses an "unexpected divorce." Paul had been best man in a friend's wedding and continued as an intimate friend of the couple for many years. Some years later, they divorced. Asked if this had any affect upon him, he replies: "I think it impacted my life by showing me that the people that you think were *made for each other,* can get a divorce, for whatever reason. And there's nothing you can do about it and *it can happen to you too. It can happen to anybody, you know.* I guess at that time I hadn't really seen too many of my old friends—I'd heard of people getting divorced, [...] but it didn't happen to us, for heaven's sakes. Ha, ha, ha. Yes it does happen, you know."

There is a formula to many of these stories: an early friendship, participation in a wedding, the newlyweds' seeming compatibility, and then the surprise divorce.[3] Because Paul's friends seemed like they were "made for each other," the surprise of the divorce presses Paul to reflect on his own vulnerability: "But I just felt so badly for him, and I just thought, my god, if this could happen to them, it could happen to anybody. And, god, I'm so *scared*. What is love? I mean, how do I know if I have *the right one*? I just don't know. And that's kind of how I felt, it really impacted my life quite a bit. Just kind of really made me, made me *very scared* and just made me think I gotta be *really careful as to who*— whereas before marriage was more of a romantic notion." Paul's fear led him to consider how he might avoid the pitfalls of his friend. Since the divorce predated his own marriage, the experience elicited vigilance and caution in mate selection. He aimed to be "really careful" about who he married.

For the already married, witnessing an unexpected divorce elicited references to luck. Because *everyone* appears susceptible to divorce, respondents often refer to "luck," "chance," or "misfortune" to explain the endurance or dissolution of marriages. Several spouses perceive friends' divorces as "bad luck." For example, one wife says of her twice-divorced best friend, "she's having bad luck." Some describe friends' divorces and conclude that "if it weren't for a few different circumstances, they'd probably still be together." Others wondered, "How did I luck out?" Lynn Shepard asks this rhetorical question as she discusses her marital happiness in her individual interview. Her husband, Stan, concurs: "Both of us feel that we've been really lucky." He adds that "despite all the hardships and hard work," he has been fortunate in finding the "right person." Mia Turner asserts, "we're pretty lucky that we have common things." Sharon Ellison remarks, "we've been married so long that we've grown in different ways but there's still a real nice interconnecting. And I think that's lucky because I know a lot of people who got married as young as we did but grew in different directions." These spouses share the assumption that there is an element of divorce that spouses cannot fully control.

The regularity with which '70s spouses invoke "luck" to account for the broken and sustained marriage is not only an indicator of divorce anxiety bred by unexpected divorces; it also signifies an inability to account for divorce. "Luck" serves as a residual category to explain the unexplainable.[4] The psychologist might explain the invocation of luck as a denial of personality defects contributing to unstable relationships. The family systems theorist might suggest that functional or dysfunctional patterns of relating are still invisible to those who talk in terms of luck. However, the sociologist will be concerned that "luck" talk overlooks social structures and systems of power that enter into the formula of marital endurance and severance. There have always been personality disorders and dysfunctional families in previous generations—yet these have not always accompanied divorce. If we are to understand emergent meanings and practices of marriage and divorce, we must uncover structural realities.

The Hypothetical Divorce

The feeling of being out of control highlights the degree to which spouses feel vulnerable to divorce, but it also elicits strategies for dealing with uncertainties. One such strategy is the "hypothetical divorce."

Paul Nakato felt vulnerable once the marriage of his friends, who seemed "made for each other," dissolved. He was cautious about marrying the "right one."[5] Earlier in his interview, when I asked him what was good about his marriage, Paul asserted that he felt he married the "right one." As if to substantiate this conclusion, he described an earlier relationship in which marriage was considered "childishly." By implication this potential spouse was the "wrong one": "I mean I almost consider that relation to be like a bad marriage. She just messed me up so badly, you know, I just, god, you know, I just really [laughs]—it's just amazing. I mean if I would have gotten married to her, *I would have gotten divorced.*"

In the above account, Paul describes what I call a "hypothetical divorce." A hypothetical divorce is a divorce that would have occurred had one married the wrong person or married at the wrong time. Because Paul adamantly asserts that "it can happen to anyone," I would argue that this hypothetical divorce represents a reduced chance for divorce in his current marriage. In a sense, he has already been vulnerable to divorce, avoided it, and mastered the potential of divorce. Paul is implicitly describing the age-old adage that "playing the field" is important for selecting the "right" partner. Yet, the number of "would be" divorces presented by spouses, in diverse contexts, led me to conclude that the "hypothetical divorce" is a *defensive* response to the emergence of "divorce culture." Whether divorce is perceived as a gateway or a threat, divorce culture means that everyone must contend with and gain mastery over the divorce option to some degree. Examples of hypothetical divorces—provided by Paul and others—shared a key contradiction: on the one hand, a sense that they were as vulnerable to fate as the next person, and on the other, a sense that they had mastered their brush with a potential divorce when they married the right person at the right time.

Beth Fenton, who desired a "marriage-like relationship," lived with her current husband, Adam, for three years and "saw" him for nearly six years before their marriage. She reports that they "would've divorced had we stayed together early on." For Beth, this hypothetical divorce would have transpired because of the wrong time rather than the wrong person. She explains that she and Adam "explored a lot of stuff" when they separated and they were fortified by having "had enough divorce experiences" by the time they got married. Through the years, she figured out what she liked, missed, and wanted with Adam. Both engaged in other relationships and witnessed the union and dissolution of relationships among friends. Beth concludes: "If we stayed together when we first lived together, it would've ended—frustrated by differences. But because we waited, it lent strength."

Like Beth, Pamela Jordan had a long-term relationship with her husband before their marriage. When I ask Pamela "what's good about your marriage?" she replies that in past relationships "there was always a threat there that something would go wrong for one reason or another." Pamela did not feel that threat with Burton, and she hypothesizes: "If I had married every other man that I had been with before, I would have been divorced ninety-six times by now, at least. [laughs] And uh, I didn't feel that. Even then, 10 years ago when I first laid eyes on him, I felt this was my soul mate." Pamela implies that she has married the right person at the right time. While he does not refer to divorce, her husband, Burton, focuses on the timing of the marriage as crucial in averting dissolution: "It was like it was a good thing that I did leave her when I did. We'd probably be the two worstest [sic] enemies of each other had I stayed there longer in our first relationship. I needed to go away for those six, seven years and go through hell and really come back around. Find myself." In sum, whether "hypothetical divorces" are embedded in the context of finding oneself, the right person, or the right time, as imaginative experiments they seem to function to control current vulnerability to divorce.

Nine respondents refer to their own hypothetical divorces. These inventive constructions allow respondents to distance themselves from a felt vulnerability to divorce. They have "imaginatively" divorced in some sense and, therefore, do not have to actually divorce.[6] These imaginative experiments simultaneously serve to support the key premise of divorce culture—that marriage is contingent—while leaving room for the possibility of marriage as forever. I would argue that the hypothetical divorce allows respondents to resolve their ambivalence about divorce by "containing" their potential for divorcing, which allows their current relationship to "contain" their chance at marital endurance. While spouses can *reconcile* their support for divorce and their desire for an enduring marriage, this strategy has the effect of reproducing divorce culture through the expectation that marriage is contingent.

Passing the Test

The more that divorce touches the perimeter of one's life, the more one's own marital endurance becomes experienced as an achievement. While the '50s spouses talked in terms of achievement in later years, they focused on endurance, rather than stories that signified a test of their commitment. In contrast, the '70s spouses are attuned to challenging moments in their marriage that they met and overcame.

Fourteen respondents referred to an experience that either they or others had "survived" as a couple. The experience symbolized potential for marital endurance. In effect, the following diverse examples demonstrate how respondents confront, then overcome, a "close call" with divorce. These divorce-prone contexts are interpreted retrospectively by spouses as proof of the relationship's past durability. I call this strategy "passing the test." The experience itself is not the focus here; rather, it is the respondents' *interpretation* of the experience that functions as a defense of marital stability in divorce culture. Their constructions of personal, social, or cultural experiences as "close calls" is another kind of protective, imaginative experiment that signifies protection from divorce in the future.

For example, Dennis and Margaret Garcia both describe a one-year period of being unemployed and living in Guatemala as a "trial." Margaret asserts that "looking back I thought . . . my train of thought [was] that because our marriage did survive Guatemala that we could survive anything." Andrew Ellison points to a turning point in his marriage when their home was stripped, damaged, and ransacked in a burglary. Andrew concludes that it was "an object lesson that we can get through anything in our marriage." Iris Sutton talks about friends' marriages that have been "tested and failed" upon the birth of the first child; she reasons, "if you survive that time, then your marriage will probably survive." In this last example, Iris not only draws upon a personal experience, but implicitly has drawn upon the unexpected divorces of friends. In short, others' experiences are often used symbolically to designate what it takes to "pass the test." Paul and Debbie Nakato talk about a "hurdle" in their marriage, when Debbie's health was threatened, which is an example of "passing the test"; yet, Paul also uses his parents' experiences to make his goal of "passing the test" appear more manageable.

As *sansei,* third-generation Japanese-Americans, Paul and Debbie are alert to the sociohistorical conditions that distinguish their own experiences from their parents' experiences as *nisei.* They recognize and respect their parents' sacrifices and courage during and after internment by the

United States government during World War II. While Paul deplores the institutional racism and the adversity incurred by the internment travesty, he also asserts that such conditions generated tenacity and strength:

> Our parents had to, you know, had their homes taken away from them, they were put in concentration camps—how can anybody go through this nonsense and come out psychologically sane? *If you can survive that, you can survive anything! Being married, what's the big deal? That's easy, see?* But for us, you know, we didn't have the easiest life either, but I'm just saying that, hey, you know, we got to go to school, we got to have jobs, like, you know, better jobs. I mean we're really coddled compared to them. [. . .] So, because of that, it's like, when something bad happens, you know, you don't really know what it's like to suffer so therefore you start blaming your spouse, saying, you know, "well, you're the one making this soap opera not work; the music is stopping because of you—because you're being greedy." Blaming the other. You don't really assess that "hey look, if we break up because of an argument here, look at all the other things we'll be giving up. And look at all the good things that we've built up. Look how grateful we should be for all the good things that we have."

For Paul, the adversity faced by his parents not only yielded survival skills, but made marriage or other troubles seem minor by comparison. Paul diminishes and thereby manages marital difficulties by placing them alongside his parents' more severe deprivations.

Leon Kramer also saw his parents' marital endurance in terms of surviving adversity. Leon's parents are Jewish survivors of the Holocaust. He says: "I don't think necessarily that there was a prescription against divorce as there is in the [wider] culture, but these marriages that I knew were cemented by adversity, by the war, so the closeness was partially pushed by that."

In sum, "passing the test" ranged from surviving unemployment in a foreign country (the Garcias) to using parents' survival to make marriage more manageable (Paul Nakato). In the latter case, Paul employs his parents' experiences to interpretively minimize the "tests" in his own marriage and to explain why divorce is on the rise among other couples in his generation: they have not been tested as rigorously and thus have not acquired the mettle to deal with marital challenges. In all cases, personal or social history is imaginatively interpreted to ensure and theorize about resilience in the face of marital conflict.

Gender Ideology as a Shield Against Divorce

As I interviewed the '70s couples, I came to expect spouses' talk about changing gender roles to blend into observations about changes in divorce—and vice versa. The meanings of these two distinct, but related, social transformations are entwined in the minds of the married. In short, there is a widespread perception that gender ideologies are central factors contributing to marital stability or, alternatively, divorce. Most spouses who suggest that divorce results from changes in gender assume that ideologies converge with practice and most use the language of roles to talk about these changes.

Some '70s spouses talk generally about generational change. For example, Roxanne Kason-Morris theorizes that the change in marital endurance is partially due to the decline of traditional roles over the generations. She observes: "Well, my grandmother and I talk about that all the time—she's 89 and we wonder why her generation's marriages—she was born in 1903—worked out. [. . .] I'm in my second marriage and literally everyone, almost everyone I know is divorced and remarried or just divorced. So um, I wonder what the adhesive quality is to what people used to have. [. . .] I think traditional roles, that's one thing."

Seventeen spouses in my sample brought up "gender ideology" to explain why their own or others' marriages did or did not last. Some spouses claim "traditional" ideologies and practices—a homemaking wife and a breadwinning husband—serve to resist the pull of divorce culture. Dan and Judy Green (who I will discuss at length in Chapter Ten) also believe that "traditional" roles are crucial to "marriage as forever." While this is also apparent in the talk of some '50s spouses (for example, Katy Stone, who thinks that the high divorce rate is due to the "roles" being "badly messed up"), the Greens and other '70s couples confront a less supportive peer context and must grapple with the challenge of gender equality earlier in their marriage than the '50s couples.

Only 5 of the 17 spouses who brought up gender suggested that a traditionalist gender ideology protects one against divorce. The other 12 spouses claimed egalitarianism ensures and is a condition of marital stability. Some of these spouses defined equality in terms of independence, and they were more likely to talk the language of individualism. Other spouses defined equality more in terms of interdependence, mutuality, and an equality of obligation or sacrifice. But all 12 spouses reflect the increasing trend toward egalitarian beliefs (Thornton 1989; Mason and Lu 1988; Simon and Landis 1989). Although beliefs do not necessarily reflect practice (Hochschild with Machung 1989), and obdurate social structures make egalitarian practice difficult (Schwartz 1994), egalitarian beliefs have certainly accompanied changing social conditions, such as the rise in married women's participation in the labor force (Cherlin 1992) and the need for two-income families (Moen 1992).

For the Fenton-Harringtons, egalitarianism was and is a condition of their marriage. For Beth, years of cohabitation with Adam represented a critique of and reaction to a perceived hard-wiring of marriage culture and male dominance. Beth stated that "egalitarianism" is the linchpin of her relationship with Adam. Beth aimed to redefine marriage:

> I wanted a marriage-like relationship whether or not it went through all the formal state stuff or the ceremony. I didn't care about that at all. I guess I went through a period when I was like 20 to 25 when I guess I said I wasn't going to have kids and that would be an oppressive experience and I didn't want to get married. You know I felt that pretty strongly that I didn't want that, but somehow I kind of got to the end of that and I thought ... I just thought marriage doesn't necessarily ... having a family doesn't have to be an oppressive experience—where people have control over their lives and you know you learn about what's oppressive about it and you sort of think about how not to make it oppressive.

Beth wants the commitment of a long-term relationship, without the oppressive freight of male dominance she associates with marriage and children. Her husband, Adam Harrington, strongly affirms in his statements and behaviors the centrality of equality in their marriage. Yet, his description of cohabitation as a "testing" ground also reflects the strategy of "passing the test." As he puts it, "I was definitely into 'the trial'— an extended period of working things out." Adam credits his parents' divorce for his caution and his more progressive political views, including gender equality. He reasons: "Get divorced. Question authority." The Fenton-Harringtons have essentially "passed the test"; however, they need practice to accompany ideology if they are to sustain their marriage, in spite of labor market limitations they both lament.

Both Adam and Beth acknowledge that job arrangements have not been fully equitable. Beth views the priority given to his job through the lens of her knowledge about social constraints. This helps her to locate the problem outside of the marriage rather than within it: "So we have sort of taken turns, but it does cause problems. I mean if there's any source of inequality I think it's the labor market. I mean there's other sources, it can definitely be in the family, but that's not where it's coming here. It's coming from the outside." Nevertheless, Beth does suggest that if it "went on for a long, long time" it might break the marriage. It probably helps that Adam gives her the gift of recognition; Adam acknowledges that their current work arrangements are "not fair to her." Yet, as the Fenton-Harrington case study implies, an individual's—or a couple's—desire to fuse marriage culture and gender equality is not enough. As Riessman (1990, 215) observed: "Without job parity, equality between women and men in marriage is difficult to sustain, despite the best efforts of individual couples. Ideology is not enough; structural change is necessary, too." Legal, economic, and political obstacles to comparable wages, jobs, and benefits hamper the best of intentions.

The "Marital Work Ethic"

"Hypothetical divorces," "passing the test," and "gender ideology" are important means of coping with marital contingency. However, the most widespread and important strategy for coping with the uncertainty of divorce culture was the "marital work ethic."

The common belief that people do not "try hard enough to make it work" is countered by the belief that, given the ease of divorce, people must work harder on marriages today. As Craig Morris ponders generational change in marriage and divorce since the 1950s, he articulates this tension regarding work in marriage:

> I guess there were a lot of people who were stuck in marriages, and very unhappy at that time, and didn't feel like they had a way out. And yet, on the other hand, um, you look at today and you say ... I think maybe a lot of people are leaving too soon, before they really look for ways to [...] save their marriage. But then again *people are working harder today to save their marriages than ever before.* Um, because you have to work hard to save it 'cause it's so easy to let it slip away, compared to 30 years ago.

Whether or not people are "leaving too soon," or actually "working harder today," nearly every spouse refers to the work entailed in maintaining a marriage.

The "marital work ethic" is the belief that people have to work harder on their marriage than ever before if they want it to last.[7] This "work ethic" came up in a variety of contexts. It was mentioned as the Younger generation described crises when intimacy broke down, lessons learned in trying times, and friends dissolving marriages. The marital work ethic came up as they discussed their previous relationships or marriages, as they described their parents' marriages, as they discussed sex, jobs, parenting, or what advice they would give their children on marriage. Twenty-eight out of thirty-four respondents mentioned the need to work on marriage.[8]

> And it was work. That's the other thing. It meant working really hard at what we had, and if we had something. And I think I took it more seriously than he did. [Pamela Jordan, Euro-American, age 38, married seven years].

> Mostly it involves effort, work, communication and tolerance. [Naomi Rosenberg, Euro-American, age 42, remarried nine years].

To make it work. Maybe that's the largest decision. It's so easy to say, "I quit." It's more difficult to stay and make it work [Rosemary Gilmore, African-American, age 38, married 13 years].

[To] do custodial things, you know, to keep myself in a sound frame of mind. And not go overboard in voicing my way of doing things. Sometimes, you know, it does go overboard and I have to reel that in. Sometimes she'll point those out to me, and sometimes I'm aware of them. And sometimes the kids bring points and stuff up—it's about my being willing to, you know, make those changes necessary to get back on course [Bill Gilmore, African-American, age 39, married 13 years].

The '70s spouses assume that contending with the pull of divorce requires effort. When Iris Sutton asserts that the biggest challenge of her marriage is "probably just staying married," and adds, "I mean there are so many reasons to get divorced, I mean that are very good reasons," she is not saying her marriage is insufferable. Iris is implying that marital endurance requires persistence. When divorce is not an option, staying in a marriage may bring suffering, pleasure, or indifference, but the work is less salient because there is the sense of "no alternative"; in fact, more effort may have been required to leave the marriage in the marital context familiar to the '50s couples. But when the gateway of divorce is readily available and deterrents are fewer, it takes more attentive effort to stay in the marriage, particularly when it is ungratifying. Recall that Kitson and Holmes (1992, 341) found that "relational complaints" are increasingly seen, by the divorced and the married, as legitimate grounds for marital dissolution.

Like the other three strategies, the marital work ethic is a mental and symbolic strategy to cope with the perceived potential of divorce. But the ethic expresses divorce culture not only by assuming marital contingency, but also by assuming that marital endurance is contingent upon a *gratifying* marriage. There are a number of forces that undermine marriages; however, as divorce is increasingly perceived as a gateway (rather than a last resort), marriage must be a gateway as well.

Of course, the '50s spouses also brought up the work of marriage. The implied work made marital endurance an increasing "achievement" and, as we saw, '50s wives in particular were monitoring marriages. In short, the "marital work ethic" is not entirely new with the '70s spouses. But it is more salient. The emergence of divorce culture and the widely shared goals of "growth" and "gratification" have fueled the ethic. Moreover, '70s wives increasingly expect that the work of marriage should be shared.

Marital Work

Despite shared beliefs in a "marital work ethic," more often than not the behavior or the work itself remains women's responsibility. Like the literature documenting women's disproportionate responsibility for family work, my research finds that women are more likely to do or to initiate the work of taking care of the marriage (Blaisure and Allen 1995; DeVault 1987; di Leonardo 1987; Goldscheider and Waite 1991; Hochschild with Machung 1989; Kitson with Holmes 1992; Oliker 1989; Thompson 1991). Marital work entails the conscious "emotion work" of monitoring marriage and communicating about marital well-being in the service of sustaining a gratifying marriage. Through this emotion work, spouses attempt to induce feelings of intimacy, connection, and attunement (Hochschild 1983). The code words of marital work are adjusting, trying, learning, growing, fulfilling needs, caring, and above all, communicating.

Every '70s spouse referred to the importance of "communication" for sustaining a marriage. When I ask Bill Gilmore what advice he would give his children on marriage, he responds: "Communication. Communication. Communication. Communication." If communication was the means of marital work lauded by all—"growth," "intimacy," and "self-development" were the ends mentioned by most. When I ask Lisa Reeves what is good about her marriage, she replies that "there is room for a process of growing, and there is room for freedom." Patrick Reeves states: "We have a sense of union and joy in that union—a feeling of something greater being available through marriage than without it." A language of relationality marks this statement. Yet, Patrick also asserts that to be happily married, you "have to be happy within yourself first." Here, he returns to the vocabulary of individualism. While it is not always clear whether growth precedes or derives from the marriage, self-development, growth, and transformation are apparent goals of marital work as described by the '70s spouses. As we will see in the next chapter, the language of therapeutic culture—both individualistic and relational—is intrinsic to marital work for the '70s couples.

COPING WITH CONTINGENCY: A TOOL KIT OF STRATEGIES

Unlike the Older generation, the Younger generation lives in a social context in which the hegemony of "marriage culture" has lapsed. They sense this. The Younger generation differs from the Older generation by their endless stories of divorce, their divorce anxiety, and their talk of contingency. In addition to this sense of vulnerability fostered by prevalence and contingency, the '70s spouses differ from the '50s spouses by being more likely to support or advocate divorce. Thus, many of them must reconcile their belief in, and support for, divorce with their desire for marital endurance and stability. To contend with this dilemma these spouses have needed and created a new "cultural tool kit."

Divorce culture provides and elicits a tool kit of habits and styles that provide "strategies of action" that are different from those of marriage culture (Swidler 1986). Thus, we see '50s couples increasingly recognizing their "achievement," yet they still largely talk the terms of traditionalism; achievement has the ring of endurance. In contrast, the idea of "working" on one's marriage is pervasive for '70s couples. Given marriage culture's legacy as an "old order," it is resilient and still tends to govern a lot of the minutiae in marriage and divorce. This means we still see '70s men proposing marriage even after extended cohabitation. Or we see spouses surprised by the divorce of friends "made for each other," even though staying married is an increasing surprise. Drawing from Swidler's (1986) analysis of culture, I argue that there is a new cultural repertoire available to '70s spouses; even so, they are "reluctant to abandon familiar strategies of action" (281). Thus we see anxiety, interplay, and contradiction as spouses talk the terms of marriage and divorce cultures today.

The '70s spouses' paradoxical position of supporting, yet mastering, their own vulnerability to divorce is partially resolved by imaginative experiments, such as the "hypothetical divorce," "passing the test," and using "gender ideology" as a protective shield. While these imaginative strategies are prevalent, the most predominant coping strategy is the belief in a "marital work ethic." If the marital work ethic is so pervasive, why have divorce rates remained high? It is important to recall that this sample focuses upon *durable* marriages which, in fact, makes their talk of uncertainty and contingency all the more noteworthy. Moreover, the simple existence of a "marital work ethic" says nothing about the variety of ways that the goals of "growth and happiness" are constituted or achieved.

9   '70s Couples Aim for Relational Equality

THE COMIC STRIP "Cathy" provides a daily slice of popular culture through the story of a white, middle-class, single woman who continually wrestles with the prospect of marriage. The particular strip below captures the way a culture of marriage competes with a culture of divorce and smuggles in gendered stereotypes in the process.[1] Cathy tabulates weddings and points to traditional meanings of marriage, including "commitment," "stability," and "nurturance." Irving's reply, by emphasizing "this season in *real* life," accords divorce a realism denied marriage and points to a competing cultural reality. When Irving comments that the spouses "by all accounts, were as perfectly matched as people can get" he reproduces the new "structure of surprise" around divorce. Divorce cannot be predicted.

Cathy's final retort that "men don't watch enough prime-time," foregrounds the issue of gender already present in the structure of the comic. Cathy, the woman, is associated with a televised fantasy of marriage, while Irving is associated with that "reality" which is divorce. The problematic relation between marriage and divorce is not only constructed as a *gendered* relation, but this relation is situated at the borders of the real and ideal.

cathy®   **by Cathy Guisewite**

At first glance, this association of women with marriage and men with divorce makes some historical sense. Men have been associated with a "flight from commitment" (Ehrenreich 1984). Men have had greater economic freedom to pursue divorce, while women have been in greater need of marriage financially. Moreover, marriage has been represented as a "ball and chain" for men economically and relationally, while women have been represented as pining for marriage emotionally. This is related to the nearly two centuries-old "doctrine of separate spheres," when marriage was women's livelihood and a veritable career for white and middle-class women (Bernard 1981; Dill 1988). Yet, the stereotypes associated with this historical legacy may be changing. The demographer Frances Goldscheider has claimed that "the real revolution" of the last 20 years is "women's growing lack of interest in marriage."[2] Do women and men come to marriage with these stereotyped traits and opposing visions today?

The '70s couples in this chapter—the Clement-Leonettis, the Ellisons, and the Walkers—suggest not. While we live in a time of competing beliefs about marriage and gender, and some of these stereotypes seep through, these couples want a marriage based on relational equality, evincing nurturance, caretaking, and interdependence. Even as they reject the traditionalism of male dominance, they embrace the traditionalism of marriage culture. Despite this embrace, they are vulnerable to divorce. Yet as they "work on" their marriages, we see a stubborn, if subtle, asymmetry between women and men: women seem to be more thoroughly attuned to marital quality.

THE CLEMENT-LEONETTIS: MARITAL WORK THROUGH THERAPY

Dana Clement and Robert Leonetti have been married for 10 years. This is a first marriage for each of them. They are a Euro-American couple struggling to maintain a middle-class lifestyle. Robert works two jobs as a policy analyst and a consultant, while Dana works part-time in a biological laboratory and is the primary parent to their three children. The Clement-Leonetti marriage illustrates how "unexpected divorces" fuel the "marital work ethic." For Robert Leonetti, the first unexpected divorce was that of his parents; for Dana Clement, it was her best friend. Children, homes, and marital length all figure into the unexpected quality of these divorces for Dana. Curiously, the topic arises when I ask Dana "what's good or happy about your marriage?" She replies:

> I think that Robert and I have certain understandings that—I think a big part of what has shaped our marriage and the reason we're still together

and all that is because he comes from a family that is divorced. His parents are divorced. And when my first child was born, my best friend from kindergarten went through a divorce. And I was totally, you know, unaccustomed to divorces in a family. And one of the things that helped us, I think, is that we both shared our feelings about both of those sets of divorces. For me, it was terribly shocking that my friend who had been married 15 years and had two kids, and a car, and a house, and a yard and a dog, and, you know, the whole American picture, to be getting divorced. At that time—this was eight years ago already—we agreed that we would never stay together with one of us unhappy, that if something was going wrong, we would at least have the respect for the other person to tell them what was happening.

Dana begins her response by assuming she should give a *reason* for still being together. When marriage culture prevailed, justifying marital endurance was less necessary. As Dana discusses the array of divorces surrounding Robert and herself, she turns a potential vulnerability to divorce on its head. For Dana, these brushes with divorce have helped them stay together, primarily by informing their strategy for averting divorce. They pledge to share their feelings with one another and keep one another abreast of encroaching unhappiness or doubts. That the goal of marital work is a "gratifying" marriage and not simply an "enduring" one is captured in Dana's statement that "we agreed we would never stay together with one of us unhappy."

In their joint interview, Dana reiterates the shock of her close childhood friend's divorce. She asserts "it did scare" her because it was at a time when Robert and she had just had their first child. In addition to this "unexpected divorce," Dana was anxious because "Robert comes from a family of so many divorces and crummy relationships." And Robert shared these fears. His parents' divorce was unexpected because, according to Robert, they had created "this ideal situation that look[ed] real good on the outside," yet the relationship abruptly disintegrated in later years. He notes, "I was pretty convinced that I didn't want it [my marriage] to go the way my parents' relationship went. I was very active in that." In sum, because Robert's father had sprung his decision to divorce on his mother, and because Dana's friend's divorce was "shocking," Robert and Dana are actively working on their relationship. As in Paul Nakato's account, these "unexpected divorces" elicit greater vigilance and an explicit strategy. To avert an unhappy marriage and subsequent divorce, they "work" at it. But how exactly do they do so?

Part of the "work" is managing emotions and their expression. When I asked Robert about how they have changed over the course of their marriage, he explains that in the early years of their relationship, their

differences were more "pronounced," and there were many more arguments: "I would have a version of what was going on and how she was
feeling about something. And then I'd have my version of how to man-
age that. [. . .] But I guess, it's sort of my imposition of my version of
how we're supposed to resolve things. And then, you know, I'd be
betrayed, and angry, and ready to leave because clearly it wasn't going—
commitment wasn't there—she wasn't going to do it *my way.*"

Initially, Robert admits he wanted to resolve differences "his way."
Over the years their interactional styles shifted. When I ask Robert how
they got through those years of conflict, he begins by laughingly reporting "years of arguing," and then elaborates:

> And we struggled with it. I don't know, maybe we grew up—I grew up, she
> grew up—together. [. . .] And I wasn't, clearly, I really wasn't asking what
> she was feeling, I was just telling her what she was feeling. And *as I watched
> that in myself, and I had to 'cause she forced me to*—and I was also kind
> of growing—[. . .] I was really forced to deal with it. I either had *to deal
> with it or leave.* [A lesson was learned] which is that there are ways that
> are different than what you want, and that I really wasn't . . . I was express-
> ing my own disappointment, my own anger in a way that didn't leave
> enough room for her [emphasis added].

Because Dana "forced" him, Robert learned to monitor himself and the
"imposition" of his "version" of a situation. In other words, he learned
to suppress or redefine his disappointment and anger. More importantly,
he learned to recognize and become attuned to Dana's feelings and to
"leave enough room for her."

At the same time, Dana reports that she was learning that arguing and
yelling did not mean the end of a relationship. Dana explains, "I wasn't
used to anybody arguing with me and then still wanting to ever talk with
me again. [. . .] Every male that I had been involved with and had an argument with—that was the end of the relationship." Dana reports that
Robert would say to her, "I just yelled, that's all there was to it, I was
angry so I yelled." She adjusted over time. Ultimately, she reports that
"Robert accepted my shortcomings and I've accepted his." She discusses
and argues more; he lets go of things more. He reiterates later that he had
to "let go of his version of resolution as right" and remind himself that
"her way of expression was okay and mine was not better." In this way,
he feels he has "grown."

The Clement-Leonettis' ability to share the emotion work of the marriage challenges the stereotype that nurturance is "natural" for women
and beyond men's capacities. Their marital dynamics resemble Blaisure
and Allen's (1995, 13–14) qualitative account of feminist marriages that

practice "reflective assessment" and "emotional involvement." Blaisure and Allen found that within marriages self-identified as feminist, those that evinced equality the most not only criticized gender injustices in society, had husbands who accommodated wives' work, and publicly demonstrated acts of equality such as separate last names, but also were able to jointly monitor respective contributions to the marriage and to verbally communicate about emotional needs and conflict. While I did not specifically ask Robert and Dana if they identified their marriage as "feminist,"—their separate names suggest a level of awareness about the pitfalls of wives merging their identities with those of their husbands. Furthermore, it was clear that their notion of equality included the emotion work of marriage.

If both partners embrace "Cathy's" vision of a nurturing and committed marriage, they also recognize "Irving's" cautions about divorce. In addition to the Clement-Leonettis' pledge to keep one another informed of their feelings about the marriage, Dana contends that her friend's divorce was "one of the reasons I went to therapy at the time I did." She observes that these divorces were "what I talked about a lot." Robert and Dana both portray therapy as part of the work they did, not only to deal with the divorces surrounding them, but to further the relational work in their own marriage. In this marriage, both partners are explicitly aware of the need to do marital work together. By relying upon therapy, they reflect a more widespread, generation-based pattern. Their *mutual* desires and efforts to take care of the marriage are less typical in this sample. However, they embody key facets of marital work through their response to the pull of divorce culture and their aims of growth and happiness.

An Indicator of Marital Work: Couples Therapy

Among the '50s spouses, we saw that "divorce thoughts" served as an indicator of monitoring marriage, and we saw that wives had more divorce thoughts and seemed to be doing more monitoring. Among the '70s spouses, however, divorce thoughts were more widespread and evenly divided—the gender difference was not as notable. Only a few more wives than husbands reported divorce thoughts.

This could be interpreted as a sign of gender convergence in monitoring marriage. And it does seem that '70s husbands are aware of the need to monitor marriage in a way that '50s husbands were not. Yet, it also seems that "divorce thoughts" do not *mean* the same thing for the Younger generation because "divorce actions" are more readily available at earlier stages in the life course. As the marital environment becomes increasingly saturated by divorce, "divorce thoughts" are hard to avoid.

Kitson and Holmes's (1992) research on the married and divorced was not controlled by generation, however. They found that by 1979 "divorce thoughts" were typical.[3] Discussing married persons with "little intention of divorcing," they stated: "As a part of the continual evaluation of the viability of their marriages, apparently virtually all married persons contemplate the consequences of divorce" (86). While divorce is more thinkable among the married, suggestions and initiation of divorce still reveal notable gender differences among the divorced. Kitson and Holmes found in their divorced sample that wives, more than husbands, had thought of divorce and its consequences; and they report on the repeated finding across research projects that women suggest and initiate divorce more than men (92). For the 9 previously married spouses among the 34 '70s spouses, 6 of their divorces were described as initiated by women, 2 were described as mutual, and 1 account was unclear.[4] Looking at the accounts of the nine previously married spouses, as well as current spouses' accounts of marital conflicts, it seems that continued initiation of divorce may reflect, in part, how marital work is still initiated, if not fully performed by wives. As Robert reported, Dana "forced" him to reflect and work on his emotions. This marital work is rooted in therapeutic culture.

In the new marital context, therapy is a more powerful indicator of marital work than thoughts of divorce, simply because so many people have "divorce thoughts." Among the '70s spouses, "couples therapy" serves as a central, though not the sole, indicator of marital work. Comparing the '50s and the '70s couples reflects this turn toward therapeutic culture. Going to couples therapy was more prevalent among the Younger generation than the Older generation. While only 2 of the most troubled couples went to therapy in the Older generation, 7 out of the 17 younger couples had relied upon couples therapy at some point during their relationship—some briefly and some at length.[5] Therapy increasingly provides a context and language for the marital "work" of communicating, learning, and growing—whether the marriage is troubled or not. While couples therapy represents an increasing tendency for the work of marriage to be shared, there were gender differences in attitudes toward therapy.

Although some of the wives criticized or resisted therapy, wives were more likely to advocate therapy, more likely to persuade husbands to go into therapy, and more likely to talk the vocabulary of therapeutic culture, using terms like "the inner child" and "co-dependency." Wives were also much more likely to feel dissatisfied with the quality of communication with their husbands.[6] In contrast, husbands were more likely to refuse, resist, or downplay the role of therapy in their marriage, less likely to talk in terms of an "inner child," and less likely to be dissatisfied with communication in the marriage.

Many of the husbands who had been in couples therapy at some point described a reluctance to participate. One husband notes that "I resisted for awhile" when his wife requested he join her in therapy. Another husband wryly complains, "she dragged me to therapy, you know, with a gun." And another husband remarks, "I never liked going. Never liked therapists, just therapy—bad, bad. [...] There were some things that came out that [helped] ... try to improve my communication skills, you know." In short, husbands were more likely to negatively evaluate or downplay the role of therapy.

Wives, on the other hand, tended to see therapy favorably. For example, Sharon Ellison—now in a 20-year marriage with Andrew—describes how 10 years ago a series of events increasingly threatened the stability of their marriage. First, the inordinate hours of Andrew's work as an attorney took a toll on their marriage. At that time she "thought our marriage was over, 'cause he was a crazy man." Then, their home was stripped and ransacked in a burglary as her husband was contemplating leaving his position as partner in a law firm. Both Andrew and Sharon turned to a therapist to deal with the burglary and the job crisis. Yet, Sharon explains that, at one point in the therapy, she shifted the focus to the marriage and said: "The robbery and the job crisis are no longer the main issues for me; the issue is I'm seeing my marriage as a casualty of this whole thing." More than once, Sharon declares that: "This therapist saved our life." Andrew puts it less dramatically; he found that therapy improved his communication skills—that the "major work of the marriage for me has been figuring out what I feel and then communicating that to Sharon." During the Ellisons' joint interview, as Sharon discusses their friends' unstable marriages, she comments that "it's almost spooky," and confidently asserts that "we're the ones looking good these days."

In short, the Ellisons credit the therapy, along with the resulting job change by Andrew, for the renewed stability of their marriage. But whereas Sharon sees it as saving their marriage, Andrew tends to frame it as simply improving their marriage. If Sharon initiated the marital work and defined the marital threat, ultimately, the stability of the marriage depended upon Andrew's willingness to assume some responsibility for the marital work. Through therapy, Andrew not only became aware of his responsibility for communicating, but also realized that his work in a high-powered law firm was undermining his marriage.

The therapeutic context appears to assist wives in their traditional tasks of monitoring the well-being of a marriage. In some ways, therapy seemed to play the role sociologist Stacey Oliker has accorded wives' best friends. Oliker (1989, 150) describes the talk of best friends as a social context for doing "collaborative marriage work," which tends toward an emphasis on "accommodative and self-changing strategies." The differ-ence between work in therapy and the "collaborative marriage work" of best friends is that the "accommodative and self-changing strategies" are also expected of *men* in couples therapy. Therapists are, in some sense, allies to many women not because they necessarily support their agenda,[7] but because they legitimate women's relational concerns and suggest that men may have to contribute to the emotion work of marriage. In the Ellisons' case, it also served to expose how occupational structures were impinging upon their ability to sustain a satisfying marriage.

The Clement-Leonettis and the Ellisons represent the way in which therapeutic culture can assist, rather than undermine, a marriage by bring-ing "relationality" and "interdependence" into focus. Therapeutic culture can help women redefine marriage by revaluing and redistributing the work of maintaining a marriage. Despite the link between divorce cul-ture and therapeutic culture discussed in Chapter Two, therapeutic cul-ture can serve as a buttress for a redefined marriage culture. And while structural and economic changes will be fundamental to effect a redistri-bution of marital work, on a cultural level therapeutic culture can help in some instances to substantiate the belief that marital work is not women's work alone.

THE "PSYCHO-RELIGIOUS" BLEND OF MARITAL WORK

Of course, therapy proper was only one vehicle and indicator of work-ing on a relationship. Couples therapy is notable because of the propor-tionate increase across generations. However, there were 10 couples in the younger cohort who did *not* avail themselves of couples therapy, but nevertheless talked about the importance of "communication" and "working on" marriages. Among the 10 couples who had never been in couples therapy, there was a tendency to be more religiously active. Five of these couples were religiously committed.[8] While this association sup-ports some scholars' contention that therapeutic culture is displacing the role of religious commitment in family life (Bellah et al. 1985; Rieff 1966; Sennett 1978), there is also evidence that therapeutic culture infuses reli-gious institutions (Bellah et al. 1985; Holifield 1983; Tipton 1982; Yankelovich 1981).

This convergence of the psychological and religious approaches to grappling with the meaning of life has been labeled "psycho-religious" in Simonds' (1992) analysis of one vehicle of therapeutic culture—self-help books. I use the term to refer not only to self-help books, but also to the weave of religious and therapeutic discourses expressed by those spouses who are committed to religious institutions; both discourses share an attempt to provide meaning despite the suffering in life (Gerth and Mills 1946). If religious faith provides ultimate salvation and rectification for unjust suffering, therapeutic language provides a more immediate means to repair and make sense of suffering and sacrifice. With respect to marital work, there are clear benefits and deficits accompanying the appropriation of the "psycho-religious" blend by spouses.

There are some signs that religious commitment accompanied by therapeutic concerns can aid wives in marital work. The religiously committed Walkers, for example, have never been to therapy of any kind, and yet therapeutic culture echoes in their talk of sustaining a marriage. And in line with what we have seen, their pattern reflects the tendency for women to initiate the marital work.

THE WALKERS: MARITAL WORK THROUGH RELIGION

The Walkers are a middle-class, dual-career couple in their first marriage. They are African-American and have two children. The Walkers are both active parents and co-providers. Jane works in middle management in a large corporation; Gordon operates a small business. Gordon asserts, "We entered into our marriage as equals. We're still equals." Indeed, he sees such equal sharing as a tradition for Black families and only a new development in the context of white families.[9] The Walkers are deeply involved in a local Baptist congregation. They report that the theme of their 17-year marriage is "we've come this far by faith." Their faith, however, is complemented, and perhaps reinforced by their "marital work ethic."

When I ask Jane Walker how she would account for all the divorce today, she replies in terms of her own marriage: "I think just keeping on top of everything. Making sure that we're in touch with each other. I still think communication is a huge factor." Her husband, Gordon Walker agrees. As he discusses how good their marriage is, he says:

> I think we both recognize—I'm pretty sure she'd tell you the same thing—
> *we worked at it.* We understand that you just don't: "okay, we love each
> other, we got married, okay, fine that's it, let's go on." Because if you are
> an individual who is *growing,* you change. And if you care about the rela-
> tionship that you're in, you're *constantly communicating* with your mate
> so that they *adjust* with you. Or if the adjustments are uncomfortable, you
> are *aware* of those changes, and you make them fit if you're concerned
> about the relationship [emphasis added].

In this passage, Gordon articulates the themes that arise in numerous interviews. Growth requires work. And work entails being aware of, adjusting to and constantly communicating with one's spouse.

The Walker's marriage was among the most gratifying marriages I witnessed. However, they too have had to contend with challenges to their marriage. After a decade of marriage, one spouse lost a parent to death and the other lost a close sister within a month's time. Jane describes this time as the "low point" in their marriage and tries to capture the estrangement in the months to follow when she says: "It's like we were going out, and we realized that something's not right here, and we came back in again." When I ask her how they realized it was "not right" and moved to make it right, she relates: "It seems like we just lost a closeness. We weren't communicating. I guess I wasn't really expressing my feelings. He wasn't expressing his. It just seems like the door was closing, like he's closing out, and I realized that—and he realized that as well—*but he wouldn't identify it as much as I would,* and say: 'Something's really wrong here. You have to let me in. You have to go down this road together.'"

Gordon describes this period of estrangement, following the death of a parent and sister, as a "drift" and explains:

> They were our rudders, and they were gone. And we just kind of drifted for awhile. Jane was real quiet. I was real quiet. And the marriage was quietly falling apart. And one night, Jane said—*she recognized it, I guess more than I did*—and she said "something's happening to us, and we need to straighten it out." So we began—I think I said earlier, "you have to work on your marriage" [KH: Right.]—we began to find new rudders. My new rudder is Jane, and Jane's rudder is Gordon. From that point, the marriage—it was already strong, but it went from being strong to totally and completely unbreakable. [...] Had it gone another couple of months, *we probably would have broken up, and we never would have known why.*

Both spouses imply that the marriage was faltering at this time and required work and monitoring to recapture "closeness" and a stability with "new rudders." When I ask how they went about working on their relationship and whether they availed themselves of therapy, Gordon states that they did not go to therapy, rather "Gordon talked to Jane, and Jane talked to Gordon and then both of us talked to the Lord." Gordon asserts that now their marriage is "completely unbreakable." In fact, despite the suggestion of an imminent divorce during their troubled times, he is one of only four respondents within the entire marital cohort who respond "death" (or "nothing") when I ask what would break their marriage, reflecting a firm belief in "marriage as forever." Furthermore, he reiterates the biblical injunction that what God has joined, no person "should put asunder."

The Walkers' accounts illustrate how marriage can "become forever" through the "marital work ethic." For them, like the Ellisons, the relational work of monitoring and communicating served to avert a divorce that "might have been," according to Gordon. And the Walkers illustrate two additional points. First, religious commitment and therapeutic culture are not mutually exclusive systems of meaning. Their shared religious commitment is clearly a primary pillar of their marriage—a pillar that has a social as well as an ideological base: they do not simply espouse a Christian faith; they are actively involved in the community of their congregation.[10] Second, as both spouses attest, Jane initiated the marital caretaking. Just as Dana Clement enlisted Robert in the marital work, Jane found a receptive and responsive spouse in her husband, Gordon. During the Walkers' crisis, marital work conforms to the pattern of women being responsible for the well-being of the marriage. However, in every other way—providing, parenting, and decision making—they model relational equality.

AN EQUALITY OF CARETAKING

Because the *ends* of marital work are growth and happiness, and the *means* of this work is communication, the marital work is, above all, informed by therapeutic culture. As many social scientists have observed, the number of therapists and the types of therapeutic services and therapeutic materials have multiplied in the last few decades (Bellah et al. 1985; Cancian 1987; Simonds 1992; Skolnick 1991).[11] Beyond therapy, television talk shows, magazine articles, advice books, 12-step programs, and even religious groups have become conduits for therapeutic culture. More abstractly, therapeutic culture refers to the evolving world view that accords psychology a place of primacy in defining the meaning of self and relationships.[12] It connotes a heightened emphasis on the awareness of feelings, self-development, and expressiveness in relationships.

Therapeutic culture has been variously characterized as the "democratization of personhood" (Clecak 1983), as "ascetic in its demands" (Bellah et al. 1985), and as "self-indulgent" (Lasch 1979). These diverse analyses reflect social analysts' interpretations of the meaning and weight accorded to individualism by therapeutic culture. Although it has been variously applauded, critiqued, or denounced for advancing individualism, it is widely agreed that therapeutic culture represents an increasing focus on the expressive quality of interpersonal relationships as well.

Family scholars have recognized that self-expression, intimacy, and flexible roles are central to marital relations today and that they remain in tension with traditional cultural values of self-sacrifice, obligation, and commitment (Bellah et al. 1985; Cancian 1987; Hochschild with Machung 1989; M. Johnson 1988; Skolnick 1991; Swidler 1986). Cancian (1987,

40) spoke to this tension when she argued that the increased weight given to self-development in the past two decades is manifest in two marital blueprints with different implications. Self-development can be understood as a precondition to a love relationship, which she calls an "independence blueprint." Or, alternatively, love can be seen as a precondition to self-development, which she calls the "interdependence blueprint." In short, self-development can result in a myopic focus on individual choices or, within the interdependence blueprint, it can mean a mutual sensitivity that deepens commitment.

My research suggests that spouses can appropriate therapeutic culture as a "language of individualism" stressing independence or as a language of "relationality" emphasizing interdependence. The language of individualism would seem to give priority to individual needs, feelings, and choices, over and above connections and commitments to others. Mia Turner spoke this language, for example, when she asserted that in her former marriage she "wasn't afforded" the opportunity to be "independent" or "know herself" and always considered her husband first. In her remarriage to Nick she asserted: "I also think of myself—I would say first—what is good for me and I know that if I make that decision that it'll fit right in with whatever it is that we're doing." In short, she talks in terms of the primacy of her individual needs. On the other hand, a language of relationality, also characterizing therapeutic culture, emphasizes that individual identity and self-development are grounded in and dependent upon connections and commitments to others. We heard the language of "relationality" when Patrick Reeves stated: "we have a sense of union and joy in that union—a feeling of something greater being available through marriage than without it." Similarly, we hear relational language when the '70s wife Anita Weiss discussed how she would be disappointed if her children did not eventually marry because "you're able to blossom" within marriage and family.

Yet, often a single spouse talks a language of individualism as well as one of relationality. While the distinction between the blueprints of independent individualism and interdependent relationality can be analytically neat, I saw ambiguity when assessing whether spouses manifested either pattern. When Robert Leonetti relates that he and Dana have been happy in their marriage because they "make these commitments to choices together," is he speaking the language of individualistic choices or committed relationality? Is Gordon Walker only speaking a relational language when he says, "if you are an individual who is growing, you change [. . .] and if you care about the relationship that you're in, you're constantly communicating . . ."? Whether self-development comes before or through the relationship, what is *un*ambiguous is that self-development is a central theme in the '70s spouses' marital work and that development within marriage requires communication.

Communication need not indicate marital work. After all, communication has always been central to any relationship. Yet, often divorce is a backdrop for spouses' talk about communication. Today, spouses assume that a reflexive interchange of thoughts and feelings is a condition for marital endurance. Therapy has undeniably been a middle-class phenomenon. Therapy is an "indulgence" requiring time and money; however, therapeutic culture represents the "reflexivity" required in modern institutions, including the institution of marriage, under conditions of uncertainty and rapid social change (Giddens 1991, 180). The '70s spouses' assumption that partners must be reflexive about relational commitments is a sign that the reach of therapeutic culture is more extensive. The cross-class reach of therapeutic culture is indicated not only by its popularity on television talk shows such as "Oprah" and best-selling advice books, but also through its integration into religious and legal institutions.[13]

One of the conditions of the newly introduced "covenant marriages" in some state laws is premarital therapy (secular or religious). Although many people object to a legal requirement for therapy, there are few who would object to the idea of communicating through a facilitator before marriage. Premarital therapy aims to avert a bad marriage and subsequent divorce; furthermore, it presumes that communication is central to the foundation of a lifelong marriage. This suggests, further, how therapeutic culture is increasingly a tool for marriage culture. From one point of view, the thread of lifelong commitment is flimsily secured by therapeutic culture because it rests upon the very assumption that undermined marriage culture in the first place: an individual's expressive self-fulfillment. From another point of view, therapeutic culture can provide one important, reflexive means toward marital communication and interaction that can effect relational equality in marriage.

The spouses in this chapter are neither cynical nor romantic idealists, but "realistic." The Clement-Leonettis and the Walkers challenge the gender stereotypes advanced by the "Cathy" comic; both women and men in these marriages want "renewed commitment to deep, stable, nurturing, long-term relationships." Men in these marriages do not see their relationships as a "ball and chain" and are willing to grapple with issues of dominance or emotional distance. The couples in this chapter are models of a redefined marriage culture—one that is not hard-wired to male dominance. Their efforts advance the notion that care is people's work and to be valued. An equality of caretaking, which includes the self and other in the compass of care,[14] implies that partners must expect marital work from each other—it is only fair.[15] Indeed, to view care as people's work is not only to challenge male dominance but also to reconstruct polarized conceptions of masculinity and femininity. Neither wives nor husbands need be shackled by gendered prescriptions that insist upon preset difference. This does not mean that gender equality is reduced to uniformity or sameness; rather, redefining marital commitment in terms of relational equality requires a recognition of one another that insists upon attunement to specificity and diversity (Scott 1986). Spouses in such marriages are free to forge particular, rather than gender-determined, commitments.

Nevertheless, like '50s wives, these '70s women still seem to initiate the marital work, their husbands' receptivity notwithstanding. Duncombe and Marsden (1993, 237) suggested that "women's demands for the emotional reciprocity of intimacy may be seen as the next frontier of the battle for gender equality." Moreover, to the degree that spouses still see marital work as "women's work," we can presume that the transition to gender equality is still underway in U.S. society.

10 The '70s Greens

Traditionalism in the 1990s

IN SPITE OF the challenges and changes represented by divorce culture and gender equality, traditionalism is alive and well in the 1990s. "Traditional," as I have used the term, refers to spouses who embrace not only the ideals of marriage culture, but also male authority. The '50s traditionalists never felt the need to defend their beliefs—even after the 1970s watershed of gender and marital change. For the Older generation, the process of defending one's ideals and practices from widespread social influences was more pertinent for the "divorcee," the "egalitarian" or the "single mother." However, the '70s traditionalists have not only experienced a society marked by growing demands for gender equality in the public sphere, but also one in which marital arrangements have been increasingly de-gendered, and divorce and cohabitation have been destigmatized.

How does the social context for the traditionalist marriage in the 1990s compare to that of the '50s? How are today's traditionalist spouses responding to the pull of divorce culture? Are they on the defensive? Are traditionalist husbands more concerned with keeping promises or keeping power? What are the implications of contested gender and marital beliefs for traditionalist wives? Even though no marital ideology or practice prevails at this time, the talk of these traditionalists indicates that they perceive themselves to be a minority. Traditionalists sense that marriage culture and male authority are no longer all-pervasive.

TRADITIONALISTS: A NEW CONTEXT

As we saw in Chapter Two, since the 1970s, economic, institutional, and legal developments have dramatically changed the social context of "traditionalism." The indicators of the decline of the "male provider role" discussed by Bernard (1981) continue unabated.[1] Above all, the ability of families to secure a "male family wage" has diminished and moved up the class ladder. For the '50s traditionalists, a belief in male breadwinning was more directly supported by a manufacturing economy, government programs and subsidies, and the law (Coontz 1992). For the '70s traditionalists, a belief in male breadwinning is harder to sustain in a service economy that pays lower wages and has yet to be widely unionized. Also, traditionalists have not felt supported by family law since the introduction of no-fault divorce in the 1970s. Reflecting cultural changes, no-fault divorce "redefined marriage as a time-limited, contingent arrangement" (Weitzman 1985, 368). This is the language of divorce culture and is not the language of the traditionalists. One can sense that some '70s traditionalists feel compelled to defend their ideals.

In recent years, traditionalists have not only been on the defensive, but have also taken the offensive by advancing laws to promote their language and views. As we have seen, Louisiana in 1997 and Arizona in 1998 instituted "covenant marriage," and a number of other states have introduced similar legislation. These laws add a covenant marriage option to the no-fault format. Individuals who select covenant marriage must undergo premarital counseling and abide by a waiting period should they desire divorce, and the terms of divorces must meet strict legal grounds (*San Francisco Examiner,* November 23, 1997). This is the language of marriage culture: marriage is forever and divorce is a last resort.[2] While the law is gender-neutral in wording, like no-fault divorce, this law has potential for gendered consequences.

Recent men's movements suggest that traditionalists are on the offensive to sustain male authority as well as marriage culture. The Promise Keepers—an organization of primarily white, middle-class, Christian men who uphold a view of masculinity based upon heterosexuality, family responsibility, and leadership—began a rise to prominence in 1990. Their membership had skyrocketed by 1997, when they marched on the nation's capital. The Promise Keepers argue that men must take more responsibility for their families. This is good news for many women who have been carrying the burden of maintaining families—rearing children without the economic or social support of fathers (Arendell 1986, 1995; Kurz 1995). By emphasizing responsibility, the movement advances marriage culture, wherein spouses are expected to keep their promises or commitments "forever." However, the movement is also bad news for women because masculine responsibility has been linked with male authority. A content analysis of writings by men in the movement, for example, revealed that a major theme is a "natural hierarchy of authority" (from God to husband to wife and children), reflecting a "degradation of egalitarianism" (Beal and Gray 1995 cited in Messner 1997, 32). Tony Evans, a leader of the Promise Keepers, argued: "I'm not suggesting that you *ask* for your role back, I'm urging you to *take it back.* . . . There can be no compromise here. If you're going to lead, you must lead. Be sensitive. Listen. Treat the lady gently and lovingly. But *lead!*" (cited in Messner 1997,

32). Through their constituencies and goals, the Promise Keepers represent what has been the prevailing or dominant ideal of masculinity in U.S. society: the white, heterosexual, professional breadwinner who is superordinate not only to women and children but to alternative and marginal masculinities (Connell 1987). Even though some Promise Keepers do not advocate male authority, the movement suggests that it is extremely difficult to sever the promotion of male commitment from the promotion of male authority.

The Million Man March on Washington, D.C. in 1995 reflected overlapping, yet distinctive, concerns about masculinity. The event, launched by Louis Farrakhan on behalf of the Nation of Islam, was constituted by African-American men concerned about racism, economic decline, social justice, and the social assault on young African-American men. The Million Man March participants and the Promise Keepers are similar in that both are "spiritually based movements that are calling on men to stop their self-destructiveness, stop their violence, and bond together with other men to retake responsibility for caring for and leading their families, their communities, and their nations" (Messner 1997, 92). However, the aim to "retake responsibility for caring for and leading their families" produces different meanings for African-American men than for the predominantly white Promise Keepers. For example, wholesale discrimination has prevented many African-American men from adopting the male provider role and enjoying its associated privileges; thus, whether such privileges are withheld or denied reflects racial and not just gender inequality. Still, calls for male leadership in the Black community are troublesome to some African-American women and men. As a result, the mission statement of the Million Man March straddled the conservative language of roles and the progressive language of equality; it called for Black men to assume a "new and expanded responsibility without denying or minimizing the equal rights, role, and responsibility of Black women in the life and struggle of our people" (Karenga 1995 cited in Messner 1997, 70). While the gender politics of the men in the March varied, the organization of the event symbolically supported a traditional public-private split; men actively testified in public while women observed a "Day of Absence" at home (Messner 1997, 71).

Another public call for traditionalism issued from the Southern Baptists in June 1998, when the church approved an amendment to the Baptist Faith and Message that called for husbands' leadership in an era of a "crisis in the family." On the basis of literal interpretations of a number of biblical passages, the amendment asserts that "marriage is the uniting of one man and one woman"; that "a husband is responsible for leading, protecting, and providing for his family"; and that a wife is to "submit graciously to the servant leadership of her husband" (*The Arizona Republic,* June 10, 1998). Again, this view was contested by some Southern Baptists—members who reject literal and selective interpretations of the Bible and emphasize "mutual" submission between husband and wife.

The Southern Baptists' assertions, the covenant marriage laws, and the men's movements of the 1990s are various attempts to invigorate traditional ideals.[3] Some of the '70s couples reflect the endurance of traditionalist beliefs in spite of beliefs in divorce culture and gender equality. The proportion of spouses who are traditionalist is smaller than it is in the Older generation. Only 3 of the 17 couples (the Woodards, the Greens, and the Weisses) advance traditionalism as a couple.[4] Most traditionalists in this study are Euro-American—though one Asian-American wife is traditional, as we will see in the next chapter. While studies show that traditionalism endures across all class strata, it is probably no accident that these '70s traditionalists enjoy an upper-middle-class income, given that it takes considerable income to practice a belief in male breadwinning today. The '70s traditionalists are also more likely than other '70s couples to depend on religious communities to support their belief in "marriage as forever" and, to some degree, their belief in male authority. The Greens' interviews reveal the dynamics behind the beliefs in male authority and marriage culture today.

THE GREENS: TRADITIONALISM IN THE 1990S

Married for 17 years and parents of three children, the Euro-American Greens live in an exclusive suburb of the San Francisco Bay Area. They are too conscious of the competing ideals of divorce culture and gender equality to "pass" for a typical '50s couple. But Dan and Judy Green disapprove of divorce for "trivial" purposes and advocate staying together for the children—at least until the children are 18—a qualification that reflects the rise of divorce culture. They are active Catholics and are raising their children accordingly. In brief, the Greens support the ideal of "marriage as forever," perceive their gendered division of labor as "separate but equal," and are religiously committed.

While Dan Green's father prospered over a number of decades, Dan had surpassed his father's standard of living by his thirties. He acquired an advanced degree, but his frustration with "liberal" academics steered him toward the banking industry, where he has been successful and has found support for his traditional ideals. The Greens' upper-middle-class status is evinced not only by their educational background, his earning power, and her full-time homemaking, but is displayed by their antique furnishings, their spectacular view of the Bay, the gardener who prunes their trees, and the nannies who travel with them during vacations. Their marital ideals are upheld and enabled by the solid bedrock of their class status.

The Greens' neighborhood and religious communities reinforce the normative model of staying together in a male-dominated marriage, and their interviews suggest that they insulate themselves against the marital *Zeitgeist* of the times. Yet, there are limits to such insulation. Like most couples in the Younger generation, the Greens have witnessed the divorces of their own friends and relatives. And like the Weisses, one of the Greens' children has appealed: "I don't want you to get divorced." This plea, according to the Greens, does not derive from intense arguments between them but, rather, emanates from their child's best friend, who experienced parental divorce. Describing her sister's marriage to a divorced man, Judy Green remarks that it is her sister's first marriage "so far." Since her sister is having a baby now, Judy thinks the marriage is "good for at least another five years." When I ask if the pregnancy has saved the marriage, she replies, "Well, [it] extended it." Thus, even as the Greens uphold traditional marital and gender ideals, they also reiterate and reproduce the contingent quality of divorce culture.

Dan Green: A Gender Deal

At the beginning of his interview, I ask Dan to compare the meaning of marriage in his parents' generation with its meaning in his own generation. He promptly addresses gender relations. His account of changing marital patterns is woven into his account of changing gender relations. He does not immediately inform me of his parents' separation; rather, he asserts that "my parents' view of marriage changed very dramatically over time." He partly attributes this "changed view" to his father's injury in a car accident, which subsequently limited his father's mobility. This meant that "the relative responsibilities changed" for his parents. He also implicitly attributes his mother's change to the women's movement. He observes that his mother changed "in her attitude" in later years as the "whole idea of how women viewed themselves changed." This, in tandem with his father's accident, meant that "she had a different power and leverage relationship with him than she might normally have had."

Dan proceeds directly to contrast Judy's social context to that of his mother's era. He begins by portraying Judy as more modern than his mother was early on in her life course:

> And Judy's gone through and lived through the uh . . . the best and the worst of the change in how women view themselves. Not that she's adopted them.

But uh ... they're out there to be looked at. [...] It's a different mindset. And she has ... I think very fortunately for me at least, I think for her too, she hasn't adopted it. She's not ... she has no particular sympathy toward—I won't say "feminism," I'm not sure what that means anymore, I think the word's been hijacked by some lunatics—but in terms of the earlier version of feminism, if you like, you know, *equal opportunity,* things like that—that's part of her being in a way that probably wasn't part of my mom's ... at the beginning. And she doesn't think anything strange— it's not unusual for women to be working and take care of themselves and that sort of thing.

While describing his wife, Dan reveals disrespect for feminism—a disrespect that, according to his wife, might be more accurately depicted as "hatred of feminists." However that may be, Dan echoes a compromise made by the older cohort regarding the changes in women's status: equality is implicitly located in the opportunity of the public sphere and distanced from the concerns of the private sphere. However, the very arrangements that would enable the attainment of equality in the public sphere—the social or parental sharing of child rearing—are implicitly rejected.[5]

Unlike the '50s spouses, Dan acknowledges that their own gendered arrangements are their "choice." He cannot avoid the reality that the majority of married mothers work. By 1994, 69 percent of married mothers with children under the age of seventeen worked for pay—a substantial contrast to the 12.6 percent who did so in 1950 (Hochschild 1997, 6). After noting that Judy does not think it strange that women are working for pay, he continues: "Now that's not the role she wants and that's not the role she and I—we're probably more, closer to the way my parents thought they were when they started out because her job's taking care of the children and my job is to make money, in that we have that unit and that's a division of responsibility that seems to work pretty well for us." Dan's conclusion that his current arrangement with Judy is similar to "the way my parents *thought* they were when they started out" suggests that his parents were not really that way.

When I ask for clarification of what he means by "the way my parents thought they were when they started out," he perceptively suggests that a traditional division of labor represented how his parents thought— "without knowing they were thinking about it that way, because I don't think there was any alternative model." The absence of "an alternative model" for his parents, the change in his mother's power, and his parents' subsequent and temporary separation all seem to contribute to the unsettled quality of his parents' gender arrangements. He never directly blames his mother's increasing power in her marriage for the marital separation and instability—after all, his father's accident was no one's fault—but he implies as much.

Dan asserts that, unlike his parents, Judy and himself entered their marriage with an explicit awareness and agreement that it would be traditional in regard to gender. If Dan's parents' initial arrangement was implicit, perhaps his own overt agreement will avert the instability that plagued his parents' marriage. While the strategy of viewing gender ideology as insurance against divorce was widespread among '70s couples,[6] traditionalists were fewer in number. The idea that gender ideology can help to secure one's marriage suggests that spouses interpret gender as central to marital (in)stability and endurance.

The Greens' marital ideal rejects feminist marital models and other alternatives that are more prevalent in society and represented in the media by the 1990s. When I ask Dan to elaborate on how the changes in women have impacted his own and other marriages today, Dan reports that he and Judy have a marital "deal" that repudiates the models represented by the likes of "Murphy Brown." He describes the difficulty of contending with these competing family ideals in today's social context:

> I think from time to time it is difficult to . . . have a particular role model held up in the media as ideal, when in fact it doesn't, it's not . . . it's not workable with the personalities involved. In other words, if Judy came in one day and said "Look, I'm going to work 12 hours a day, I'm going back to be a lawyer, and I'm going back this, and I'm putting the kids in child care all day, every day, and that's the way it's going to be," that would not be acceptable. That's a role model, but that's not one that we bargained for. That's not the deal we made. You can always get out of a deal, but that's not the deal. And, and I don't make a value judgment for other people, it just wouldn't work for me. That's not what I want in a wife.

Most important to note here is that Dan attaches conditions to "marriage as forever": if Judy decided to pursue a full-time career, she would threaten the "deal" and no longer conform to what he wants "in a wife."

When I ask if these broader gender changes "insinuate" themselves into "the interior of his marriage," Dan replies: "Yeah, from time to time it does because you can't escape it. [. . .] Insinuate's a good word. Insidious is another good word. [. . .] I've seen it with other people where I think it's very destructive of relationships." I ask about how gender changes have been destructive for others' relationships. He does not describe these "other people," but he does reveal yet another strategy taken by traditionalists: "Friends that have had marital problems from time to time. I think um . . . the happiest, the, you know, we don't—we live in an area where people are *families*. And when they're not families, they sort of disappear. Because they can't afford—you know, one half or the other can't usually afford to stay here. [...] But in terms of uh ... it is, *in this particular area the ideal is to be the mom raising children*—not to get [a job], not to be a working mom." Dan implies that divorced parents and their children are not "families." More important, Dan indicates how the insularity of upper-middle-class and upper-class communities functions to preserve role-differentiated gender ideals. While he admits the replacement of divorced families by remarried families is a bit "phony," it is clear that the reproduction of gender-traditional marriages is enabled by the intersection of class and gender interests.[7] Communities segregated by race and class—in this case, white and upper-middle class—can function to insulate and resist the sometimes threatening models manifest in other communities and the mass media.[8]

Judy Green: Balancing Family Needs

Judy Green believes in the ideals of marriage culture. In her individual interview she asserts: "I think of marriage as being eternal. It's probably the only—*the* stable force." When I ask Judy if she thinks it means the same thing to be married today as it did in her parents' generation, she responds by addressing their division of labor by gender:

> I would typify our marriage as being very traditional. I am not working and I think that's a function of that I don't need to work. It's also a function of our desire [for] bringing up the kids in a traditional household where I am home for them, able to help them with homework, get them to after school activities, to manage them, really. On the other hand, I have been able to have some freedoms of my own that are probably not traditional. Every so often I take a long weekend and go to a spa resort alone or with a friend. [...] So the fact that he was open enough *to allow me* to take some time off on my own [is not traditional] [emphasis added].

Here Judy employs the term "traditional" to describe their role-differentiated marriage—though she uses it in other contexts to describe enduring, rather than dissolved, marriages. The malleability of this term functions to link the conceptually distinct domains of gender and marriage politics. She recognizes that their class status underlies their traditional arrangements when she says, "I don't need to work." But she goes on to attach values—their child-centered "desires"—to the practice of traditional homemaking. When she notes that Dan "allows" her to take off once a year, her words imply that freedom is not traditional for wives and acknowledge Dan's authority over her. Dan is "open" compared to men of the Older generation. Among the '50s couples, many spouses simply assumed that wives could not take off for recreation with buddies like husbands could. Nevertheless, the weight of male dominance can be felt in Judy's assumption that Dan could veto her activities if he so desired.

When I ask Judy if one spouse dominates, she does not assert that he is the "head of the household" with the vigor of the Older generation. Instead, she describes fluctuation and a division of "realm": "It shifts from time to time. There are times when I would say Dan is much more dominant and me submissive, on the other hand, there are times . . . when I'm, when I'm stronger and I make decisions about where we should live—what house, what school, those kind of things are mostly my realm." Judy almost gives the impression that dominance-subordination are "half and half"—perhaps because of the growing validation accorded egalitarianism. It is also clear that "much more dominant," which she uses to describe Dan and "stronger," which she uses to describe herself, are not equivalent terms. And, as many family scholars have pointed out, the division of realms—home and school versus the public and economic realm—are not domains of equal power (Thorne with Yalom 1982).

But then Judy wanted to avoid a female-dominated marriage, and this seems to shape her ideas about egalitarian marriages. She describes her parents' marriage as "nontraditional" and "unhappy" because her mother dominated her father and her father was a "wimp." She explains that this influenced her own choice of spouses and her marriage and then claims: "My husband is a much stronger—I think I chose someone who was stronger than I, and more the leader. He was more knowledgeable about the world than my father." Like Dan, Judy reasons that it was the "nontraditional" arrangements of her parents that destabilized their marriage. Conversely, she implies that her "informed choice" of traditional roles may avert unhappiness and divorce.

Interestingly, like many egalitarian wives, Judy was initially disappointed that Dan was not more involved with child rearing. She liked the fact that her "wimpy" father was nurturing toward children. She came to the marriage expecting Dan to be more involved:

> [Dan] wasn't expecting that. And so then he said . . . you know, we just sort of realized each other's expectations and [pause] and, you know, it's very difficult being a single parent and doing all the work yourself, so, we would either have a live-in nanny, or when we traveled we would take a nanny with us. So that relieved my stress [. . .] So, consequently it worked out. I wasn't bitter to him for not changing diapers because there was someone else helping me.

Judy describes a joint realization of mismatched expectations. She pauses, solicits a shared understanding ("you know"), and then describes the difficulties of being a "single parent."[9] Like other '70s mothers, Judy draws on the term "single parent" as a metaphor to describe how she *felt* at that time.[10] She might have become "bitter" if he had not provided for paid help. As other analysts have observed, class-based resources, rather than Dan's compromises, deflected conflicts over the "second shift" and the emotional consequences of those conflicts (Hochschild with Machung 1989; Ostrander 1984; Rollins 1985). Further, although Judy prefers her father's nurturance of children to Dan's authoritarian distance from the children, she does not explicitly link the limited nurturance to constructions of masculine power.

Dan's authority is confirmed throughout the interviews. They go to the church he prefers; they buy a mountain cabin he wanted, and they move when his career demands. Judy adapts to his agenda. When I ask them each to describe the biggest compromise of their marriage, it is clear who heads the household. Dan replies, "I don't think I've really compromised in her direction," and then states that Judy's compromise has been geographic relocation. Judy affirms this compromise and mentions another: his insistence that they raise the children Catholic.

To describe the Greens' marriage as male-dominated is not to say that Judy wields no power at all, but it is the limited power of the subordinate party. At one point, the Greens lived in Los Angeles and faced a decision about career options and an inevitable move. When I ask Judy how she successfully persuaded Dan to refuse a career opportunity in India and move back to the Bay Area, she describes two strategies. First, she says: "passive resistance," then she illustrates an appeal to the needs of the children. She mimics herself as she describes her strategies for encouraging the move:

> "Yes dear, anything you want, I understand, it's for your career" and then the lower lip comes out. It's a very hard line to, to walk along—what's best for you, what's best for the family, what's best for your husband. And it's very difficult to weigh and I'm very much a balancer. So much of my life is, is trying to keep those balanced. [. . .] I just had such a strong emotional gut feeling that moving to India would be to the detriment of the kids. It would be fine for me because I've moved so many times that I've become very adaptable. I could live in India. But I really didn't think that it be suitable for the kids or their contact with their grandparents. So I felt very strongly. . . .

Judy employs "passive resistance" as a wife, but it was most likely her advocacy as a mother that enabled her to prevail in this case. While she has "become very adaptable" as a wife, she draws on her genuine relational concerns for her children's stability to legitimate her resistance to a distant move. She reflects Miriam Johnson's analysis that "women are strong as mothers but made weak by being wives" (1988, 269).

Judy describes her role as the "balancer." Like many wives, she absorbs the conflicts between family members' needs, and between work and family (Degler 1980; Ferree 1990; Thorne with Yalom 1982). One formula that Judy relies upon when potential conflicts arise resonates with the reasoning of therapeutic culture: "If I'm happy, then the kids will be happy, then the family will be happy."[11] For Judy, "happy" is imbued with the conditions of being a mother, that is, her happiness and her children's happiness are interdependent. Yet, "happy" is also delimited and even contradicted by the context of being a wife. Asked what she would have done if Dan had insisted upon the move, she states unambivalently: "I would have gone." If Dan had insisted, the formula linking the happiness of children and mothers suggests that neither she nor her children would have been happy.

Given their wealth and despite his dominance, when I ask Judy if their arrangement feels "fair," Judy responds, "Oh, I think I have the better deal."[12] Later on, she elaborates on and then grounds her marital satisfaction in their financial resources: "I think reality was far greater than my expectations just because of our financial security enabled us to make motherhood easier and purely a relaxed ... I don't know, comfortable, by being able to afford baby sitters, we have been able to either get out, so I could come back refreshed ... I mean we were very, absolutely centered on the babies—attention wise." Most women can only dream of an experience of motherhood described as "purely relaxed"—a relaxation that overcomes the "time bind" and is based on extraordinary financial security (Hochschild 1997). Under such optimal conditions, it is no wonder that Judy embraces traditionalism. Ostrander (1984, 152) found that married mothers of the upper class tend to reproduce traditional gender practices despite "strains and contradictions." She suggests they will continue to do so "in part because the gains of *gender* equality would not be enough to balance the losses of *class* equality." Ostrander's study suggests that if upper-class wives directly challenge male dominance, they risk their class and marital status.

Shared Traditionalism and Divergent Conceptions of Relationship

The Greens share the "traditionalisms" of marriage culture and male dominance. Despite the explicit convergence of their ideologies, a divergence in their conceptions of relationship arises when I separately ask Judy and Dan what would break their marriage. Initially, Judy responds: "Probably infidelity."[13] Then she digresses to explain both her lack of opportunity and interest in pursuing an affair: "Well being a housewife you don't see a whole lot of men to begin with. Secondly ... secondly, I have come to the conclusion that *women often make better companions anyway*. As I get older . . . I don't know, I, I don't know—if my husband heard this he would absolutely cringe—but he has an absolute hatred of feminists. And yet, in this day and age *it's difficult not to be influenced, but* . . . I don't know, I've come to respect women a great deal more than men." Here, Judy ventures to challenge their seemingly shared gender ideology; the risk entailed in this challenge is represented by "I don't knows" in triplicate. She does not identify as a feminist, but admits the influence of feminism upon her and implies that it has increased her respect for women. Yet, when I inquire how that increased respect for women has come about, she relies neither on her lived experience nor on a social explanation (e.g., feminism); rather, she resorts to a biological explanation (i.e., hormones): "Well, I just think it's sort of a *natural order* that I see men as, as—well as *being like children*. That they have these hormones and they have to go out and conquer [I laugh], and ambitious and . . . they're just little boys. I don't know, I guess—I go for hikes with female friends and [. . .] *we can just talk about a great deal more and understand and have a more communal agreement*" (emphasis added). Since power is withheld from the wife role by definition, Judy appropriates a natural maternal identity to counter male dominance. This view of men "as being like children" is actually a conventional response for the subordinated wife (Dinnerstein 1976; Rubin 1983, 126). On the one hand, this response represents an awareness of male dependence; it can be understood as a defensive response for wives who are "juvenilized" vis-à-vis their husbands (M. Johnson 1988, 269). On the other hand, this view advances a rift that reproduces gender inequality: men are "ambitious conquerors," driven by hormones and cut off from relational understanding, and women are communal cooperators, cut off from independent assertion.[14] By relying on notions of the "natural order" and "hormones," Judy reinforces the impossibility of men and women ever finding common ground; "naturalizing" suggests immutability and a powerlessness to change the situation.

Yet, as Judy's description of female friendships implies, her ideal relationship is neither to be an object of other women's power nor to exercise power over other women; rather, she seeks and garners talk, understanding, and "a more communal agreement" from women. This is Judy's "hidden agenda." In her female relationships, she feels recognized, connected, and on an equal plane. Judy privileges the female model of relationship, even as she seeks a husband who is "stronger" than herself. This tension represents the "heterosexual knots" or asymmetrical relational needs of women and men fostered by male-dominated marriage (Chodorow 1978).[15] Essentially, Judy turns to her female friendships and to her children to satisfy the relational needs unmet by heterosexual marriage alone. Female friendships and motherhood contribute to the Greens' marital stability insofar as they fulfill Judy's needs. At the same time, these relational needs hold potential for marital conflict. If Judy is ever caught between the contradictory needs of her children and Dan, if he were to become threatened by her friendships, or if the Greens ever suffer a financial catastrophe undercutting Judy's ability to pay for child care and time for her needs, Judy might find she is unable to maintain the "balance."

When Dan is asked what would break his marriage he, too, speculates about the possibility of "infidelity"—a long-standing ground for divorce in our monogamous society. He then reiterates what he does not want in a wife—that is, the conditions that he attaches to "marriage as forever": "Or *breaking a fundamental deal,* in other words, if the *contract* is that you take care of the children and I go do this, and suddenly you say to me, 'I really want to go back to work and I'm going to hire baby sitters to do that,' I don't think that would be acceptable. I don't know whether it would break the marriage, but it would certainly put a huge stress on it and I would fight it pretty vigorously." Dan hesitates to state that a change in the bargain could break the marriage; this reflects his belief in marriage culture. Yet, his conception of marital commitment here is imbued with contingency—a contingency founded upon male terms. If Judy attempted to redefine gender arrangements, the marriage would be on the line and she would be faulted for "breaking a fundamental deal." This is Dan's "hidden agenda"—hidden insofar as he espouses "marriage as forever" but then implies that there are conditions attached to this "unconditional commitment." When traditionalism is defined as a belief not only in marriage culture, but also in male dominance, then the terms of marriage are ultimately set by men. From here, it is not a large step to the belief in contingent marriage that lies at the heart of divorce culture.

IS THERE A MALE-DOMINATED DIVORCE CULTURE?

Male dominance untempered by the responsibilities of marriage culture remains unseemly to most; thus it is not surprising that the husbands I interviewed did not embrace this package of beliefs. Among the '50s spouses, Vincent Dominick's belief system came closest to combining male dominance with divorce culture. Had it not been for his child's trauma and the children of his mistress, he probably would have left his first wife; his rights were ultimately tempered by responsibilities.

Among '70s spouses, the package of male dominance and divorce culture is not claimed explicitly; spouses do talk in terms of divorce culture, yet belief in male authority is less common among the Younger generation—among both women and men. By and large, the '70s spouses want to make a claim for equality in marriage. Their beliefs in male dominance are more submerged than those of '50s spouses and are expressed either through "separate-but-equal" or "gender-neutral" language.

Dan Green was a committed traditionalist at the time of the interview, yet his interviews suggest that he has the potential to embrace divorce culture, particularly if his wife resists his terms. Dan talks the vocabulary of contingency even as he reproduces marriage culture. He attaches conditions to "marriage as forever" when he asserts that "breaking a fundamental deal" might end his marriage. And the fundamental deal that concerns him is a gendered deal: "If the *contract* is that you take care of the children and I go do this, and suddenly you say to me, 'I really want to go back to work' [...] I don't think that would be acceptable."

Dan Green, however, is not the only husband who talked in terms of "marriage as a contract." Two other professional husbands who were marriage culture advocates explicitly used this language.[16] The '70s husbands are more likely than '70s wives to use contract language. Of course, egalitarians who talk divorce culture also speak as if marriage were a contract. While wives who used contract talk invariably believed in equality and divorce culture, husbands used contract language across gender and marital ideologies—even when advancing marriage culture.

Schneider (1996, 205) points out that the problem with "contract language" is not only that individuals are likely to set the terms of relationships in ways that damage or undermine a social institution like the family, but it also encourages individuals to maximize their self interests and "to enforce the rights they have won." Whatever their gender ideology or marital ideology, contract vocabulary represents men's awareness of their individual choice and male prerogatives in marriage.

Projecting a Male-Dominant Divorce Culture on "Others"

The assumed privilege to break a contract if one's rights have been transgressed is most apparent in stories about other people's divorces. Several respondents tell stories of the divorces of friends or relatives that suggest a male-centered, contingent approach to marriage.[17] For example, Dan Green describes a friend of his who ran into marital troubles and divorced: "I could understand her being unhappy with him because of how driven he was, but I could also understand he being unhappy with her. He was a very driven, particular kind of guy. He always, he only dated redheads, he only wanted to be married to a redhead—that's all that was acceptable to him. Had to have a certain figure, a certain way, just absolutely his way or no way. [...] And it's still that way." Dan explains that this wife could not tolerate the "strains" of her husband's career. One might presume that she had difficulties with "his way or no way" as well; this male friend was setting the terms of marriage whether it was work-related or appearance-related. Dan remarks that "she took off, I mean in the financial sense, at exactly the wrong time." Dan speculates that "she was trying to make a point and the point got—she was overwhelmed by her own action [. . .] I'm not sure she meant for it to end the way it did." The man has gone on to marry another "beautiful redhead" and have more children.

Dan seamlessly continues with the story of "another friend of mine." This is a case of an older couple; the wife left, they reunited, and then, Dan continues: "Only this time he found somebody else in the meantime, and said goodbye and now they'll both be bankrupt. She'll be in her '50s, totally unable to work, you know, on her way to being suicidal, if she's not already, and you know she pulled the game and she lost." His examples reveal the obstacles for women who attempt to redefine marriage in divorce culture. Dan assumes that these marital struggles occurred on a level or gender-neutral playing field. However, as these wives attempt to assert their needs and desires, they transgress the norm of subordination. In both cases, wives incur substantial financial and emotional losses that reflect a broader pattern of socioeconomic inequality.

CAUTIONARY TALES FOR WIVES

The rise of divorce means that all couples invariably experience the divorces of friends, colleagues, and family. For many '70s spouses, these stories of divorce serve as cautionary tales. Both Judy and Dan Green have witnessed upper-middle-class mothers divorce and experience subsequent "downward mobility" (Arendell 1986; Weitzman 1985). Judy saw her friends experience a "frenzied" rather than "purely relaxed" motherhood and describes many female friends who "are in trouble," and whose troubles clearly serve as a "cautionary tale" in her life. Indeed, these may be the same women Dan Green described who "pulled the game and lost." Such storytelling may give pause to married women who want to redefine marital terms.

Hochschild and Machung (1989, 86) argued that "cautionary tales of divorce" can deplete women's power when women are "chastened by the memory of [a] mother's struggle as a single mother" or "chilled by tales of divorce among contemporary women friends." These stories can serve to increase the gratitude of wives who have not been "left" by their husbands. Because women need marriage more than men for financial support—for themselves and for their children—divorce reduces married women's power. Hochschild (preface to Arendell 1986, xii) described how male dominance is transformed in an era of divorce: "A newer, more pervasive, more impersonal form of oppression is partly replacing an older, more personal form. [...] In the older form of female oppression, a woman was forced to obey an overbearing husband in the privacy of an unjust marriage. In the newer form, the working single mother is economically abandoned by her former husband and ignored by society at large."

Many mothers, across class and race, have discovered that a more "impersonal" male dominance awaits mothers on the other side of divorce (Hochschild with Machung 1989). The excessive impoverishment of women and their children after divorce testifies to this vulnerability. Moreover, given that men experience fewer economic disincentives to divorce, and given the age-gradient in marriage, the traditional wife is vulnerable to being left for "a younger model" with no right to legal or financial compensation from the man who is, more often than not, the higher-earning partner. Economically, few families today can easily sustain a middle-class standard of living on one income—particularly if it is the average woman's income. Also, women are still more likely than men to sacrifice their educational aspirations and earning power for the purposes of primary parenting (Coontz 1997). In these ways, the rise of divorce disempowers married women by serving as a cautionary tale and reinforcing submission in marriage. Thus, the calls for abiding commitments in a reinvigorated marriage culture—by men's movements, by advocates of covenant marriage, and by some religious organizations—would seem to be good news for women.

Yet, marriage culture also contains a "cautionary tale" for wives. Judy asserts that their marriage is "unconditional." Dan's discourse on marriage suggests otherwise: he attaches some conditions. Dan's contractual language represents his power in the relationship, rather than any sign of impending divorce. Further, Dan talks as if "the deal" is a personal choice rather than a socially constructed reality. To talk about the "personalities involved" in marriage conceals the degree to which this "deal" has a history and continues to be socially reconstructed on a daily basis. While both genders exercise greater choice regarding employment and marriage than ever before, individuals do not proceed to "freely contract" from equivalent social positions; gender (as well as age, class, sexuality, and race) shapes the direction and meaning of these chosen "contracts" or "commitments." Dan's use of these personal, individual-based terms obscures the inequality underlying such gendered patterns.

When the Promise Keepers urge men to take back their leadership, such gendered patterns are not obscured; they clearly aim to bolster men's manifest power in marriage (Komter 1989). Yet, when Promise Keepers urge men to keep commitments—a seemingly benign and de-gendered proposal—they may obscure how latent and invisible power can be maintained through these calls (Komter 1989). Latent power means wives, such as Judy, must anticipate their husbands' needs ("Yes dear, anything you want, I understand, it's for your career"). Invisible power is the power hidden in the taken-for-granted assumptions about the nature of reality, when, for example, Judy legitimates Dan's behaviors, including dominance, by drawing upon the "natural order." Promise keeping represents power keeping—whether male dominance is explicit or implicit—because marital commitment has historically been on male terms.[18] Precisely because social supports favor men outside of marriage, husbands theoretically have greater power in *all* types of marriages, regardless of ideology.[19]

Husbands' power can be amplified by the divorce option, particularly for traditionalist wives. If traditionalist wives dare to question men's terms, they risk losing the conventionally male responsibilities that have accompanied marriage culture.[20] Yet, divorce has been an important power lever for wives too—a lever women have pulled through time in spite of economic perils. As Coontz (1997, 84) points out, "it is *women* more than men who have historically needed the protection of divorce." Studies continue to find that men are more maritally satisfied than women and that the vast majority of women who do divorce report greater satisfaction in their family situation afterwards (Hetherington, Law, and O'Connor 1993; Riessman 1990; Stewart et al. 1998). Such findings indicate that marriages are still arranged around men's terms more than women's. The '70s wives who embrace the tenets of an egalitarian divorce culture have more power than traditionalist wives—if not always more power than husbands supported by social structures at large. Thus, divorce is not merely a cautionary tale that disempowers wives; it can also embolden and empower wives to set the terms of marriage. While critics who lament a lapse in family values are most troubled by marriage becoming contingent, my research suggests that contingency is not really new to marriage; rather, divorce culture expands who determines what marriage is contingent upon.

11 "Topsy-Turvy" Marriages Among '70s Spouses

WHEN 39-year-old, Euro-American Roxanne Kason-Morris is asked to address the meaning of marriage in the 1990s, she notes the high divorce rates and wonders about changing roles in recent generations:

> In the old times, no one questioned what the woman's and the man's role is. *Now it's all topsy-turvy* and uh ... then who's going to take care of the children is a big question and um, two working parents, of course, you have to divide the responsibility and the woman is forever resentful toward the man who doesn't take his full share—or half the share. [...] And I resent him because I'm home with a [temporary] job and I'm expected to take now 100 percent. Before, it was 50 percent [emphasis added].

To illustrate the "topsy-turvy" nature of constructing a marriage today, Roxanne points specifically to the changing division of labor on the "first" and "second" shifts. When she asserts that "you have to divide the responsibility" and that the "woman is forever resentful toward the man who doesn't take his full share" she expresses the emotional consequences of practices that fall short of equality. Her woman-centered perspective on "equality" is evident in her presumption that it is men, not women, who fall short on assuming marital responsibilities.

Despite Roxanne's egalitarian ideology, she assumes that traditional roles are more conducive to marital stability. Why does she make this interpretive connection? Why does she not see "equality" as divorce insurance and target role traditionalism as the current culprit? To some degree, she expresses her own ambivalence; she has, after all, "chosen" to all but withdraw from the labor force. In other ways, her interpretation draws on the historical association between marriage culture and traditional roles; like others, she sees the correlation between the rise of women's participation in the labor force and rise in divorce and imputes a causal connection. A third explanation for this contradiction is that *her* marriage would be more stable if she were to embrace, rather than resist and resent, traditional roles.

Roxanne's view is shaped by where we have been. We proceed from a history of male-dominated, role-differentiated marriages as we redefine gender relations in marriage today. Reconstructing gender in marriage is not, however, a well-coordinated or uniform process. Spouses are changing in different ways and at different rates in a cultural climate also marked by contestation between marriage and divorce cultures. How do '70s spouses cope in a culture of divorce when their gender ideologies are at odds? Does it matter whether it is the wife or the husband who advances gender equality in contrast to male authority? Overall, '70s spouses appear to experience more conflict than '50s spouses when it comes to beliefs about gender or marriage, and among '70s spouses, by and large, wives seem to talk equality and divorce culture more. As many family scholars have noted, this may be a mark of women changing faster than men in their gender ideologies and family practices (Hochschild and Machung 1989; LaRossa 1988; Coltrane 1995).

The two portraits of marriage in this chapter—the Kason-Morris marriage and the Nakato marriage—reveal the contradictions between ideology and practices that emerge in the quest for equality in the context of divorce culture. The Kason-Morris marriage represents the more typical dynamics of the wife changing faster than the husband. The Nakatos are a "negative case" because Paul Nakato seems to be changing faster than Debbie Nakato. I argue that this kind of asymmetry may be less problematic than the more typical asymmetry of wives changing faster.

THE KASON-MORRIS MARRIAGE: HETEROSEXUAL KNOTS AND DIVORCE CULTURE

Roxanne and Craig have been married for five years and are raising two daughters (one from Roxanne's previous marriage). They are Euro-American, nonreligious, and college educated, and live in a middle-class Bay Area suburb. They met when a mutual friend suggested Roxanne contact Craig, an accountant, for help with her taxes; she had begun to set up a word processing business through her home. Both have been married before, were leery of remarriage, but hope that this "second chance" will succeed.

Now that Roxanne works at home, with intermittent contracts doing word processing, she is expected by Craig to do 100 percent of the second shift. Given that her contributions to breadwinning are minimal, it is worth asking what Roxanne is complaining about. Surely she has more time than her husband to devote to child rearing and other domestic tasks. Why do these arrangements feel unfair to her? And if they are so unfair, why is she not working more? Her feelings about "fairness" grow out of the dynamics between Craig and herself. But they also grow out of her earlier experiences—her first marriage and divorce.

During her individual interview, Roxanne asserts that: "divorce is hell." Roxanne's first marriage was passionate and short-lived. Roxanne describes what was at first a gratifying marriage at age 23 to a musician. They met as students, lived together for six months, and married on the wave of infatuation. The birth of their daughter, however, rapidly undermined the joy and sense of equality that had initially characterized their relationship. Her divorce in 1983, when she was 30, was due to the "stress of child rearing." Her account of this marriage—like Mia Turner's first marriage—is a story of an unequal division of parenting labor. So too, is her story of life after divorce.

Roxanne's divorce was followed by a period of single motherhood and reliance upon Aid to Families with Dependent Children (AFDC). She experienced firsthand the "downward mobility" that characterizes divorce for many middle-class white women (Kurz 1995; Newman 1988; Weitzman 1985). As she describes it: "I had no nothing. It was the most humiliating circumstance. I . . . AFDC, wow. [. . .] And my family didn't help me, you know, at all." Eventually, she was able to get a job in word processing. She could make ends meet, even if times were tight.

Roxanne also represents the relative "upward mobility" that can follow remarriage, particularly for white women—an economic security she does not want to put at risk again.[1] She reiterates three times that she does *not* want to be a single mother again. These assertions suggest that one experience of divorce can deter another. Avoiding single motherhood is, above all, a financial issue for Roxanne: "No, I don't want to be a single mother again, with another . . . I figure that I can support myself with the kids. That's why I had only one. Because I knew that I could get divorced again, or get widowed, and I could do okay. 'Cause I got a job—I finally found a job where I could make enough money, scratch by, and I could actually do it myself. And I know now, that I could live by myself. I got over that hump. I can live as a single mother." In spite of her personal experience with this "economic cautionary tale," Roxanne has considered divorce in her current marriage. Divorce rates testify that remarriages are more vulnerable to divorce (Amato and Booth 1997; Martin and Bumpass 1989). Once again, Roxanne feels that the birth of a child has undermined the possibility for equality in this remarriage. According to Roxanne, it could be his "moodiness, pouting, and childlike behavior" that would break her marriage. She is tired of Craig's pouting, his refusal to answer her, and his business trips. She speculates that as the kids get older, she might get fed up and consider divorcing him. She is not staying together for the children's well-being per se; rather, she foresees the financial free fall that might befall her and the kids.

Roxanne's irregular employment is a "choice" that reflects structural conditions; she is trying to avoid the conflict between work and family responsibilities that emerges from a social context in which neither businesses nor governments truly support family-friendly policies. Craig has the higher-paying job and their children are young; one child is not yet in school. Moreover, Roxanne feels anxious about leaving her children in "mediocre" day care. She wants to be "really present" for her second child; she felt like she shortchanged her first child when she was working full-time. She has learned to trade baby sitting with friends for a break from the responsibilities of caretaking.[2]

Whether speaking of child care, household labor, or market labor, Roxanne is frustrated that responsibilities are not shared in her current marriage. Roxanne experiences her minimal work commitments as a forced choice; if she were to work more, her husband might help more at home, but not enough to compensate for the hours she would put in at work. When I ask Roxanne about the biggest compromise of her marriage, she asserts: "Housework. It's my compromise, not his." Later, she describes the choice *not* to work full time as the biggest "concession" of her marriage: "It's really a powerless situation in a marriage when you're barely working." This is because "you have no monetary power" and "you're at their beck and call." Finally, when I ask what is not good about the marriage, she says, "He complains that I strap him with the load of child care when he comes home from work, [. . .] which isn't true, but that's what he thinks."

While it might seem that Roxanne's claimed sacrifices, compromises, and concessions are an array of separate issues, in many ways her account suggests that the division of housework, paid work, child care, and emotion work are all of a piece. In her first marriage, Roxanne repeatedly vented her anger about the second shift. In this marriage, she says, "I'm not going to do that anymore, I'm not going to lower myself and I'm not going to get that angry." She has learned, as she puts it, to "press down my anger when he won't do the dishes." She embodies Hochschild and Machung's (1989, 56) point that "[a]cross the nation at this particular time in history, this emotion work is often all that stands between the stalled revolution on the one hand, and broken marriages on the other." Roxanne is caught between her ideals of an equality based on independence, her interdependent practices of motherhood, and her dependent practice as an underemployed wife.

In some ways, Roxanne is not "changing" as fast as other wives; she is not doing a full-time paid job and a second shift, as were many of the wives I interviewed. Yet, her limited unemployment is a temporary stopgap while her children are young. In contrast to the egalitarian Mia

Turner, Roxanne is an egalitarian who is currently caught in the web of traditional gender arrangements. This explains why arrangements feel unfair to her; she wants to stay home as a mother, but not as a wife. These arrangements, however, have practical and emotional consequences for Craig as well. To practice role-traditionalism is to enter into traditional standards of fairness.

Craig's View of the Second Shift

While the biggest compromises of Roxanne's marriage have been the homemaking role and primary responsibility for child care, Craig feels the biggest compromises of *his* marriage have been his contribution to child care and housework. As Craig says, "In my view, I do a lot around the house, and I help a lot, and I do a lot of the work around the house, and in my wife's view I don't do anything." His repetition serves to emphasize his belief in his contribution. He goes on to illustrate: "I do all my own laundry, I take care of all my own clothes. If I ask Roxanne to cook a meal—I probably get her to cook a meal, maybe two times a week. And I, I will eat on my way home, because if I don't she won't have dinner and I don't want to learn how, and she doesn't want to do it for me, and so. . . ." Craig wants more appreciation and recognition for his domestic efforts. He is already taking care of his own laundry. He feels neglected. Craig demonstrates his resentment of Roxanne's neglect by eating on the way home and refusing to learn to cook. In Craig's view, his contributions are already above and beyond "traditional" standards.

Roxanne, as an egalitarian, might object in two ways to Craig's account. Doing his own laundry is a given, not a gift. Furthermore, taking care of one's own laundry or dinner is not the same as everybody taking care of everybody's laundry or dinner. Does Craig ever wash her shirts? Does he cook for the family? While she can refuse to cook his dinner, she cannot force him to cook hers. In sum, their divergent ideals about responsibility for domestic upkeep mean that both spouses feel shortchanged.

As Craig expresses his marital disappointments, he reports that Roxanne is forever pointing to the practices of other husbands. Craig not only feels neglected, he does not feel "recognized" for his contributions:

> I wish that Roxanne were more appreciative of the things that I do around the house or would recognize the things, my contributions. She's often telling me about this husband or that husband and the wonderful things that they're doing for their wife and you know, 'did you know that Mr. so and so watches the kids every Saturday so [that] Mrs. so and so can go, you know, to aerobics? Did you know that?' You know, and so I, you

know, I wish that, I wish that um, she were, would recognize more my contributions around the home.

From Craig's report, we can infer that Roxanne is engaged in the "politics of comparison." Hochschild and Machung (1989, 51) argue that this
reflects "a semiconscious sense of the going rate for a desirable attitude
or behavior in an available member of the same and opposite sex." Such
comparisons inform their "economy of gratitude." If the "going rate" is
for fathers to assume the responsibilities of child care on Saturdays, then
Craig is falling short. The effect of Roxanne's comparisons are, however,
to make Craig feel even more underappreciated and unrecognized. Moreover, the standard Roxanne attempts to create with her reference group
of husbands is countered by Craig's "politics of comparison." Craig's
standards are partly informed by his first marriage.

Craig reports that he did *not* do the "second shift" in his first marriage, even though his first wife worked full-time. His first wife's independence may have been problematic for him: "I saw her change a lot as
she advanced in her work. She worked very hard to, to be successful in
a man's environment, you know, and I felt it kind of um, toughened her,
jaded her, made her—she got aggressive and I didn't really like that." In
addition, Craig reports that she earned more money than he did. While
she was occupationally successful in spite of responsibility for the second
shift, their eventual divorce suggests that his first wife was not satisfied
with the arrangement either.[3] Craig describes the marital dissolution as a
"slow drift"—no one really initiated it.

In comparison to his first marriage, Craig feels that he contributes
more than enough now. Indeed, in child care, like housework, he is too
active for his own liking:

> I guess the biggest compromise is the amount of time that I spend taking
> care of the baby, you know, I, I, I think I—it's not enough from Roxanne's
> point of view, but I feel like I—and I've complained to her many times, "*I
> feel like I'm your baby sitter,* you know, I'm the child care." [...] That's
> what needs to be done I guess. So I wish that—that's, that's a compromise,
> because I would like to come home and I would like to read the paper. I
> would like to have a minute to do some work or to pay the bills or do some-
> thing, you know, but I, I feel like the children are kind of, the baby espe-
> cially, is kind of foisted on me as soon as I walk in the door. She doesn't
> feel that she does that . . . at all.

Like wives who believe in equality, Roxanne would critique the idea that
being a parent to one's child should be depicted as "baby sitting." Yet,
Craig implicitly perceives his primary contribution to the family as being
the "breadwinner." And Craig puts in very long hours, sometimes at two

jobs. When Roxanne "foists" the baby on him when he comes in the door, it ignores the contribution Craig has already made in his eight-to-ten-hour day.

Unlike domestic responsibilities, Craig does not resent breadwinning. However, he does want appreciation for it. His breadwinning, an instrumental demonstration of his love, is not sufficiently recognized by Roxanne. In line with Cancian's (1987) argument that the "feminization of love" renders the instrumental and physical aspects of love invisible, Craig wants recognition for his practices of love. Ironically, Craig may be working ever harder at his job to garner this recognition from Roxanne. Speaking generally, Cancian observes that what women need and what men need are often at odds with what they think they need: "When they are unhappy, women usually think they need more love, but the objective evidence suggests that they need more independence. Men typically are too independent and too focused on achievement at work. They think they need more success, but studies of illness and death rates indicate that they need more close relationships" (81). Craig needs to cut back on his work hours to strengthen his marriage; instead, he redoubles his efforts at the male breadwinning role and denies the harm and privileges these practices entail. Yet, these are the very practices that Roxanne feels ultimately constrain her options, leave her at his "beck and call," and make her feel like a "single mother" again. Craig's long hours at work prompt Roxanne to claim, "I am really a single mother still. He is rarely home." Of course, Roxanne is well aware that financially she is not a "single mother"—she draws on this metaphor of divorce culture to describe relational issues here.

Despite gendered issues, expectations, and compromises, when I ask Craig whether women or men have any advantages or disadvantages in marriage today, he repeats several times: "I can't really see how one could have an advantage over the other." He also claims: "It doesn't matter to me in terms of, you know, where the money comes from and who does the work and who stays home." Yet, at another point he asserts, "I really love my work." He works overtime as a rule. Moreover, he refuses to learn to cook, does not do the dishes, and feels like a "baby sitter" when watching his own children. It is not clear that Craig would be willing to switch places with Roxanne. He talks in a "gender-neutral" fashion. The language of gender-neutrality was used by '70s husbands more than by the '50s husbands. Such language tends to assume, rather than question, gender equality. Craig's gender-neutral talk obscures his submerged ideals, his "hidden agenda," as well as enduring inequalities in society at large.

Hidden Agendas in a Conflicted Context

Social institutions remain arranged primarily for the worker who is "family-free" or wife-supported (Hochschild 1975; Moen 1992). For upper-middle-class couples such as the Greens, who share traditional beliefs, family goals can proceed more seamlessly. However, this context presses husbands to construct expectations based on traditional role differentiation even if they have egalitarian wives. Social structures act to support Craig's ambivalent gender ideology; while he talks gender-neutrality, he practices a "separate-but-equal" traditionalism. He implicitly resists equality in practice; indeed, it seems that his "hidden agenda" of male authority is hidden even to himself.

At the same time, institutional structures still press wives like Roxanne to meet the demands of being a wife and mother, whether or not they are also breadwinners (Coltrane 1998). In addition, the cultural mandate is for women to put family priorities first (Coser 1991). Roxanne already felt powerless as a wife and mother when her first husband, family, and society neglected to support her. Today, she advises young adults that "there's nothing like, *nothing like,* kids to make or break a marriage." Roxanne blames motherhood for disempowering women in marriage, yet she focuses on individual solutions, rather than cultural mandates and social arrangements. She currently resolves the family/work conflict by being a "stay-at-home" mom in practice, talking "rights equality," and harboring her own hidden agenda of relationality.

Both Roxanne and Craig testify to a mutually satisfying sex life. Yet, for Craig, "great sex" represents intimacy; moreover, he wants Roxanne to be more appreciative of things as they are. In contrast, Roxanne perceives "talk" as constituting emotional intimacy and she wants more of it. When I ask what is missing in the marriage, Roxanne replies: "One thing that I would want more of is more intimacy, just on a, on a daily basis. More visiting. More communication. More talking. Sharing." Intimacy, as Lillian Rubin (1983, 79) defined it, is the "wish to know another's inner life along with the ability to share one's own."

This wish and this ability are gendered, according to Chodorow (1978), whose psychoanalytic theory of gendered personality differences suggests that women's desire for connection tends to conflict with men's need to maintain separation, resulting in "heterosexual knots." One does not have to agree with this psychoanalytic account, however, to recognize this typical gendered construction. Indeed, these heterosexual knots reflect the "feminization of love," which Cancian (1987) described as a social construction.

"Heterosexual knots" or "feminized love" are not new. Yet wives are increasingly likely to press for their vision of a fulfilling marriage, a vision that is marked by relational responsibilities and a wished-for intimacy that requires shared marital work. While expectations inherited from male-dominated practices inform men's "hidden agenda," relational expectations inform women's "hidden agenda." And therein lies a dilemma.

Cancian (1987, 80) astutely argued that the "feminization of love contributes to overspecialization and unequal power between the sexes." Many women face a dilemma upon trying to correct for this "overspecialization." Of course, some wives reproduce this "expert status" on love and shut men out. Other wives try to redefine love by opting out of this specialty and embracing traditionally male signifiers of love—sex and instrumental practices—that, because they are male-identified, are not devalued. Yet, wives such as Roxanne cannot force husbands such as Craig to adopt the female-identified practices and signifiers that are crucial not only to redefining love, but to doing marital work. And there is less incentive for husbands to do so, because these practices exist in a devalued sphere. While the feminization of love contributes to unequal power, defeminizing love can also require power.

Wives' relational responsibilities have them searching for strategies to procure intimacy and recruit husbands into marital work. As we have seen, one vehicle for sharing marital work is to participate in couples therapy. Roxanne has tried to get Craig to go to therapy with her, and she "would still like to," but "he hated it." She says, "we got in our worst arguments after each session." She "decided it would be the ruin of our marriage if we continued."[4] This concession represents one obstacle to de-gendering labors of "love."

Craig laments their communication dynamics too. However, the change Craig would like to see in their communication is not more talk, but more understanding. For Craig, therapy was not a means to overcome, but rather a setting to reenact, these difficulties. He states that he "doesn't care for" therapy and that he is uncomfortable with a lot of talk.[5] Moreover, Craig felt manipulated into therapy and felt that Roxanne was hauling him into therapy to focus on *his* problems. In some ways he was right. Roxanne is focused on how Craig should change; she wants him to take more responsibility for marital work. Craig may sense that therapy legitimates her relational concerns. But his resistance to therapy blinds him to therapy's potential for averting a growing breach between Roxanne and himself; while it might legitimate her relational concerns, the process would not necessarily support her agenda. Indeed, it could expose her contradiction; she wants equality yet lives a traditional life. While Roxanne's contradiction, like Craig's, issues from a social structure that constrains more than enables equality, it explains why her expectations feel unfair to Craig. Furthermore, Craig's refusal to participate in therapy does not change the degree to which therapeutic culture influences Roxanne's vision of marital relationships. What it does change, however, is whether she attends to the message of relationality or individualism.

By choice or default, Roxanne is attuned to the message of individualism. She aims, as she says, to conquer her "codependency," that is, a "dysfunctional" tendency to take care of others at the expense of taking responsibility for oneself. Since wives have traditionally been expected to sacrifice for the sake of the family, this criticism of self-denial and the call to attend to oneself resonates for many women like Roxanne. This form of therapeutic culture has been criticized for focusing on the regressive, rather than the life-affirming aspects of women's caretaking tendencies (Haaken 1993). It also locates the solution in the individual, thereby ignoring the structural conditions that sustain heterosexual knots and channeling women's energies in the direction of a male model of independence. Because Roxanne cannot make her husband monitor the marriage or "sacrifice" for the family in the way she would like, she presses down her anger, aims to secure her independence, and establishes an equality of nonsacrifice.

While Roxanne desires a marriage contingent upon a sense of autonomy and connection, in actuality, she is neither very autonomous nor connected right now. She draws on "single mother" as a metaphor for the limited time Craig gives to their marriage and her resulting sense of emotional isolation. Roxanne's fears for the future are "unhappiness and isolation." Women's complaints that men do not "care about their emotional lives" (Thompson and Walker 1989) and the fact that "relational complaints" are increasingly seen as legitimate grounds for marital dissolution by the married and divorced (Kitson with Holmes 1992, 341) are closely linked. If one believes in divorce as a gateway, as Roxanne does, one is pressed to experience marriage as a gateway to emotional connection and relational equality as well.

Craig represents the difficult transitions faced by husbands today. The legacy of traditionalism confers advantages on Craig, although he does not fully see or want to recognize them. He does not want to let go of male-associated prerogatives or to assume female-associated responsibilities. Craig did not create the enduring structural inequalities. Indeed, he cannot effect a single-handed reversal of these structures any more than can egalitarian husbands such as Adam Harrington. Still, his denial that men continue to have advantages over women in marriage today helps to sustain these inequalities through his gendered expectations with respect to productive, reproductive, emotional, and marital labor. Craig may recognize that "people are working harder than ever to save their marriages," yet he redoubles his efforts at breadwinning and leaves the marital work to Roxanne, who is growing tired of it. Craig's blinders also render Roxanne's "hidden agenda" of relationality invisible; this influences her to aspire to a male model of independence, even as she relies upon his earning power. Craig's resistance to marital work contrasts sharply with another husband, Paul Nakato, who promotes marital work.

THE NAKATO MARRIAGE: A HUSBAND CHANGES FASTER

The Nakatos participated in this research because, as Paul says, they are "proud" of their marriage. Marriage was a given; they always wanted and expected to marry and have children. They did not live together, but dated for two years before this first marriage. By the interview, they have been married for five years and have two young children. Both Paul and Debbie Nakato are college educated, work full-time, and commute long distances in order to be homeowners and sustain a middle-class lifestyle. Both are on the job Monday through Friday. She works as a loan officer for a mortgage company; he works as a computer technician. Assistance with child care from both sets of parents enable the Nakatos to forego the high emotional and financial costs of institutional child care. They are moderately satisfied with their work, but both speak with more enthusiasm when the conversation turns to their families.

As a traditionalist, Debbie relies on the elasticity of the term "traditional" to capture the nature of their marriage; she uses it to describe ethnic traditions, gender arrangements, and "family morals." When I ask Debbie what is good about their marriage, she focuses on commonalities: "We have a lot in common. Same type of background. We're both third-generation Japanese-Americans, raised uh—him in a diverse community and myself here in, I was raised in a pretty much all Caucasian, you know, type of . . . but we were both raised with the same, raised very similarly and uh, I think that's what's probably made our—we have a lot in common. We have a lot of strong family background and lot of—more family morals. Very traditional, we're very conservative, traditional." Here, Debbie conveys, but downplays, differences between the communities in which they grew up. She notes the different racial demographics of their neighborhoods; in his interview, Paul also highlights the class differences between their childhood communities. Debbie is from a middle-class background; her mother was a homemaker and her father a professional. Paul's parents were working class and both had to work hard to sustain a decent standard of living. Paul is acutely aware of their sacrifices and appreciates his upward mobility. While Paul notes his commonalities with Debbie, he also relies on his class background to account for the differences they do have.

Debbie's reference to "family morals" is meant, in part, to capture her adherence to "marriage as forever." She asserts without solicitation early on in the interview that "we've never considered any divorce or anything like that." When I ask what would break her marriage, she replies with the conventional "last resort" response, "adultery," and then immediately adds, "but he won't though." Finally, there is little contingency in her marriage talk. When speaking of the future, she talks as if the marriage will endure without question. However, she does feel the press of divorce culture around her. In her view, married parents are in the minority now. She fears that once her children are in school, she and Paul will have less influence with regard to traditional values. Her impressions are shaped not only by developments among friends and family, but by popular culture:

> When I read *People* magazine and kind of everybody who's successful out there—they all come from single parents [...] Wendy and Ricki are going to be in the minority—they're going to be the only people with two parents. [slight laugh] That's sad. [KH: Does that concern you?] I think so, because other people are supposed to be their classmates and peers and that's where, I think, you can raise a child to the best of your ability and ... after they start going to school, you lose control. And, and um ... those peers have an influence.

In this passage, she wonders whether the divorced are reaping greater rewards; this suggests that Debbie hears the message "divorce is a gateway." She fears her children will be in the minority because, as she presumes, they will be the only parents still married. When she discusses her children's more distant future, she returns to their traditionalism and presumes her marital endurance: "I hope that they exhibit traditional values that their grandparents, you know, ourselves—that we'll try and instill in them."

Debbie and Paul are less "traditional" when it comes to breadwinner/homemaker roles. Debbie works full-time, but she talks like Judy Green in her emphasis upon being a traditional mother. Early in the interview she asserts that "I like to stay at home, in fact, with a baby it requires a person to stay at home—and I'm home most the time." Confusion followed in the interview, because I thought she meant that she did not work. What she meant, however, was that she is "at home" when she is *not* at her full-time job.[6] Her focus is on being a mother. She explicitly asserts: "Our marriage is and will be child-centered." There is no question that she needs to work in their view, but she does betray some concern about being a dual-career family when I ask her about models of good marriages in the media. She first asserts, "George and Barbara" and then adds, "Arnold and Maria—they're a two-career marriage and they seem to be happily married."[7] For Debbie, two careers challenge traditional gender arrangements, but need not challenge a good or model marriage.

Interestingly, both Debbie and Paul claim that with the birth of their children the gendered division of labor became more, rather than less, fair. While Cowan and Cowan (1992) found that the transition from "partners to parents" can undo gender "equality" in a couple's division of labor—in line with Roxanne Kason-Morris's experience—both Nakatos claim a move to more equal arrangements with the arrival of children. Debbie says she used to "pretty much take command of the house," but now "he's got more responsibility." Debbie describes the strains of having a toddler and an infant and asserts that this explains shifts in domestic responsibilities: "Well, he's taken on that responsibility in terms of— you know, I just don't have time, I'm still feeding [the baby] and, you know, the majority of his care is, is myself right now. Because I am still nursing him. Doing dishes—and Paul has to do, has to go grocery shopping and change the sheets and all that kind of stuff." At this time, child rearing is not shared, nor does that seem to be an explicit goal. Currently, Debbie sees it as her domain. After the first birth, she reports, Paul took a week off of work and she had to tell him, "I won't be offended if you go back to work." In sum, these adjustments have been pragmatic ("I just don't have time"), stage-dependent ("I am still nursing him"), and implicitly ideological; that is, the mother should be the primary parent at this stage.

According to Debbie, Paul sometimes moves too slowly on chores; however, she values his contribution around the house. In fact, like the Older generation she locates sources of "inequality" primarily in the work world, not in her home life. Compared to her parents' generation, Debbie perceives equity at home; as she puts it: "In our parents' generation, the moms did everything for the husbands." Using asymmetrical role terms here—moms versus husbands—is meaningful insofar as Debbie draws upon her identity as a mother, much more than her identity as a wife, in these interviews. Perhaps Debbie intuits that more power resides in motherhood than wifehood.[8]

Both Debbie and Paul accord the mother more knowledge about parenting at this stage in the life course. Paul claims that Debbie "does it better." And Debbie has read advice books on parenting. Paul asserts that he intended to read the books too, but did not, adding, "I guess I kind of trust her to do things right, so that's why I always go to her for the answers 'cause I know she's reading all that." Like other fathers at these early stages of parenthood (Coltrane 1998), Paul intends to be more involved when the children are older. His tempered involvement now is partly a function of his deference to Debbie, her appropriation of the expert role, and a culture at large that supports such appropriation in spite of the images of the "new fatherhood ideals" (Coltrane 1998; LaRossa 1988).

Both spouses describe themselves as "traditional." However, Paul primarily uses the term not when discussing gender, but when he is referring to ethnic and religious traditions. Their "traditionalism" is reflected in their active commitment to and participation in a Buddhist congregation, support for lifelong marriage, and, as these early years of parenting suggest, a tendency toward differential gender ideology and practices. On a questionnaire, they would probably reflect the tenets of traditionalism. Debbie is a traditionalist. However, in-depth and open-ended interviews reveal that Paul Nakato is deeply ambivalent about changes in gender and in marriage.

Paul is more drawn to equality and more ambivalent about divorce culture than his wife. He seems to take the lead in terms of redefining marriage in an egalitarian direction. He draws upon his working-class background to account for the difference between himself and his more conservative wife. Two other factors related to his liberalism—growing up in a dual-job family and witnessing more divorce—can also be traced to his working-class background. It is only in recent years that socioeconomic class has lost its once robust predictive power regarding divorce. In short, Paul bore witness to the marital strains wrought by financial limits. He questions "cultural givens" more than Debbie. From meritocracy to male authority, he is more critical of mainstream norms and assumptions. Perhaps his class background and race consciousness account for his shift in ideology—and for the fact that he changes faster than his wife. His reflexivity seems to have contributed to his reluctance to take Debbie for granted and his commitment to "marital work."

Paul rejects male dominance in marriage. He does not explicitly use "equality" as insurance for an enduring marriage, as the Turners and the Clement-Leonettis do. However, he implicitly and earnestly suggests that attention to equity in labor and in communication is essential to maintaining a vital marriage. When I ask Paul what is not good about his marriage, he replies "I probably need to work harder around the house. [. . .] I feel that I try to do my share, I'm not trying to be your typical Japanese-American male. I think that I still don't do enough."

In addition to the "second shift," Paul is sensitive to the damage done by male prerogatives in the past. When I ask him if there are more threats to marriage in this day and age than in his parents' generation, he responds:

> Yeah, I think there are a lot more risks than in their generation. Some of the ones that I, that I feel is that women are no longer kind of this—as everyone knows—they're not as enslaved like they were then. I mean, you know, like—god, a lot of my mom's friends couldn't even—never learned how to drive, they weren't allowed to work, you know, and even when they did work they got some crappy job somewhere. [...] So I mean, you know, I think it was easier then, for a man to keep a woman as a slave, because, you know, she had nowhere else to go. So yeah, so even though she had a lousy husband, okay, well, I have to—'he owns me,' like, like property, see? So it's not like that now, thank god, and women don't deserve that—there's still a lot more strides to be made, but because of this I feel that women don't have to take this crap anymore. 'Cause if they start acting like a jerk, hey, just kick them right in the butt—and see you later. So, so that's one thing that's, that's bad—well, not bad, but I'm just saying that—if I'm out of line, hey, you know, Debbie could take off right now. I mean, it's no big deal for her, you know. Her parents live pretty close by, she could survive very easily.

Paul relies on the analogy of slavery to depict women's subordination in marriage in preceding generations. He deplores previous male domination and women's lack of alternatives, and yet when he links this change to marriage, he labels it as "bad." He immediately corrects himself, realizing that this is "bad" *for him*—as a man—and that these reconstructions of gender influence marital stability. On the one hand, this changing context serves as a "cautionary tale" for Paul. Unlike previous generations of men, he knows Debbie has alternatives. He implies that men today, including himself, have less leeway to "get out of line." On the other hand, while he implies that equality is problematic, he does not simply blame women's changes for marital instability; rather he points to *men's reluctance to change* to account for rising divorce.

Shifting power relations between women and men and unexpected divorces come together in his interpretation. Paul's talk about others' divorces illustrates wives' new alternatives. However, his stories are not focused on women's options to leave a marriage; rather, they concern men's refusals to "work on" marriage. While the Nakatos have not been to any kind of therapy, they affirm a place for marriage counseling. Paul claims that "I think that everybody—even us—could probably stand to go." A central problem in marriages is that men are not willing to communicate. He remarks:

> And to me I feel that a lot of Japanese-American friends that I have—the males—they're just like their dads, they think that there's this big macho

thing about not communicating, being quiet, being strong. "Hey, nothing bothers me," you know. You know, "I don't want to talk about it." And these are the guys that are getting divorced because they can't communicate. They can't communicate and that's why they're getting divorced.

Of course "macho" and "noncommunicative" ideals are not unique to Japanese-American men.[9] However, Paul does see himself as challenging this version of masculinity. In this he sounds like Robert Leonetti and Gordon Walker, and reflects Gottman and colleagues' (1998) findings. In their study of marriages, Gottman et al. found that newly wed men who were "active listeners" and were willing to be influenced by their wives were in enduring, stable, and happy marriages six years later.[10] At another point, Paul criticizes the male individualism that has marked traditional marriages and conveys that he does not intend to emulate that model of marriage.

> If I started acting like some of my friends and feel so comfortable about the marriage that I kind of further sink into the degradation of being um ... so egotistical and think I'm so great that "I can do any damn thing I want—I can go to the bar every night, and the hell with you, and you know, if you don't like it, if you don't know me by now, the hell with you." See? And I *constantly have to monitor myself* because I tend to think that I'm pretty considerate and I'm doing things, you know, *thinking of both of us*, but you know, after a while you start—you do start to get comfortable [...] See, *so I am trying to monitor myself* and I know there's a lot of room for improvement in myself that I know that if I had the wrong wife it would be a problem. Right now, nothing's a problem because *she's the right one* [emphasis added].

Paul "monitors" himself in the service of the relationship. He rejects male prerogatives and believes in taking responsibility for the marriage. Like the Walkers and Fenton-Harringtons, Paul believes in an equality of sacrifice, rather than an equality of nonsacrifice. While Paul does not take Debbie for granted, Debbie's traditional beliefs ensure that Paul's sacrifices will be reciprocated.

Before closing the three-hour individual interview, I ask Paul if there is anything else I should know about their marriage. His reply reflects the difficulties of sustaining "marriage as forever" in a climate of divorce. He remarks that he realizes that "we tend to be kind of old-fashioned in our views on marriage." He links this to the fortune of having "parents who have been married over 40 years—have stayed together no matter what."[11] Despite being a proponent of marriage culture, he goes on to observe:

> We have excellent examples to follow. Most people don't have that. Most people consider divorce to be a very normal phenomenon. Having seen so

many good people get divorced, I am a firm believer that it's better to be divorced than to stay and *gaman*—and be miserable the rest of your life with somebody you absolutely cannot stand, you know? So, so in my opinion, especially now as opposed to before, it's okay—it's okay to be divorced, it's okay to find a better spouse the second time, third time, fourth time around. Ummm, you know, that's okay, and it's just part of your growing process.

In this passage, Paul reproduces "divorce as a gateway" when he says that "it's okay to find a better spouse the second time, third time, fourth time around"—that it is "just part of your growing process." Yet, Paul must reconcile his firm belief in "marriage as forever" with his reluctance to criticize divorces by "good people"—particularly as it has become a "normal phenomenon." His ambivalence emerges as he continues: "So, I think that we've been very fortunate to be this way, *if we do turn out to be married forever,* which I certainly am confident that we will be, but you know, you never know, *but I'm confident of it,* I consider ourselves very lucky. *But I also say, we're no better than anybody else.* And that, uh, we just happen to be one of the fortunate few that could do it. . . ." Paul swings from contingency to certainty and back again with regard to his confidence in "marriage as forever." He refers to good fortune and luck three times in this short passage. "Luck"—including the luck of good parental models—functions to differentiate his capacity for "marriage as forever" and his friends' marital contingency. When Paul continues, he asserts that "getting divorced for the wrong reason is not right" and that people should "try to work it out." He is quick to add that if divorce is necessary, one should not be subjected to social stigma.

As Paul closes his monologue, it is clear that he feels that he must be on the defensive as a believer in "marriage as forever" in a climate of contingency. Moreover, while he agrees with the value of "happiness" advanced by divorce culture, he wants to redefine it:

I'm hoping that we can pass down [to our children] the fact that it's not a crime to be married for 40 years if you're happy. And that happiness comes in many different forms. You can still argue—I mean, my opinion of marriage is, is that having seen my parents—I know they love each other very much, but, you know, they argue. They don't see eye to eye on a lot of things. Even still. They never will. But see, as long as you can deal with it, that's love and that's marriage. And I think with some people still have this notion that unless you're just lovey-dovey all the time, you know, that if you're fighting, that if you're disagreeing too much, then it's not a good marriage! They don't—that's not right. A good marriage is based on constant discussion, on constantly trying to work out things that will bother you for the rest of your life. And we're going to be working on this forever—forever, she's going to not like this, I'm not going to like that. But we'll work it out.

In contrast to his earlier statement regarding divorce and remarriage as a "growing process" for individuals, Paul presents a new account of marital happiness here. He describes happiness as an achievement that takes "many forms" and requires "constant discussion" and "work." When he says, "we're going to be working on this forever," he is reproducing marriage culture.

Depending on the passage, Paul reproduces divorce culture, then marriage culture. He has witnessed "good people" divorce unexpectedly. He feels as susceptible as the next person. To diminish his vulnerability, he relies, like other '70s spouses, on a series of strategies: the "marital work ethic," "the hypothetical divorce," "luck," "passing the test," and good parental "models." While he reproduces divorce culture, his support for marriage culture prevails.

The configuration of a more egalitarian husband and a traditionalist wife was atypical in my sample. Paul makes sense of his differences from Debbie in terms of his class background. This does explain his liberal and flexible orientation; he critiques the status quo. The wavering in ideologies may also be a mark of their stage in the life course; they married later and have a "younger family" than most couples I interviewed. Finally, Paul's critique may represent a male prerogative in their more conservative circles; as a woman, Debbie may have less leeway to be critical than Paul; that is, she may be more subject to social censure should she give voice to these liberal ideals.

While the "causes" for this configuration are debatable, the implications of the combination are more favorable for marital endurance. When it comes to power dynamics, the combination of a traditionalist wife and an egalitarian husband is less problematic for a marriage than the reverse, particularly when both spouses work full time. First, spouses are less likely to default to individualism and an equality of nonsacrifice; both privilege mutuality, obligation, and interdependence. Second, an egalitarian husband can compensate for the inequities of society because he does not deny that inequities exist and he has some power to counter them. Alternatively, if the husband is traditionalist and the wife egalitarian, the inequities that make their way into a marriage seem to have an additive effect—as in the Kason-Morris marriage.[12] Third, unless she feels that her husband is excessively encroaching on her traditional domain of responsibilities, the traditional wife is more likely to appreciate the "gifts" of the husband who actively monitors and assists with marital labors. Paradoxically, the traditionalist wife defers to her husband's prerogative to promote egalitarian relations. This suggests that redefining masculin-ity—by allowing for multiple and nurturant forms—could have a sizable effect on the rate at which gender relations change.

Conclusion: Gender and "Topsy-Turvy" Marriages

Most all of the '70s couples wrestle with a breach between ideologies or practices within themselves (ambivalence), between the marriage and soci-ety at large (cultural and structural contradictions), or within the dyad (beliefs at odds). This chapter has focused on the last split. Asymmetri-cal beliefs were more common among '70s than '50s couples. The beliefs of 2 out of 12 couples were distinctly at odds in the Older generation; 6 out of 17 couples disagreed in the Younger generation.

This generational difference could be explained by marital duration. The Older generation had been married many more years and had more time to construct aligned accounts through their "marital conversation" (Berger and Kellner 1964). Of course, aligned accounts do not mean men and women had shared expectations or experiences; the high number of '50s wives who had "divorce thoughts" compared to '50s husbands tes-tifies to disappointed expectations. Nevertheless, more middle-class women and men among the '50s couples upheld gender-differentiated practices and the male authority those practices implied. Moreover, while the '50s couples registered the rise of divorce culture, they still reproduced marriage culture. Marrying in an age of greater cultural consensus (the 1950s) regarding marital and gender ideologies probably contributed to a greater convergence in beliefs between '50s spouses. Conversely, a lack of cultural consensus on the meaning of gender and marriage created divergence between '70s spouses.

Where there is divergence in gender ideology, the more typical asym-metry is that of wives "changing faster" than husbands toward equality. In one case, this was not true. Paul Nakato was not the fastest-changing husband—the most egalitarian; however, what is notable was that he seemed to be changing faster than Debbie. These patterns require more investigation, but my research suggests that when men change faster on the dimension of equality, then the marriage is less likely to be conflicted. Other research shows that husbands who move toward nontraditional gender-role attitudes tend to report better marital quality (Amato and Booth 1995). The pattern of women changing faster on the dimension of equality is not only more prevalent, but more problematic for marital sta-bility. In cases, such as Roxanne Kason-Morris, in which equality is an issue for the wife, particularly when she is financially dependent, conflicts over conventional divisions of labor are more likely to yield conflict. Amato and Booth (1995) also found that wives who change toward nontraditional attitudes about gender roles also tend to express more marital strain. Craig Kason-Morris talks in terms of gender-neutrality, but this conflicts with his traditional practices and obscures his "hidden agenda." Unlike Dan Green, Craig does not advocate manifest power; however, Craig does have the potential to construct a male-dominated divorce culture, based more upon latent and invisible power (Komter 1989).

Changes in gender enter into new marital meanings in at least three ways in this younger marital cohort. First, gender ideology is explicitly used as insurance against divorce. This is more typical among couples holding "symmetrical" beliefs; however, Roxanne Kason-Morris assumes that traditional roles are insurance against divorce. Second, gendered "hidden agendas"—assumptions of male authority by some men and orientations toward relationality by some women—implicitly influence the gendered expectations of marriage and, when combined with divorce culture, can shape legitimization for divorce. Third, a couple's beliefs interact with shifting cultural conceptions that shape their practice of marital labors.

Roxanne Kason-Morris rightfully observes that marriages are "topsy-turvy" today. Marriages are "topsy-turvy" not only because there is a lack of cultural consensus on what constitutes "marriage," but also because there is a lack of cultural consensus on the meaning of "gender" in marriage. As a result, contradictions between spousal ideals and practices seem to have increased for '70s couples. Further, social structures often demand practices at odds with spousal ideologies; the work world still privileges the worker who is "family-free" (single or wife-supported) and the independent egalitarian over and above the relational egalitarian. Debbie Nakato's dual-career practices and traditional ideology sharply contrast with Roxanne Kason-Morris's homemaking practices and egalitarian ideology. Both wives live contradictions related to social structures; the stability of their marriages differs not only because of their husbands' differences in their practice of marital work, but also in their willingness to reconstruct notions of manhood or masculinity.

As middle-class women increasingly reconstruct and expand the meanings of womanhood or femininity—through their participation in the labor force, political activities, and their expectations of marriage— we witness a shifting "politics of comparison" (Hochschild with Machung 1989). Perhaps, as Miriam Johnson (1988, 259) suggests, "as women gain power as people, they gain power within marriage itself." While the challenge of gender equality can destabilize some marriages, it is important to recollect that equality has rarely been achieved with ease or finality.

12   Divorce Culture

A Quest for Relational Equality in Marriage

WHEN people marry they do not simply tie a knot, but weave a complex of relationships according to pre-existing patterns. In U.S. history, the institution of marriage has been like a loom through which several threads of social relations have been woven. Marriage has been a monogamous, lifelong commitment that has regulated gender, sexuality, and the physical and social reproduction of the generations. This Western marital pattern is being redesigned. We are still responding to the tapestry of old, but the various threads are being disaggregated and rewoven. Our society is deeply divided regarding the value and meaning of these new and partially woven designs.

Over the past decade, family scholars have debated whether we should be optimistic or pessimistic about marital and family life (Glenn 1987, 349).[1] Optimistic theorists have argued that families are not falling apart, but simply changing and adapting to new socioeconomic conditions (Riley 1991; Scanzoni 1987; Skolnick 1991). They stress the value of embracing family diversity and removing structural obstacles for the well-being of all families. Optimists emphasize the oppression that has attended women's sacrifices in marriage and point to the potential for greater self-determination and happier relationships today (Cancian 1987; Coontz 1992, 1997; Riessman 1990; Skolnick 1991; Stacey 1990, 1996). These theorists are concerned about threads that have regulated gender and sexuality and have subordinated women in marriage.

Pessimistic theorists have argued that the institution of marriage is a cause for concern—that divorce rates signify an unraveling of social bonds (Bellah et al. 1985; Glenn 1987; Lasch 1979; Popenoe 1988; Popenoe, Elshtain, and Blankenhorn 1996; Spanier 1989; Whitehead 1997a). Above all, pessimists argue that divorce suggests an increasingly tenuous thread of commitment and a growing "individualism" among today's adults, particularly since marital dissolution by divorce, rather than death, entails individual choice. In this view, marriage represents the singular commitment that sustains intergenerational family relationships, especially parenthood. Indeed, several recent books urge a return to lifelong marriage for the sake of children (Blankenhorn 1995a, 1995b; Popenoe, Elshtain, and Blankenhorn 1996; Whitehead 1997a).

Pessimists fear that with the advent of divorce culture we have forsaken nurturance, commitment, and responsibility. Because these are the very virtues that have traditionally been valorized in women, these divorce debates are always implicitly, if not explicitly, about gender. As one optimistic scholar has argued, "when commentators lament the collapse of traditional family commitments and values, they almost invariably mean the uniquely female duties associated with the doctrine of separate spheres for men and women" (Coontz 1992, 40). Critics of divorce do not always or necessarily reject gender equality in marriage, but they do tend to set it apart. Many scholars assume that the thread of gender ideology can be easily disentangled from the thread of commitment.

The middle-class '50s and '70s couples in this study, in combination with those in other studies, enhance our knowledge of the newly constructed meanings of marriage. Among the '70s spouses, I found a reproduction of divorce culture among the married, a growth in a marital work ethic, and fluid, even contradictory, beliefs regarding marital and gender ideologies. These findings validate the concerns of both optimists and pessimists.

Pessimists may be dismayed by the sense of contingency in the talk of married couples and may be confirmed in their belief that commitments are unraveling. On the other hand, optimists may feel validated in their views that spouses do not take divorce lightly; rather, "working" on marriages is the prevailing belief among spouses—though wives are still trying to equalize this work. A full-blown marital work ethic has arisen because of divorce anxiety and marital instability, yet it has also arisen because of instabilities in beliefs about gender. Spouses must be reflexive about the nature of marriage since the authority of marriage culture and male dominance have lost their hegemonic hold. The fluid beliefs among '70s spouses suggest that spouses do not wholly embrace either marriage or divorce culture. This may disturb pessimists more—at least those who would like to see marriage culture regain the hegemony of generations past.

At this point in time, marriage does not seem to be forever for almost half of all marriages. Is this a result of culture and the decline of values such as commitment, or are there other factors contributing to marital contingency today? Could divorce culture be transitional—a means to the goals of equality and new tapestries of commitment, rather than an end in itself? While the individualism of divorce culture has brought new problems, we should neither overlook the structural sources of these troubles nor forget the costs of marriage culture, particularly to women.

THE COSTS OF MARRIAGE CULTURE

Women's greater participation in the labor force, increased activity in the political sphere, and greater initiation of divorces suggest that women like Mia Turner and Roxanne Kason-Morris are claiming their rights and appropriating a model of individualism. However, my research suggests that women's increasing "individualism" needs to be understood in context. Because we proceed from a history of male-dominated marriages, individualism does not *mean* the same thing for women as for men.

Historically, we know that as heads of the household, even when not primary breadwinners, most husbands have had greater authority, and therefore greater freedom to be independent, than wives. Economic and legal structures have not only firmly anchored a white man's family authority in the public sphere, but have recognized and applauded his individualism. His autonomy, integrity, rights, and self-expression were never constrained to the same degree as those of wives, though he carried heavy financial responsibilities. Not all men have been able to accomplish or benefit from the provider role—working-class men and men of color have often been thwarted by economic and racial injustice. However, for those able to realize the ideal of the male provider role, these responsibilities have optimized men's freedoms and prerogatives.

Wives who are more individualistic are often trying to counter the legacy of male dominance in marriage. At face value, "contingent marriage" dilutes commitment by making it conditional. Marital commitment and contingency stand in an uneasy relation to one another. The unconditional commitment requires flexibility and a long-range view of reciprocity and rewards over time; it permits conflict, serendipity, and unforeseen developments without threatening the commitment; it builds trust that only a sustained history can provide. Yet, "marriage as forever" can also obscure the latent terms of commitment that have prevailed under conditions of male dominance. Paradoxically, a sense of contingency can enable wives to elicit values such as commitment, responsibility, caretaking, and equality. In short, it provides a powerful lever to set the terms of marriage.[2]

Of course, both men and women can use the lever of contingency in heterosexual marriage. Indeed, a male-dominated divorce culture may be a greater threat to the values of responsibility, caretaking, and equality than a male-dominated marriage culture. Yet, as I have suggested, securing power through individualism is not a new means for men within divorce culture. Thus, this lever is more important for women, who have had less economic and political power in the marital relationship. In fact, contingent marriage may be crucial for redefining marriage in an egalitarian direction. Most women are hungry not for power but for "the absence of domination" (M. Johnson 1988, 261). Yet, how can wives challenge domination without engaging the power of individualism?

A belief in equality is more widespread today—the '70s spouses did not generally embrace male dominance as their '50s counterparts did, but rather voiced support for gender equality.[3] Yet, ongoing conflicts over gender equality are apparent in husbands' and wives' "hidden agendas." When there is evidence of rights equality—such as a wives' participation in the labor force—husbands tend to assume that equality has been achieved; they are unaware of ongoing inequalities, such as marital work, and their enduring privileges to set the terms of marriage. Rights equality has more often been a masculinist discourse in U.S. law and culture (Arendell 1995; Coltrane and Hickman 1992; Weitzman 1985).

Many wives also embrace rights equality, yet women's conventional responsibilities for caretaking, child rearing, kin work, and marital work continue to incline women toward a vision of equality that focuses upon relational responsibilities, expressiveness, equity, and interdependence. Relational equality has been more often feminized in U.S. society (Cancian 1987; Riessman 1990). It is not that women are "essentially" relational, but rather that they have been expected and positioned to accomplish relationality. While some women are undoubtedly more individualistic today, as critics of divorce culture argue (Hewlett and West 1998, 200; Whitehead 1997a, 172, 181), more women increasingly want to share the marital and family labors that optimists have documented. Women are frustrated by men's lack of participation in marital work—and the emotion work, kin work, and housework that such reflexive assessment encompasses (Blaisure and Allen 1995; Cancian 1987; DeVault 1987; di Leonardo 1987; Goldscheider and Waite 1991; Hochschild 1983; Hochschild with Maching 1989; Oliker 1989; Thompson and Walker 1989; Thompson 1991).

These gendered marital visions are also apparent in the retrospective accounts of the divorced. Among divorced women and men, Riessman (1990, 164–65, 184) found that "freedom" encapsulated the positive meaning of divorce, but this gateway to freedom did not necessarily hold the same meaning. Women reported a freedom from subordination and the freedom for self-development—reflecting limits to equality in marriage; men reported freedom from obligations demanded by wives and a freedom from wives' scrutiny—reflecting some dissatisfaction with marital labors. Also, while former wives described their "transformations in identity" as learning to balance relatedness with self-reliance, former husbands discovered the value of "talk" and becoming more relational (199). This latter change by some husbands is ironic for former wives if, as I have argued, relational inequality contributes to marital instability and contingency.

In their suburban divorced sample, Kitson and Holmes (1992) found that ex-husbands and ex-wives similarly ranked a "lack of communication or understanding" as the top marital complaint (though wives ranked this higher) and similarly ranked "joint conflict over roles" as a key complaint.[4] Most interesting, however, was a notable gender difference on the marital complaint "not sure what happened"; for ex-husbands it ranked third, for ex-wives it ranked 28th (123). This suggests that men were less attuned to what the marriage lacked—a prerequisite for doing marital work.

Some '70s husbands—such as Robert Leonetti, Gordon Walker, and Paul Nakato—do marital work. Yet, more often than not, wives initiate and try to redistribute the actual "marital work" of communicating, caring, fulfilling needs, adjusting, and planning for marital well-being. To advocate shared marital work is to de-gender the rights and responsibilities conventionally attached to marital practices, to challenge male authority, and to disrupt power relations. Recent research that aims to predict marital happiness and divorce, as well as to improve the efficacy of marital therapy, reveals that a husband's refusal to accept influence from his wife is a key factor for predicting divorce (Gottman et al. 1998, 14, 19).

The above research suggests that marital work and the relational equality that it entails may be as important as rights equality for wives in a culture of divorce. The cultural irony is that even though wives may want a relational marriage, they may need to draw upon individualism to secure it. If secured, that is, if husbands keep up with wives' changes, wives may change the power dynamics of their marriage. Yet, ultimately what many wives want is not freedom from commitment, but freedom within an egalitarian and relational marriage. However, if relationality is unsecured, these wives may choose the gateway of divorce.

It is worth recalling that it was primarily the wives and not the husbands who thought about divorce among '50s couples ensconced in marriage culture. What does this reveal about the gendered costs of marriage culture? Writing about marriage and the nuclear family, Stacey (1996, 69) noted: "It seems a poignant commentary on the benefits to women of that family system that, even in a period when women retain primary responsibility for maintaining children and other kin, when most women continue to earn significantly less than men with equivalent cultural capital, and when women and their children suffer substantial economic decline after divorce, that in spite of all this, so many regard divorce as the lesser of evils." In light of women's postdivorce commitments to children, to charge such mothers with an egoistic or self-centered individualism reveals a refusal to recognize the costs of marriage culture to women.

Are there no costs for men in marriage culture? While research continues to find that marriage is better for men than women in terms of overall health and mortality rates (Hu and Goldman 1990), men are adjusting to new gender ideologies and practices too. Historically, the ability to provide and the ability to head a household have rooted men's identities. Working women and growing beliefs in equality are increasingly uprooting these means to manhood, as distinct from womanhood. As Furstenberg (1988, 239) has observed: "Men looking at marriage today may sense that it offers them a less good deal than it once did. This is the inevitable result of reducing male privileges, female deference to men, and a range of services that were customarily provided as part of the conjugal bargain. The loss of these privileges has persuaded some men to opt out of family life altogether." Paul Nakato's observation that some '70s men would rather be "right" than "married"—echoes Goode (1992, 124) on the sociology of superordinates: "Men view even small losses of deference, advantages, or opportunities as large threats and losses." Craig Kason-Morris felt increasingly underappreciated for all his work; yet his solution was to devote more energy to breadwinning, risking the relational needs of his marriage.

If we ignore the emotional costs of marriage culture and its connection to gender inequality, we will fail to see that divorce culture is a transitional phenomenon. We will also advance the costs of divorce culture—the impoverished single mothers, estranged fathers, and affected children—of concern to pessimists and optimists alike.

The Costs of Divorce Culture

The gendered patterns of divorce follow from those of marriage. Just as women usually do the primary parenting during a marriage, they generally obtain custody of children after divorce. Fathers are overwhelmingly noncustodial parents—only 14 percent of custodial parents are fathers (Sugarman 1998, 15). Just as fathers help support children during marriage, they are expected to contribute to child support upon divorce. Yet, many noncustodial fathers have become estranged from their children and delinquent on child support. Single, custodial mothers must often raise children on one slim paycheck. More widespread divorce seems to have increased women's and children's impoverishment, undermined fathers' economic and emotional commitment to children, and deprived children of the emotional and economic goods that two parents can provide.

Pessimists acknowledge structural impediments to marital commitments—the decline of the male wage and the need for two wage earners in a postindustrial economy. Yet, they see the decline in cultural and family values, such as commitment, as the more pivotal factor fostering these new social problems. On the other hand, optimists regularly argue that our failure to respond to the new global and postindustrial economy—the low priority given to families by corporate and government entities—is more basic to these problems, and that these new conditions demand solutions that do not discriminate on the basis of marital status. Although structural solutions are central, optimists are also concerned with cultural and family values—though the values of equality or justice are of greater concern than commitment.

Optimists and pessimists alike are concerned about the economic costs of divorce for mothers and their children. About a third of female-headed households are in poverty—six times the rate of married-couple households (U.S. Bureau of the Census 1995, P60-187). A re-evaluation of one study's claims about the economic consequences of divorce a year after divorce, finds that women's standard of living declines by 27 percent and men's increases by 10 percent (Peterson 1996, 534).[5]

A key solution to poverty for many pessimistic family scholars is reinforcing marriage and the nuclear family structure (Blankenhorn 1995b; Hewlett and West 1998; Popenoe et al. 1996; Whitehead 1997a). Marriage has functioned to redistribute economic resources in the past.[6] Also, today more than ever, two earners are necessary to secure a middle-class standard of living. However, to imply that unmarried motherhood or divorce are the *cause* of poverty among women and children, and marriage the only solution, is to use family structure to solve problems generated by the social structure. Such an approach overlooks the enduring gender inequality in economic structures. Also, marriage does not necessarily reverse poverty, particularly for working-class women and women of color. For instance, Brewer (1988, 344) noted that "an emphasis on female-headed households misses an essential truth about black women's poverty: black women are also poor in households with male heads." Higher wages in female-dominated jobs may be a more effective solution than marriage. This would not only help married, nuclear family households, but all families and households.

Similarly, marriage culture will not solve the larger economic problem of declining wages for working- and middle-class men brought by a postindustrial, service, and global economy.[7] Indeed, we could transform divorce culture by repairing wage declines for those most disadvantaged by this postindustrial economy—including many working-class men, especially men of color. This could remove sources of conflict and resentment within and across family groups. Yet, to address structural sources of inequality would only mitigate, and not reverse, divorce culture unless we attend to cultural beliefs about gender as well.

Pessimists advocate marriage culture in part because it would seem to solve so many problems of divorce culture at once, most especially divorced men's failure to provide and care for their children. Of all policies, child support has received the most attention by legislators and media over the last two decades. Only about half of custodial mothers with child support orders receive the full amount (Arendell 1995, 39). In 1991 the "average monthly child support paid by divorced fathers contributing economic support" was only $302 (for an estimated 1.5 children), and "child support payments amounted to only about 16% of the incomes of divorced mothers and their children" (Arendell 1997, 162). As a result of the Family Support Act of 1988, the mechanisms for securing child support from fathers have become more rigorous (Furstenberg and Cherlin 1991, 109); there are established formulas for calculating child support payments and, since 1994, all new child support payments are withheld from the paychecks of absent parents (mostly fathers). Yet, as Hewlett and West (1998, 180) observe, in spite of all the policies and prison terms, "the number of deadbeat dads has declined only slightly since 1978."[8]

We need new ways to address fathers' "failure to provide"—clearly, some fathers partly withdraw from marriage and children because they cannot be "good providers."[9] Yet, to focus on the provider role is to limit fatherhood to a model that evolved during the industrial era and is at odds with a postindustrial economy. One could say that this approach merely exchanges a "fragmented" fatherhood for its predecessor: a "shrinking" fatherhood (Blankenhorn 1995a).[10] Indeed, to focus on providing alone will only sustain men's detachment from parenting. "Studies do show that fathers who visit more regularly pay more in child support" (Furstenberg and Cherlin 1991, 274). Whether these payments are due to visiting or greater commitment, attention to the relational aspects of fathering would seem crucial.

Both optimistic and pessimistic scholars are concerned about the lack of paternal participation in children's lives. Most research shows a substantial and unacceptable decline over time in father-child contact after a divorce (Furstenberg and Cherlin 1991). Data from the recent National Survey of Families and Households reveals that about 30 percent of children of divorce have not seen their fathers at all in the preceding year, and many more see their fathers irregularly and infrequently (Arendell 1995, 38). Speaking of unmarried as well as divorced fathers, Hewlett and

West (1988, 168) report that "close to half of all fathers lose contact with their children."

Thus, all family scholars see a need to revitalize and redefine fatherhood. For example, a supporter of divorce culture, Arendell (1995, 251) protests: "Why should it be so difficult to be a nurturing, engaged father? Where are the institutional and ideological supports for parenting?" Arendell adds: "That caring fathers are subject to criticism and stigmatization points to a seriously flawed ideological system" (251). Also, advocates of marriage culture Hewlett and West (1998, 173) assert that "a withering of the father-child bond devastates children, stunts men, and seriously erodes our social capital." In spite of shared concerns, the means to a revitalized fatherhood are contested.

Just as critics of divorce culture suggest that marriage will alleviate the impoverishment of single mothers, they argue that fathers cannot be effective parents outside of the marriage structure (Blankenhorn 1995a; Hewlett and West 1998; Popenoe 1996; Wallerstein and Blakeslee 1989; Whitehead 1997a). For example, Hewlett and West (1998, 171–72) note that single males are more likely to die prematurely due to self-neglect, more likely to abuse drugs and alcohol, and are responsible for a disproportionate share of violence—including murder, robbery, and rape. They reason, like Durkheim, that marriage and children have a "civilizing" effect upon men.[11] In Blankenhorn's (1995a) view, both co-residence and a parental alliance with the mother are preconditions for effective fatherhood.

Undoubtedly, co-residence assists in the building of relationships—including, and especially, parent-child relationships. Yet, there is evidence to suggest it is not a precondition for effective fatherhood. In her study of divorced fathers, Arendell (1995) describes "innovative" divorced fathers (not all of whom had single custody) who were able to detach being a father from being a partner, separate anger at an ex-wife from their love for their children, focus on the children's needs rather than adult rights, and combine breadwinning with caretaking in ways that developed their nurturing and relational skills. While such fathers are too rare, fathers who parent effectively after divorce suggest that marriage or co-residence are not prerequisites—though alliances between parents do seem to be important whether outside or inside the marriage structure. Further, studies on nonresidential mothers show they are more active participants in their children's lives (Maccoby and Mnookin 1992, 212; Arendell 1997, 170). Finally, even if custody determinations were divided equally between women and men, co-residence would not always be an option for father and child. Suggesting marriage as the solution for divorce—and effective fathering—is empty advice for those compelled to divorce.[12]

Divorced fathers' flagging commitment seems to have exposed a tenuous responsibility for children in the first place. This may represent a "male flight from commitment" that started in the 1950s (Ehrenreich 1984); even so, this too should be understood as a legacy of separate spheres that identified masculinity with the provider role and devalued men's caretaking capacities (Bernard 1981; Coontz 1992). Since women still do the bulk of child rearing during a marriage, many divorced fathers have to learn how to be a primary parent after divorce (Arendell 1997, 163). As optimists and pessimists alike have observed, men appear to depend upon wives to mediate their relationship to their children (Arendell 1995, 33; Furstenberg and Cherlin 1991, 275; Wallerstein and Blakeslee 1989; Whitehead 1997b).[13] This may explain why marriage seems like the only solution for effective fathering for the pessimists.

Another route for expanding paternal participation—and overcoming the historical equivalence between breadwinning and masculinity[14] — would be to construct men as nurturers, caretakers, and responsible fathers. Arendell (1995, 251) calls for "a more vocal and widespread critique of the conventions of masculinity." A construction of masculinity that goes beyond putting all of men's eggs into one "breadwinner" basket (Bernard 1981) is long overdue. Perhaps marriage has an important "civilizing function" for men because of a flawed construction of masculinity in the first place; men have been deprived of the expectation or opportunity to advance their relationality—from boyhood to manhood.

Reinforcing marriage by compelling "divorce as a last resort" would obscure, not solve, this paternal disability. Rather than advocating marriage or reinforcing the provider role as pessimists do, many optimists argue that men need to combine providing with caretaking just as women have combined caretaking with providing. In the aggregate, women are changing faster than men. To keep up with wives' changes means that husbands must be willing to recognize the legitimacy of a wife's relational concerns, embrace what has been largely a devalued sphere, and to share power with their wives.

If a redistribution of relational responsibilities were to take place in marriage, this might extend fathers' involvement with their children in the event of divorce. More important, this could prevent divorces based on relational inequalities in the first place.[15] Indeed, in my research, paternal participation is part of the "marital labor" that egalitarian wives wanted to share. Reconstructing masculinity (and therefore gender in marriage) might provide the stronger deterrent to divorce for which pessimists have been searching.

IS DIVORCE EVER A GATEWAY FOR CHILDREN?

Given children's attenuated relations with their fathers and the downward mobility most children share with their mothers, is divorce ever a gateway for children? Not only do two-thirds of divorces involve children (U.S. Bureau of the Census 1995, P60-187), but few people object to divorce by childless couples today. Because it is children that electrify the divorce debates, I only sampled married parents. Are children paying the price for adults' individualism and lapsed family values, as the critics of divorce culture would argue? Or, could they be paying the costs of marriage culture and the quest for equality—interpersonal and institutional—that I have described?

Divorce is rarely experienced as a "gateway" for children—even perhaps, when it should be. It is, however, a turning point that is distinct from the adult experience. There is a tendency in the debates about the effects of divorce upon children to project adult experiences and capacities onto children. One recent study found that parents' and children's experiences were generally "out of synch" (Stewart et al. 1997, cited in Arendell 1998, 227). Parents may overestimate their child's well-being. Kitson with Holmes (1992, 227) found that most parents attribute very low levels of distress to their children, even though we know that the early period is hard for children. Whether divorce is due to a spouse's adultery, violence, or self-centeredness, the decision is not the child's to make. Of course, children survive and thrive after the temporary crisis of parental divorce, just as they survive other crises. Yet, the assumption that children are resilient should be tempered with the view that the endurance of parental relationships (even if they divorce) matters to children. Neither "divorce as a last resort" nor "divorce as a gateway" capture the divorce turning point for children, because they both presume some choice in the matter.[16]

Many studies agree upon some costs borne by children after a parental divorce, yet the source, extent, and meaning of these costs are fiercely debated (Wallerstein and Kelly 1980; Wallerstein and Blakeslee 1989; Amato and Booth 1997; Maccoby and Mnookin 1992; Hetherington, Law, and O'Connor 1993; Furstenberg and Cherlin 1991; Whitehead 1997a). The conditions preceding, surrounding, and following divorce matter a great deal, including the quality of parent-child relationships, custodial arrangements, the quality of the ex-spousal and coparenting relationships, the economic and social supports available, and the child's own psychological strengths (Furstenberg and Cherlin 1991; Kelly 1988, 134). The age and gender of the child may matter—though gender effects have been questioned (Arendell 1997, 175; Wallerstein and Kelly 1980; Kelly

1988; Wallerstein and Blakeslee 1989). Remarriage and new stepfamily relations affect a child's adjustment over time; indeed, some research suggests remarriage may be more of an adjustment than divorce (Ahrons and Rodgers 1987, 257).

Drawing upon an analysis of 92 studies involving 13,000 children, Amato (1994, 145) reports consistent findings that children of divorce experience "lower academic achievement, more behavioral problems, poorer psychological adjustment, more negative self-concepts, more social difficulties, and more problematic relationships with both mothers and fathers. Also, children of divorce are reported to become pregnant outside of marriage, marry young, and divorce upon becoming adults (McLanahan and Bumpass 1988; Glenn and Kramer 1987).

Taken together, these findings would seem to be alarming. The pessimists are alarmed. Yet, we should not assume that divorce is the "cause" when divorce is correlated with undesirable effects among children. Research on the adverse effects of divorce for children consistently finds that other factors that accompany divorce may be more important than the divorce itself. For example, "income differences account for almost 50 percent of the disadvantage faced by children in single-parent households" (McLanahan and Sandefur 1994; Coontz 1997, 101). Changes of residence and schools help to explain the other 50 percent of disadvantage. Above all, prospective and longitudinal studies of families suggest that marital conflict is more crucial than divorce in explaining behavioral and emotional problems for those children who are troubled (Amato and Booth 1996, 1997; Block, Block, and Gjerde, 1986; Coontz 1997, 102). Longitudinal studies have discovered that children's problems are apparent over a decade before the parents' divorce. Thus, in some cases, divorce and a single-parent household is better for children than continued marital conflict (Amato, Loomis, and Booth 1995).

Furthermore, Amato's (1994) analysis of multiple studies also reveals that the effects of divorce are very weak and that differences between children of divorce and children in continuously intact families are quite small (Amato and Keith 1991; Amato 1994; Amato and Booth 1996, 1997). As the optimist Coontz (1997, 99) clarifies, this research does not suggest that children of divorced parents have *more problems*, rather that *more children* of divorced parents have problems than do children of married parents. Yet, children of divorce show greater variability in their adjustment (Amato 1994). This means that some children of divorce do better than children of married parents. Children from all kinds of families fare well and poorly. When we focus on the difference between family structures, we overlook the extensive overlap in children's well-being across family structures. Further, research increasingly suggests that the quality and consistency of family life, and not family structure, influences children's well-being (Arendell 1997, 187).

Most of the '70s couples I interviewed did not believe in staying together "for the sake of the children" if there was marital conflict. Parents sense that if their marriage is continuously in conflict, then this harms children too. Divorce is not a singular solution to conflict or violence since both can be exacerbated upon separation and divorce (Arendell and Kurz, 1999). Yet the gateway is crucial for such troubled marriages. Recall that the '50s Dominicks stayed together miserably for thirty years in spite of extramarital affairs, separation, and indications of violence—all for the sake of the children. These were justifiable conditions under the terms of marriage culture. One wonders to what degree the "sake of the children," among other deterrents, inhibited divorces that should have been when marriage culture reigned uncontested.[17]

Kurz's (1995, 52) random sample of divorced mothers revealed that 19 percent pursued divorce specifically because of violence; however, an astonishing 70 percent reported at least one incident of violence during the marriage or separation. Most research shows that violence remains a graver problem for wives than husbands—particularly in terms of injuries (Gelles and Straus 1988; Kurz 1989; Straton 1994). Also, research increasingly finds that witnessing spouse abuse *is* child abuse—even when a child is not physically violated (Holden, Geffner, and Jouriles 1998). Thus, removing children from the perpetrator, however much he (or she) is loved, is arguably for the sake of the children.

Believers in "divorce as a gateway" may want to make parental happiness equivalent to children's happiness when it is not. Pessimists correctly stress that the child's experience of divorce is distinct from the parents' experience. Thus, scholars are increasingly advocating parenting education classes for divorcing parents (Arendell 1995; Wallerstein 1998). Yet, believers in "divorce as a last resort" also mistakenly presume that the maintenance of marriage and a nuclear family is equivalent to children's happiness. We should not ignore the injuries that have attended marriage culture—particularly a male-dominated marriage culture. When egalitarian spouses become parents there is often a shift toward "increased traditionality of family and work roles in families of the 1980s and 1990s," and this "tends to be associated with *more* individual and marital distress for parents" (Cowan and Cowan 1998, 184). This represents the pinch between egalitarian beliefs and the structural impediments to equality in practice. Further, to the degree that we idealize a male-dominated, nuclear family model we cannot fail to reproduce such constructions of inequality among children. While some children are paying a price for the quest for equality, children also pay a price when the thread of commitment is tangled with the thread of male dominance. Moreover, children do find happiness and another vision of equality in alternative family forms.

THE FUTURE OF DIVORCE CULTURE

From Durkheim (1961) to Giddens (1979, 1991), sociologists have regularly addressed transitional periods such as our own. Norms, ideals, and authorities that guided our marital practices in the past are inadequate to families' needs in today's socioeconomic context. Could divorce culture represent a new tapestry of ideals and norms for guiding today's family lives? Even as the practices of '70s spouses are shaped by novel conditions, spouses attempt to shape them in turn—drawing alternatively, selectively, and even haphazardly on available ideologies and practices. Although divorce culture seems to be replacing marriage culture, it should be seen as a transitional means for "people to make sense of the circumstances in which they find themselves" (Mullings 1986), providing alternative strategies for action when marriage culture falls short. Still, like the '70s spouses, many people are ambivalent about divorce culture. Moreover, marriage culture endures.

Because divorce culture is new and unsettling there is a tendency to inflate its power and prevalence. Marriage culture is widely embraced. "Marriage as forever" is a belief that is not only sustained by married couples, but also the divorced (Riessman 1990). The reintroduction of grounds in "covenant marriages" represents a political effort to value the old tapestry that sustained "divorce as a last resort." Finally, "marrying as a given" lives on. While rates of marriage and remarriage have decreased since the mid-1960s (U.S. Bureau of the Census, 1992, P23-180, 8)—suggesting that fewer people experience marriage as an imperative—the majority of people eventually marry. Also, the two-parent family continues to be the predominant family form—so concern with its decline can be overstated (Cowan and Cowan 1998, 189).

Marriage culture also lives on in the next generation's aspirations. The majority of young people say they value marriage and plan to marry (Landis-Kleine et al. 1995). A 1992 survey, showed that of all extremely important goals in life, the most valued by 78 percent of the high school respondents was "having a good marriage and family life"(Glenn 1996, 21). "Being able to find steady work" was ranked a close second by 77 percent of these students, and "being successful in my line of work" and "being able to give my children better opportunities than I've had" tied for third, at 66 percent.

Will the '90s spouses continue, reverse, or transcend the advance of divorce culture? How will they cope with the rise of divorce culture and its problems? Because a culture of divorce creates "divorce anxiety," premarital counseling would seem to be increasingly important. One valuable component of "covenant marriage" advanced by pessimists (in spite of critiques of therapeutic culture) has been to encourage religious or secular premarital counseling. Instituting therapy before marriage might prepare '90s spouses for the reflexive process and the marital work that characterizes marriage in an era of change, choice, and uncertainty.[18] Such counseling should not only attune spouses to one another's hopes, dreams, and desires, but should also provide information on the social conditions faced by married couples today. For example, the arrival of children is a vulnerable period of transition in marriage even when children are deeply desired (Cowan and Cowan 1998). Also, '90s spouses should know that aspirations for lifetime marriage, for thriving children, and a good job are not new; most people getting married share these hopes for themselves even as they harbor doubts about others. What thwarts their resolve and aspirations? Do they simply become individualistic?

This analysis of divorce culture has tried to situate the charges that a high divorce rate represents increased individualism in recent generations. On the one hand, like the pessimists, I agree that divorce culture is marked by individualism. Individualism clearly links and underlies the tenets of divorce culture: the choice to marry, to set conditions, and the chance to unmarry all speak to the primacy of the individual to redesign his or her life. However, my research complicates these claims. Individualism is not in a zero-sum relationship with commitment. It can be morally responsible rather than egoistic, it has not been absent for men in marriage culture, and it is not necessarily an end in itself. Divorce culture exposes how the terms of marital commitment reflect a legacy of male dominance. For married women, individualism can be a tool to resist old and enforce new terms of marital commitment—including nurturance, commitment, and relational responsibility shared by both spouses. When mothers use the power of individualism for relational ends—by working to provide, by removing children from violent households, or by refusing to be subordinated—individualism is neither an end in itself nor easily severed from committed responsibility. The meaning of pulling the individualistic lever of divorce culture cannot be stripped from interactional or institutional contexts. Thus, '90s spouses would also do well to take the insights of optimists into account. Our quest for equality is ongoing.

Finally, an overemphasis on the individualism of women or men diverts our attention from the ways our social structures obstruct this quest for equality. The variety of families today may not represent a failure of commitment as much as individuals' valiant struggles to sustain commitments in a society that withholds structural supports from workers and families. Indeed, until the 1993 Family and Medical Leave Act, the United States had no family policy at all.[19] Other scholars have suggested an array of family policies—from easing work and family conflicts to providing economic and social supports—for today's burdened families, which I will not repeat here (see Arendell 1995; Burggraf 1997; Hewlett and West 1998; Hochschild 1997; Mason, Skolnick, and Sugarman 1998). Yet, two things are clear—when we allow corporate and government policies to neglect the needs of working parents, we are undermining marriage culture, and when we ignore enduring gender inequalities we advance divorce culture.

While divorce culture is flawed, I see it as a means to propel marital and family relationships in an egalitarian direction. Both "optional marriage" and "divorce as a gateway" recognize commitments apart from marriage, expose the costs of marriage culture, and legitimate diverse family arrangements. Critics of divorce culture advocate a return to the singular design of the nuclear family structure; however, in many ways this sustains a white, middle-class ethnocentrism,[20] and a heterosexism[21] that has marked our family ideals. By challenging "marriage as a given" and "divorce as a last resort," divorce culture helps to destigmatize unmarried families.

As we reconstruct the terms of marriage culture with the tool of divorce culture, we risk sacrificing relationality for rights equality. Rights language is essential for justice, dignity, and self-determination. Yet, it is not an unmitigated good, and only the young, childless, wealthy, or powerful can indulge in a sense of independence and obscure interdependence by relying upon others to sustain the illusion. Only when the relational responsibilities, still constructed as "feminine," are practiced and valued by men, and by the society at large, will we be able to move beyond the individualism of divorce culture and beyond a notion of equality limited to individual rights and obscuring relational responsibilities. Whether divorce culture eventually supplants rather than contests marriage culture, or generates "family cultures" that transcend this contestation, will depend upon social structural change and the quest for relational equality in the next generation.

Appendix
Methodological Notes

RESEARCH DESIGN: DATA SOURCES

To analyze the meaning of marriage for women and men married before and after the 1970s, I compared archival in-depth and longitudinal interviews with matched wives and husbands born around 1928 and married around 1950 to my own in-depth interviews with matched wives and husbands born around 1953 and married after 1970. Altogether, I analyzed a series of interviews with 26 individuals whom I have referred to as the "'50s spouses," and I conducted interviews with 34 matched "'70s spouses."[1] Neither sample can be said to fully represent the general population of married couples from the '50s or the '70s. Still, I took care to select a range of couples and experiences.

The '50s Couples

I selected 12 couples from a longitudinal study at the Institute of Human Development at the University of California, Berkeley. My sample is a small subset of 248 individuals who were selected by every third birth born to residents surveyed in a San Francisco Bay Area city between January 1928 and June 1929. Researchers collected enormous amounts of physical and psychological data throughout these subjects' childhoods; by around 1946, as they were about to graduate from high school, about 60 percent of the original sample were still involved in the study. By the time they were 30 years of age, the subjects were recalled for further data collection, which included interviews discussing their educational, occupational, marital, and parental careers. At this time, in 1958, subjects' spouses were included irregularly. Between 1969 and 1971, the original subjects (now about 40 years of age) and their spouses each participated in an in-depth interview.[2] Finally, between 1981 and 1983, both subjects and spouses were recalled for two more sets of interviews: a structured interview and a clinical interview.[3] On the average, I read seven interviews for each of the twelve couples across the decades. Altogether, I read 86 interviews ranging from 20 to 120 pages each, averaging about 50 pages.

The data collection for the '50s couples primarily occurred between the fall of 1991 and the spring of 1992. Of the 12 couples I studied, 10 were selected for their enduring marriages, on the basis of marital satisfaction scores compiled in 1982.[4] Two couples were divorced and remarried and were selected for comparative purposes. The current *and* former spouses of these two original subjects (a man and a woman, divorced and remarried by 1970), had been interviewed around 1971 along with the subject; by the 1982 interviews, only the second spouse was interviewed with the subject. Selection of cases was partially determined by the number of subjects and spouses who fully participated at all three follow-ups. Therefore, this sample may be constituted by people who are more committed to social research.

The policy of the Institute of Human Development prohibited the removal of these interviews from the archives. Thus, I dictated the selected passages into a tape recorder and then selectively transcribed these for analysis. I substantially winnowed the data in three stages. First, I read through all the interviews, coding relevant passages and sections where subjects talked about their spouses, marriages, divorces, marital life, gendered observations and responsibilities, the women's movement, their children, etc. In the structured interviews, these topics were likely to be addressed under relevant subheadings, such as "marital history," although sometimes relevant passages were discovered under categories such as "military career." In the open-ended, clinical interviews, spouses' talk about gender, marriage, and divorce could be located anywhere in the transcript.

After reading the interviews in their entirety, I returned to the coded interview passages, taking notes of essentially two kinds: verbatim notes (quotes and interviewers' observations) and theoretical memos (conceptual links that occurred to me as I read). These memos were useful guides as I reviewed earlier interviews, reading them in light of the later interviews. For example, it was only in 1982 that spouses began to describe "getting married" as "a given"; if they described reasons for getting married earlier, the "givenness" of the marriage was not mentioned, even after 8 or 20 years of marriage in 1958 and 1970, respectively. I began to conclude that their retrospective accounts of "getting married" were shaped and made visible by the rise of the alternative vocabulary of "marrying as an option." I could not incorporate analysis into data collection because this was archival data; yet, I returned to the '50s data when I began my intragenerational analysis, much later. In sum, I followed the procedures of "grounded theory" within the limits of my data (Corbin and Strauss 1990; Glaser and Strauss 1967; Schwartz and Jacobs 1979; McCracken 1988; Strauss 1987).

The demographic characteristics of the '50s spouses varied to a degree. My sample was limited not only by the selection of spouses based on marital satisfaction scores, but also by the nature of the longitudinal sample (see Table 1). Overall, more upwardly mobile and middle-class couples continued their participation in this longitudinal sample over time. Eichorn (1981, 41) points out that by the adult interviews 90 percent of the longitudinal samples were middle class, due to funding restrictions, deaths, and selective attrition. Above all, the participants experienced enormous social mobility over the course of the study. The majority of the '50s spouses in my study are, likewise, middle class.[5] Education ranges from some high school to college graduates and beyond (10 to 18 years); the majority have some college experience. Occupations include executives and professionals, business managers and teachers, administrative personnel, homemakers, and clerical workers.

Racial and ethnic diversity was negligible in the larger sample; thus, I oversampled for some racial/ethnic variation, resulting in a group of 20 European-American and four African-American spouses. There was no intermarriage by

Table I. Characteristics of Older and Younger Generation Samples

Demographics	'50s Spouses	'70s Spouses
Class Status		
Working	3 (11%)	2 (6%)
Lower-middle	4 (15%)	2 (6%)
Middle	13 (50%)	22 (65%)
Upper-middle	6 (23%)	8 (23%)
Race-ethnicity		
African-American	4 (15%)	5 (15%)
Asian-American	0 (0%)	5 (15%)
Euro-American	22 (85%)	21 (62%)
Biracial	0 (0%)	3 (8%)
(Native American, African American, Latino, Euro-American)		
Education		
Less than 12 yrs.	1 (4%)	2 (6%)
High school graduate	8 (31%)	7 (21%)
Some college	5 (19%)	0 (0%)
College graduate	5 (19%)	11 (32%)
Professional (16+ yrs.)	6 (23%)	14 (41%)
Unknown	1 (4%)	0 (0%)
Religious affinity		
Buddhist	0 (0%)	4 (12%)
Jewish	2 (8%)	4 (12%)
Protestant	11 (42%)	9 (26%)
Catholic	8 (31%)	3 (9%)
Mormon	3 (11%)	0 (0%)
None	2 (8%)	14 (41%)
Percent remarried	6 (23%)	9 (26%)
Average year of marriage	1950	1979
Children		
Mean number	3	2
Range	0–6	1–4
Total N	26	34

race. Most of the 26 individuals were affiliated with Christianity at some point in their lives, though two were raised within Judaism, and two reported no religious affiliation.

While white, middle-class Americans have been over-studied, it remains pertinent to analyze the middle class because middle-class behaviors and beliefs still tend to be perceived and represented as "normative" (Skolnick 1991). Paradoxically, the rise of "normlessness" regarding marriage and divorce patterns can be increasingly perceived as "normative" when practiced by whites and the middle class (Peters and McAdoo 1983; Stacey 1990).

Table 2. Historical Location of Generations

	1950	1958	1970	1982	1990–92
Generation					
'50s spouses*	Married	(1st interview, subject only)	(2nd interview, each spouse)	(3rd interview, each spouse)	
'70s spouses		Born		Married	Interviewed (separately and jointly)
Sociocultural context	Marriage culture hegemony		Marital watershed**		Marriage and Divorce cultures

* Born 1928
** Demographic, legal, social, and economic developments

Among the '50s couples, the mean year of marriage was 1950 and the mean age at first marriage was 21.7. The twelve couples averaged three children each. By 1970, their children were generally teenagers, and a few were adults. By 1982, they were considering retirement.

This design allowed me to uncover the "conditional matrix," or how structural conditions enter into the daily interactions and meanings that make a marriage (Corbin and Strauss 1990). As Table 2 suggests, the post-1970 interviews for the Older and Younger generation are almost a decade apart. While it would have been preferable to have 1990 interview data for the Older generation, recontacting these spouses was not an option. This is a limitation in my research design, yet the two samples do allow for an analysis of meanings before and after the 1970 watershed. In terms of life stage, the 1970 interviews are most comparable to the interviews with the '70s couples in the 1990s.

The '70s Couples

The '70s couples were selected with an eye toward generational comparison. I wanted a sample of individuals who conceivably could be the children of the older sample. I built a sample that was similar to the Older generation in terms of regional influence, marital and parental status, and class status, but regularly varied by at least twenty years of age. I wanted the couples to have children and to be in long-term relationships—to have surpassed both the current mode (about two years) and mean (about seven years) durations of marriages for those who divorce. I reasoned that such a sample would be more resilient vis-à-vis divorce, and yet would have confronted the reality of widespread divorce since 1970.

The 34 spouses were born in the early 1950s and married in the late 1970s. For 10 of the 17 couples, one spouse is an alumnus from a 1971 or 1972 graduating class of a San Francisco Bay Area high school. In order to locate individuals who were born in the early 1950s and were from the same region as the Older generation, I pursued high school graduating classes of the early 1970s. I gained access to the reunion listings for the classes of 1971 and 1972—listings which contained recent names and addresses.

To locate *married,* as opposed to single or divorced, alumni, I relied on addresses, names, photographs indicating couples, and referrals from others within the high school class. I began by mailing out a letter to every third eligible couple on the list explaining my research, requesting their participation, and asking them to call or write me with a response at their convenience. While I obtained some responses this way, most of my letters seemed to disappear into a void. Thus, the next batch of letters was not only delimited in terms of region and likelihood of being married, but also in terms of the availability of their phone numbers. Thus, the sample could be described as nonmovers, reuniongoers, and people who list their phone numbers, implying people who prefer stability to mobility, sustain old contacts, and are accessible in the community. Yet, these differences should not be overplayed, since I also included seven couples selected in a different context.

In August 1990, I was hired as one of four interviewers for the Marriage Project, a study conducted by Dr. Judith Wallerstein that eventually formed the basis for her book *The Good Marriage* (1995). Every interviewer was assigned to interview couples who were in her "area" of the Bay, to reduce transportation costs around the Bay Area. Dr. Wallerstein agreed that I could use my interview data for the purposes of my research because several of our sample parameters (married couples with children), methods (the in-depth interviewing of matched couples—separately and then together), and areas of inquiry (about the nature of the marriage) overlapped.[6]

Of the 12 couples I interviewed for the Marriage Project, I selected seven to include in this research.[7] These seven couples conformed to the average age of my spouses and allowed for a range of differences important to "theoretical sampling" in the grounded theory tradition. For example, these individuals were less likely to be from the Bay Area; five were from out of state.

Interviews with couples from the Marriage Project occurred from the summer of 1990 to the spring of 1991, while interviews with the other couples began in the spring of 1992 and were concluded in the fall of 1992. The structure of the interview process for both samples of '70s spouses was virtually identical. After participants agreed to be interviewed, three interviews were scheduled for each couple. The husband and wife were each interviewed separately. After these individual interviews were completed, a joint interview was scheduled. Three couples were not scheduled for a joint interview due to scheduling conflicts and time limitations. In sum, for the '70s spouses, I conducted 34 individual interviews and 14 joint interviews, totaling 48 interviews.[8] All the interviews were tape-recorded and transcribed.

Individual interviews lasted an average of two and one-half hours each, and joint interviews lasted an average of two hours. A brief questionnaire solicited information regarding births, marriages, income ranges, race/ethnicities, levels of education, etc. I also introduced a release form at the beginning of every individual interview that explained my study and their rights as respondents. Spouses were not only guaranteed confidentiality in future publications, but were promised confidentiality in the individual interviews vis-à-vis the joint interview. I did not bring up issues in the joint interview that had been raised in their individual interviews, although spouses were free to mention the individual interviews and most of them did. In this book I have left out emphatically confidential material (such as sexual affairs) and have changed information that other people could conceivably use to identify the couple.

Interviewing the couple together was a small, but significant, attempt to introduce the advantages of participant observation. I was able to see how what they *said* about the marriage related to what they *did* within the marriage. I was able to get a sense of their marital dynamics, see how they dealt with conflict, avoided or approached topics, exercised humor, and often, how they interacted with their children. I did not have the resources to devise the "component marital satisfaction scores" that were available for the Older generation, but the joint interview enabled me to assess their marital quality. My subjective sense of a couple's marital well-being is as problematic as self-reports (Krokoff 1989; Skolnick 1981). Still, by monitoring my own subjective level of tension or pleasure in joint interviews I was able to "tell" whether a couple was essentially happy or not at that time and can safely assert that these 17 couples ranged in marital satisfaction. A sense of their marital satisfaction influenced my interpretations of some "divorce talk," yet new cultural meanings seemed to be shared across levels of marital stability. Indeed, the meaning of "marital happiness" is part of what is being redefined in divorce culture.

Studying married couples naturally included and excluded people on three demographic parameters: marital status, gender, and sexual orientation. My aim here was to understand the meaning of divorce from the standpoint of those eligible to divorce: heterosexual married couples. The average age of the '70s spouses was 39 at the time of the interview. Three-quarters of the sample were in their first marriage, and the average age at first marriage was 26. About half of the couples had married in the late 1970s and about half married in the 1980s. Six couples had been married less than 10 years, and eleven couples had been married 10 or more years. All of the couples were raising children.

The mean length of marriage was 11 years, yet these couples also had known each other for an average of 5 years before marrying. Perhaps reflecting the liberal Bay Area region, 11 of the couples had lived together before marriage. Although 11 out of 17 couples is high, Goode (1993, 159) pointed out that by the mid-1980s, half of the married population aged 30–34 (the age of my '70s spouses) had cohabited at some time.

Thirteen of the '70s couples were in dual-job or dual-career marriages. Thus, 76 percent of the '70s wives worked, compared to the national average of 57.8 percent of wives in the labor force in 1992 (Reskin and Padavic 1994, 143). Occupations ranged from clerical, social work, teaching, and small businesses, to work requiring professional degrees, such as law. As Table 1 shows, educational background varied as well.

Because of the middle-class status of the '50s couples (and changing marriage and divorce patterns among the middle class), I decided to maintain a comparable middle-class sample for the '70s couples. However, I did not anticipate or select for the relatively high class status of many of the couples. The class *background* of the spouses ranged considerably, but their *current* class status was relatively high and varied less. The modal income range for the younger sample was from fifty to seventy-five thousand dollars a year. This is higher than the Bay Area averages taken as a whole. The median income for the San Francisco metropolitan areas was $41,459 in 1989 (1993 County and City Extra: Annual Metro, City and County Data Book 1992–93). Most individuals were college graduates and some had master's degrees. All but three of the couples were homeowners; in contrast, about 57 percent of housing units were owner-occupied in 1989 in this same area. Education, income, occupations and home ownership all indicated a middle- to upper-middle-class standing. (See Table 1 for more details.)[9]

The relative affluence of this sample seems to be, first of all, a product of self-selection. It was easier for those with more resources to participate since they had more control over their time and child care. These interviews demanded that both spouses participate and be able to schedule a joint interview when the children were not present. Also, the more highly educated are apt to see value in social research and likely to be higher earners. A higher class status may have followed from using a reunion list as a sampling frame (assuming reunions appeal to those who feel successful in their lives) and from some sampling through professional associations in the Marriage Project. Finally, married couples—particularly long-term married couples—tend to be better off financially because they have had the opportunity to accumulate resources. A sample of long-term married couples automatically eliminates the divorced, who are likely to be less affluent.

Although the 1950s spouses were largely white, I decided it was crucial to include some racial and ethnic variation to avoid creating yet another study theorizing on the basis of the experiences of European-Americans alone. I wanted racial/ethnic variation to inform my "grounded theory," even though I did not systematically examine racial/ethnic differences in marital meanings. While interracial marriages had skyrocketed in the San Francisco Bay Area, I did not expect a preponderance of interracial marriages (4 of the 17 marriages).[10] An integrated high school experience may have favored these relationships. Also, there was a tendency for people of color to state that they wanted to participate in my marriage study because they were "proud" of their marriage, and interracial couples may have been motivated by similar reasons. This desire to positively represent family lives can be understood in light of the distorted representations of families of color by white researchers and the media. Given the oppressive uses to which past social research has been put, I valued the trust that spouses of color extended to this white researcher from a predominantly white research institution—though I also have no doubt that my identity as a white, middle-class woman influenced the nature of the interaction and the data collected (Anderson 1993; Edwards 1990; Riessman 1987; Rollins 1985).[11]

As with the '50s couples, religious variation emerged naturally. Spouses' religious upbringing was often different from their current religious practice. One clear pattern emerged: religious identification was more salient as a child than as an adult; the primary category of identification in childhood was Christian (18), but the primary category reported as adults was None (14). By adulthood, 14 reported no religious identification, 9 reported being Protestant, 3 Catholic, 4 Jewish, and 4 Buddhist.

PROCESSES OF ANALYSIS

Grounded theory advocates the use of "sensitizing concepts," but also encourages an open-ended approach to the field or one's data. It is an approach that involves modifying hypotheses as the analysis proceeds, trying to disprove hypotheses, and making comparisons between and within cases (Gilgun 1992; Glaser and Strauss 1967). My analysis was guided by grounded theory in four ways. First, I relied upon theoretical sampling (I assumed that degrees of marital satisfaction, religious involvement, therapeutic participation, and a first marriage versus a remarriage would be relevant conditions for analyzing variable meanings of divorce). Second, I relied upon the "constant comparative" method by going back and forth between interviews to see whether and how the concepts of, for example, "divorce as a means to growth" clustered with other concepts, such as "never fantasized about marriage." Third, I looked for negative cases: for example, after seeing that women seemed to be changing faster in terms of gender and marital ideologies, I found exceptions to this relationship. Finally, concepts emerged in the process of doing the research; for example, I had not theorized about the strategies that spouses used to cope with divorce before I entered the field.

I proceeded with post-positivist assumptions to the degree that I aimed for a research design that would yield two generations of married couples that would be alike in nearly every way except for their generational difference.[12] However, I have also been influenced by feminist and constructivist paradigms that submit that the interviewing process is an interactive, co-construction of meaning (Oakley 1981; Reinharz 1992; Stacey 1988).[13] I aimed not only to create a context for a focused conversation (rather than a stiff interchange implied by structured interviews), but also to view the focused conversation as a joint production of meanings by the participant(s) and myself. An open-ended approach allowed the spouses to shape the direction of the interview. Every interview touched upon the key areas in the interview guide, but the wording and order of the questions varied widely. I always opened with the question "What's good about your marriage?" but the interviews went in various directions as I pursued their responses to this question.[14] Also, I reserved questions about divorce for later in the interview, unless the spouses volunteered information, opinions, or thoughts about divorce—which they frequently did. Finally, I was continuously reflexive about my influence on the interactions with spouses. I was as attuned to the "halting, hesitant, tentative talk" of spouses as I was to the articulate speech, both while interviewing and while doing analysis (DeVault 1990, 103).

The Emergence of Concepts and Categories

I began to analyze the data by repeatedly poring over the interviews to create a matrix of responses to each of the key questions by each of the individual spouses.

I listed each wife by each husband so that I could compare their responses in the process. Several clusters of responses gradually began to serve as indicators of emergent concepts. For example, in answer to questions regarding how they viewed marriage when they were in high school (or if they imagined themselves married when they reached adulthood) answers varied from "I never thought about marriage," or "I just wanted to live with someone," to "I always knew I'd marry and have a family." These responses became indicators of the concepts "marrying as an option" and "marrying as a given." These concepts, in turn, informed the categories of "marriage culture" and "divorce culture."

The concepts of "marriage as forever" and "divorce as a last resort" versus "marriage as contingent" and "divorce as a gateway" were similarly indicated by an array of statements that emerged in a variety of contexts. Thus, after my initial matrix responses, I constructed new matrices of concepts rather than indicators. For example, under "divorce as a gateway" I entered the various contexts in which spouses talked about the liberating and growth potential of divorce.

Some emergent indicators and concepts were unanticipated and less straightforward than others. For example, I did not preconceive the idea of the "hypothetical divorce." This notion of divorces that "could have been" (in their own personal histories of relationships) was initially obscured among the competing reasons why spouses felt their own marriage would endure (the same interests, married young, married old, right person, right time, etc.). As people repeatedly drew upon these instances to serve as a contrast to their current marital well-being, I concluded that this was in fact a strategy specific to divorce culture. It became apparent that these strategies were significantly related to spouses' claims regarding the premises of marriage and divorce culture.

"Gender ideology" was indicated by statements about who should head the household, who made final decisions, how labor was divided in the marriage, and whether they felt their marriage was "equal" or "fair." It also emerged as spouses reported their marital disappointments. Furthermore, as spouses discussed reasons for rising divorce in the society at large, many spouses pointed to gender ideology (either belief in the male as head of the household or in equality) to explain enduring or dissolving marriages (their own or others).

Initially, I used "ideal types" as a heuristic device in the Weberian tradition to explain how spouses are variously defining and redefining marriage in the context of widespread divorce and to emphasize the salience of gender equality; a two-by-two table with male dominance or gender equality on one axis and marriage culture and divorce culture on another axis helped me to situate the ideological tendencies of spouses. Yet, spouses' ambivalence, changes over time, and the contradictions between their beliefs and reported practices meant that people did not easily fit such types. Thus, in the book I describe a range of ideological tendencies in a marital context marked by contestation between marriage and divorce culture and negotiation over the meaning of gender in marriage. While a typology is neat, life is not so clear-cut.

INDIVIDUAL INTERVIEW GUIDE FOR '70S SPOUSES

I. Opening Questions

What's good about your marriage? What would your spouse say? What would your children say?

What's not good? What would your spouse say? What would your children say? How easy/difficult has it been to have a good marriage? What does it mean to be married? Do you and your spouse share the same idea of what it means to be married?

II. Story of Relationship

How did you meet? Year? Ages? What attracted you to each other? Was desire balanced early on?

How would others have described you early on? Later? What were the delights of your relationship? The problems? Why did you decide to marry the person you did? Of all factors, which encouraged or discouraged, influenced you to get married? Not get married? Did you ever live together?

III. Early Loves

Did you have any early loves? Any major losses in love? Anyone you almost married?

Or, story of divorce if remarried—Was anything learned from this relationship?

IV. Familial Reactions to Marriage

Who asked whom to marry? Who told which families? What did it mean to your parents that you made this choice? What did you communicate to your parents by your choice? Did they all attend the wedding? Was anyone important absent?

V. Parents' Marriage

How would you compare marriage today to your parents' generation? How was their marriage as a model for you? How would you characterize their marriage? What made you proud, sad, embarrassed about their marriage? How do you want your own marriage to be like theirs, or different?

When you were in high school, how important was marriage to you when you imagined yourself grown? Did you envision it? Did you anticipate becoming a parent?

VI. Work and Leisure

How much time do you and your spouse spend together and apart? What activities/interests do you share? What values do you share? are there values that clearly differentiate the two of you?

How have you made decisions regarding money, jobs, home maintenance, religion, child care, kin care, etc.?

Does your marriage feel fair or equal to you? To your spouse?

What are the good things about being a woman/man? How have changes in women's roles affected your marriage?

VII. *Sex Life*

How has sex been for the two of you? Was your spouse your first sexual partner?

Did sex change with marriage, pregnancy, children? How important is sex to you (1–10)? To your spouse (1–10)?

To what extent have you been satisfied with the frequency of sex? The quality?

Have you had fantasies of affairs, or had affairs? Have these affected your marriage?

Would you tell spouse if you had an affair? What would happen?

VIII. *Parenthood*

Were children an expected part of your marriage?

How and when did you decide to have children?

How has becoming a parent changed you and your spouse?

What's your spouse like as a parent? Does your spouse think you are a good parent?

In what ways do you hope your children will be like your spouse? And you?

What advice will you give your children about marriage when the time comes?

IX. *Marital Challenges*

What would break your marriage? Has your marriage ever been threatened? Have you ever been close to calling it quits? Ever discussed separating or been separated?

How do you deal with conflicts? Have you ever sought any sort of therapy? Read articles on therapy?

What's been the biggest disappointment in your marriage? Your spouse's?

What's been the biggest surprise? What's been the most important decision?

What's been the biggest compromise for you? Your spouse?

If your spouse died/divorced you what would you lose? What's possible only with this spouse?

X. *Reflections on Marriage/Divorce*

What are the biggest threats to marriages today?

When were you first exposed to divorce? Through family, friends? Were there any divorces in your family? In your spouse's? How would your family, friends, community respond to your divorce? Have you seen any close friends go through divorce?

How did you support them? (And they you?)

Any ritualistic observances that you have engaged in, such as sending a card upon a divorce?

How do first and later weddings differ?

What do you know about current divorce law? Is it too lenient or strict in your opinion?

Are there any good models of marriage in the public eye today? In TV, films, or literature? Are there any shows that capture what it means to be married today? To experience divorce?

XI. Overview and Closing Questions

What have you learned about yourself and about your spouse over the course of your relationship?

How have you changed? How has your spouse changed?

How do others view the two of you now? Have there been other major changes that have impacted your relationship (deaths, illnesses, moves, job changes, etc.)?

What dreams have you realized? What dreams have gone unrealized?

What fears/hopes do you have regarding the future? Do you anticipate any major decisions?

Is there anything important to understanding you and your marriage that I've missed?

JOINT INTERVIEW GUIDE FOR '70s COUPLES

Introductory Statement

1. *Review:* I have met with each of you separately. I do not bring up material from the individual interview portion of our interactions (rules of confidentiality).

2. *Overview:* The aim of this interview is to think with you about the span of your relationship and how you and your spouse have developed over time as a couple and as individuals. To discuss your unique family heritage and family histories. What did you each bring with you in the way of expectations, traditions, aspirations?

I. Marital Ups and Downs

[Each individual is provided with cards on which to write their responses. The spouses trade the cards for reflection and discussion after Question IVA.]

A. Thinking over the course of your relationship/marriage, what event or experience has been the marital high point? Approximate year?

B. Thinking over the course of your marriage, what's been the marital low point? Year?

II. *Individual*

A. Thinking over your individual experiences, apart from the marriage, what experience, event has been your individual high point?

B. Again, thinking of your individual experience what's been your individual low point?

III. *Other*

A. Thinking about your spouse's individual life over the course of the marriage, what do you think has been his/her individual high point?

B. His/her individual low point?

IV. *Chapters*

A. If you were to break down the story of your relationship into chapters, how many would there be and what would you name them? [*trade cards*]

1. What do you see? Are there some similarities/differences?

2. Does your III A and B match their II A and B? What do you think of each other's responses? Any surprises?

FAVORITE FAMILY PHOTOS

1. How did you come to select these pictures?

2. What do they represent for you about these people, this place, and this time?

3. What do you make of the expressions? The arrangement? Are there any pictures you wanted to show but didn't get to?

FAMILY HERITAGE

1. Looking at your family backgrounds, how similar or different were you and your spouse in terms of: (a) economic status, (b) ethnic/racial background, (c) religion, (d) education, (e) occupation, (f) emotional styles?

   How important was the difference or similarity to you early in the relationship and how important is it now?

2. What values do your families share and what values would you say differentiate them?

3. What kinds of traditions from your own families do you recreate with your children? Are the traditions of one side of the family more prominent than those of the other (e.g., religious beliefs and practices, holiday celebrations, meal times, games, stories)?

4. Who, if any, were the outcasts in your family? Why?

5. Whose marital relationship was most broken down? Were they separated or divorced? Why was it troubled?

6. When you think of your respective families, who had a model marriage? How was it a model? Where did you look for a model? Was this model marriage one you would like to or have recreated in some way?

7. Are there any points during the course of your relationship when you think other family has been particularly important to your marriage—strongly supporting the marriage or possibly undermining the relationship?

8. Who, if anyone, was the first person to divorce in your families that you know about? Each of your parents? Siblings? Others?

9. How many of your close friends are divorced? None, few, most, all?

   Have you ever been to a wedding twice for the same person? Have you ever sent or received a divorce card?

   Have any of your relationships changed as a result of someone else's divorce?

10. Are there any movies, television shows, novels that come to mind that have captured what it means to be married? What it means to be divorced?

11. What is the most recent famous marriage or divorce you took note of?

12. If you had to say there's been a theme to your marriage, what would it be? How would you symbolize your marriage? A song?

Notes

INTRODUCTION

1. Reaching a "tipping point" means that there were sufficient numbers of people divorcing to designate divorce as a behavioral norm or standard. Social norms have changed when as many, if not more, marriages dissolve as endure. Bernard (1982) designated 1980 as the "tipping point" for the "two-earner marriage" because at that time the employed wife became the numerical standard.

2. Sweet and Bumpass (1987) document that by the 1970s it became more common for an adult to lose a spouse through divorce than through death.

3. Although marriage culture endures, I am implying a decline in the hegemony of marriage culture here. Gramsci's (1971) term captures the fact that not only material conditions, but also ideological influences, made marriage culture the desirable and "common sense" ideal, whether attainable or not, for women and men across class, race, and other axes of stratification.

4. This is a C.B.G. advertisement. It can be found in the May 1992 issue of *Glamour* magazine.

5. Divorce as a gateway signifies not only a step away from a miserable life, but also a step toward a promising one. Furthermore, the umbrella concept of "divorce culture" emerged as a category with particular and sometimes contradictory meanings in the course of my research in the early 1990s and is not meant to convey either positive or pejorative meanings. Barbara Dafoe Whitehead's, *The Divorce Culture* (1997), published since that time, has imbued the phrase with pejorative connotations not intended here.

6. In fact, some rates may not change. For example, the proportion of those who intend to marry has remained high in past decades. Thornton (1989, 878) reports that "between 1960 and 1980 the percentage of female high school seniors expecting to remain single increased only from 3% to 5% and for male seniors the increase was only from 8% to 10%." However, the meaning of marrying may change when release from marriage is pervasively modeled and relatively accessible.

7. Note that "first-time" is an important qualification in a culture of divorce.

8. Riessman (1990) coined the term "divorce talk." However, my use of the term is slightly different. Riessman used it to describe the accounts that the divorced provided of their own divorce experiences. In contrast, I focus on the married, using the term more broadly to describe the talk—by people divorced, married, single, straight or gay—that reflects a social context of divorce and the premises of divorce culture, such as seeing marrying as an option or divorce as a gateway.

9. Male dominance, as opposed to patriarchy, arose with industrial capitalism. Male dominance is identified here with the "male-headed nuclear family," which was distinguished by new gender arrangements as well as by the contradiction between expectations of wifely obedience and "companionate" marriage (M. Johnson 1988, 231). Companionate marriage, which emphasized friendship, partnership, and mutual respect, arose in the nineteenth century and continued into the twentieth century (Burgess and Locke 1945; Skolnick 1991).

10. Women's economic independence also increases men's alternatives; the potential self-sufficiency of wives can ease husbands' departures from marriages.

11. Stacey (1990), Coontz (1992), and Kurz (1995) also challenge this claim.

12. Snitow (1990) describes this centuries-old debate in terms of those who would "maximize" gender difference and those who would "minimize" gender difference in the name of equality. The "maximizers" tend to celebrate women's unique qualities, such as relationality; the "minimizers" tend to focus on similarity and want to extend the same rights to white women and people of color that have been the prerogatives of white men.

13. Demographers would refer to these as "marriage cohorts" because the couples of the Older generation were married in the early 1950s, while the couples of the Younger generation were married after 1970, mostly around 1979. Both samples, however, were gathered as "birth cohorts"—that is, people were selected by their shared birth year, and their spouses were then included in the research project. See Appendix for details.

14. The '50s spouses were classified according to racial/ethnic group by the original investigators at IHD. I asked the '70s spouses to classify themselves. The term "racial/ethnic" denotes the social structural discrimination and the common cultural heritage that shape the identities, practices, and material possibilities of people in society (Baca Zinn and Eitzen 1993, 111). Although racial categories have been formed to denote differences in physical features such as skin color, through history they have been used for economic and political purposes and have sustained and yielded common cultural practices associated with ethnicity. I use the terms "European-American" (or "Euro-American"), "African-American," "Japanese American," and "Latino" to describe the racial/ethnic identities of individuals. I use "Asian," "Black," "Latino," and "white" as I discuss social groups and occasionally in response to the usage preferred by spouses. As social constructions, these terms are in flux and marked by contradictions, as many scholars have observed (Amott and Matthaei 1991; Baca Zinn and Eitzen 1993).

CHAPTER ONE

1. All names of the couples in both generations are pseudonyms to protect identities.

2. By 1982, the Stones' marital satisfaction scores are in the top third within the entire sample of couples participating in the longitudinal study at the Institute of Human Development.

3. Spouses of the original subjects were interviewed in 1970 and 1982 and not interviewed in 1959. Therefore, this is a retrospective statement by Evan.

4. In *Intimate Strangers*, Lillian Rubin (1983) discusses this conventional gendered pattern, whereby women experience sex as an outcome of intimacy and relationship, while men experience sex separate from relationship and as a means to feel intimate.

5. Kin work is more thoroughly defined by di Leonardo (1987, 442–43) as "the conception, maintenance, and ritual celebration of cross-household kin ties ...; the organization of holiday gatherings; the creation and maintenance of quasi-kin relations; decisions to neglect or to intensify particular ties; the mental work of reflection about all these activities; and the creation and communication of altering images of family and kin vis-à-vis the images of others, both folk and mass media."

6. It should be noted that Evan locates palpable conflict a few years after 1971, when Katy has her divorce thoughts; also, he was one of only two husbands who admitted to divorce thoughts. In contrast, Katy was one of 7 wives among the 12 couples.

7. Judith Stacey (1990) discovered when she studied evangelical marriages in Silicon Valley that wives seemed to appropriate fundamentalist principles for feminist purposes, enabling them to share relational responsibilities within and across their families.

8. The Turners were one of four interracial couples I interviewed. The high proportion of interracial marriages in my sample was unexpected. There was a 365 percent jump in the number of interracial marriages between 1970 and 1992 in the San Francisco Bay Area (*San Francisco Chronicle*, July 26, 1993); still, this is an over-representation. This high proportion may have affected my findings, in that interracial marriage is still relatively rare; thus, in addition to changing gender ideologies, spouses must be reflexive about the racial/ethnic meanings of their marriage.

9. Kitson and Holmes (1992, 123) found that in men's accounts this complaint followed "lack of communication or understanding" and "joint conflict over roles." They also found other gender differences in marital complaints.

Chapter Two

1. This summary paragraph draws from Weitzman (1985, 27), who specified the innovations entailed by this new permissive law; these innovations are also described in Glendon (1987), Kay (1987), and Mason (1988).

2. These gender assumptions had informed many of the "grounds" since the nineteenth century. As Weitzman (1985, 8) reports: "While the most ritualistic 'evidence' of misbehavior varied from state to state, husbands charged with cruelty, the most commonly cited ground, were often alleged to have caused their wives bodily harm, while wives charged with cruelty were more typically accused of neglecting their husbands, homes, or wifely duties. Along the same lines, allegations of a wife's desertion were typically supported by evidence of a wife's withdrawal of affection, refusal to do housework, or attention to outside interests, but the same behavior would not be considered as desertion by the husband unless he also stopped supporting his wife financially."

3. Weitzman's (1985, 323) estimate that divorced men experienced a 42 percent rise and divorced women (and their children) experienced a 73 percent decline in standard of living after their first year divorced has been criticized (Hoffman and Duncan 1988; Peterson 1996). Although less severe, the direction of the change she indicated was correct. Upon reevaluating Weitzman's data, Peterson (1996, 534) found a 27 percent decline in women's standard of living, and a 10 percent increase in men's standard of living after divorce.

4. This rule-changing is reflected in Newman's (1988) data. She found that older divorced women still felt entitled to some support from their ex-husbands after years of homemaking, while younger divorced women wanted a complete break from ex-husbands and expected self-sufficiency from themselves, in spite of the fact that they had been homemakers.

5. The combined influence of economic conditions and government policies is important for understanding the "lack of affluence" and decline of divorce rate during the Great Depression. Economic hardship would seem to explain low divorce, yet declining divorce rates were not registered in other countries hit by the Depression (Phillips 1991, 209). Social and political policies specific to the United States may have delimited women's options in particular, and may help explain why severe recessions in recent years have not depressed divorce rates. Phillips reports that during the Depression, "welfare assistance was given more readily to families than individuals, and men with families were given priority in employment on relief projects" (210). Phillips also points out that "married women whose husbands were in paid employment were often fired or denied employment." In short, women's loss of financial independence probably deterred divorce, particularly since at this time "two-thirds of American divorces were sought by women."

6. Cherlin also notes that there are a few exceptions. For example, since 1980, birth rates for women in their thirties have been particularly high; this has not been true for women in their twenties. This is probably explained by the marked postponement of childbearing by women born in the 1950s (Cherlin 1992, 34). Another exception that Cherlin does not discuss is cohabitation—which I address below. Cohabitation is much more marked among people born after the 1950s than those born before. Also, while period effects are partially substantiated by the direction of statistical trends, that does not necessarily imply that the behaviors hold the same meaning across cohorts.

7. McLaughlin et al. (1998, 120) also show a similar increase for *married* mothers of young children. Contrasting different decades and populations, Cowan and Cowan (1998, 172) point out that: "Whereas only 18 percent of women with a child under six were employed outside of the home in 1960, more than 50 percent of women with a child *under one* were working at least part time in 1990."

8. Cherlin (1992, 61) reports that: "By the mid-1980s a majority of families in the upper half of the income distribution had working wives. A second income became increasingly necessary to stay in the middle class."

9. Cherlin (1992, 53) argues that the participation of young women in the labor force in the 1960s and 1970s "is stronger and more suggestive than that linking any other concurrent trend with the rise in divorce." He does not com-

pletely reject alternative explanations, such as cohort influences, reproductive control, and men's declining wages (63). However, he does see three areas of research results as suggestive, though somewhat "circumstantial": "(1) a married woman may be more likely to divorce if she is in the labor force; (2) the labor force participation rate for younger married women rose sharply after 1960; and (3) younger married women are in general more likely to divorce than are older married women" (53).

10. In contrast to the Euro-American wife, the African-American wife experienced neither the privileges nor the detriments associated with the "feminine mystique." Racial discrimination compelled a dual-job scenario long before it gained ascendance in Euro-American communities. While one-quarter of all married women were labor force participants, one-third of African-American wives worked in 1950 (Jones 1985, 269).

11. As Evans (1979, 24) and others document, the "struggle for racial equality has been midwife to a feminist movement" twice in U.S. history. The ideals of equality and justice for the racially oppressed exposed parallel contradictions, if dissimilar oppressions, in gender following the nineteenth-century abolitionist movement and the twentieth-century Civil Rights movement.

12. In my view, the unprecedented reach and availability of the mass media and the simultaneous changes occurring in the society at large—particularly women's participation in the labor force, but also the institutionalization of women's organizations—suggest that feminist advances cannot be as easily reversed as in earlier eras. Lopata (1993) similarly argues that the current backlash will not overturn the progress and momentum of changes.

13. Gay and lesbian marriage is perhaps a more radical challenge to marriage culture than divorce culture because it questions "compulsory heterosexuality" (Rich 1980).

14. Thornton (1989, 883) reported a 45 percent decrease between 1965 and 1972 to about 22 percent of young men and women who agreed with the statement that premarital sex was always or almost always wrong.

15. These figures refer to the '50s and '70s generations in my samples, respectively.

16. Colleen Leahy Johnson's (1988) illuminating research findings are limited by small samples and the liberal San Francisco Bay Area research site. Furthermore, because she is tracing family networks, she samples divorced people and then solicits the participation of their parents. Because most of the parents had remained married, the independent influences of marital history and generation upon attitudes toward marriage and divorce are conflated.

17. It is beyond my aims to explore variations in histories, beliefs, practices, and institutional vehicles within the Judeo-Christian tradition. However, see Joan Aldous and William D'Antonio, eds., *Families and Religions* (1983) for articles on Protestant, Catholic, and Jewish faiths, as well as Black and Hispanic churches. Also, see Ammerman and Roof (1995).

18. There are exceptions. For example, there are the well-known polygamous practices among Mormons in the past. There has long been ongoing tension between the virtues of celibacy and those of marriage in the Roman Catholic

tradition. In fact, marriage was not a sacrament until the fifteenth century (D'Antonio and Cavanaugh 1983, 144).

19. Mormonism, for example, contends that marriage is eternal, rather than lifelong or "till death do us part," and, as such, marriages cannot be undone. For those who marry within the Temple, the divorce rate is unusually low (Albrecht, Bahr, and Goodman 1983).

20. D'Antonio (1983, 102) asserts that "religiosity does predict differences in attitudes and behavior regarding such phenomena as interreligious marriage, fertility, abortion, premarital sex, and divorce, but the relationship is not one to one; social class, education, and occupation are often more important variables. The amount of the variance religion explains has been steadily decreasing."

21. Evangelical Protestantism and Catholicism are among the most conservative. Yet male dominance is repudiated altogether in some branches of Christianity, such as Quakerism.

22. Chesler (1972) provided an early indictment of mental health systems' discrimination against women. Also, see Howell and Bayes, eds., *Women and Mental Health* (1981) and Renzetti and Curran (1995) for continuing critiques of sexist biases in mental health systems and clinicians.

23. A "psychological" or "therapeutic" culture implicitly distinguishes itself from cultures in which meaning is traced primarily and predominantly to nonpsychological sources—that is, social positions or roles and collective myths, beliefs, religions, or rituals pointing to a metaphysical reality perceived as primary and external to the individual—from the feudal economic system to Hindu belief systems. Nonpsychological cultures are not without psychologies; however, a psychological orientation is not the center of gravity. The term "therapeutic culture" was originally coined by Philip Rieff (1966).

24. While more troubled couples may have gone to therapy, these figures also suggest that therapy may encourage divorce to a degree. These are not mutually exclusive explanations. I suspect both are true, though this has yet to be established.

25. While many books and articles on "how to save the marriage" seem to reflect marriage culture, many of them, such as Weiner-Davis's *Divorce Busting* (1992), are responding to divorce culture and, as such, reproduce it. See Hackstaff (1994) and Whitehead (1997a) for discussions of print and electronic media reflecting divorce culture.

26. It is interesting to note that one of Cancian's (1987, 43) indicators for assessing flexible roles was the acceptability of divorce. This links gender equality and divorce culture by suggesting that divorce tolerance has helped to usher in flexibility in gender roles.

27. As many scholars have observed, these ideals raise the standards for marital happiness and are recent manifestations of the long-term rise in "affective individualism" (Bellah et al. 1985; Cancian 1987; Skolnick 1991; Swidler 1986; Whitehead 1997a).

28. As multicultural and postmodern theories have made clear, what have been passed off as "absolute values" in society more generally have often been the preferences of one group—and these preferences have not only been the by-

product of political power, but have ensured that it is maintained. As we will see, the seemingly objective good of "equality" becomes problematic in this context.

29. These would extend from the efforts of a few elite couples such as John Stuart Mills and Harriet Taylor in white, middle-class Victorian society, to an affinity for equality between the genders among African-Americans, drawn from either African traditions or the "equality of oppression" experienced by both sexes (Collins 1990; Crosbie-Burnett and Lewis 1993; Dill 1988; Rose 1983).

30. Somewhere between one-quarter to one-third of divorces are mutual according to the research, and the initiator of divorce is more frequently the wife than the husband (see Kitson with Holmes 1992; Kelly 1982; Wallerstein and Blakeslee 1989).

31. To understand the degree to which fathers are uninvolved is more complicated than simply interpreting low rates of paternal custody, visitation, or support payments as "individualistic." Aggregate rates obscure the cultural and economic stories behind them. For example, Niobe Way and Helena Stauber (1996) argue that urban adolescent girls have more significant relationships with fathers who do not live in their households than the recent literature suggests. Still, the degree of involvement by mothers is not questioned or debated. As Philipson (1993) and Blankenhorn (1995a) argue in different contexts, men seem to be "vanishing" from the family, in a way that women are not.

32. Even for committed egalitarians, it is difficult to share parenting equally when wage structures suggest that the husband's job should be favored over the wife's (Ehrensaft 1980; Schwartz 1994). It is difficult for wives to compete within certain occupations when the "clockwork of male careers" collides with the biological clock of childbearing and rearing (Hochschild 1975). Moreover, it is hard to get family-friendly legislation and policies passed when governing bodies and executive boards are still dominated by men whose experiences are not located at the points of greatest stress between work and family.

33. The dimension of difference(s) examined matter enormously here. For example, those who focus on several axes of difference—such as sexual preference, race/ethnicity, class, and gender—attempt to foreground marginalized and diverse discourses; some of these theorists are social constructionists (Epstein 1988), while others are postmodern theorists who reject universal theories and emphasize the variability of experiences across all dimensions (hooks 1990; Nicholson 1990), and still others are multiracial feminists who emphasize the dynamic, interlocking nature of systems of inequality or what Collins (1990) calls the "matrix of domination" (Baca Zinn and Dill 1996). Those who highlight gender difference—across these dimensions—are often categorized as "essentialists," whether emphasizing the biological or the social-psychological aspects of gender difference.

34. Collins (1990, 161) describes this as a defining feature of black feminist thought and suggests that a "both/and" conceptual orientation will help us rethink many social divides and debates between action and thought and between axes of oppression. For example, she notes that black nationalism and racial integration have long been opposing positions, when "autonomy and coalition should be [viewed] as complementary and essential parts of the same process. . . ."

35. I draw from Tronto (1993) here regarding the importance of a more encompassing notion of care that breaks down many of the current "boundaries" around morality and goes beyond gender difference.

36. Riessman (1990, 36) reports that while two-thirds of the women in her study mentioned a lack of communication or emotional intimacy in their divorce accounts, only one-third of men did so.

37. Cancian traces this exclusion to industrialization, which effected a split between public and private spheres; men and women have been associated, respectively, with an instrumental public sphere and an expressive private sphere.

38. As Rothman (1984, 329) insightfully states in a different context: "The question is not whether choices are constructed but *how* they are constructed. Society, in its ultimate meaning, may be nothing more and nothing less than the structuring of choices."

CHAPTER THREE

1. The crude divorce rate, based on the entire population, overlooks the many who are not eligible for marriage or divorce; furthermore, it conceals variations between generations. In 1970, when the Younger generation was around 19 years of age (i.e., barely eligible for marriage and divorce) and the Older generation was around 42 years of age, the rates of divorce per 1,000 married women were 28 and 14, respectively. By 1980, when the younger cohort was 29 years old, their divorce rate per 1000 married women was 43. For the Older generation, now about 52 years of age, the rate was 10 (Glick and Lin 1986, 738). In short, the Younger generation is more clearly surrounded by the rise in divorce among their peers.

2. Moen (1992, 13) cites some of the more telling statistical indicators of changing practices by wives and the concomitant decline of the male breadwinner/female homemaker model. The number of working wives tripled between 1950 and 1980 (from 8 to 29 million); and "over half (64.6%) of the wives of Hispanic origin were in the labor force in 1989; ever larger proportions of white (57.0%) and black wives (65.7%) were working."

3. I am not implying that the increasing democratization of family relations began in the twentieth century. It has been a slow and piecemeal process. The rise of individualism related to democratization can be traced back to the Protestant Reformation. Patriarchal family relations based on age and sex hierarchies have eroded gradually. Edward Shorter (1975), Lawrence Stone (1977), and Philippe Aries (1962) all address the gradual change in the quality of family relations. Looking at the case of Massachusetts, historian Nancy Cott (1978, 130) documents "a retreat from hierarchical models and an advance toward ideals of complementarity in the prevailing conceptions of the marriage relationship" by the end of the eighteenth century. She finds that not only husbands, but wives, were able to divorce because of adultery. And she reports the "consonant change" of a shift "away from parental control in the direction of individual autonomy in marriage choice" beginning in the years of the American Revolution (130). Cott recognizes, however, that equalizing the consequences of adultery by the last quar-

ter of the eighteenth century "indicated an improvement in the position of wives, although it did not change their economic status, the *essence* of their dependency" (131, emphasis added). In short, changes in the economic status of women have been crucial for dismantling the lingering dependence of wives within hierarchical family relations.

4. The number of divorced per 1000 married women in 1958, when these couples came for their first adult interviews, was at a low of 8.9 (Kitson with Holmes 1992, 21). In 1970 the rate was 14.9, and by 1985 it had risen to 21.7 (U.S. Bureau of the Census, Series P-23, No. 162, 1989).

5. Social class was assessed at the 1970 and 1982 follow-ups according to the Hollingshead Social Class Scale, but I draw from social class categories that were assessed in 1982.

6. As we will see in later chapters, many younger spouses raised the issue of divorce in answer to questions that did not specifically address divorce. For example, a favorite reply to the question, "What's the biggest surprise of your marriage?" was the joke: "that we're still married" or "that we're not divorced."

7. The "I" does not represent myself but rather the interviewer, during the various follow-up interviews conducted through the Institute of Human Development. In later chapters I designate myself with "KH."

8. That marriage is being redefined—in terms of what is damaging or beneficial—can be observed by looking at changing marital complaints. Kitson and Holmes (1992, 92–93, 124–29) found that the complaints of married couples who reconcile and those who go on to divorce are similar. If we look at marital complaints among the divorced as indicators of generational issues for married couples, studies suggest that among older cohorts of divorcing couples, marital complaints were different in nature ("nonsupport," "authority," "out with the boys/girls") and by gender. The nature of marital complaints has become more affective/emotional with younger divorcing cohorts (e.g., "personality," "home life," and "values") and somewhat less gender-differentiated.

9. In her study of this same generation, May (1988, 187) found more evidence of the growing therapeutic influence in the 1950s than I did in my small sample. She reports heavy reliance upon professional help. She points out, however, that the psychological advice of the times was gender-differentiated; men were to look homeward to relieve their anxieties, while women were to look to psychology to aide them in overcoming their "pathologies." With the rise of the women's movement, the New Age movement, and a plethora of self-help literature, this particular double standard has diminished. Psychology has increasingly, if not sufficiently, integrated a woman-centered viewpoint in its popular advice on marital monitoring (Rampage 1994). In part, this is because gendered practices are decreasingly taken for granted in marriage (Schwartz 1994).

10. This replicates May's (1988, 193) results for this same generation. May reports: "Women were twice as likely as men to report that they were dissatisfied or regretted their marriages. Nearly half the women, but only a third of the men, said they had considered divorce. In response to the question, 'If you had your life to live over, would you marry the same person?' about half the men and women said 'definitely.' Yet nearly twice as many women as men said they would

definitely *not* marry the same person. These findings are consistent with other studies that have demonstrated that, in general, men are more happily married than women."

11. However, it has been amply demonstrated that economically women have more to lose upon divorce because of wage inequity, labor force sex-segregation, material responsibility for children, and legal changes ignoring these structural conditions.

12. Among married couples, Kitson and Holmes (1992, 93) found that wives suggested divorce more frequently than husbands. And among their divorced couples, they found that both wives and husbands agreed that the wives suggested divorce more frequently. The authors assert that "study after study suggests that women are more likely to suggest and to file for the divorce." Historically, however, "suggesting divorce" should be distinguished from "filing for divorce," because the latter is especially influenced by family law. Women commonly filed for divorce in past generations because as plaintiffs they were less financially vulnerable—that is, they were more likely to receive some financial assistance in the form of alimony or child support. When no-fault divorce was instituted, the proportion of men filing for divorce increased substantially. From 1966 to 1974, the percent of female plaintiffs dropped from 78 percent to 68 percent in California (Riley 1991, 165).

13. Arland Thornton found that in 1962 only 32 percent of a sample of young married women disagreed with the assertion "Most of the important decisions in the life of the family should be made by the man of the house." By 1985, as many as 78 percent of these same women, still married to the same men, disagreed (Cited in Goldscheider and Waite 1991. See also Modell 1985, 186).

14. Linda also seemingly contradicts his version of decision making when she states that she would prefer that he was home and "more involved with the children, mostly not that I resent making the decisions, but that I'd like to share responsibility of making decisions." Here, Linda not only suggests that she would like help with, and possibly some credit for, all the decision making, but she is also foregrounding the decisions that are invisible to Roger because of the social construction of what constitutes "heading the household."

15. Chodorow (1989) similarly finds that even as women psychoanalysts of the 1930s accorded "equality" to the public sphere, they withheld it from the domestic sphere.

16. It is worth noting in this regard that while the majority of wives are not working for pay in 1958, by 1982 10 out of 12 wives are working—and most are not driven by financial need. These women reflect the forefront of the trend toward increasing participation in the labor force—working mothers whose children are older or grown. As Moore, Spain, and Bianchi (1984) document, a key change in employment patterns of wives occurred in the 1960s and 1970s when *young* mothers increased their participation in the labor force; this change is reflected among the '70s couples.

17. There is some debate in the literature concerning the strength of the egalitarian ideal in African-American families (Dugger 1988). Many historians and sociologists have argued that historical and structural conditions (such as the fact

that the majority of African-American wives have always worked) have augmented the ideal of gender equality within marriage (Davis 1981; Dill 1988). As Dugger (1988) points out, other scholars argue that the ideal of male dominance is similar among African-Americans and Euro-Americans. Contradictory findings are reflected in my tiny sample as well. The Johnsons, another African-American couple, adhere to the male-dominant model. As Dugger (1988) and Hunter and Davis (1992) suggest, contradictions may be a function of the interaction of racist and sexist systems; when dominant white ideologies have been used to define African-American families as pathological (as with the "matriarchy" thesis), rejections of equality and embracing the ideal of male dominance are going to carry a different meaning.

18. Pat Ross was Pat Holstein; she divorced Gary Holstein in the 1960s and was married to Neil Ross by 1970.

CHAPTER FOUR

1. I use "patriarchy" here to refer to the historically specific form of male domination that preceded the rise of industrialization (M. Johnson, 1988). Patriarchal conditions represent the roots of this sexual double standard. However, during the nineteenth century, the "tender years doctrine" gave divorced mothers rights to their children under seven years of age and the "Married Women's Property Act" redefined women as legal persons apart from their husbands. Under patriarchy, wives and children were viewed as the property of fathers/husbands, and this was inscribed into the law. See Nancy Cott (1978), Eli Zaretsky (1982), Roderick Phillips (1988), and Glenda Riley (1991) for in-depth historical accounts.

CHAPTER FIVE

1. The Hamptons score in the middle third in the marital satisfaction component scores and were selected because of this. The Stevens were selected to include some African-Americans in my sample, yet they were not included in Skolnick's study, which developed the marital satisfaction component scores; however, they did self-report a middle range of satisfaction (see Appendix). Finally, the Franks were selected to represent '50s spouses who had experienced divorce, so they were not a part of the study that constructed "marital satisfaction component scores." Their level of satisfaction is drawn from their accounts, but is also a function of my interpretation.

2. See Chapter 3 for a more lengthy discussion of the egalitarian terms that marked their marriage even in the 1950s; Julia Stevens explains this quality in terms of her African-American background.

3. Of the five spouses I studied who divorced (Larry Frank, Nancy Franks, Gary Holstein, Pat Holstein Ross, and Neil Ross) all except one (Nancy Franks) eventually refer to individual "growth" and retrospectively accord "gateway" potential to divorce.

4. Interestingly, Larry's first wife, Wilma, provides an almost identical description of this kind of marital trajectory in her 1971 interview.

5. I would argue that as the cultural grounds for divorce have expanded, wife abuse not only justifies a divorce or is a sufficient ground as in the past, but staying in a violent marriage is decreasingly acceptable. The support that divorce culture provides for leaving violent marriages is a valuable and overlooked contribution of divorce culture's tolerance for divorce. Alternatively, there is an unsympathetic tendency to blame the victim who stays, as was suggested by a recent exchange in "Dear Abby," when a writer "Sick and Tired of Voluntary Victims in Oregon" argued that abused women are "stupid" if they don't leave batterers (*The Arizona Republic,* July 12, 1997). Today, there may be decreasing tolerance for the wife who does not leave such a marriage and a misunderstanding of the hurdles such wives confront.

6. In *Adultery,* Annette Lawson (1988, 74) discusses the difficulty of measuring the prevalence of adultery among men or women. She points out that about 50 percent of husbands are estimated to have an affair (or affairs, usually many) at some point in their marriage, while about 30 percent of wives are estimated to have an affair(or affairs, usually few) at some point. Behaviors seem to be changing with generation as well as attitudes—particularly among women. Lawson points out that since the 1970s women have become more liberal in their attitudes and less supportive of the double standard that allowed men extramarital affairs—even if women are not as liberal as men in their behavior. She states: "*Now* women and men express similar attitudes [. . .] that is, they are more like than unlike one another when they are divided according to the year when first they married."

7. Claims regarding the import of "communications," suffuse his interview by 1983. When he is asked if he would like his children's marriages to be like his own, Larry replies that he would like their marriages to be like his first marriage in terms of raising a family and like his second marriage in terms of "communications. Being able to communicate with one another." However, he adds that he would advise his children "not to spend too much time away from home with other involvements."

8. West and Zimmerman (1987, 126) explain that gender is not a trait, but rather an interactional accomplishment: "Doing gender involves a complex of socially guided perceptual, interactional, and micropolitical activities that cast particular pursuits as expressions of masculine and feminine 'natures.'" Gender is not something individuals "have," but something individuals produce through patterned interactions, and for which they are held accountable by others in particular contexts. Thus, what is considered "natural" and "accountable" varies with situation, historical era, and culture.

CHAPTER SIX

1. As Riessman's (1990) research would suggest, Martha could be projecting her own reactions. Riessman found that divorced men were less likely to interpret extramarital affairs as a "lack of love" and were more concerned with

whether they were primary enough in their wife's life. Regardless, the terms of the McIntyre marriage rest more heavily upon feelings by the early 1980s.

CHAPTER SEVEN

1. While all divorce rates were on the rise during the 1970s, the rates at any one point in time varied greatly across racial/ethnic groups. Thus, in 1980 the percent divorced among all women who had married 10 to 14 years earlier was 52.7 percent for African-Americans, 45.5 percent for Puerto Ricans, 47.9 percent for American Indians, 39.2 percent for Hawaiians, 37.4 percent for non-Hispanic whites, 33 percent for Cubans, 30.5 percent for Mexican-Americans, 21.8 percent for Japanese-Americans, 14.4 percent for Chinese-Americans, and 7.3 percent for Asian Indians (Cherlin 1999, 377–78).

2. This is drawn from Margaret Mead's 1947 article "The Implications of Cultural Change for Personality Development," in *American Journal of Orthopsychiatry,* 17, cited in Arlene Skolnick's *The Intimate Environment* (1987, 317). Yet, the idea was inspired by Eli Sagan, who remarked to me that spouses are like Polish immigrants who must reflect on the new ways even as they maintain the old ways; in other words, everyone must increasingly reflect on the meaning of marriage in a culture of divorce.

3. I believe this remark originates with Groucho Marx, not with Stan's cousin.

4. Twelve out of 34 respondents' parents did not remain married, but only 7 of these were due to divorce.

CHAPTER EIGHT

1. Thanks to Arlie Hochschild for this phrase capturing the internal corollary to a shifting marital context.

2. The Nakatos are a middle-class, dual-career couple, both working full-time; he is a computer technician and she is a loan officer. They rely upon relatives for child care. They are third-generation Japanese-Americans and very active Buddhists.

3. Bill Gilmore discussed the divorce of a couple who had been married for four years. Bill was the best man at their wedding. Despite the short length of marriage, Bill reports that at the time "it looked like something that could last forever."

4. Claudia Card (1990, 647) defines luck as "factors, good or bad, beyond the control of the affected agent: matters of chance and predictable results of social practice." Like the '70s spouses, I would not deny that some events are a matter of chance; yet other events can be the "predictable results of social practice"— and it is the job of sociologists to uncover such social practices.

5. This is a response found by researchers studying remarried couples as well. Writing about remarried couples, Furstenberg and Spanier (1987, 83) report that "central to the reorganization of their view of marriage is the belief that they have now married the right person." While they find this pattern among the

divorced and remarried, I would argue that the "right one" is an important interpretation for the first-married as well in a marital environment of divorce culture.

6. Thanks to Eli Sagan for clarifying this distinction. I would add that this contrasts with the '50s couples, who primarily distanced themselves from divorce by denying the divorces around them and by emphasizing their circle of married friends. In contrast, divorce culture elicits imaginary experiments from the '70s couples.

7. The marital work ethic is a second-order category that I derived from '70s spouses' various references to work and effort in maintaining a marriage (Daly 1992, 9). Daly draws from Schütz (1962) here, as I do. Schütz states: "The thought objects constructed by the social scientists refer to and are founded upon the thought objects constructed by the common-sense thought of man living his everyday life among his fellow men. Thus, the constructs used by the social scientist are, so to speak, constructs of the second degree, namely constructs of the constructs made by the actors on the social scene, whose behavior the scientist observes and tries to explain...." (6). Talk about "working" on a marriage is common. The construct of a "marital work ethic" draws attention to the context of divorce culture as a ground for such talk.

8. Interestingly, the six spouses who did not talk about the marital work ethic consider themselves "traditional"—traditional denoting both a strong belief in "marriage as forever" and in a male-dominated marriage. Perhaps this means that those spouses who heartily embrace marriage culture presume that the marriage will endure whether one works or not. But it might also indicate that such "work" is less visible and recognized because it is a presumed aspect of a wife's duties and not, therefore, constructed as "work."

CHAPTER NINE

1. The comic strip is authored by Cathy Guisewite, and this particular strip ran in the *San Francisco Chronicle,* May 2, 1992.

2. She was quoted in *The New York Times* by Jane Gross in 1992. A Canadian study in 1997 of 5,000 women "found that more than half of the women (57.3 percent) who had entered into their first serious relationship from 1990 to 1995 had chosen common law"—a rise from 40.5 percent in 1984. The study suggests that the common law choice was more likely among women with separated and divorced parents, women who did not go to church, and women with jobs (*The Arizona Republic,* December 11, 1997).

3. Kitson and Holmes do not hold generation constant, yet three-quarters of their married sample is younger than my "Older generation sample" would have been in 1979.

4. Kitson and Holmes (1992, 93) found that regardless of gender, matched ex-spouses were in agreement about wives being the primary initiators of the divorce.

5. This does not include individual therapy, which would increase the numbers. I would add here that some couples went more than once. For example, one

couple went to therapy while cohabiting and trying to decide about marriage and then returned again years later after other issues arose in their relationship.

6. Women's dissatisfaction with men's communicative skills is a typical find-ing in the literature on heterosexual relationships. Blaisure and Allen (1995) note that this is a key challenge, even in self-identified feminist marriages. Duncombe and Marsden (1993) and Morgan (1991) cite research that documents that women often feel that men do not reciprocate disclosure, tenderness, or emotional care-taking. And Cancian and Gordon (1988) conclude from their review of advice literature from 1900 to 1979 that because women are the primary readers of this literature, they are still held responsible for communicating about emotions in the marriage.

7. As we will see in later chapters, the agenda itself is often gendered—par-ticularly regarding concerns about the "second shift," as manifested in parent-ing, homemaking, and other work to sustain a home. As Hochschild and Machung (1989, 46) observed, the revolution in gender arrangements appears to have "stalled." They argue: "Across the nation at this particular time in history, this emotion work is often all that stands between the stalled revolution on the one hand, and broken marriages on the other."

8. The religious affiliations of these five couples included Judaism, Catholi-cism, Buddhism (2), and Baptist Christianity. There were others who also went to church, temple, or synagogue occasionally, but it was less clearly a part of their marital work. Among the spouses who went to therapy, more than half were not affiliated with a religion in adulthood; interestingly, the other half were couples that did not share the same religious affiliation, such as a Catholic married to a Lutheran or a Quaker married to an atheist.

9. Gordon noted: "What I've always felt to some degree, especially in black households—they talk about how in the last 20 years how women have had to go to work. I've said, 'Wait a minute.' I said, 'Wait a minute.' There are times because of economics, because of racism, whatever, the only one that can get a job was [the woman]." Gordon also discussed the importance of being a model husband and father in the context of society that disparages Black men's family responsibilities in the media. Gordon Walker's insights are also reflected in the recent literature on African-American families (Collins 1990; Taylor et al. 1990; Crosbie-Burnett and Lewis 1993; Way and Stauber 1996).

10. The Walkers reflect Carolan's (1995) qualitative study and the twine of intimacy and spirituality. "African-American Couples at Midlife: Life Course and Gender Perspectives." (Dissertation. Virginia Polytechnic Institute and State Uni-versity.) Also, see Gilkes (1995) and hooks (1993) for a discussion of the support and healing provided in African-American churches and communities. Thera-peutic culture has been thought of as a white phenomenon, yet healing, recovery, and self-actualization are not unique to whites. In her self-help book addressing African-American women, hooks (1993) observes that self-actualization is intrin-sic to building "communities of resistance" and has often occurred in the context of the church.

11. For example, Cushman (1995, 6) reports: "In 1994 in California alone there were approximately 6,500 psychiatrists, 13,800 clinical psychologists,

13,000 clinical social workers, and 21,600 marriage, family, and child therapists."

12. While the roots of a psychological orientation among Americans has been traced back to the previous centuries (Bellah et al. 1985; Holifield 1983; Sennet 1978), or traced to the twentieth century (Cushman 1995; Rieff 1966), scholars have increasingly highlighted the growth of therapeutic culture in the last few decades (Bellah et al 1985; Clecak 1983; Giddens 1991; Lasch 1979; Simonds 1992).

13. Chapter Two addressed the historical relationship between therapeutic culture and religion. Some examples of the legal deployment of therapeutic culture include the mandate of therapy or treatment programs for offenders who use illegal drugs or who physically abuse others.

14. This draws from Gilligan's (1982) portrait of the apex of moral development for women in European and American cultures; she argued that as women have taken care of others, they have tended to exclude themselves from their caretaking activities—they need to move toward an ethic of justice. Gilligan asserted that if women need to recognize their needs as individuals, men's trajectory of moral development requires intimacy and the ability to move beyond an ethic of justice toward an ethic of care. Gilligan's model of moral development has been criticized for suggesting gender difference is essential and for writing as if this gender difference were universal when her sample is white. As scholars have argued, the ethic of care is not necessarily limited to *women* across all racial, ethnic, and cultural groups (Collins 1990; Spelman 1988; Tronto 1993). Still, Gilligan's work has been a key catalyst for an extended debate about our constructions of morality and gender.

15. Such couples aim to mend what has been unfortunately severed in Western cultural history: distinctions such as individualism and relationality, autonomy and nurturance, separation and connection, public and private as well as justice and care, that have been symbolically, if not always actually, gendered as masculine and feminine, respectively (Benhabib 1986, 743; Friedman 1987, 668).

CHAPTER TEN

1. Bernard (1981) addresses the rise of the two-job couple, the increase in married women's participation in the labor force, the rise in female-headed households, the elimination of the category of the male-headed household by the Census Bureau in 1980, and the increasing beliefs in equality.

2. "Marrying as a given" is not expressed through covenant marriage; instead, to some degree, the law stresses marriage as an option with lifelong ramifications through the requirement of premarital counseling.

3. A recent debate among family scholars about the content of "marriage and family textbooks" also reflects a fear that marriage culture and traditional beliefs have been short-changed in college textbooks. (See Glenn 1997. *Closed Hearts, Closed Minds: The Textbook Story of Marriage.* New York: Institute for American Values, as well as American Sociological Association. 1998. "Sociologists Differ About Family Textbooks' Message." *Footnotes* 26, 7, 10, 12.)

4. In four additional couples, four husbands are traditional insofar as they combine male dominance and marriage culture, but the couples are split on their beliefs; the wives either uphold gender equality or divorce culture and exhibit great ambivalence about these ideologies (the Kason-Morris, Hawkins-Rose, Ellison, and Gilmore marriages). There is also one traditionalist wife married to a husband who believes in gender equality.

5. "Equal opportunity" is usually based on the assumption of individual effort and applied to the public sphere of work, even though providing equal opportunity at work, as many feminists have shown, is not really viable without structural changes that would provide for equal opportunity on the home front. For example, Lopata (1993) argues that the separate-sphere ideology is more prescriptive than descriptive of social reality; it functions to restrict gender involvements. See Rubin (1976), Zavella (1987), Thompson and Walker (1989), Ferree (1990), Coontz (1992) and Hansen (1987) for analyses of how paid work and family work across class, race, and gender reveal the artificial nature of the division between private and public spheres.

6. Overall, this strategy was used by 17 of the 34 spouses; however, 12 of the 17 believed "egalitarianism" would ensure a lasting marriage.

7. Susan Ostrander's (1984, 110) analysis of *Women of the Upper Class* shows how wives/mothers reproduce class interests and class interests maintain traditional gender arrangements. Ostrander describes the process of maintaining upper-class exclusivity, which allows some new people entry, but ensures conformity to "the general way of life." This process "insulates the class from fundamental change; but it protects the class from complete stagnation." The Greens can be considered new members, who conform to the "general way of life."

8. Ironically, this "resistance"—associated with the oppressed—is being practiced by a white, upper-middle-class couple. The media are generally held to advance the interests of white, male, and upper-class citizens; nevertheless, some "conservative" spouses suggest that the media do not represent their interests. As noted earlier, they *feel* as though they are in the minority, most likely because their practices are no longer hegemonic, even though no marital practices prevail at this time.

9. This stalled and roundabout account may reflect her realization that she never got the "nurturant father" from her husband; she later states that she wishes Dan were more "sensitive." Judy's use of "single parent" is a bit ambiguous, yet she does not seem to be threatening to become a single parent if Dan does not pitch in (with emotional or financial resources).

10. She is not the only wife to do so. For example, Sharon Ellison described an unhappy phase in her marriage as being a "single parent but with child support." Roxanne Kason-Morris says at one point that she is a "single mother still."

11. Colleen Johnson (1988) describes how her sample of divorced respondents overtly expressed the sentiment "My children can't do well or be happy unless I am happy," and discusses the therapeutic influences on this viewpoint.

12. While Judy refers to a "better deal" here, she does not describe her marriage like a contract at any point; in short, she does not talk about her marriage as contingent upon this arrangement. While my question about fairness might

have elicited her reference to "deals," this did not necessarily elicit such a response from others.

13. Infidelity was the most common reply of all respondents among '70s spouses. Despite more behavioral exceptions to this norm, monogamy remains an important norm in marriage (Lawson 1988; Thornton 1996). Many spouses saw "infidelity" as more deplorable in their generation given the rise of AIDS; others said it was "symptomatic" of an already-troubled marital relationship.

14. In *The Mermaid and the Minotaur* (1976), Dinnerstein discussed this "rift" and the reciprocal "infantalizing" done by men and women toward one another; from a feminist psychoanalytic perspective, she theorizes that this is a result of mother-dominated child rearing.

15. Chodorow (1978) theorizes that women have more complex relational needs and capacities than men (object relational and intrapsychic). She argues that family structure in which girls and boys are mother-raised produces men and women with asymmetrical relational needs and wants; this leads people to form heterosexual unions that contain these contradictions. In contrast to men who must repudiate identification with their mother and deny relational needs, women's continuous identification with their mothers makes for a self defined in relationship and "triadic" relational needs. Heterosexual relationships cannot address these needs. Wives are likely to turn to female friendships and, most importantly, to having children to meet their relational needs. Mother-raised men and women go on to reproduce "heterosexual knots" which, in turn, reproduces male-dominated marriage and female-dominated child rearing (191–205). Thus, it is symbolic that the only other event that Judy thought could break their marriage would be the death of the children.

16. The two husbands were Andrew Ellison and Ira Hawkins—both professionals and believers in marriage culture. The contractual language of these married husbands, a language that presumes individual rights, is reminiscent of Weitzman's (1985) study. Weitzman's study also uncovered a tendency for men to talk in terms of "the law" and their "rights" upon divorce. Even as they discussed economic arrangements, women talked more in relational terms and were more likely to talk in terms of compromise. Furthermore, wives were found to "shy away from negotiation and conflict" (see 313–17). One of the lawyers I interviewed confirmed these gendered tendencies in her experience of practicing family law. And, upon comparing her study of divorced mothers and her study of divorced fathers, Arendell (1986, 1995) found that women did not use "rights talk" as men did (1995, 49). Finally, Coltrane and Hickman (1992) also found a language of rights used by men and not women in relations to child custody and child support issues.

17. This also came through when respondents described others' affairs. Several husbands talked about "bachelor parties" and/or one-night stands where committed husbands would secretly take a night or a weekend for a secret liaison. While two wives admitted affairs to me, three husbands implied, but did not state that they had had affairs. One husband slyly stated, "I'll never tell." As a woman, I may have made husbands feel more threatened and wives feel safer about confiding an affair. Yet, in one couple removed from my sample because of age, a husband did report having affairs.

18. A qualified belief in the value of commitment is apparent in traditionalists' resistance to legalizing same-sex marriages. Also, promoting traditionalist marriages through the law overlooks the problems that continue to haunt marriage, in spite of the legal ease of departure represented by no-fault divorce. For example, research shows wife abuse is more likely in highly traditional marriages (Dobash and Dobash 1992; Arendell and Kurz 1999; Gelles and Straus 1988); Kurz's representative sample revealed that 70 percent of divorced mothers had experienced violence at least once during marriage or separation (Kurz 1995, 53).

19. Husbands' actual power will depend upon many factors, including the fit between a husband's and a wife's marital ideology, gender ideology, economic resources, earning power, educational resources, etc. Within marriages, a husband's power is augmented if a wife adheres to "marriage as forever." If earnings and educational levels are taken as indicators of power struggles in dyads, then marriages departing from the male-dominant models appear to be at greater risk for divorce. Research finds that husbands' *un*employment and wives' employment contribute to divorce. The Census Bureau found that when both spouses worked full time, the rate of divorce or separation was 1 in 12; in contrast, when the husband worked full time and the wife part time, the rate dropped to 1 in 20, a 60 percent decrease (*San Francisco Chronicle*, January 15, 1993). Findings are mixed concerning how women's earning power is associated with divorce (White 1990). But research suggests that among *women,* those with high education and earning power are more likely to marry and to divorce (Carlson, 1990 cited in Baca Zinn and Eitzen 1993, 371; Coontz 1997, 82). Among *couples,* when husbands earn less and wives earn more, they are more likely to divorce (Kitson, Babri, and Roach 1985). Finally, some research has found that husbands who earned less than their wives in dual-job marriages were *less* likely to share the "second shift" than husbands who earned more or the same—a finding that suggests that men may make up for loss of power in one domain by exercising it in another (Hochschild with Machung 1989; Brines 1994).

20. With the rise of divorce culture, the historical practice of having a mistress on the side more easily translates into a second wife and serial marriage.

CHAPTER ELEVEN

1. Brewer (1988) points out that while marriage can make the difference between poverty and a comfortable standard of living for white mothers, this is not necessarily true for mothers of color, because racial discrimination restricts opportunities for men of color to garner decent wages. (See also McAdoo and McAdoo, 1993.)

2. The conflict between work and family depends heavily upon occupational, class, gender, and family resources. Unlike the Greens, the Kason-Morrises cannot afford regular baby sitters. Unlike Mia Turner, Roxanne's ex-spouse has not taken any responsibility for her daughter. And unlike the Fenton-Harringtons the Kason-Morrises do not share parenting. Finally, as we will see, unlike the Nakatos, she does not have extended family to reduce child care costs.

3. Although there is no way of knowing the dynamics of his first marriage without his first wife's interview, Craig's account suggests that before the divorce, his first wife may have done the second shift to compensate for her occupational achievement—that is, relied on the principle of "balancing" (Hochschild with Machung 1989). These conditions suggest that Craig lost power in the relationship; losing power in one way may have compelled him to retain his power in other ways. Even as their marriage unraveled, Craig thought marriage counseling was inappropriate; he explains that he never considered it because he supported his first wife "in whatever she wanted to do." But his descriptions suggest that gender issues infused Craig's first marriage as well, and that he brings these standards and conflicts into his remarriage. It also suggests, though it does not prove, that Roxanne's claim that it was 50/50 when she worked full-time is a retrospective exaggeration. Having another child and withdrawing from full-time work probably made the inequities appear to increase. Indeed, when Roxanne asserted in the opening paragraph that domestic labor used to be divided 50/50, my sense is that she idealizes the sharing that occurred while she was working full-time.

4. Roxanne was not the only wife to say that therapy threatened to dissolve her marriage. The implication is not that this derived from individualism, but that the husbands felt too threatened, angered, and manipulated by the demands of relationality. If gendered tendencies are extreme, addressing these tendencies in couples therapy is bound to be a minefield for a counselor. (See Goldner 1985.)

5. Craig was hesitant to participate in my research, he tells me, because it resembles therapy. While an in-depth interview does not share the structure or the aims of therapy, Craig is right that the processes are similar in that in-depth interviewing asks respondents to "share their inner life." It is this very aspect, I believe, that made Craig reluctant to participate. He participated for his wife. While in many couples the desire to participate was mutual, when it was not mutual the husband claimed to participate for his wife more often than the reverse.

6. This reflects the findings of Anita Garey's research on working mothers. She found, for example, that working mothers tend to construct themselves as "stay-at-home" moms, even when they work full time. (See Garey 1995.)

7. The first example, the Bush marriage, is clearly a conservative model based on a breadwinner/homemaker division of labor. My sense is that Debbie offers the second model—Arnold Schwartznegger and Maria Shriver—in order to convey that her own gender arrangements also reflect a model marriage.

8. For example, in the joint interview I asked the spouses to independently record on an index card the highs and lows of their relationship and their individual lives, and to describe their spouse's individual ups and downs. Then, they exchange cards and talk about their responses (see Appendix). Debbie designates her relational and individual high points to be the birth of their children and her pregnancies, respectively; Paul puts down their children's births as a relational high and their marriage and the children's births as individual high points. While Paul had recorded the children's birth for Debbie's high point, he wishes he would have thought of pregnancy: "I probably should have put that." Debbie replies that pregnancy is "an experience that *no man* will ever know" (emphasis in original). In

response, Paul not only affirms that he is barred from the experience, but gives Debbie the respect she has, in some ways, solicited: "[At the first birth] I realized, god, I don't think I could ever do this if I was pregnant—I would have just caved in."

9. Euro-American Patrick Reeves is another adherent to egalitarian marriage culture, but he is married to a wife who agrees with him. When he discusses male friends' divorces, he too refers to an unwillingness to communicate. As he discusses one couple's conflicts, Patrick asserts: "He would rather 'win' than stay married."

10. Conversely, Campbell and Snow (1992, 84) found that "men who have lower levels of marital satisfaction are less able or willing to express emotions, have higher levels of conflict between work or school and family relationships, and have lower levels of family cohesion."

11. Earlier in his interview, Paul reports on how his views regarding marital endurance changed as he grew up: "I guess when I was growing up I kind of used to think, 'well okay so you've been married'—like they celebrate their 25th anniversary when I was still in college; 'well, okay, 25th, big deal.' Because most everybody else that, you know, that they knew, was married 25 years. So what?! I mean some parents were celebrating their 50th, what's the big deal? So what, you know? Now that I look, I said, 'man, one year is a miracle.' Five years is a miracle. So I just have an even more—a newfound respect for—both them as parents and them as being able to stay with each other and do the right thing, and put other people's priorities above their own [...] I think I was very lucky to, to have been exposed to such positive behavior on their part."

12. In addition to Roxanne Kason-Morris, three egalitarian wives are married to husbands who show leanings toward male dominance, even as they talk gender neutrality.

CHAPTER TWELVE

1. Glenn (1987) refers to this conflict between family scholars as either "concerned" or "sanguine." I refer to these groups as pessimists and optimists because I see both groups as concerned. Pessimists represent those who see mostly problems and little promise in new patterns of marital and family life and optimists see the valuable facets in these new patterns. Also, there could be cause to describe these different viewpoints as liberal or conservative. However, some pessimistic scholars, such as Hewlett and West (1998) are liberal in their political orientations, and many of the political solutions advanced by pessimists concern government regulations, which are often considered anathema to conservatives.

2. Taking a more economistic view of marriage, Burggraf (1997) also argues for the importance of an exit option in *The Feminine Economy and Economic Man*.

3. Because these samples are not representative, these frequencies are only indicative of widespread changes. However, it might be useful for future researchers to have a report of the changing ideological patterns. While 73 percent of the older spouses believed in marriage culture, this was down to 61 percent for the younger

spouses. Among those who talked marriage culture, those who believed in male dominance had declined by a 17 percentage-point difference (from 46 among the '50s spouses to 29 percent among the '70s spouses), while those who believed in equality had increased by a 5 percentage-point difference (from 27 to 32 percent). Further, those spouses who believed in divorce culture had increased by an 11 percentage-point difference (from 27 to 38 percent). Beliefs in a male-dominated divorce culture were more often part of men's hidden agendas. Those who believed in equality and divorce culture increased by a 19 percentage-point difference (from 19 to 38 percent).

The '70s wives were more likely than husbands to espouse the virtues of egalitarianism and slightly more likely to embrace the premises of divorce culture. These patterns and the qualitative text suggest wives are changing faster; however, this small and unrepresentative sample cannot be generalized. Among the older couples, wives constituted half of those sharing beliefs in marriage culture and male dominance; wives constituted 57 percent of those believing in marriage culture and equality and 60 percent of those believing in divorce culture and equality (note that this represents 3 out of 5 spouses). Among the younger couples, wives constituted 55 percent of those believing in marriage culture and equality (6 out of 11 spouses) and 54 percent of those believing in divorce culture and equality (7 out of 13 spouses). Younger wives only made up 40 percent of the traditionalists embracing marriage culture and male authority (4 out of 10), whereas they constituted 50 percent of traditionalists among the older couples (6 out of 12).

4. It should be noted, however, that husbands rated "joint conflict over roles" second, while women found alcohol, untrustworthiness and immaturity, and extramarital sex slightly more important complaints than joint conflict over roles. In many ways these reveal relational concerns that have prevailed in traditional marriage culture.

5. This was a re-evaluation of Weitzman's (1985) figures based on a California sample that overestimated women's downward mobility upon divorce. A conservative estimate from a nationally representative sample following five thousand families found that intact families had a 21 percent increase in standard of living, divorced men had a slightly retarded increase of 17 percent; divorced women had a 7 percent decrease in their standard of living over a seven-year period (Hoffman and Holmes 1976, cited in Weitzman 1985, 337).

6. Historically, marriage represented social commitment and duty for both women and men, however, for women it has also represented a livelihood. As Christopher Jencks has observed: "As long as most American men and women married and pooled their economic resources, as they traditionally did, the fact that men received 70 percent of the nation's income had little effect on women's material well-being" (cited in Weitzman 1985, 355).

7. While still higher than female wages, male wages have stagnated significantly. Hewlett and West (1998, 173) report that "wages are down 25 percent for men twenty-five to thirty-four years of age." They also report that: "Over the last twenty years, the tide has risen (real per capita GNP went up 29 percent between 1973 and 1993), yet 80 percent of the boats have sunk. Equalizing trends

of the period from 1930 to 1970 reversed sharply in the early 1980s, and the gap between the haves and have-nots is now greater than at any time since 1929" (174).

8. Hewlett and West (1998, 180) go on to argue: "The fact is, we don't need a bigger crackdown—we need a new approach." They propose "A Parents' Bill of Rights" with an array of commendable and problematic policies addressing structural and cultural impediments to families—notably missing is any attention to the gender equalities in marriage addressed here.

9. For example, Wilson (1987) has argued that declining marriage in African-American communities is related to the declining numbers of "marriageable males," that is, young men who are not jobless, dying, or incarcerated. Lack of education and job opportunities combine to severely restrict marriage as an option for men. Material means to marriage remain important for it to be an option one embraces or repudiates. Still, "marriageability" in this analysis rests on constructing "husband/father" ideals in terms of the male provider role; clearly, poor women are parenting and providing at once. In this context the female-headed household can be understood as a strategy to contend with the lack of a marriage option (Baca Zinn 1989). While some have blamed welfare for displacing fathers, female-headed households have been increasing across the class system and in industrialized nations throughout the world with policies very different from our own.

10. Blankenhorn (1995a) describes the historically diminishing role of fathers as the shrinking of fatherhood, and the more recent noninvolvement and absence of fathers (including being reduced to their sperm in sperm banks) as the fragmentation of fatherhood. While I agree with Blankenhorn that fathers' participation has diminished and should be expanded and made more robust, I do not agree that we need to return to the role of fatherhood that implies patriarchal authority or biological primacy.

11. These assertions reflect the research that found that marriage generally improves men's well-being more than women's (Hu and Goldman 1990). It also suggests that "his" marriage has generally been better than "hers" (Bernard 1982).

12. As Skolnick (1997a, 94) observed: "It is hard to find a liberal or feminist who argues that a loving, harmonious, two-parent family is not preferable to a post-divorce single or recombined family. But that's beside the point. Loving, harmonious families are unlikely to break up." As Skolnick notes, this echoes the "Just Say No" campaign against drug abuse.

13. More recent research questions the degree to which fathers' relationships with children are mediated by mothers, particularly in stepfamilies. (See Lynn White's paper on "Affective Relationships between Parents and Young Adult Children: Stepfamilies, Gender, and Context." Paper presented at the annual meeting of the American Sociological Association, August 21, 1998.)

14. As Faludi (1991, 457) discovered upon analyzing survey data, being a good provider continues to be the leading trait of masculinity recognized by women and men. Blankenhorn (1995) also found that men still highlight the good provider role in defining manhood.

15. Research shows that some fathers are increasing their parental participation within egalitarian marriages—though this is not the prevailing pattern (Blaisure and Allen 1995; Coltrane 1998; Hochschild with Machung 1989; Gerson 1993). For example, about one-fifth of Hochschild and Machung's sample of working married parents shared the second shift of housework and child care equally.

16. While those who believe in divorce as a last resort often base this on the sake of the children—the "children's sake" is still being determined by adults' perceptions and interests and is framed as "staying together" rather than "parting" for the children's sake.

17. The hidden benefits of a contested rather than a hegemonic marriage culture may be reflected in recent research. Amato (1994, 149) notes that compared to older research, recent research shows less disparity in adjustment between continuously married and divorced families for both children and adults; he reasons that this probably reflects reduced stigma, less acrimony due to no-fault divorce, and, finally, the sum total of divorces may be constituted by relatively fewer desperate, highly conflicted, and violent divorces.

18. Giddens (1991, 180) has described therapy as "an expression of generalised reflexivity" that "exhibits in full the dislocations and uncertainties to which modernity gives rise."

19. The 1993 Family and Medical Leave Act provides only 12 weeks of *unpaid* leave for family responsibilities like childbirth or adoption—if the worker is employed by a business with 50 or more workers. About one-third of adults are simply not covered by this policy—and many more cannot afford the unpaid leave. As Hewlett and West (1998) point out, not only is this leave policy anemic compared to most European nations—which provide at least twice the leave time and offer pay—but we would need an overhaul of government and corporate policies to manifest the support for families that we express. See Hewlett and West's comprehensive "A Parents' Bill of Rights," which concludes their book.

20. Such ethnocentrism is apparent in the definitions of family and household used by the U.S. Census Bureau. For example, the rate of out-of-wedlock births is very high among the Navajo, yet formalized or legal marriage is not "the" magic linchpin; what might be labeled single parenthood and a lack of family values by outsiders represents a high regard for motherhood and commitment to the community in the context of matrilineal support networks for many Navajo (Deyhle and Margonis, 1995). As other researchers have observed, African-Americans have a tradition of relying upon extended family for shared parenting, as well as a greater acceptance of single parenthood (Fine and Schwebel 1988; Stack 1974; Taylor, Chatters, and Tucker 1990). The marital relationship may be important, but it is not the only relationship in which one can accomplish committed support. This may also explain why African-American children of divorced or single parents may manifest fewer problems than European-American children of divorce in some research on self-esteem (Fine and Schwebel 1988). Peters and McAdoo (1983) made a point about two-job married couples that is relevant to the new family forms brought by divorce; when this pattern became widespread among European-Americans it was decreasingly perceived as "pathological" and

increasingly perceived as "alternative." Further, Crosbie-Burnett and Lewis (1999) observe that for centuries African-American family life has required role flexibility, relations across households, bicultural socialization, and contended with a "deviant" label. They argue that postdivorce Euro-American families could learn a great deal about nontraditional families from African Americans.

21. Increasing cohabitation among heterosexual couples and the rise of domestic partnership laws have probably reduced the marginality of gay and lesbian couples and families. Many lesbian and gay couples choose to marry ceremonially and make commitments through legal contracts. Through the language of choice, the premises of divorce culture are, in some sense, "friendlier" than marriage culture toward gay and lesbian couples (Weston 1991). Choosing to participate in wedding ceremonies or to draw up contracts are activities shaped by structural obstacles to legal marriage. While not all lesbian and gay scholars promote legal marriage (Sherman 1992), many were thrilled in 1993 when Hawaii's Supreme Court was the first state in the country to rule (in *Baehr v. Lewin*) that denying marriage to lesbians and gays is unconstitutional because it violates the equal-protection clause through gender discrimination (F. Johnson 1996). Congress and state legislatures reacted by securing the frayed borders of the old tapestry. The Defense of Marriage Act, passed by Congress in 1997, retains rights and benefits for male-female unions only and grants states the right to refuse to recognize marital unions in other states. By questioning the heterosexual imperative (Rich 1980), lesbian and gay marriages may be a more radical challenge to the old tapestry. Same-sex marriages challenge the threads of heterosexuality and institutionalized male authority that have been sustained through religious and secular laws and economic arrangements, while affirming the threads of monogamy and commitment. However, if the resistance to same-sex marriage were overcome, it could help undo the enduring, if ever-changing, gender stratification that has defined marriage (Blumstein and Schwartz 1983; Arendell 1995).

Appendix

1. I also relied upon exploratory interviews with and observation of "experts" in marriage and divorce (including clergy, attorneys, psychologists, and mediators), attended a workshop on divorce mediation, and collected and analyzed products of popular culture on marriage and divorce; all of this is considered supplementary data.

2. After 1969, the Guidance Study was merged with another longitudinal study at the Institute of Human Development, the Oakland Growth Study.

3. The 1958 interviews are referred to as the Adult-I follow-up, the 1969–1971 interviews are the Adult-II follow-up, and the 1981–1982 interviews are known as the Adult-III follow-up. These multiple interview schedules and guides for the Longitudinal Studies are not reproduced here, but can be obtained from the Institute of Human Development at the University of California, Berkeley.

4. These scores include self-report as well as ratings by clinicians on the basis of the Adult-III data. I am indebted to Dr. Arlene Skolnick at the Institute for Human Development for allowing me to use these ratings to select my sample.

5. According to Hollingshead scale assessments, they range from Social Class I to IV by 1982; however, the central tendency of the majority of couples is to be middle class, that is, 19 respondents fall into Social Class II or III.

6. Dr. Wallerstein's interview guide was quite similar to my own interview guide in several areas. Where our questions were similar, I tended to pursue questions as she devised them, not only for her "Marriage Project" but also thereafter when I interviewed people from the High School Reunion Sample. Some of her questions that were dissimilar from my own (such as "What is the biggest surprise of your marriage?") ended up being quite important to my study of the meaning of divorce. Other dissimilar and more psychological questions were dropped when I turned to the High School Reunion interviews.

7. Dr. Wallerstein's larger sample (constituted by more than 50 couples) was gathered through a variety of sources, including professional associations, schools, and references through colleagues and participants. While I solicited some participation, sampling decisions were Dr. Wallerstein's. Couples were solicited to participate if they felt that they had "happy marriages." Despite the self-reported happiness, of couples in this sample, I did not find that my "Reunion Sample" was any more or any less happy in their marriages. I was more interested in talking to couples in a range of marriages—from unhappy to happy, than I was in happiness per se. A range of "satisfaction" was discernible in both the Married Project and the Bay Area Reunion samples.

8. Most of the interviews (38) took place in the spouses' homes. Seven interviews took place at the respondent's work site (two of these were joint), two individual interviews were at a cafe, and one individual interview took place in my home at the respondent's request.

9. Of course, defining "middle class" has been problematized in recent decades. With the shift from a manufacturing to a service economy, traditionally blue-collar jobs indicating "working class" status are on the decline, as pink-collar jobs with low pay and benefits have been on the rise (Reskin and Padavic 1994; Sacks and Remy 1984). Also, as many feminist scholars have observed, it is no longer valid to determine a wife's class status on the basis of her husband's income. Wives in this sample, like the population at large, tended to be less educated and have less earning power than their husbands. While most of these wives' class status would decline if they were to divorce, they are nevertheless mostly college-educated, mostly employed, and currently living a middle-class to upper-middle-class lifestyle, as evidenced by their homes and communities. Among three couples, the wife had the same or more education and/or earning power as the husband. I designated class status by individual income, education, and occupational status, but when neighborhood, children's schooling, home ownership, and lifestyle are taken into account, spouses' class status converged.

10. Interracial marriage remains relatively rare. This is not surprising given that miscegenation laws were not overturned until 1967. Nevertheless, between 1970 and 1992 there was a 365 percent jump in the number of interracial marriages (*San Francisco Chronicle*, July 26, 1993). A more diverse and tolerant Bay Area population both supports interracial relationships and enables supportive communities once married.

11. My identity as a white researcher was more salient in interactions with people of color. When I asked Gordon Walker, for example, what is good about being a man in marriage today, he began by saying that he must talk in terms of being a Black man. In the joint interview, when I asked about ethnic family traditions, spouses of color and white spouses in interracial marriages talked at length. However, white couples tended to look puzzled—like white students who have not realized how race enters into, shapes, and privileges their lives (McIntosh 1988). My identity as a woman was also more salient when interviewing men; research suggests that men confide in women more than they confide in other men, so this "difference" may have been an advantage (Rubin 1983).

12. Indeed, initially I even hoped to ask similar questions of the '70s interviewees to those that had been asked of the '50s interviewees in earlier decades. However, I soon realized that identical questions would no longer convey the same meaning. For example, even in the 1982 interviews, spouses were asked to describe "the way you felt about your spouse during your (first) courtship." The term "courtship" does not have the same meaning today, particularly as more and more couples live together before marriage.

13. While my research reflects concerns I share with constructivists, such as recognizing how the researcher and the researched interact and construct data together in the interview process, my research design and sampling also reflect ongoing concerns I share with post-positivists. I am aware that these paradigms are logically irreconcilable. (See Guba and Lincoln 1994, 116). Still, in practice, we shift from one paradigmatic lens to another in order to communicate with others, and so I report and recount these orientations in spite of the theoretical contradiction.

14. This was a terrific entree into the interview that I borrowed from Dr. Wallerstein's marriage research. While the question stumped a few spouses—as open-ended questions can—for the most part, it was a positive way to begin to talk about marriage.

Bibliography

Ahlburg, Dennis A., and Carol J. De Vita. 1992. "New Realities of the American Family." *Population Bulletin* 47(2). Washington DC: Population Reference Bureau, Inc.

Ahrons, Constance R., and Roy H. Rodgers. 1987. "The Remarriage Transition." In Arlene Skolnick and Jerome Skolnick, eds., *Family In Transition,* 9th ed. New York: Longman, 1997, pp. 185–96.

Ahrons, Constance. 1994. "What Divorce Is and Is Not: Transcending the Myths." In Susan J. Ferguson, ed., *Shifting the Center: Understanding Contemporary Families.* Mountain View, CA: Mayfield Publishing Company, 1998, pp. 400–412.

Albrecht, Stan L., Howard M. Bahr, and Kristen L. Goodman. 1983. *Divorce and Remarriage: Problems, Adaptations, and Adjustments.* Westport, CT: Greenwood Press.

Aldous, Joan. 1983. "Problematic Elements in the Relationships Between Churches and Families." In Joan Aldous and William V. D'Antonio, eds., *Families and Religions.* Beverly Hills, CA: Sage Publications, pp. 67–80.

Aldous, Joan, and William V. D'Antonio. 1983. "Introduction: Families and Religions Beset by Friends and Foes." In Joan Aldous and William V. D'Antonio, eds., *Families and Religions.* Beverly Hills, CA: Sage Publications, pp. 9–16.

Amato, Paul R. 1994. "Life-Span Adjustment of Children to Their Parents' Divorce." *The Future of Children: Children and Divorce* 4(1): 143–64.

Amato, Paul R., and Alan Booth. 1995. "Changes in Gender Role Attitudes and Perceived Marital Quality." *American Sociological Review* 60: 59–66.

————. 1996. "A Prospective Study of Divorce and Parent–Child Relationships." *Journal of Marriage and the Family* 58: 356–65.

————. 1997. *A Generation at Risk: Growing Up in An Era of Family Upheaval.* Cambridge, MA: Harvard University Press.

Amato, Paul R., and B. Keith. 1991. "Parental Divorce and the Well-Being of Children: A Meta-Analysis." *Psychological Bulletin* 100: 26–46.

Amato, Paul R., L. S. Loomis, and Alan Booth. 1995. "Parental Divorce, Marital Conflict, and Offspring Well-Being During Early Adulthood." *Social Forces* 73: 895–915.

American Sociological Association. 1998. "Sociologists Differ About Family Textbooks' Message." *Footnotes* 26: 7–12.

Ammerman, Nancy Tatom, and Wade Clark Roof, eds. 1995. *Work, Family, and Religion in Contemporary Society.* New York: Routledge.

Amott, Teresa L., and Julie A. Matthaei. 1991. *Race, Gender & Work: A Multicultural Economic History of Women in the United States.* Boston: South End Press.

Anderson, M. L. 1993. "Studying across Difference: Race, Class, and Gender in Qualitative Research." In Maxine Baca Zinn, Pierrette Hondagneu-Sotelo, and Michael A. Messner, eds. *Through the Prism of Difference: Readings in Sex and Gender.* Boston: Allyn and Bacon, 1997, pp. 70–78.

Anderson, Tamara, and Beth Vail. 1999. "Child-Care Dilemmas in Contemporary Families." In Stephanie Coontz, Maya Parson, and Gabrielle Raley, eds., *American Families: A Multicultural Reader.* New York: Routledge, pp. 359–70.

Arber, Sara, and Jay Ginn. 1995. "The Mirage of Gender Equality: Occupational Success in the Labour Market and Within Marriage." *British Journal of Sociology* 46(1): 21–43.

Arendell, Terry. 1986. *Mothers and Divorce: Legal, Economic and Social Dilemmas.* Berkeley, CA: University of California Press.

————. 1987. "Women and the Economics of Divorce in the Contemporary United States." *Signs: Journal of Women and Culture in Society* 13(1): 121–35.

————. 1992. "The Social Self as Gendered: A Masculinist Discourse of Divorce." *Symbolic Interaction* 15(2): 151–81.

————. 1995. *Fathers and Divorce.* Thousand Oaks, CA: Sage.

————. 1997. "Divorce and Remarriage." In Terry Arendell, ed., *Contemporary Parenting: Challenges and Issues.* Thousand Oaks, CA: Sage Publications, pp. 154–95.

————. 1998. Review of *Separating Together: How Divorce Transforms Families,* by Abigail J. Stewart, Anne P. Copeland, Nia Lane Chester, Janet E. Malley, and Nicole B. Barenbaum. *Contemporary Sociology* 27(3): 226–28.

Arendell, Terry, and Demie Kurz. 1999. "Divorce, Gender, and Violence." Paper presented at Women's Worlds International, 1999. Tromo, Norway. June 1999.

Aries, Philippe. 1967. *Centuries of Childhood.* New York: Vintage Books.

Baca Zinn, Maxine. 1989. "Family, Race, and Poverty in the Eighties." In Arlene Skolnick and Jerome Skolnick, eds., *Family In Transition,* 9th ed. New York: Longman, 1997, pp. 316–29.

Baca Zinn, Maxine D., and D. Stanley Eitzen. 1993. *Diversity in Families,* 3rd ed. New York: Harper Collins College Publishers.

Baca Zinn, Maxine, and Bonnie Thornton Dill. 1996. "Theorizing Difference from Multiracial Feminism." *Feminist Studies* 22(2): 321–31.

Beal, B., and J. Gray. 1995. "Bill McCartney and the Promise Keepers: Exploring the Connections among Sport, Christianity, and Masculinity." Paper presented at the annual meeting of the American Alliance for Health, Physical Education, Recreation, and Dance, Portland, Oregon.

Bellah, Robert N., Richard Madsen, William M. Sullivan, Ann Swidler, and Steven M. Tipton. 1985. *Habits of the Heart.* Berkeley, CA: University of California Press.

Benhabib, Seyla. 1986. "The Generalized and the Concrete Other: The Kohlberg–Gilligan Controversy and Moral Theory." In Diana Tietjens Meyers, ed., *Feminist Social Thought.* New York: Routledge, 1997, pp. 735–56.

Benjamin, Jessica. 1988. *The Bonds of Love: Psychoanalysis, Feminism, and the Problem of Domination.* New York: Pantheon Books.

Berger, Peter L., and Thomas Luckmann. 1965. *The Social Construction of Reality.* Garden City, NY: Anchor Books.

Berger, Peter, and H. Kellner. 1964. "Marriage and the Construction of Reality: An Exercise in the Microsociology of Knowledge." In Hans Peter Dreitzel, ed., *Recent Sociology No. 2: Patterns of Communicative Behavior.* New York: Macmillan, 1970, pp. 178–89.

Bernard, Jessie. 1981. "The Good-Provider Role: Its Rise and Fall." In Arlene Skolnick and Jerome Skolnick, eds., *Family In Transition*, 9th ed. New York: Longman, 1997, pp. 99–119.

————. 1982. *The Future of Marriage.* New Haven, CT: Yale University Press.

Blaisure, Karen R., and Katherine R. Allen. 1995. "Feminists and the Ideology and Practice of Marital Equality." *Journal of Marriage and the Family* 57: 5–19.

Blankenhorn, David. 1995a. *Fatherless America: Confronting Our Most Urgent Social Problem.* New York: Basic Books.

————. 1995b. "The Diminishment of American Fatherhood." In Susan J. Ferguson, ed., *Shifting the Center: Understanding Contemporary Families.* Mountain View, CA: Mayfield Publishing Company, 1998, pp. 338–55.

Block, J., J. H. Block, and P. F. Gjerde. 1986. "The Personality of Children Prior to Divorce: A Prospective Study." *Child Development* 57: 827–40.

Blumstein, Philip, and Pepper Schwartz. 1983. *American Couples.* New York: William Morrow and Company, Inc.

Breines, Wini. 1986. "The 1950s: Gender and Some Social Science." *Sociological Inquiry* 56(1): 69–92.

Brewer, Rose M. 1988. "Black Women in Poverty: Some Comments on Female-Headed Families." *Signs: Journal of Women and Culture in Society* 13(2): 331–39.

Brines, Julie. 1994. "Economic Dependency, Gender, and the Division of Labor at Home." *American Journal of Sociology* 100(3): 652–88.

Bumpass, L. 1990. "What's Happening to the Family? Interactions Between Demographic and Institutional Change." *Demography* 27(4): 483–98.

Bumpass, Larry, James A. Sweet, and Andrew Cherlin. 1991. "The Role of Cohabitation in Declining Rates of Marriage." *Journal of Marriage and the Family* 53: 913–27.

Burgess, E. W., and Harvey J. Locke. 1945. *The Family.* New York: American Book Co.

Burggraf, Shirley P. 1997. *The Feminine Economy and Economic Man.* New York: Addison-Wesley.

Campbell, James L., and Brent M. Snow. 1992. "Gender Role Conflict and Family Environment as Predictors of Men's Marital Satisfaction." *Journal of Family Psychology* 6(1): 84–87.

Cancian, Francesca. 1987. *Love in America: Gender and Self-Development.* New York: Cambridge University Press.

Cancian, Francesca M., and Steven L. Gordon. 1988. "Changing Emotion Norms in Marriage: Love and Anger in U.S. Women's Magazines Since 1900." *Gender & Society* 2: 308-42.

Caplow, Theodore, Howard M. Bahr, Bruce A. Chadwick, Reuben Hill, and Margaret Holmes Williamson. 1982. *Middletown Families: Fifty Years of Change and Continuity.* Minneapolis: University of Minnesota Press.

Card, Claudia. 1990. "Gender and Moral Luck." In Diana Tietjens Meyers, ed., *Feminist Social Thought.* New York: Routledge, 1997, pp. 646–62.

Carlson, Christopher. 1990. *Perspectives on the Family: History, Class, and Feminism.* Belmont, CA: Wadsworth.

Carolan, Marsha T. 1995. "African-American Couples at Midlife: Life Course and Gender Perspectives." Ph.D. diss., Virginia Polytechnic Institute and State University.

Chafetz, Janet Saltzman. 1980. "Conflict Resolution in Marriage: Toward a Theory of Spousal Strategies and Marital Dissolution Rates." *Journal of Family Issues* 1(3): 397–421.

Chafetz, Janet Saltzman, and Jacqueline Hagan. 1996. "The Gender Division of Labor and Family Change in Industrial Societies: A Theoretical Accounting." *Journal of Comparative Family Studies* 27(2): 187–219.

Cherlin, Andrew. 1981. *Marriage, Divorce, Remarriage.* Cambridge, MA: Harvard University Press.

_____. 1992. *Marriage, Divorce, Remarriage.* (Revised and enlarged edition). Cambridge, MA: Harvard University Press.

_____. 1999. *Public and Private Families: An Introduction.* 2nd ed. Boston: McGraw-Hill College.

Chesler, Phyllis. 1972. *Women and Madness.* Garden City, NY: Doubleday and Company, Inc.

Chodorow, Nancy J. 1978. *The Reproduction of Mothering.* Berkeley, CA: University of California Press.

_____. 1986. "Toward a Relational Individualism: The Mediation of Self Through Psychoanalysis." In T. Heller, M. Sosna, and D. Wellbery, eds., *Reconstructing Individualism.* Palo Alto, CA: Stanford University Press, pp. 197–207.

_____. 1989. *Feminism and Psychoanalytic Theory.* New Haven, CT: Yale University Press.

Clausen, John A. 1993. *American Lives: Looking Back at the Children of the Great Depression.* Berkeley, CA: University of California Press.

Clecak, Peter. 1983. *America's Quest for the Ideal Self.* New York: Oxford University Press.

Colletta, Nancy Donohue. 1983. "Stressful Lives: The Situation of Divorced Mothers and Their Children." *Journal of Divorce* 6(3): 19–31.

Collins, Patricia Hill. 1990. *Black Feminist Thought: Knowledge, Consciousness, and the Politics of Empowerment.* Boston: Unwin Hyman.

Coltrane, Scott, and Neal Hickman. 1992. "The Rhetoric of Rights and Needs: Moral Discourse in the Reform of Child Custody and Child Support Laws." *Social Problems* 39: 400–420.

Coltrane, Scott. 1995. "Stability and Change in Chicano Men's Family Lives." In M. Kimmel and M. Messner, eds., *Men's Lives*. Boston: Allyn and Bacon, pp. 469–84.

———. 1998. *Gender and Families*. Thousand Oaks, CA: Pine Forge Press.

Connell, Robert W. 1987. *Gender and Power*. Palo Alto, CA: Stanford University Press.

Coontz, Stephanie. 1992. *The Way We Never Were: American Families and the Nostalgia Trap*. New York: Basic Books.

———. 1997. *The Way We Really Are: Coming to Terms with America's Changing Families*. New York: Basic Books.

Corbin, Juliet, and Anselm Strauss. 1990. "Grounded Theory Research: Procedures, Canons, and Evaluative Criteria." *Qualitative Sociology* 13(1): 3–21.

Coser, Rose Laub. 1991. *In Defense of Modernity: Role Complexity and Individual Autonomy*. Stanford, CA: Stanford University Press.

Cott, Nancy. 1978. "Divorce and the Changing Status of Women in Eighteenth-Century Massachusetts." In Michael Gordon, ed., *The American Family in Social-Historical Perspective*, 2nd ed. New York: St. Martin's Press.

Cowan, C. P., and P. A. Cowan. 1992. *When Partners Become Parents: The Big Life Change for Couples*. New York: Basic Books.

Cowan, Philip, and Carolyn Pape Cowan. 1998. "New Families: Modern Couples as New Pioneers." In Mary Ann Mason, Arlene Skolnick, and Stephen D. Sugarman, eds., *All Our Families: New Policies for a New Century*. New York: Oxford University Press, pp. 169–92.

Crosbie-Burnett, Margaret, and Edith A. Lewis. 1993. "Use of African-American Family Structures and Functioning to Address the Challenges of European-American Postdivorce Families." In Stephanie Coontz, Maya Parson, and Gabrielle Raley, eds. *American Families: A Multicultural Reader*. New York: Routledge, 1999, pp. 455–68.

Cushman, Philip. 1995. *Constructing the Self, Constructing America: A Cultural History of Psychotherapy*. New York: Addison-Wesley.

Daly, Kerry. 1992. "The Fit Between Qualitative Research and Characteristics of Families." In Jane Gilgun, Kerry Daly, and Gerald Handel, eds., *Qualitative Methods in Family Research*. Newbury Park, CA: Sage Publications.

D'Antonio, William V. 1983. "Family Life, Religion, and Societal Values and Structures." In Joan Aldous and William V. D'Antonio, eds., *Families and Religions*. Beverley Hills, CA: Sage Publications, pp. 81–108.

D'Antonio, William V., and Mark J. Cavanaugh. 1983. "Roman Catholicism and the Family." In Joan Aldous and William V. D'Antonio, eds., *Families and Religions*. Beverley Hills, CA: Sage Publications, pp. 141–62.

Davis, Angela. 1981. *Women, Race and Class*. New York: Vintage Books.

Degler, Carl. 1980. *At Odds: Women and the Family in America from the Revolution to the Present*. New York: Oxford University Press.

Denzin, Norman, and Yvonna S. Lincoln, eds. 1994. *Handbook of Qualitative Research*. Thousand Oaks, CA: Sage Publications.

DeVault, Marjorie. 1987. "Doing Housework: Feeding and Family Life." In Naomi Gerstel and Harriet Engle Gross, eds., *Families and Work*. Philadelphia: Temple University Press, pp. 178–91.

DeVault, Marjorie L. 1990. "Talking and Listening from Women's Standpoint: Feminist Strategies for Interviewing and Analysis." *Social Problems* 37(1): 96–116.

Deyhle, Donna, and Frank Margonis. 1995. "Navajo Mothers and Daughters: Schools, Jobs, and the Family." *Anthropology and Education Quarterly* 26(2): 135–67.

di Leonardo, Micaela. 1987. "The Female World of Cards and Holidays: Women, Families, and the Work of Kinship." *Signs: Journal of Women and Culture in Society* 12(3): 440–53.

Dill, Bonnie Thornton. 1988. "Our Mother's Grief: Racial Ethnic Women and the Maintenance of the Family." *Journal of Family History* 13(4): 415–31.

Dinnerstein, Dorothy. 1976. *The Mermaid and the Minotaur: Sexual Arrangements and Human Malaise*. New York: Harper and Row.

Dobash, R. Emerson, and Russell P. Dobash. 1992. *Women, Violence and Social Change*. New York: Routledge.

Dugger, Karen. 1988. "Social Location and Gender-Role Attitudes: A Comparison of Black and White Women." *Gender & Society* 2(4): 425–48.

Duncan, Greg J., Richard D. Coe, Mary E. Corcoran, Martha S. Hill, Saul D. Hoffman, and James N. Morgan. 1984. "An Overview of Family Economic Mobility." In Arlene Skolnick and Jerome Skolnick, ed., *Family in Transition*, 5th ed. Boston: Little, Brown, and Company, 1986, pp. 104–20.

Duncombe, Jean, and Dennis Marsden. 1993. "Love and Intimacy: The Gender Division of Emotion and 'Emotion Work': A Neglected Aspect of Sociological Discussion of Heterosexual Relationships." *Sociology* 27(2): 221–41.

Durkheim, Emile. 1951. *Suicide*. New York: The Free Press.

———. 1961. *Moral Education*. Translated by Everett K. Wilson and Herman Schnurer. New York: The Free Press.

Easterlin, Richard A. 1980. *Birth and Fortune: The Impact of Numbers on Personal Welfare*. New York: Basic Books.

Edwards, Rosalind. 1990. "Connecting Method and Epistemology: A White Woman Interviewing Black Women." *Women's Studies International Forum* 13: 477–90.

Ehrenreich, Barbara. 1984. *The Hearts of Men: American Dreams and the Flight from Commitment*. Garden City, NY: Anchor Books.

Ehrenreich, Barbara, and Frances Fox Piven. 1984. "Women and the Welfare State." In Irving Howe, ed., *Alternatives: Proposals for America from the Democratic Left*. New York: Pantheon Books.

Ehrensaft, Diane. 1980. "When Women and Men Mother." *Socialist Review* 49: 37–73.

Eichorn, Dorothy H. 1981. "Samples and Procedures." In Dorothy H. Eichorn, John A. Clausen, Norma Haan, Marjorie P. Honzik, and Paul H. Mussen, eds., *Present and Past in Middle Life*. New York: Academic Press, pp. 33–50.

Elder, Glen H. 1974. *Children of the Great Depression.* Chicago: University of Chicago Press.

Epstein, Cynthia Fuchs. 1988. *Deceptive Distinctions: Sex, Gender, and the Social Order.* New York: Russell Sage Foundation.

Evans, Sara. 1979. *Personal Politics: The Roots of Women's Liberation in the Civil Rights Movement and the New Left.* New York: Vintage Books.

Faludi, Susan. 1991. *Backlash: The Undeclared War Against American Women.* New York: Crown Publishers.

Ferree, Myra Marx. 1990. "Beyond Separate Spheres: Feminism and Family Research." *Journal of Marriage and the Family* 52: 866–84.

Fine, Mark, and A. Schwebel. 1988. "An Emergent Explanation of Different Racial Reactions to Single Parenthood." *Journal of Divorce* 11(2): 1–15.

Fineman, Martha. 1991. *The Illusion of Equality.* Chicago: University of Chicago Press.

Flax, Jane. 1981. "The Conflict Between Nurturance and Autonomy in Mother-Daughter Relationships and Within Feminism." In Elizabeth Howell and Marjorie Bayes, eds., *Women and Mental Health.* New York: Basic Books, pp. 51–69.

Freud, Sigmund. 1926. *Inhibitions, Symptoms and Anxiety.* James Strachey, ed., and Alex Strachey, trans. Reprinted 1959. New York: W.W. Norton and Company.

Friedan, Betty. 1963. *The Feminine Mystique.* New York: W.W. Norton and Company.

Friedman, M. 1987. "Beyond Caring: The De-Moralization of Gender." In Diana Tietjens Meyers, ed., *Feminist Social Thought.* New York: Routledge, 1997, pp. 664–79.

Furstenberg, Frank. 1988. "Good Dads–Bad Dads: Two Faces of Fatherhood." In Arlene Skolnick and Jerome Skolnick, eds., *Family in Transition,* 9th ed. New York: Longman, 1997, pp. 221–41.

Furstenberg, Frank, and Andrew Cherlin. 1991. "Children's Adjustments to Divorce." in Arlene Skolnick and Jerome Skolnick, eds., *Family In Transition,* 9th ed. New York: Longman, 1997, pp. 267–77.

Furstenberg, F., and A. Cherlin. 1991. *Divided Families: What Happens to Children When Parents Part.* Cambridge, MA: Harvard University Press.

Furstenberg, F., and G. Spanier. 1987. *Recycling the Family.* Newbury Park, CA: Sage Publications.

Garey, Anita. 1993. "Constructing Identities as 'Working Mothers': Time, Space, and Family in a Study of Women Hospital Workers." Ph.D. diss. University of California, Berkeley.

———. 1995. "Constructing Motherhood on the Night Shift: 'Working Mothers' as 'Stay-at-Home Moms.'" *Qualitative Sociology* 18(4): 415–38.

Geertz, Clifford. 1973. *The Interpretation of Cultures.* New York: Basic Books.

Gelles, Richard, and Murray Straus. 1988. "Profiling Violent Families." In Arlene Skolnick and Jerome Skolnick, eds., *Family in Transition,* 9th ed. New York: Longman, 1997, pp. 445–62.

Gerson, Kathleen. 1993. "Dilemmas of Involved Fatherhood." In Susan J. Ferguson, ed., *Shifting the Center: Understanding Contemporary Families.* Mountain View, CA: Mayfield Publishing Company, 1998, pp. 355–71.

Gerson, Judith M., and Kathy Peiss. 1985. "Boundaries, Negotiation, Consciousness: Reconceptualizing Gender Relations." *Social Problems* 32: 317–31.

Gerstel, Naomi. 1987. "Divorce and Stigma." *Social Problems* 34(2): 172–86.

———. 1988a. "Divorce, Gender, and Social Integration." *Gender & Society* 2(3): 343–67.

———. 1988b. "Divorce and Kin Ties: The Importance of Gender." *Journal of Marriage and the Family* 50: 209–19.

Gerstel, Naomi, Catherine Kohler Riessman, and Sarah Rosenfield. 1985. "Explaining the Symptomatology of Separated and Divorced Women and Men: The Role of Material Conditions and Social Networks." *Social Forces* 64(1): 84–101.

Gerth, H., and C. Wright Mills. 1946. *From Max Weber: Essays in Sociology.* New York: Oxford University Press.

Giddens, Anthony. 1979. *Central Problems in Social Theory.* Berkeley, CA: University of California Press.

———. 1991. *Modernity and Self-Identity.* Stanford, CA: Stanford University Press.

Gilgun, Jane F. 1992. "Definitions, Methodologies, and Methods." In Jane F. Gilgun, Kerry Daly and Gerald Handel, eds., *Qualitative Methods in Family Research.* Newbury Park, CA: Sage Publications, pp. 22–40.

Gilkes, Cheryl Townsend. 1995. "The Storm and the Light: Church, Family, Work, and Social Crisis in the African-American Experience." In Nancy Tatom Ammerman and Wade Clark Roof, eds., *Work, Family, and Religion in Contemporary Society.* New York: Routledge, pp. 177–98.

Gilligan, Carol. 1982. *In a Different Voice: Psychological Theory and Women's Development.* Cambridge, MA: Harvard University Press.

Glaser, Barney G., and Anselm L. Strauss. 1967. *The Discovery of Grounded Theory.* Chicago: Aldine Publishing Company.

Glendon, Mary Ann. 1987. *Abortion and Divorce in Western Law: American Failures and European Challenges.* Cambridge, MA: Harvard University Press.

Glenn, Norval D. 1987. "Continuity Versus Change, Sanguineness Versus Concern." *Journal of Family Issues* 8(4): 348–54.

———. 1991. "The Recent Trend in Marital Success in the United States." *Journal of Marriage and the Family* 53: 261–70.

———. 1996. "Values, Attitudes, and the State of American Marriage." In David Popenoe, Jean Bethke Elshtain, and David Blankenhorn, eds., *Promises to Keep: Decline and the Renewal of Marriage in America.* Lanham, MD: Rowman and Littlefield, pp. 15–33.

———. 1997. *Closed Hearts, Closed Minds: The Textbook Story of Marriage.* New York: Institute for American Values.

Glenn, Norval D., and Kathryn B. Kramer. 1987. "The Marriages and Divorces of the Children of Divorce." *Journal of Marriage and the Family* 49: 811–25.

Glenn, Norval D., and Charles N. Weaver. 1988. "The Changing Relationship of Marital Status to Reported Happiness." *Journal of Marriage and the Family* 50: 317–24.

Glick, P. C., and Sung-Ling, Lin. 1986. "Recent Changes in Divorce and Remarriage." *Journal of Marriage and the Family* 48: 737–47.

_____. 1987. "Remarriage After Divorce." *Sociological Perspectives* 30(2): 162–79.

Glick, Paul. 1979. "Children of Divorced Parents in Demographic Perspective." *Journal of Social Issues* 35(4): 170–82.

Goldner, Virginia. 1985. "Feminism and Family Therapy." *Family Process* 24: 31–47.

Goldscheider, Frances K., and Linda J. Waite. 1991. *New Families, No Families?* Berkeley, CA: University of California Press.

Goode, William J. 1956. *After Divorce.* Glencoe, IL: The Free Press.

_____. 1982. "Why Men Resist." In Barrie Thorne and Marilyn Yalom, eds., *Rethinking the Family.* New York: Longman.

_____. 1993. *World Changes in Divorce Patterns.* New Haven, CT: Yale University Press.

Gottman, John, James Coan, Sybil Carrere, and Catherine Swanson. 1998. "Predicting Marital Happiness and Stability from Newlywed Interactions." *Journal of Marriage and the Family* 60: 5–22.

Gramsci, Antonio. 1971. *Selections from the Prison Notebooks.* New York: International Publishers.

Guba, Egon G., and Yvonna Lincoln. 1994. "Competing Paradigms in Qualitative Research." In Norman Denzin and Yvonna Lincoln, eds., *Handbook of Qualitative Research.* Thousand Oaks, CA: Sage Publications, pp. 105–17.

Gwartney-Gibbs, Patricia A. 1986. "The Institutionalization of Premarital Cohabitation: Estimates from Marriage License Applications, 1970 and 1980." *Journal of Marriage and the Family* 48: 423–34.

Haaken, Janice. 1993. "From Al-Anon to ACOA: Codependence and the Reconstruction of Caregiving." *Signs: Journal of Women and Culture in Society* 8(2): 321–45.

Hackstaff, Karla B. 1994. "Divorce Culture: A Breach in Gender Relations." Ph.D. diss. Department of Sociology, University of California, Berkeley.

Hansen, Karen. 1987. "Feminist Conceptions of Public and Private: A Critical Analysis." *Berkeley Journal of Sociology* 32: 105–28.

Hareven, Tamara. 1982. "American Families in Transition: Historical Perspectives on Change." In Arlene Skolnick and Jerome Skolnick, eds., *Families in Transition,* 5th ed. Boston: Little, Brown and Company, 1986, pp. 40–58.

Hargrove, Barbara. 1983. "Family in the White American Protestant Experience." In Joan Aldous and William V. D'Antonio, eds. *Families and Religions.* Beverly Hills, CA: Sage Publications, pp. 113–40.

Hartmann, Heidi. 1976. "Capitalism, Patriarchy, and Job Segregation by Sex." *Signs: Journal of Women and Culture in Society* 1(3): 137–69.

Hetherington, E. Mavis, Tracy C. Law, and Thomas G. O'Connor. 1993. "Divorce: Challenges, Changes, New Chances." In Arlene Skolnick and Jerome

Skolnick, eds., *Family In Transition*, 9th ed. New York: Longman, 1997, pp. 176–85.

Hewlett, Sylvia Ann, and Cornel West. 1998. *The War Against Parents: What We Can Do for America's Beleaguered Moms and Dads*. New York: Houghton Mifflin Company.

Hochschild, Arlie R. 1975. "Inside the Clockwork of Male Careers." In Florence Howe, ed., *Women and the Power to Change*. New York: McGraw Hill, pp. 47-80.

_____. 1983. *The Managed Heart: The Commercialization of Human Feeling*. Berkeley, CA: University of California Press.

_____. 1997. *The Time Bind: When Work Becomes Home and Home Becomes Work*. New York: Metropolitan Books.

Hochschild, Arlie R., with Anne Machung. 1989. *The Second Shift: Working Parents and the Revolution at Home*. New York: Viking Press.

Hoffman, Saul, and Greg Duncan. 1988. "What Are the Economic Consequences of Divorce?" *Demography* 25(4): 641–45.

Hoffman, Saul, and John Holmes. 1976. "Husbands, Wives, and Divorce." In *Five Thousand American Families—Patterns of Economic Progress*. Ann Arbor, MI: Institute for Social Research.

Holden, George W., Robert A. Geffner, and Ernest N. Jouriles. 1998. *Children Exposed to Marital Violence: Theory, Research, and Applied Issues*. Washington, DC: American Psychological Association.

Holifield, E. Brooks. 1983. *A History of Pastoral Care in America*. Nashville, TN: Abingdon Press.

hooks, bell. 1981. *Ain't I a Woman: Black Women and Feminism*. Boston: South End Press.

_____. 1984. *Feminist Theory: From Margin to Center*. Boston: South End Press.

_____. 1990. *Yearning: Race, Gender, and Cultural Politics*. Boston: South End Press.

_____. 1993. *Sisters of the Yam*. Boston: South End Press.

Howell, Elizabeth, and Marjorie Bayes, eds. 1981. *Women and Mental Health*. New York: Basic Books.

Hu, Y., and N. Goldman. 1990. "Mortality Differentials by Marital Status: An International Comparison." *Demography* 27(2): 233–50.

Hull, Gloria T., Patricia Bell Scott, and Barbara Smith, eds. 1982. *All the Women Are White, All the Blacks Are Men, but Some of Us Are Brave*. Old Westbury: The Feminist Press.

Hunter, Andrea, and James Earl Davis. 1992. "Constructing Gender: An Exploration of Afro-American Men's Conceptualization of Manhood." *Gender & Society* 6(3): 464–79.

John, Daphne, Beth Anne Shelton, and Kristen Luschen. 1995. "Race, Ethnicity, Gender, and Perceptions of Fairness." *Journal of Family Issues* 16(3): 357–79.

Johnson, Colleen Leahy. 1988. *Ex-Familia*. New Brunswick, NJ: Rutgers University Press.

Johnson, Fenton. 1996. "Wedded to an Illusion: Do Gays and Lesbians Really Want the Right to Marry?" *Harpers Magazine,* November 1996, pp. 43–50.

Johnson, Miriam. 1988. *Strong Mothers, Weak Wives: The Search for Gender Equality.* Berkeley, CA: University of California Press.

Jones, Jacqueline. 1985. *Labor of Love, Labor of Sorrow: Black Women, Work and the Family from Slavery to the Present.* New York: Vintage Books.

Kalter, Joanmarie. 1993. "Finding a Good Therapist to Save Your Marriage—and When Not to Bother." *Cosmopolitan,* August, 82–86.

Kaminer, Wendy. 1992. *I'm Dysfunctional, You're Dysfunctional: The Recovery Movement and Other Self-Help Fashions.* New York: Addison-Wesley.

Karenga, M. 1995. "The Million Man March/Day of Absence Mission Statement." *The Black Scholar* 25: 2–11.

Kay, Herma Hill. 1987. "An Appraisal of California's No-Fault Divorce Law." *California Law Review* 75(29): 291–319.

———. 1990. "Beyond No-Fault: New Directions in Divorce Reform." In Stephen Sugarman and Herma Hill Kay, eds., *Divorce Reform at the Crossroads.* New Haven: Yale University Press, pp. 6–36.

Kelly, Joan Berlin. 1982. "Divorce: The Adult Perspective." In Arlene Skolnick and Jerome Skolnick, eds., *Family in Transition,* 5th ed. Boston: Little, Brown and Company, 1986, pp. 304–37.

———. 1988. "Longer-Term Adjustment in Children of Divorce: Converging Findings and Implications for Practice." *Journal of Family Psychology* 2(2): 119–40.

Kimmel, Michael S. 1996. *Manhood in America: A Cultural History.* New York: The Free Press.

Kitson, Gay C., Karen Benson Babri, and Mary Joan Roach. 1985. "Who Divorces and Why: A Review." *Journal of Family Issues* 6(3): 255–94.

Kitson, Gay C., and William Holmes. 1992. *Portrait of Divorce: Adjustment to Marital Breakdown.* New York: The Guilford Press.

Kitson, Gay C., with Leslie A. Morgan. 1990. "The Multiple Consequences of Divorce: A Decade Review." *Journal of Marriage and the Family* 52: 913–24.

Komter, Aafke. 1989. "Hidden Power in Marriage." *Gender & Society* 3(2): 187–216.

Kressel, Kenneth, M. Lopez-Marillas, M. Weinglass, and M. Deutsch. 1978. "Professional Intervention in Divorce: A Summary of the Views of Lawyers, Psychotherapists, and Clergy." *Journal of Divorce* 2(2): 119–55.

Krokoff, Lowell J. 1989. "Predictive Validation of a Telephone Version of the Locke-Wallace Marital Adjustment Test." *Journal of Marriage and the Family* 51: 767-75.

Kurz, Demie. 1989. "Social Science Perspectives on Wife Abuse." *Gender & Society* 3(4): 489–505.

———. 1995. *For Richer, For Poorer.* New York: Routledge.

Landis-Kleine, Cathy, Linda A. Foley, Loretta Nall, Patricia Padgett, and Leslie Walters-Palmer. 1995. "Attitudes Toward Marriage and Divorce Held by Young Adults." *Journal of Divorce and Remarriage* 23(3–4): 63–73.

Laosa, Luis M. 1988. "Ethnicity and Single Parenting in the United States." In E. Mavis Hetherington and Josephine D. Arasteh, eds., *Impact of Divorce, Single Parenting, and Stepparenting on Children.* Hillsdale, NJ: Lawrence Erlbaum Associates, pp. 23–49.

LaRossa, Ralph. 1988. "Fatherhood and Social Change." In M. Kimmel and M. Messner, eds., *Men's Lives.* Boston: Allyn and Bacon, 1995, pp. 448–60.

LaRossa, Ralph, and Jane H. Wolf. 1985. "On Qualitative Family Research." *Journal of Marriage and the Family* August 47: 531–41.

Lasch, Christopher. 1979. *The Culture of Narcissism.* New York: W.W. Norton and Company.

Lawson, Annette. 1988. *Adultery.* New York: Basic Books.

Lee, Gary R., Karen Seccombe, and Constance L. Shehan. 1991. "Marital Status and Personal Happiness: An Analysis of Trend Data." *Journal of Marriage and the Family* 53: 839–44.

Lewis, Diane K. 1977. "A Response to Inequality: Black Women, Racism, and Sexism." *Signs: Journal of Women in Culture and Society* 3(2): 339–61.

Lindner, Robert. 1956. *Must You Conform?* New York: Grove Press.

Lopata, Helena Znaniecka. 1993. "The Interweave of Public and Private: Women's Challenge to American Society." *Journal of Marriage and the Family* 55(1): 176–90.

Lye, Diane N., and Timothy J. Biblarz. 1993. "The Effects of Attitudes Toward Family Life and Gender Roles on Marital Satisfaction." *Journal of Family Issues* 14(2): 157–88.

Lynd, Robert S., and Helen Merrell Lynd. 1929. *Middletown: A Study in American Culture.* New York: Harcourt and Brace.

Maccoby, Eleanor E., and Robert H. Mnookin. 1992. *Dividing the Child: Social and Legal Dilemmas of Custody.* Cambridge, MA: Harvard University Press.

Markman, Howard J., Louise Silvern, Mari Clements, and Shelley Kraft-Hanak. 1993. "Men and Women Dealing with Conflict in Heterosexual Relationships." *Journal of Social Issues* 49(3): 107–25.

Martin, Teresa Castro, and Larry L. Bumpass. 1989. "Recent Trends in Marital Disruption." *Demography* 26(1): 37–51.

Mason, Karen Oppenheim, and Yu-Hsia Lu. 1988. "Attitudes Toward Women's Familial Roles: Changes in the United States, 1977–1985." *Gender & Society* 2(1): 39–57.

Mason, Mary Ann. 1988. *The Equality Trap.* New York: Simon and Schuster.

————. 1998. "The Modern American Stepfamily: Problems and Possibilities." In Mary Ann Mason, Arlene Skolnick, and Stephen D. Sugarman, eds., *All Our Families: New Policies for a New Century.* New York: Oxford University Press.

Mason, Mary Ann, Arlene Skolnick, and Stephen D. Sugarman, eds. 1998. *All Our Families: New Policies for a New Century.* New York: Oxford University Press.

May, Elaine Tyler. 1980. *Great Expectations: Marriage and Divorce in Post-Victorian America.* Chicago: University of Chicago Press.

_____. 1988. *Homeward Bound: American Families in the Cold War Era.* New York: Basic Books.

_____. 1995. *Barren in the Promised Land: Childless Americans and the Pursuit of Happiness.* New York: Basic Books.

McAdoo, Harriete Pipes, ed. 1988. *Black Families,* 2nd ed. Newbury Park, CA: Sage Publications.

McAdoo, John Lewis, and Julia B. McAdoo. 1993. "The African-American Father's Roles Within the Family." In M. Kimmel and M. Messner, eds., *Men's Lives.* Boston: Allyn and Bacon. 1995.

McCarthy, James. 1979. "Religious Commitment, Affiliation, and Marriage Dissolution." In Robert Wuthnow, ed., *The Religious Dimension.* New York: Academic Press, pp. 179–97.

McCracken, Grant. 1988. *The Long Interview.* (Qualitative Research Methods, Vol. 13.) Newbury Park, CA: Sage Publications.

McIntosh, Peggy. 1988. "White Privilege and Male Privilege: A Personal Account of Coming to See Correspondences Through Work in Women's Studies." In Margaret Anderson and Patricia Hill Collins, eds., *Race, Class, and Gender,* 2nd ed. New York: Wadsworth Publishing, 1995, pp. 76–87.

McLanahan, Sara S., and Larry L. Bumpass. 1988. "Intergenerational Consequences of Family Disruption. *American Journal of Sociology* 94: 130–52.

McLanahan, Sara S., and Gary Sandefur. 1994. *Growing Up with a Single Parent.* Cambridge, MA: Harvard University Press.

McLaughlin, Steven D., Barbara D. Melber, John O.G. Billy, Denise M. Zimmerle, Linda D. Winges, and Terry R. Johnson. 1988. *The Changing Lives of American Women.* Chapel Hill, NC: University of North Carolina Press.

Mead, Margaret. 1935. *Sex and Temperament in Three Primitive Societies.* New York: Morrow.

Messner, Michael A. 1997. *Politics of Masculinities: Men in Movements.* Thousand Oaks, CA: Sage Publications.

Mills, C. Wright. 1940. "Situated Actions and Vocabularies of Motive." *American Sociological Review* 5: 904–13.

_____. 1959. *The Sociological Imagination.* New York: Oxford University Press.

Modell, John. 1985. "Historical Reflections on American Marriage." In Kingsley Davis and Amyra Grossbard-Schechtman, eds., *Contemporary Marriage: Comparative Perspectives on a Changing Institution.* New York: Russell Sage Foundation.

Moen, Phyllis. 1992. *Women's Two Roles: A Contemporary Dilemma.* New York: Auburn House.

Moore, Kristen, Daphne Spain, and Suzanne Bianchi. 1984. "Working Wives and Mothers." In Beth B. Hess and Marvin B. Sussman, eds., *Women and the Family: Two Decades of Change.* New York: Haworth Press, pp. 77–98.

Moraga, Cherrie, and Gloria Anzaldua, eds. 1981. *This Bridge Called My Back.* Watertown, MA: Persephone Press.

Morgan, David. 1991. "From 'the Problem of Divorce' to 'the Problem of Marriage'; the Sociological Work of One Plus One, Marriage and Partnership Research, 1971–1991." *Journal of Social Work Practice* 5(2): 193–97.

Mullings, Leith. 1986. "Anthropological Perspectives on the Afro-American Family." *American Journal of Social Psychiatry* 6: 11–16.

Newman, Katherine. 1988. *Falling from Grace: The Experience of Downward Mobility in the American Middle Class.* New York: The Free Press.

Nicholson, Linda J., ed. 1990. *Feminism/Postmodernism.* New York: Routledge.

Nobles, Wade. 1976. "Extended Self: Rethinking the So-Called Negro Self-Concept." *The Journal of Black Psychology* 2(2): 15–24.

Oakley, Ann. 1981. "Interviewing Women: A Contradiction in Terms." In Helen Roberts, ed., *Doing Feminist Research.* Boston: Routledge, Kegan, and Paul, pp. 30–61.

Oliker, Stacey. 1989. *Best Friends and Marriage.* Berkeley, CA: University of California Press.

Ostrander, Susan A. 1984. *Women of the Upper Class.* Philadelphia: Temple University Press.

Pagnini, Deanna L., and Ronald R. Rindfuss. 1993. "The Divorce of Marriage and Childbearing: Changing Attitudes and Behavior in the United States." *Population and Development Review* 19(2): 331–47.

Peters, Marie F., and Harriette P. McAdoo. 1983. "The Present and Future of Alternative Lifestyles in Ethnic American Cultures." In Eleanor D. Macklin and Roger H. Rubin, eds., *Contemporary Families and Alternative Lifestyles.* Beverly Hills, CA: Sage Publications, pp. 288–307.

Peterson, R. 1996. "Statistical Errors, Faulty Conclusions, Misguided Policy: Reply to Weitzman." *American Sociological Review* 61(3): 539–42.

Philipson, Ilene. 1993. *On the Shoulders of Women: The Feminization of Psychotherapy.* New York: Guilford Press.

Phillips, Roderick. 1988. *Putting Asunder: A History of Divorce in Western Society.* New York: Cambridge University Press.

———. 1991. *Untying the Knot: A Short History of Divorce.* New York: Cambridge University Press.

Popenoe, D. 1988. *Disturbing the Nest: Family Change and Decline in Modern Societies.* New York: Aldine De Gruyter.

———. 1996. *Life Without Father: Compelling New Evidence that Fatherhood and Marriage are Indispensable for the Good of Children and Society.* New York: Martin Kessler Books.

———. 1997. "Family Trouble." *The American Prospect* 34(September–October): 18–19.

Popenoe, David, Jean Bethke Elshtain, and David Blankenhorn, eds. 1996. *Promises to Keep: Decline and Renewal of Marriage in America.* Lanham, MD: Rowman & Littlefield Publishers, Inc.

Rampage, Cheryl. 1994. "Power, Gender, and Marital Intimacy." *Journal of Family Therapy* 16(1): 125–37.

Reinharz, Shulamit. 1992. *Feminist Methods in Social Research.* New York: Oxford University Press.

Renzetti, Claire M., and Daniel J. Curran. 1995. *Women, Men, and Society.* Boston: Allyn and Bacon.

Reskin, Barbara, and Irene Padavic. 1994. *Women and Men at Work.* Thousand Oaks, CA: Pine Forge Press.

Ribbens, Jane, and Rosalind Edwards. 1995. "Introducing Qualitative Research on Women in Families and Households." *Women's Studies International Forum* 18(3): 247–58.

Rich, Adrienne. 1980. "Compulsory Heterosexuality and Lesbian Existence." In Elizabeth Abel and Emily Abel, eds., *The Signs Reader: Women, Gender, and Scholarship.* Chicago: University of Chicago Press, pp. 139–68.

Rieff, P. 1966. *The Triumph of the Therapeutic: Uses of Faith After Freud.* Chicago: University of Chicago Press.

Riesman, David, Nathan Glazer, and Reuel Denney. 1950. *The Lonely Crowd: A Study of the Changing American Character.* New Haven, CT: Yale University Press.

Riessman, Catherine Kohler. 1987. "When Gender is Not Enough: Women Interviewing Women." *Gender & Society* 1(2): 172–207.

————. 1990. *Divorce Talk: Women and Men Make Sense of Personal Relationships.* New Brunswick, NJ: Rutgers University Press.

Riley, Glenda. 1991. *Divorce: An American Tradition.* New York: Oxford University Press.

Robiner, W. N. 1991. "How Many Psychologists Are Needed? A Call for a National Psychology Human Resource Agenda." *Professional Psychology: Research and Practice* 22(6): 427–40.

Rollins, B. C., and H. Feldman. 1970. "Marital Satisfaction over the Family Life Cycle." *Journal of Marriage and the Family* 32: 20–28.

Rollins, Judith. 1985. *Between Women: Domestics and Their Employers.* Philadelphia: Temple University Press.

Rose, Phyllis. 1983. *Parallel Lives.* New York: Vintage Books.

Rosenfelt, Deborah, and Judith Stacey. 1987. "Review Essay: Second Thoughts on the Second Wave." *Feminist Studies* 13(2): 341–61.

Rothman, Barbara Katz. 1984. "The Meanings of Choice in Reproductive Technology." In Alison Jaggar, ed., *Living with Contradictions: Controversies in Feminist Social Ethics.* Boulder, CO: Westview Press, 1994.

Rubin, Lillian. 1976. *Worlds of Pain: Life in the Working-Class Family.* New York: Basic Books.

————. 1983. *Intimate Strangers: Men and Women Together.* New York: Harper and Row.

Sacks, Karen Brodkin, and Dorothy Remy, eds. 1984. *My Troubles Are Going to Have Trouble with Me: Everyday Trials and Triumphs of Women Workers.* New Brunswick, NJ: Rutgers University Press.

Sagan, Eli. 1988. *Freud, Women, and Morality: The Psychology of Good and Evil.* New York: Basic Books.

San Francisco SMSA. 1993. County and City Extra: Annual Metro, City and County Data Book, 1992–93.

Santi, Lawrence L. 1988. "The Demographic Context of Recent Change in the Structure of American Households." *Demography* 25(4): 509–19.

Scanzoni, J. 1979. "A Historical Perspective on Husband-Wife Bargaining Power and Marital Dissolution." In George Levinger and Oliver Moles, eds., *Divorce and Separation: Context, Causes and Consequences*. New York: Basic Books, pp. 20–36.

———. 1987. "Families in the 1980s: Time to Refocus Our Thinking." *Journal of Family Issues* 8(4): 394–421.

Schneider, Carl. 1996. "The Law and the Stability of Marriage: The Family as a Social Institution." In David Popenoe, Jean Bethke Elshtain, and David Blankenhorn, eds., *Promises to Keep: Decline and Renewal of Marriage in America*. Lanham, MD: Rowman & Littlefield Publishers, Inc., pp. 187–214.

Schütz, A. 1962. *Collected Papers* (Vol. I). The Hague, Netherlands: Martinus Nijhoff.

Schwartz, Howard, and Jerry Jacobs. 1979. *Qualitative Sociology: A Method to the Madness*. New York: The Free Press.

Schwartz, Pepper. 1994. *Peer Marriage*. New York: The Free Press.

Scott, Joan. 1986. "Gender: A Useful Category of Historical Analysis." *American Historical Review* 91: 1053–75.

———. 1988. "Deconstructing Equality-Versus-Difference." *Feminist Studies* 14(1): 35–50.

Seeley, John R., R. Alexander Sim, and Elizabeth Loosley. 1956. *Crestwood Heights*. Toronto: University of Toronto Press.

Sennet, Richard. 1978. *The Fall of Public Man*. New York: Random House, Vintage Books.

Sherman, Suzanne, ed. 1992. *Lesbian and Gay Marriage: Private Commitments, Public Ceremonies*. Philadelphia: Temple University Press.

Shorter, Edward. 1975. *The Making of the Modern Family*. New York: Basic Books.

Simon, Rita J., and Jean M. Landis. 1989. "Report: Women's and Men's Attitudes About a Woman's Place and Role." *Public Opinion Quarterly* 53(2): 265–76.

Simonds, Wendy. 1992. *Women and Self-Help Culture: Reading Between the Lines*. New Brunswick, NJ: Rutgers University Press.

Skolnick, Arlene. 1981. "Married Lives: Longitudinal Perspectives on Marriage." In Dorothy H. Eichorn, John A. Clausen, Norma Haan, Marjorie P. Honzik, and Paul H. Mussen, eds., *Present and Past in Middle Life*. New York: Academic Press, pp. 270–97.

———. 1987. *The Intimate Environment*, 4th ed. Boston: Little, Brown, and Company.

———. 1991. *Embattled Paradise*. New York: Basic Books.

———. 1992. *The Intimate Environment*, 5th ed. New York: Harper Collins.

———. 1997a. "Family Values: The Sequel." *The American Prospect* 32(May–June 1997): 86–94.

———. 1997b. "Family Trouble." *The American Prospect* 34(September–October, 1997): 19–21.

_____. 1998. "Solomon's Children: The New Biologism, Psychological Parenthood, Attachment Theory, and the Best Interests Standard." In Mary Ann Mason, Arlene Skolnick, and Stephen D. Sugarman, eds. *All Our Families: New Policies for a New Century.* New York: Oxford University Press, pp. 236–55.

Smith, Rebecca M., Mary Anne Goslen, Anne Justice Byrd, and Linda Reece. 1991. "Self-Other Orientation and Sex-Role Orientation of Men and Women Who Remarry." *Journal of Divorce and Remarriage* 14(3–4): 3–32.

Snitow, Ann. 1990. "A Gender Diary." In M. Hirsch and E. Fox Keller, eds., *Conflicts in Feminism.* New York: Routledge.

Spanier, Graham B. 1989. "Bequeathing Family Continuity." *Journal of Marriage and the Family* 51: 3–13.

Spelman, Elizabeth V. 1988. *Inessential Woman: Problems of Exclusion in Feminist Thought.* Boston: Beacon Press.

Stacey, Judith. 1988. "Can There Be a Feminist Ethnography?" *Women's Studies International Forum* 11: 21–27.

_____. 1990. *Brave New Families: Stories of Domestic Upheaval in Late Twentieth Century America.* New York: Basic Books.

_____. 1996. *In the Name of the Family: Rethinking Family Values in the Postmodern Age.* Boston: Beacon Press.

_____. 1998. "Gay and Lesbian Families: Queer Like Us." In Mary Ann Mason, Arlene Skolnick, and Stephen D. Sugarman, eds., *All Our Families: New Policies for a New Century.* New York: Oxford University Press, pp. 117–43.

Stack, Carol. 1974. *All Our Kin: Strategies for Survival in a Black Community.* New York: Harper and Row.

_____. 1990. "Different Voices, Different Visions: Gender, Culture, and Moral Reasoning." In F. Ginsberg and A. Tsing, eds., *Uncertain Terms.* Boston: Beacon Press. pp. 19–27.

Staples, Robert. 1982. *Black Masculinity: The Black Male's Role in American Society.* San Francisco, CA: The Black Scholar Press.

Stein, Arlene. 1997. *Sex and Sensibility: Stories of a Lesbian Generation.* Berkeley, CA: University of California Press.

Stewart, Abigail J., Anne P. Copeland, Nia Lane Chester, Janet E. Malley, and Nicole B. Barenbaum. 1997. *Separating Together: How Divorce Transforms Families.* New York: Guilford Press.

Stone, Lawrence. 1977. *The Family, Sex, and Marriage in England 1500–1800.* New York: Harper and Row.

_____. 1989. "The Road to Polygamy." *The New York Review of Books,* March 2, 12–15.

Straton, Jack C. 1994. "The Myth of the 'Battered Husband Syndrome.'" In Maxine Baca Zinn, Pierrette Hondagneu-Sotelo, and Michael A. Messner, eds., *Through the Prism of Difference: Readings in Sex and Gender.* Boston: Allyn and Bacon, 1997, 118–20.

Strauss, Anselm. 1987. *Qualitative Analysis for Social Scientists.* New York: Cambridge University Press.

Sugarman, Stephen. 1998. "Single-Parent Families." Mary Ann Mason, Arlene Skolnick, and Stephen D. Sugarman, eds., *All Our Families: New Policies for a New Century.* New York: Oxford University Press, pp. 13–38.

Sweet, James A., and Larry L. Bumpass. 1987. *American Families and Households.* The Population of the United States in the 1980s; A Census Monograph Series. New York: Russell Sage Foundation.

Swidler, Ann. 1986. "Culture in Action: Symbols and Strategies." *American Sociological Review* 51: 273–86.

Taylor, Robert J., Linda M. Chatters, and Belinda Tucker. 1990. "Developments in Research on Black Families: A Decade Review." *Journal of Marriage and the Family* 52: 993–1014.

Thompson, Linda. 1991. "Family Work: Women's Sense of Fairness." *Journal of Family Issues* 12(2): 181–96.

Thompson, Linda, and Alexis Walker. 1989. "Gender in Families: Women and Men in Marriage, Work, and Parenthood." *Journal of Marriage and the Family* 51: 844–71.

_____. 1995. "The Place of Feminism in Family Studies." *Journal of Marriage and the Family* 57: 847–65.

Thorne, Barrie, and Marilyn Yalom, eds. 1982. *Rethinking the Family: Some Feminist Questions.* New York: Longman.

_____. 1992. *Rethinking the Family: Some Feminist Questions,* rev. ed. Boston: Northeastern University Press.

Thornton, Arland. 1988. "Cohabitation and Marriage in the 1980s." *Demography* 25(4): 487–508.

_____. 1989. "Changing Attitudes Toward Family Issues in the United States." *Journal of Marriage and the Family* 51: 873–93.

_____. 1996. "Comparative and Historical Perspectives on Marriage, Divorce, and Family Life." In David Popenoe, Jean Bethke Elshtain, and David Blankenhorn, eds., *Promises to Keep: Decline and Renewal of Marriage in America.* Lanham, MD: Rowman & Littlefield Publishers, Inc., pp. 69–88.

Thornton, Arland, Duane F. Alwin, and Donald Camburn. 1983. "Causes and Consequences of Sex-Role Attitudes and Attitude Change." *American Sociological Review* 48: 211–27.

Tipton, Steven M. 1982. *Getting Saved from the Sixties: Moral Meaning in Conversion and Cultural Change.* Berkeley, CA: University of California Press.

Townsend, Nicholas. 1992. "Paternity Attitudes of a Cohort of Men in the United States: Cultural Values and Demographic Implications." Ph.D. diss. University of California, Berkeley.

Tronto, Joan C. 1987. "Beyond Gender Difference to a Theory of Care." *Signs: Journal of Women and Culture in Society* 12(4): 644–63.

_____. 1993. *Moral Boundaries: A Political Argument for an Ethic of Care.* New York: Routledge.

Turner, Ralph. 1976. "The Real Self: From Institution to Impulse." *American Journal of Sociology* 81(5): 989–1016.

Utall, Lynet. 1996. "Custodial Care, Surrogate Care, and Coordinated Care: Employed Mothers and the Meaning of Child Care." *Gender & Society* 10(3): 291–311.

U.S. Department of Commerce, Bureau of the Census. *Child Support and Alimony: 1987.* Current Population Reports, Series P-23, No. 167. Washington, DC: U.S. Government Printing Office.

————. 1989. *Studies in Marriage and the Family.* Current Population Reports, Series P-23, No. 162. Washington, DC: U.S. Government Printing Office.

————. 1992. *Marriage, Divorce, and Remarriage in the 1990's.* In Current Population Reports, Series P23-180. Washington, DC: U. S. Government Printing Office.

————. 1995a. *Child Support for Custodial Mothers and Fathers: 1991.* In Current Population Reports, Series P60-187. Washington, DC: U.S. Government Printing Office.

————. 1995b. *Household and Family Characteristics: March 1994.* In Current Population Reports, Series P20-483. Washington, DC: U.S. Government Printing Office.

————. 1996. *Household and Family Characteristics: March 1995.* In Current Population Reports, Series P20-488. Washington, DC: U.S. Government Printing Office.

Veroff, Joseph, Elizabeth Douvan, and Richard A. Kulka. 1981. *The Inner American: A Self-Portrait from 1957 to 1976.* New York: Basic Books.

Wallerstein, Judith S. 1998. "Children of Divorce: A Society in Search of Policy." In Mary Ann Mason, Arlene Skolnick, and Stephen D. Sugarman, eds., *All Our Families: New Policies for a New Century.* New York: Oxford University Press, pp. 66–94.

Wallerstein, Judith, and Sandra Blakeslee. 1989. *Second Chances: Men, Women and Children a Decade After Divorce—Who Wins, Who Loses and Why.* New York: Ticknor and Fields.

————. 1995. *The Good Marriage: How and Why Love Lasts.* New York: Houghton Mifflin.

Wallerstein, Judith, and Joan Berlin Kelly. 1980. *Surviving the Breakup: How Children and Parents Cope with Divorce.* New York: Basic Books.

Way, Niobe, and Helena Stauber. 1996. "Are 'Absent Fathers' Really Absent? Urban Adolescent Girls Speak Out About Their Fathers." In Margaret L. Anderson and Patricia Hill Collins, eds., *Race, Class and Gender,* 3rd ed. Belmont, CA: Wadsworth Publishing Company, 1998, pp. 298—311.

Weber, Max. 1976. *The Protestant Ethic and the Spirit of Capitalism.* (Introduction by Anthony Giddens.) New York: Charles Scribner's Sons.

Weiner-Davis, Michele. 1992. *Divorce Busting: A Revolutionary and Rapid Program for Staying Together.* New York: Summit Books.

Weiss, Robert. 1984. "The Impact of Marital Dissolution on Income and Consumption in Single-Parent Households." *Journal of Marriage and the Family* 46: 115–27.

Weitzman, Lenore. 1985. *The Divorce Revolution.* New York: The Free Press.

West, Candace, and Don Zimmerman. 1987. "Doing Gender." *Gender & Society* 1(2): 125–51.

Weston, Kath. 1991. *Families We Choose: Lesbians, Gays, Kinship.* New York: Columbia University Press.

White, Lynn. 1990. "Determinants of Divorce: A Review of Research in the Eighties." *Journal of Marriage and the Family* 52: 904–12.

———. 1998. "Affective Relationships between Parents and Young Adult Children: Stepfamilies, Gender, and Context." Paper presented at the annual meeting of the American Sociological Association, August 21, 1998.

Whitehead, Barbara Dafoe. 1993. "Dan Quayle Was Right." *The Atlantic,* April.

———. 1995. "The Decline of Marriage as the Social Basis of Childrearing." In David Popenoe, Jean Bethke Elshtain, and David Blankenhorn, eds. *Promises to Keep: Decline and Renewal of Marriage in America.* Lanham, MD: Rowman & Littlefield Publishers, Inc., 1996, 3–14.

———. 1997a. *The Divorce Culture.* New York: Alfred A. Knopf.

———. 1997b. "Family Trouble." *The American Prospect* 34(September–October, 1997): 16–18.

Whyte, William J., Jr. 1956. *The Organization Man.* New York: Simon and Schuster.

Wilson, William Julius. 1987. *The Truly Disadvantaged: The Inner City, The Underclass, and Public Policy.* Chicago: University of Chicago Press.

Yankelovich, D. 1981. *New Rules: Searching for Self-Fulfillment in a World Turned Upside Down.* New York: Bantam Books.

Zaretsky, Eli. 1982. "The Place of the Family in the Origins of the Welfare State." In *Rethinking the Family,* Barrie Thorne and Marilyn Yalom, eds. New York: Longman.

Zavella, Patricia. 1987. *Women's Work and Chicano Families.* Ithaca, NY: Cornell University Press.

Index

The letter *t* after a page number indicates a table; *n* indicates a note.

125, 127, 128, 130, 132, 164, 166, 196, 201, 202, 213; as a gateway, 146, 189; gay and lesbian, 2, 27, 249n. 18, 255n. 21; as a given, 13, 18, 38, 121, 124, 132, 213, 246n. 2; illusory, 25; influences on, in the 1950s, 35; influences on, in 1970, 36–39; interracial, 223, 233n. 8, 256–57n. 10, 257n. 11; meanings of, 200, 201, 231n. 6; optimism concerning, 200, 201, 206, 251n. 1; as optional, 2, 7, 18, 38, 44, 102, 113, 122, 124, 246n. 2; patriarchal, 79, 241n. 1; period effects on, 33, 234n. 6; pessimism concerning, 200–201, 206, 251n. 1; power dynamics in, 6–8, 10, 11, 85–86, 100, 101, 115, 188, 197–98, 199, 202–3, 204, 251n. 12; and religious institutions, 39, 40–42, 45, 178, 235–36n. 18, 236nn. 19–20; serial, 2, 76; socially constructed selves in, 11–12; and socioeconomic status, 57, 249n. 1; stigma of, 124; two-earner, 27, 31, 34, 143, 231n. 1, 234n. 8, 246n. 1, 253–54n. 20; unacceptable, 64–65, 239n. 8
"Marriage and the Construction of Reality" (Berger and Kellner), 11
marriage culture: beliefs encompassed by, 1–2; and cautionary tales for women, 178; costs of, 202–5, 212; cultural influences associated with, 8; decline of, 1, 231n. 3; defined, 1; future of, 213, 214, 254n. 18; and gender equality, 39–40, 47, 50, 53, 88, 144, 204, 205, 237n. 29; and generational membership, 2, 8; hegemony of, 147; and patience, 99–100, 101; and structural and cultural changes, 53–55, 238n. 38; and therapeutic culture, 39–40, 42–44, 161, 236n. 25, 236n. 27; and traditionalism, 163, 175, 180; viewed by the Younger generation, 9; and the Younger generation, 9, 150

Marriage Project, 221, 256nn. 6–7
marriage talk, 2, 231n. 8
Marx, Groucho, 243n. 3
masculinity, 53
May, Elaine Tyler, 33, 35, 239n. 9, 239–40n. 10
McLaughlin, Steven D., 33, 234n. 7
men: associated with divorce, 149–50; breadwinning viewed by, 35, 205, 209, 253n. 14; cautionary tale for, 7; children neglected by, after divorce, 237n. 31; civilized by marriage and children, 208, 209, 253n. 11; and communication, 154, 195, 245n. 6, 251n. 10; contract language used by, 176, 248n. 16; declining wages of, 206–7, 252–53n. 7; divorce thoughts of, 239–40n. 10; divorce viewed by, 48, 52, 206, 238n. 36; financial impact of divorce on, 234n. 3, 252n. 5; and gender equality, 48–49, 188, 199, 203; hidden agenda of, 203, 251–52n. 3; and individualism, 3, 46, 48, 49, 202, 214; marital complaints among, 54, 252n. 4; marital satisfaction of, 54, 66–67, 179, 239–40n. 10; and marital work, 203, 204; and the marriage culture, 205; marriage viewed by, 48, 51, 203–4; and relationality, 215; stereotypes of nurturance and, 152; and therapeutic influence, 154–56, 239n. 9, 245n. 7, 250nn. 4–5. See also fathers
men's movements, 164, 166, 178
The Mermaid and the Minotaur (Dinnerstein), 248n. 14
Messner, Michael, 164–65
methods and methodology, 5–6, 232nn. 13–14; analysis of, 224–25, 257nn. 13–14; data sources for, 58, 217–24, 255nn. 1–3, 256nn. 4–7
Million Man March, 165
Mills, C. Wright, 54, 120
Mills, John Stuart, 237n. 29